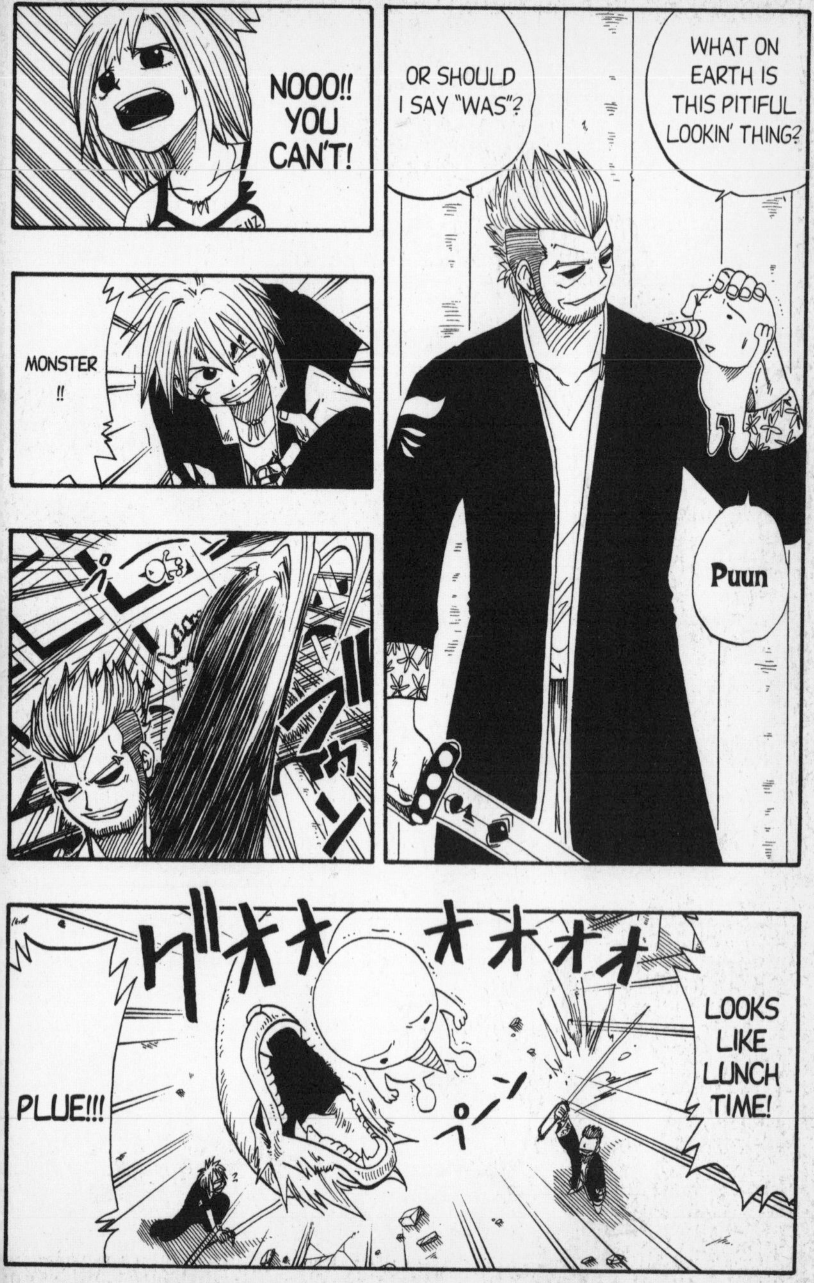
WHAT ON EARTH IS THIS PITIFUL LOOKIN' THING?
OR SHOULD I SAY "WAS"?
Puun
NOOO!! YOU CAN'T!
MONSTER !!
LOOKS LIKE LUNCH TIME!
PLUE!!!

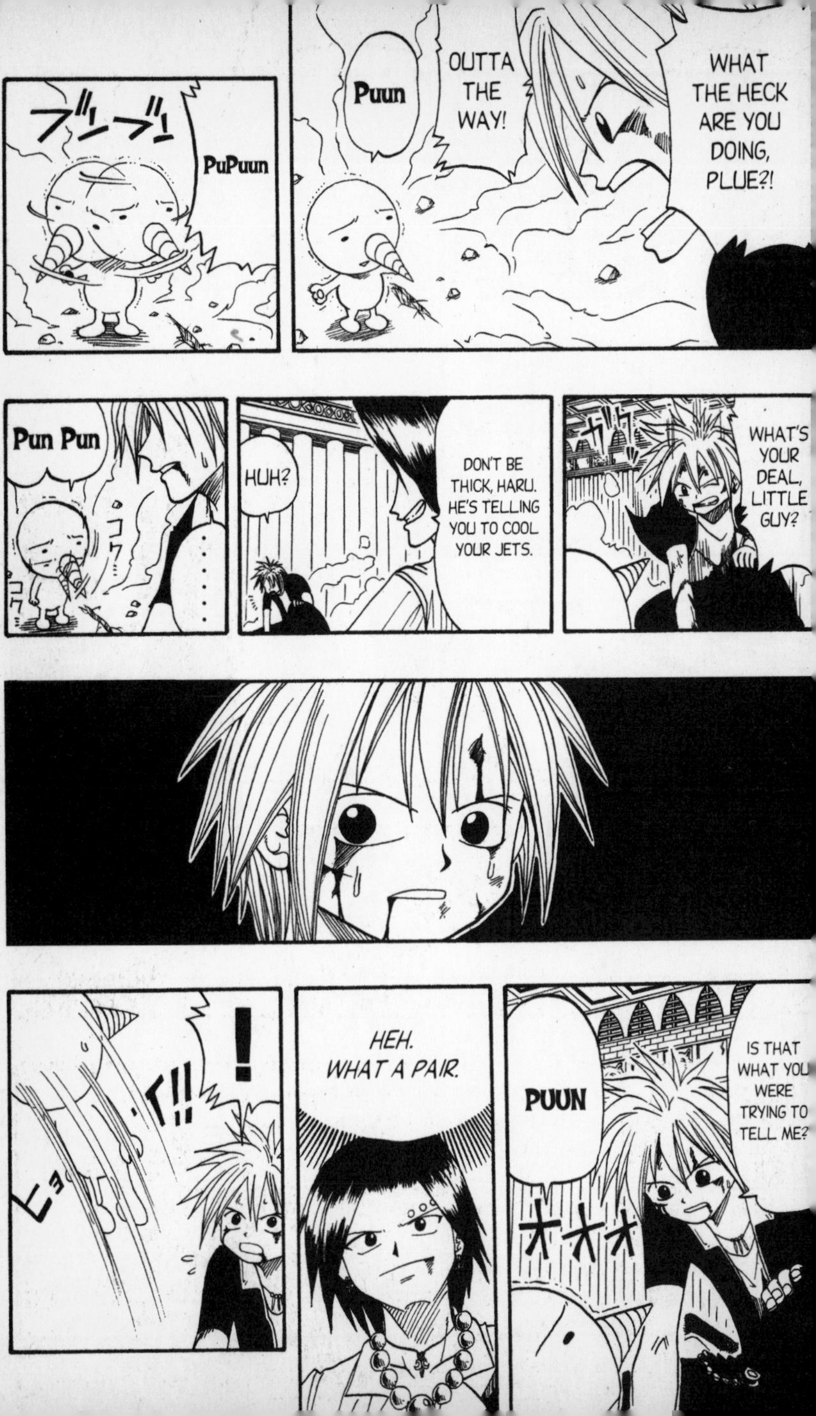
WHAT THE HECK ARE YOU DOING, PLUE?!
OUTTA THE WAY!
Puun
PuPuun
WHAT'S YOUR DEAL, LITTLE GUY?
DON'T BE THICK, HARU. HE'S TELLING YOU TO COOL YOUR JETS.
HUH?
Pun Pun
コク
コク
IS THAT WHAT YOU WERE TRYING TO TELL ME?
PUUN
HEH. WHAT A PAIR.
!

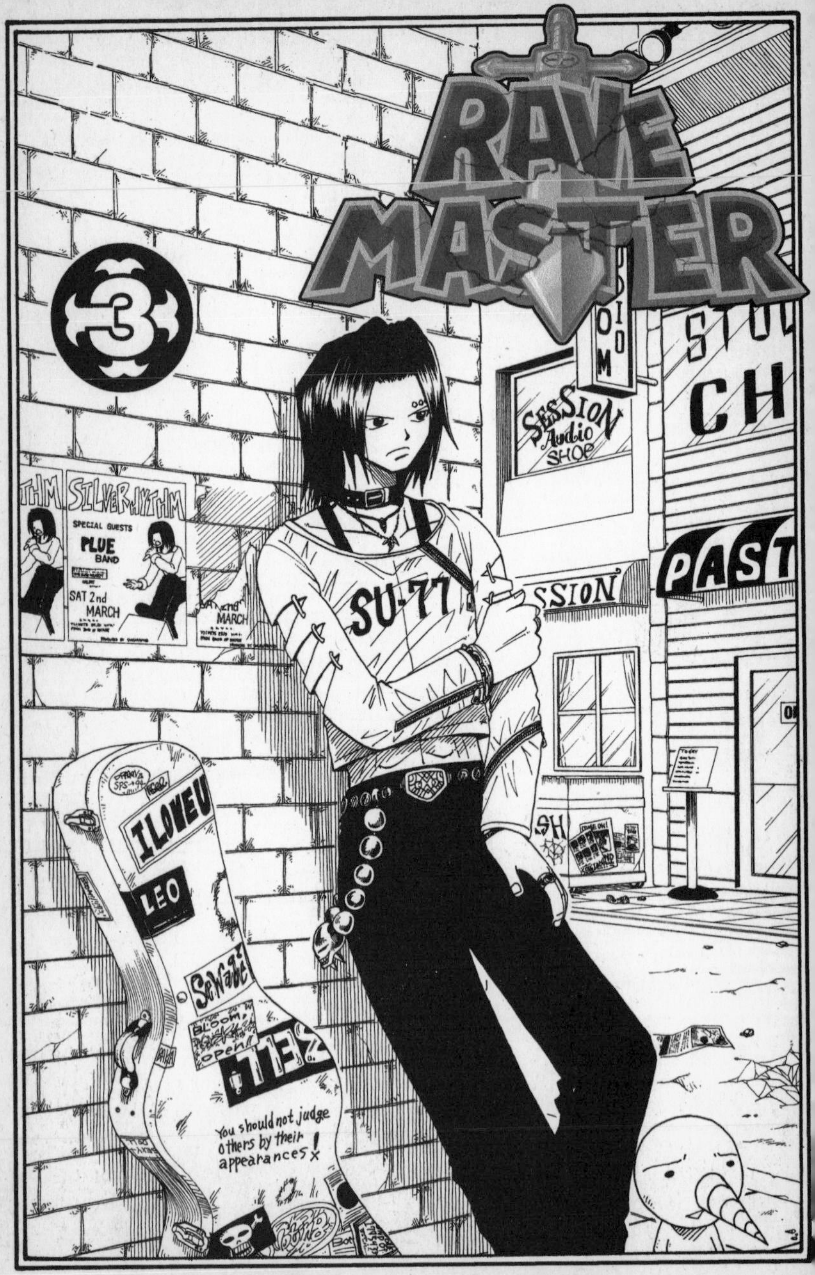
RAVE MASTER
3
SILVER RYTHM
SPECIAL GUESTS
PLUE BAND
SAT 2nd MARCH
SESSION Audio SHOP
SU-77
SSION
CH
PAST
ILOVEU
LEO
You should not judge others by their appearances!

ALSO AVAILABLE FROM 🔷 TOKYOPOP®

MANGA

@LARGE (August 2003)
ANGELIC LAYER*
BABY BIRTH* (September 2003)
BATTLE ROYALE*
BRAIN POWERED*
BRIGADOON* (August 2003)
CARDCAPTOR SAKURA
CARDCAPTOR SAKURA: MASTER OF THE CLOW*
CHOBITS*
CHRONICLES OF THE CURSED SWORD
CLAMP SCHOOL DETECTIVES*
CLOVER
CONFIDENTIAL CONFESSIONS* (July 2003)
CORRECTOR YUI
COWBOY BEBOP*
COWBOY BEBOP: SHOOTING STAR*
DEMON DIARY
DIGIMON*
DRAGON HUNTER
DRAGON KNIGHTS*
DUKLYON: CLAMP SCHOOL DEFENDERS*
ERICA SAKURAZAWA*
ESCAFLOWNE* (July 2003)
FAKE*
FLCL* (September 2003)
FORBIDDEN DANCE* (August 2003)
GATE KEEPERS*
G GUNDAM*
GRAVITATION*
GTO*
GUNDAM WING
GUNDAM WING: BATTLEFIELD OF PACIFISTS
GUNDAM WING: ENDLESS WALTZ*
GUNDAM WING: THE LAST OUTPOST*
HAPPY MANIA*
HARLEM BEAT
I.N.V.U.
INITIAL D*
ISLAND
JING: KING OF BANDITS*
JULINE
KARE KANO*
KINDAICHI CASE FILES, THE*
KING OF HELL
KODOCHA: SANA'S STAGE*
LOVE HINA*
LUPIN III*
MAGIC KNIGHT RAYEARTH* (August 2003)

MAGIC KNIGHT RAYEARTH II* (COMING SOON)
MAN OF MANY FACES*
MARMALADE BOY*
MARS*
MIRACLE GIRLS
MIYUKI-CHAN IN WONDERLAND* (October 2003)
MONSTERS, INC.
NIEA _7* (August 2003)
PARADISE KISS*
PARASYTE
PEACH GIRL
PEACH GIRL: CHANGE OF HEART*
PET SHOP OF HORRORS*
PLANET LADDER*
PLANETES* (October 2003)
PRIEST
RAGNAROK
RAVE MASTER*
REALITY CHECK
REBIRTH
REBOUND*
RISING STARS OF MANGA
SABER MARIONETTE J* (July 2003)
SAILOR MOON
SAINT TAIL
SAMURAI DEEPER KYO*
SAMURAI GIRL: REAL BOUT HIGH SCHOOL*
SCRYED*
SHAOLIN SISTERS*
SHIRAHIME-SYO: SNOW GODDESS TALES* (Dec. 2003)
SHUTTERBOX (November 2003)
SORCERER HUNTERS
THE SKULL MAN*
TOKYO MEW MEW*
UNDER THE GLASS MOON
VAMPIRE GAME
WILD ACT* (July 2003)
WISH*
WORLD OF HARTZ (August 2003)
X-DAY* (August 2003)
ZODIAC P.I. * (July 2003)

*INDICATES 100% AUTHENTIC MANGA (RIGHT-TO-LEFT FORMAT)

CINE-MANGA™

CARDCAPTORS
JACKIE CHAN ADVENTURES (COMING SOON)
JIMMY NEUTRON (September 2003)
KIM POSSIBLE
LIZZIE MCGUIRE
POWER RANGERS: NINJA STORM (August 2003)
SPONGEBOB SQUAREPANTS (September 2003)
SPY KIDS 2

NOVELS

KARMA CLUB (July 2003)
SAILOR MOON

TOKYOPOP KIDS

STRAY SHEEP (September 2003)

ART BOOKS

CARDCAPTOR SAKURA*
MAGIC KNIGHT RAYEARTH*

ANIME GUIDES

COWBOY BEBOP ANIME GUIDES
GUNDAM TECHNICAL MANUALS
SAILOR MOON SCOUT GUIDES

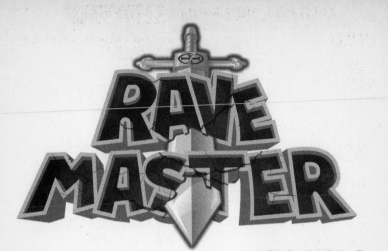

VOLUME 3

Story and Art by
HIRO MASHIMA

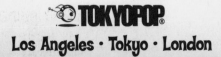

Los Angeles · Tokyo · London

Translator - Amy Forsyth
English Adaptation - James Lucas Jones
Editor - Jake Forbes
Associate Editor - Paul Morrissey
Copy Editor - Jennifer Wagner
Retouch and Lettering - Rob Settles
Cover Layout - Raymond Makowski
Cover Colors - Pauline Sim

Managing Editor - Jill Freshney
Production Coordinator - Antonio DePietro
Production Manager - Jennifer Miller
Art Director - Matthew Alford
Director of Editorial - Jeremy Ross
VP of Production & Manufacturing - Ron Klamert
President & C.O.O. - John Parker
Publisher & C.E.O. - Stuart Levy

Email: editor@TOKYOPOP.com
Come visit us online at www.TOKYOPOP.com

A 🍩 **TOKYOPOP**® Manga

TOKYOPOP® is an imprint of Mixx Entertainment, Inc.
5900 Wilshire Blvd. Suite 2000, Los Angeles, CA 90036

ISBN: 1-59182-210-6

First TOKYOPOP® printing: June 2003

10 9 8 7 6 5 4 3 2 1

Printed in the USA

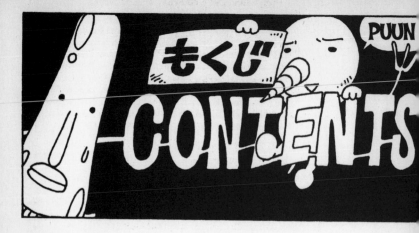

PUUN

もくじ

CONTENTS

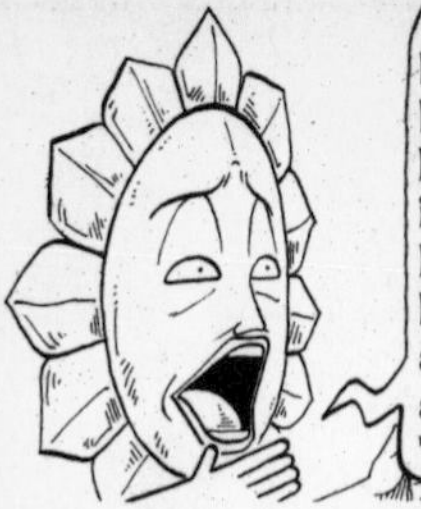

The Story So Far...

Haru Glory never wanted to be a hero, but when the evil society Demon Card came to his home of Garage Island, he realized they had to be stopped. His weapon, the Ten Powers Sword, was broken in a battle with the Demon Card general Shuda. So with his guide, Plue, he traveled to Punk Street to have the sword repaired by Musica, the Legendary Blacksmith. On the way he was joined by Elie, a girl with no memories. All was going well until Lance, a Demon Card agent, kidnapped Elie and held her for ransom. With the reforged Ten Powers, Haru came to Lance's mansion to rescue Elie.

HARU GLORY: The Rave Master. Haru is the heir to Rave, the only one capable of wielding it and destroying Dark Bring. Impulsive and headstrong, he's not afraid to put himself in danger to do what is right. His father disappeared in search of Rave when he was very young.

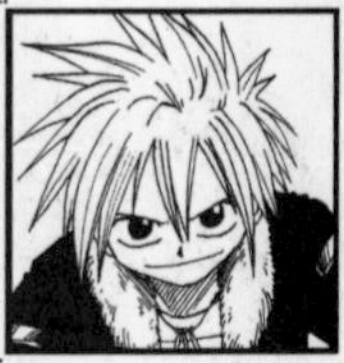

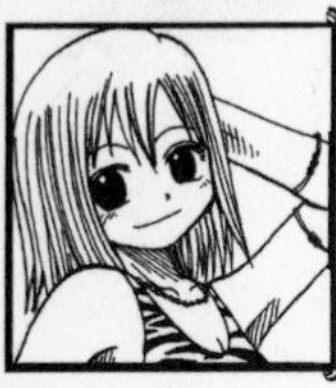

ELIE: A Girl with no past. Elie travels the world in search of the key to her forgotten memories. Outwardly cheerful, she hides a great sadness from her past. She's hot-headed, so when she pulls out her explosive Tonfa Blasters, bad guys watch out!

MUSICA: Leader of the Silver Rhythm Gang. An orphan whose family was slaughtered when he was a baby, Musica became a street-fighting petty thief, but he has a good heart.

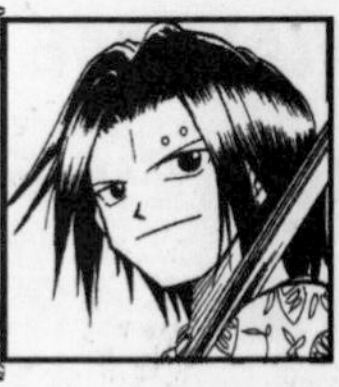

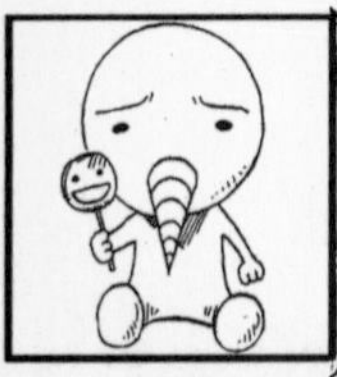

PLUE: The Rave Bearer. Plue is supposed to be Haru's guide in finding the Rave Stones, but so far he's just gotten him in and out of trouble. No one knows what exactly Plue is, but he seems to have healing abilities and is smarter than your average...whatever he is.

LANCE: The Beast Swordsman. Lance is the Demon Card operative who runs Punk Street. He killed Musica the blacksmith's family with a sword he had forged. Now he's under orders to capture the Rave Master–dead or alive.

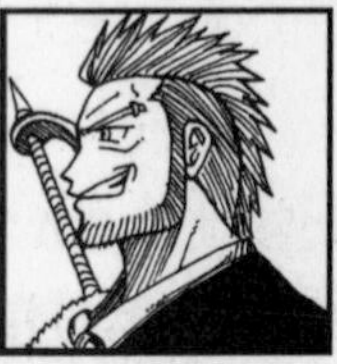

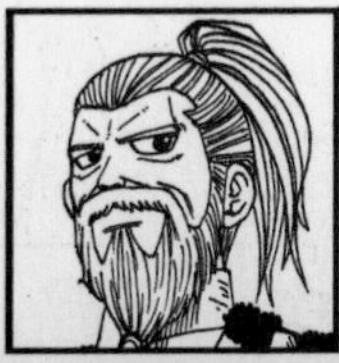

GALEIN MUSICA: The Legendary Blacksmith. Musica forged the Ten Powers Sword and reforged it for Haru when it was broken. After his family was killed, he became depressed and did whatever Demon Card told him to. Haru inspired him to follow his heart.

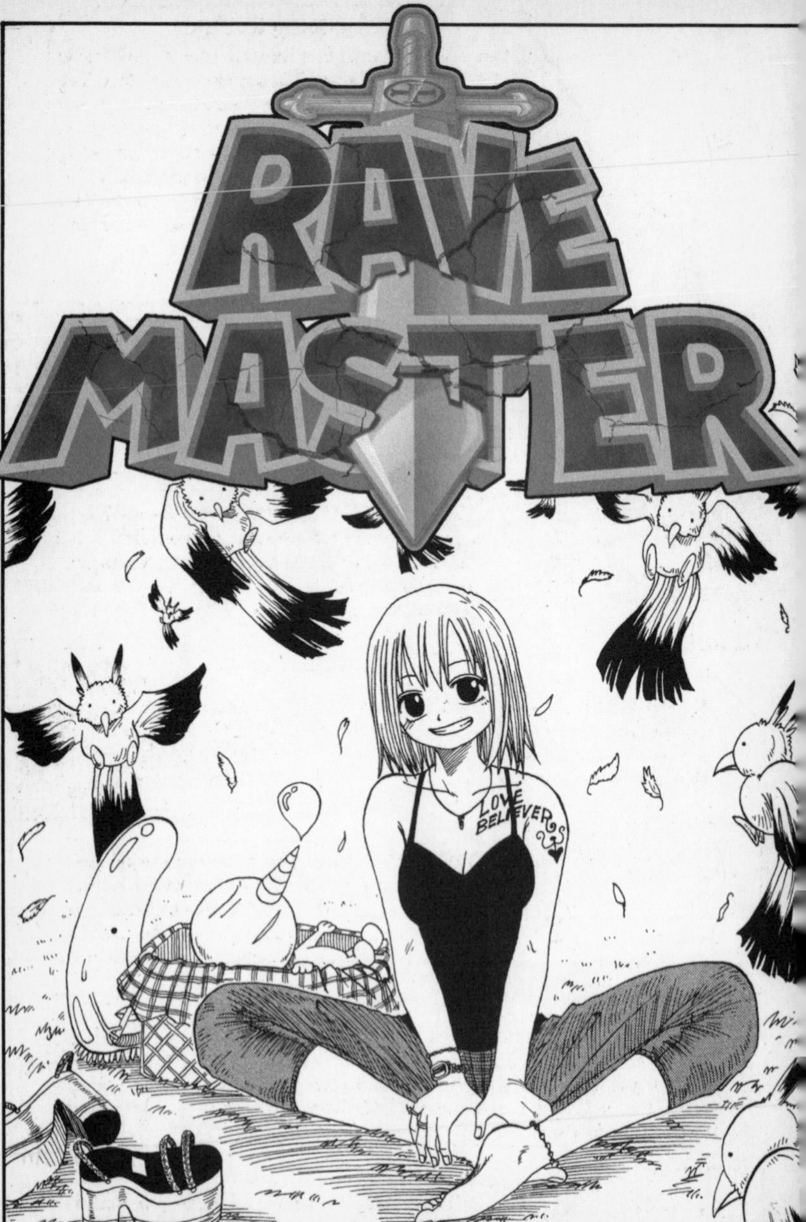
RAVE MASTER
LOVE BELIEVERS

RAVE 14 APPROACHING DARKNESS

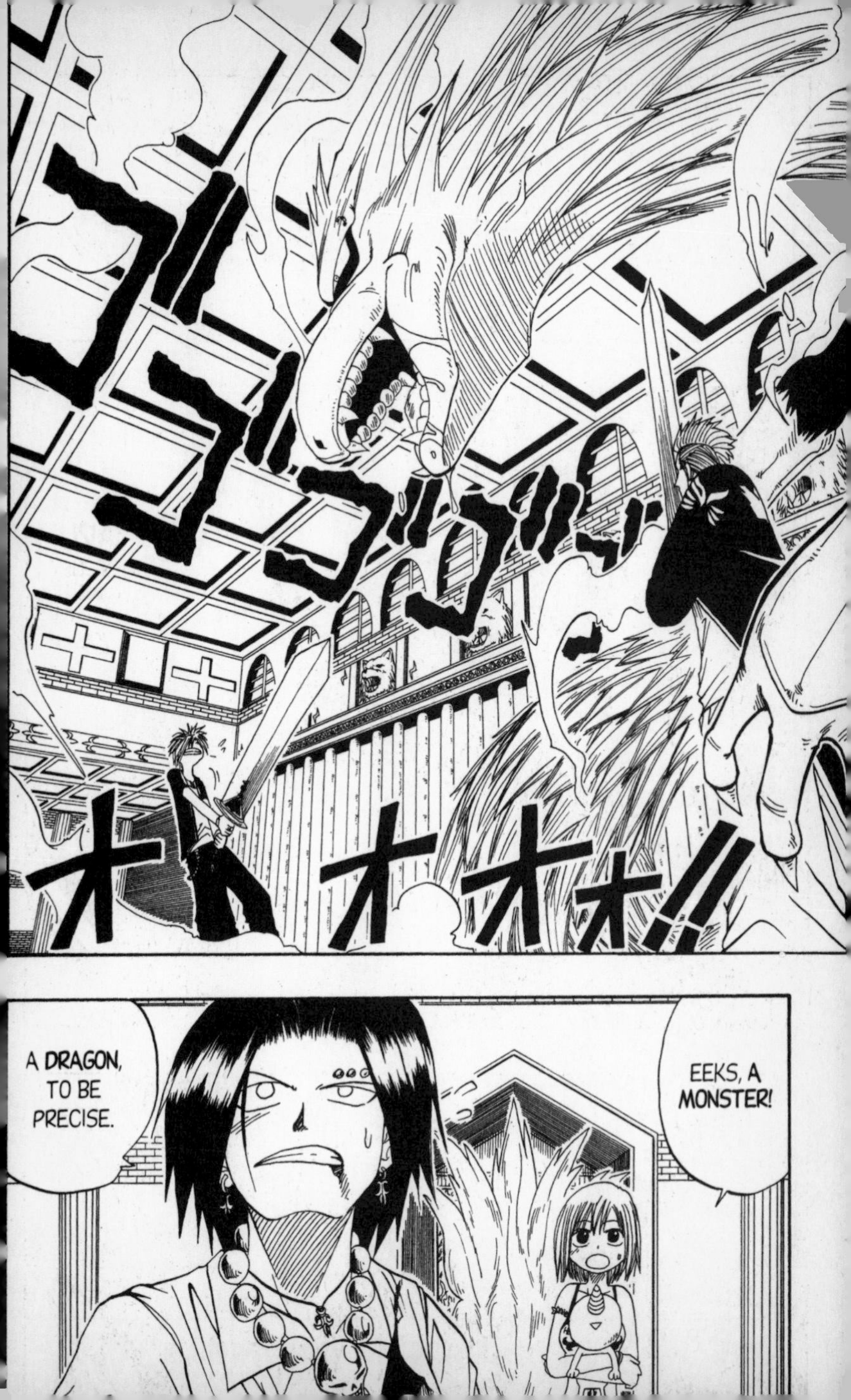
オオオオ!!
EEKS, A MONSTER!
A DRAGON, TO BE PRECISE.

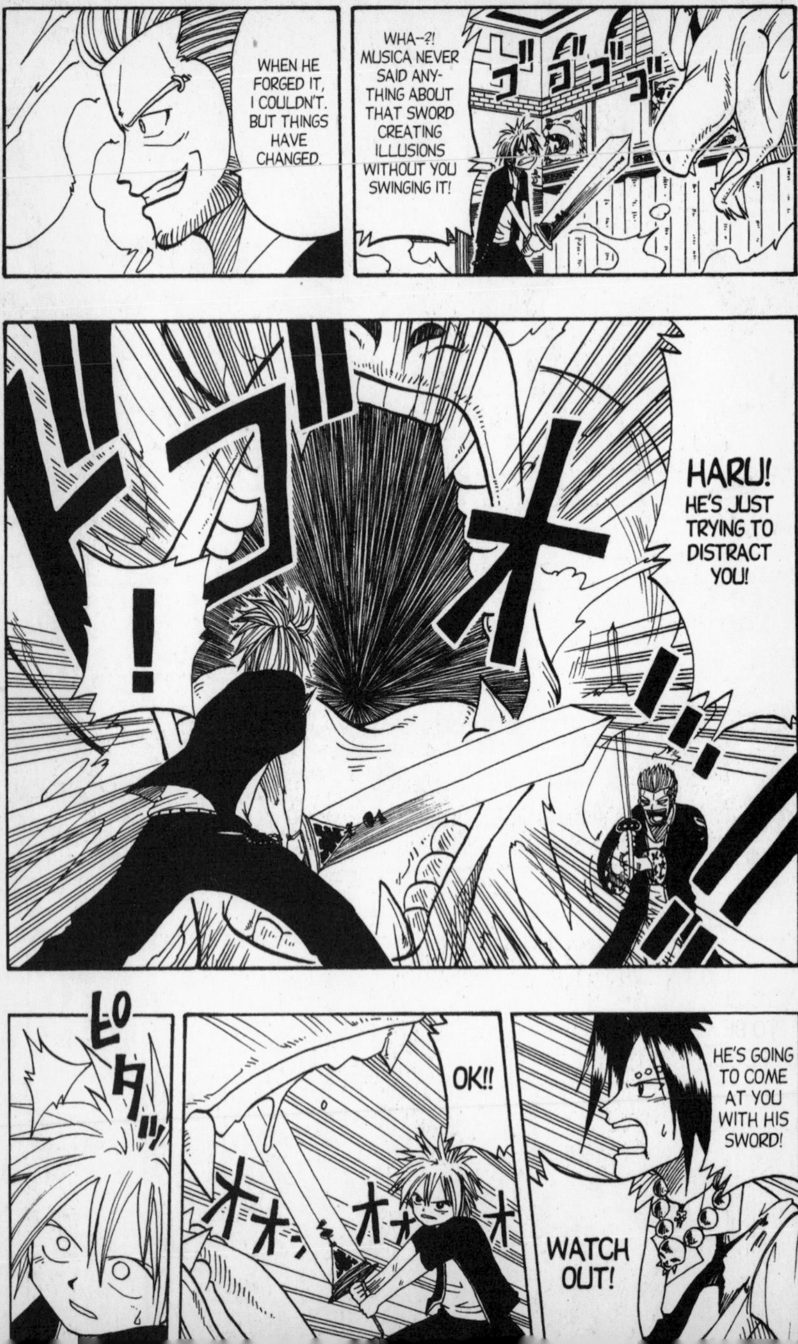
WHA--?! MUSICA NEVER SAID ANY-THING ABOUT THAT SWORD CREATING ILLUSIONS WITHOUT YOU SWINGING IT!
WHEN HE FORGED IT, I COULDN'T. BUT THINGS HAVE CHANGED.
HARU! HE'S JUST TRYING TO DISTRACT YOU!
HE'S GOING TO COME AT YOU WITH HIS SWORD!
WATCH OUT!
OK!!

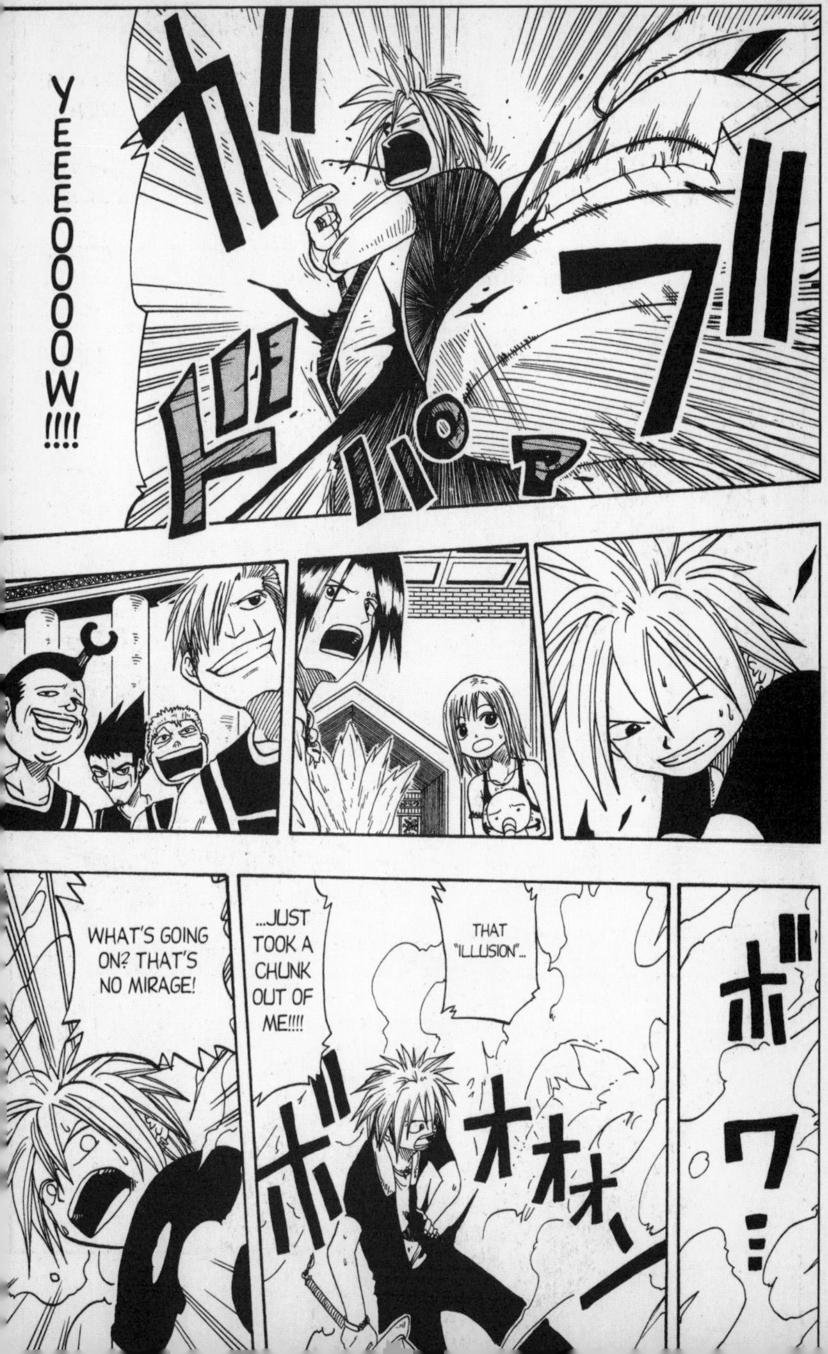
YEEEOOOOOW!!!!
THAT "ILLUSION"...
...JUST TOOK A CHUNK OUT OF ME!!!!
WHAT'S GOING ON? THAT'S NO MIRAGE!

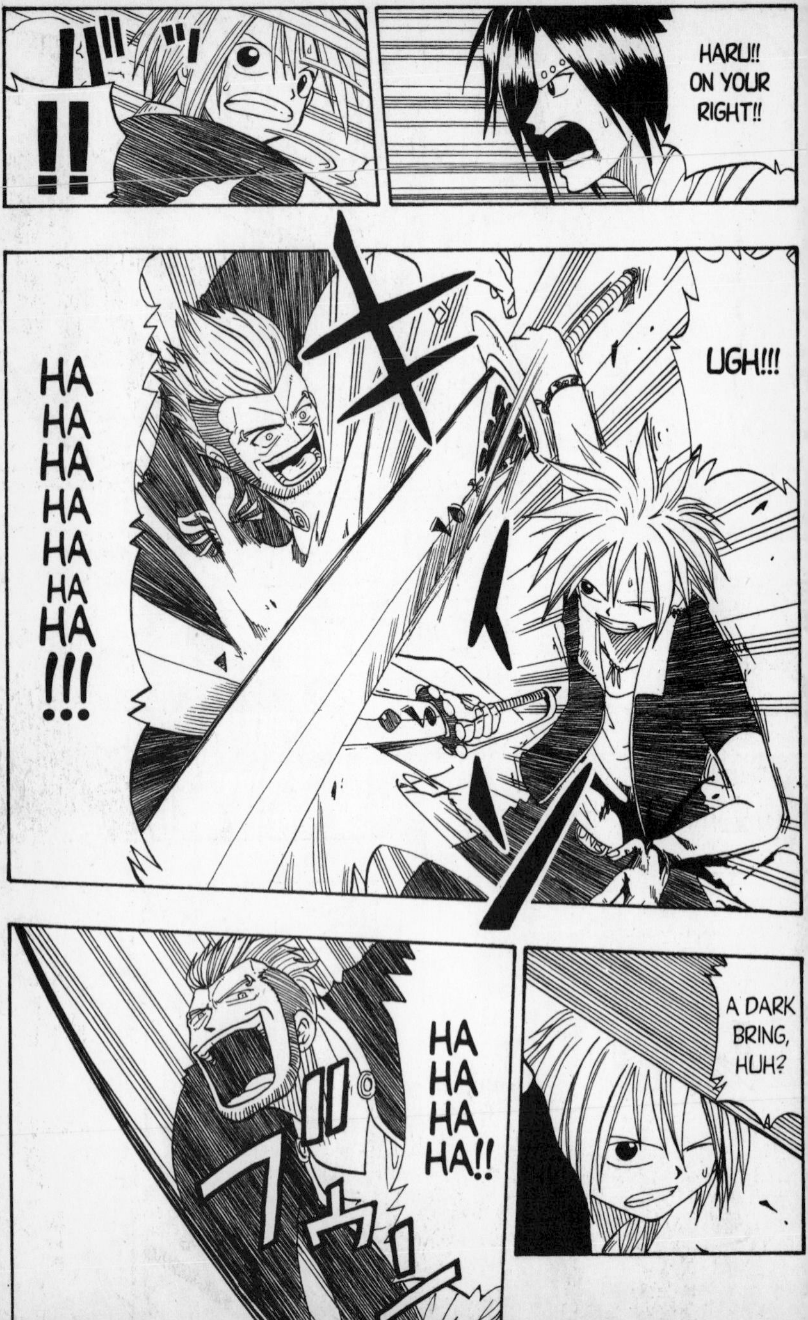
HARU!! ON YOUR RIGHT!!
UGH!!!
HA HA HA HA HA HA HA!!!
A DARK BRING, HUH?
HA HA HA HA!!

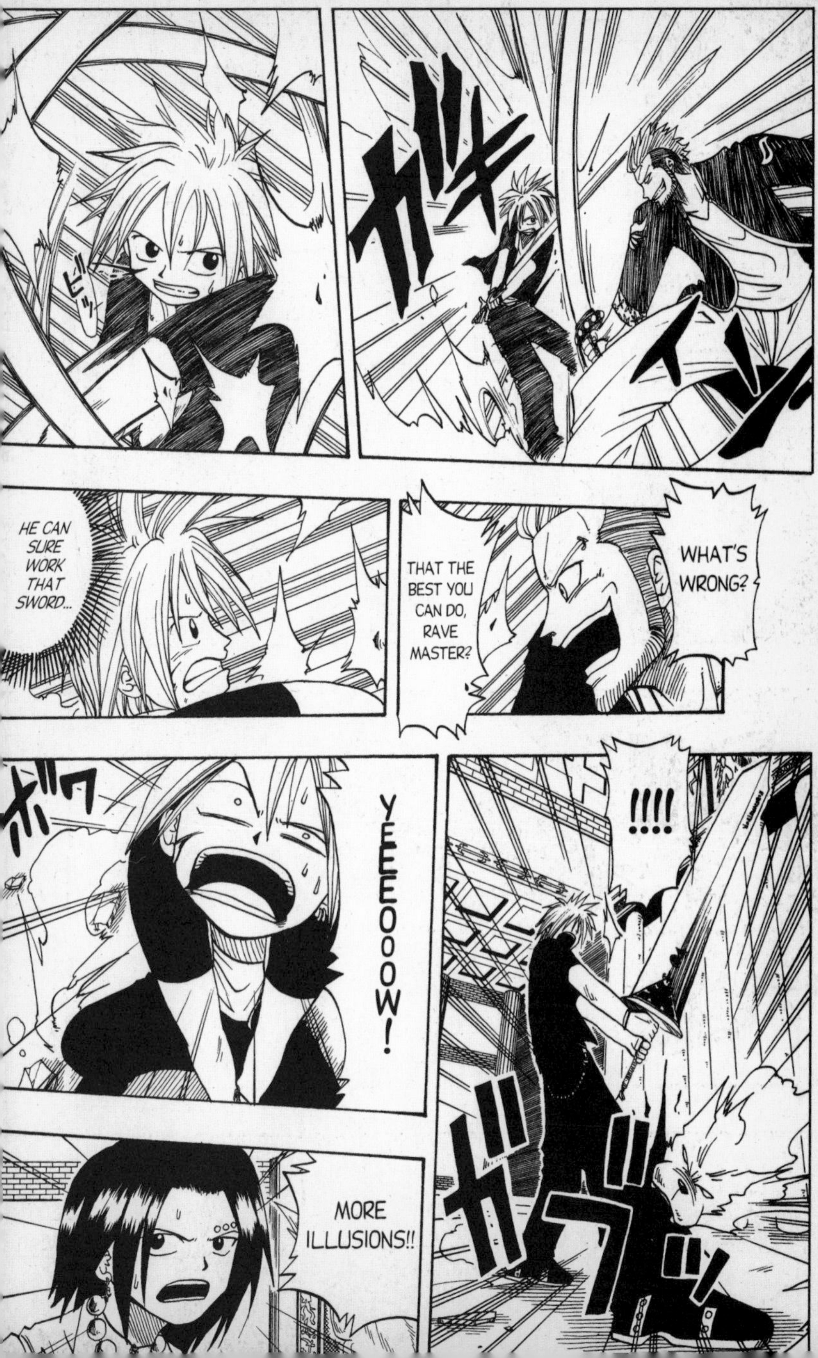
WHAT'S WRONG?
THAT THE BEST YOU CAN DO, RAVE MASTER?
HE CAN SURE WORK THAT SWORD...
!!!!
YEEEOOOOW!
MORE ILLUSIONS!!

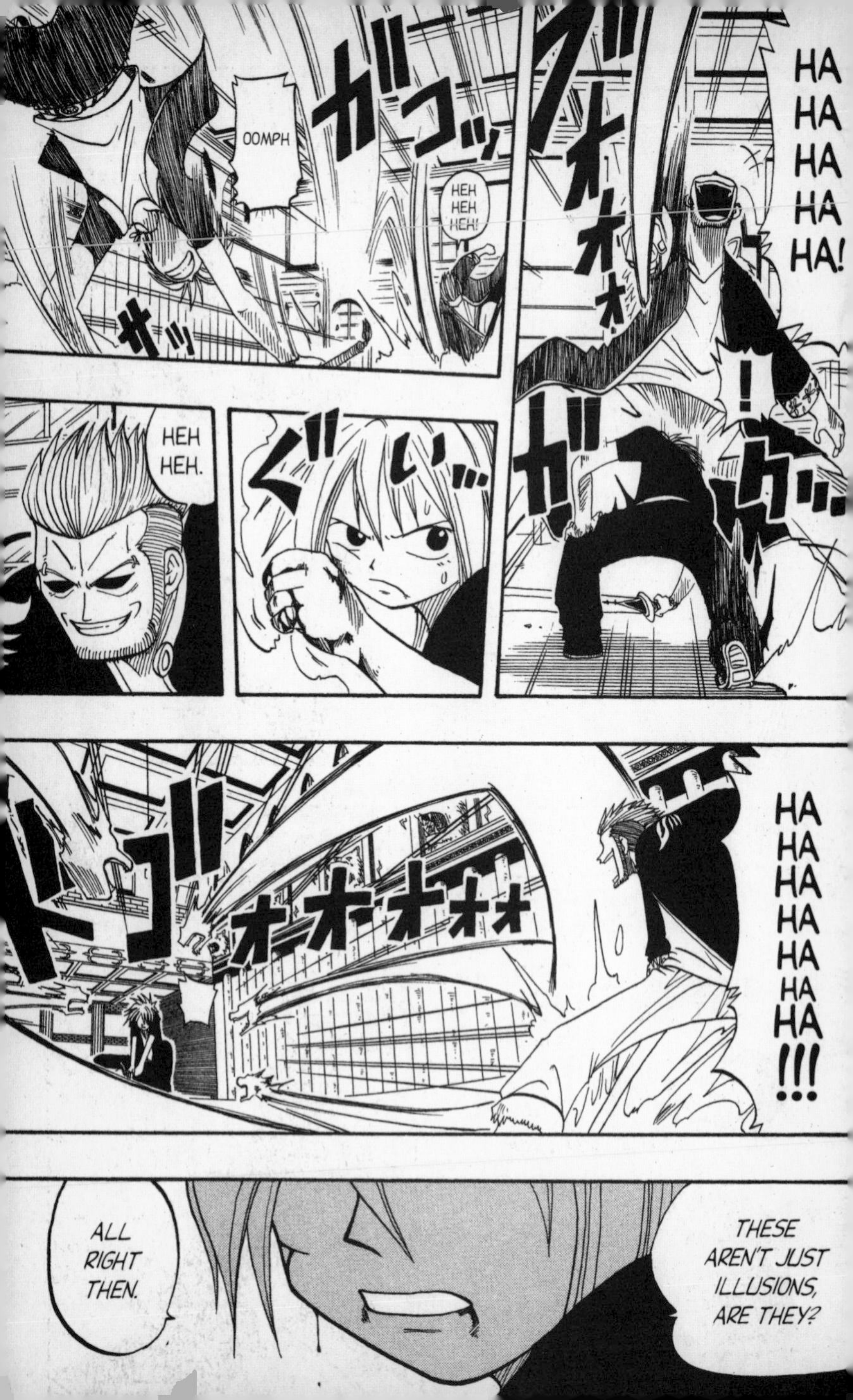
HA HA HA HA HA HA!
!
HEH HEH HEH!
OOMPH
HEH HEH.
HA HA HA HA HA HA HA HA!!!
THESE AREN'T JUST ILLUSIONS, ARE THEY?
ALL RIGHT THEN.

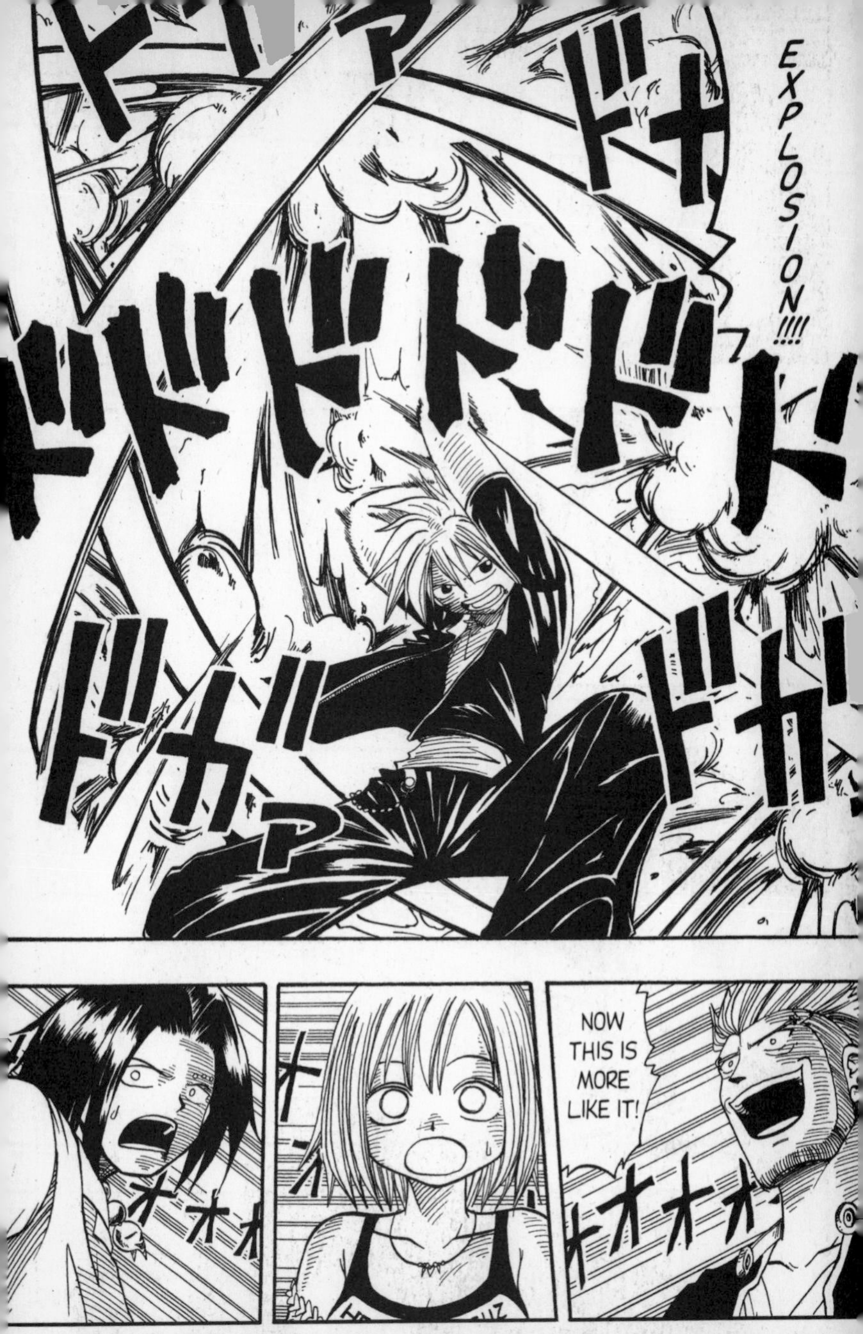
EXPLOSION!!!!
NOW THIS IS MORE LIKE IT!

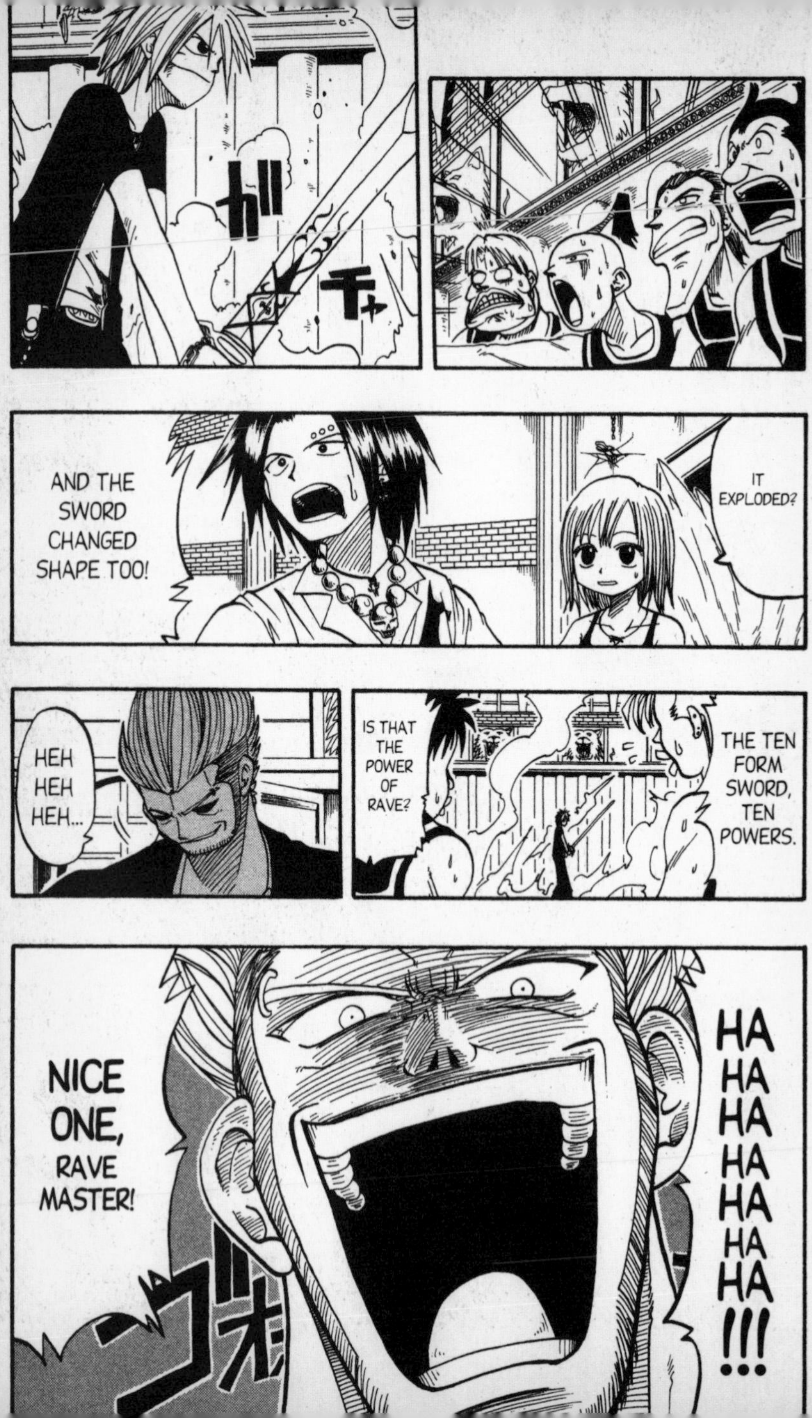
IT EXPLODED?
AND THE SWORD CHANGED SHAPE TOO!
THE TEN FORM SWORD, TEN POWERS.
IS THAT THE POWER OF RAVE?
HEH HEH HEH...
HA HA HA HA HA HA HA HA!!!
NICE ONE, RAVE MASTER!

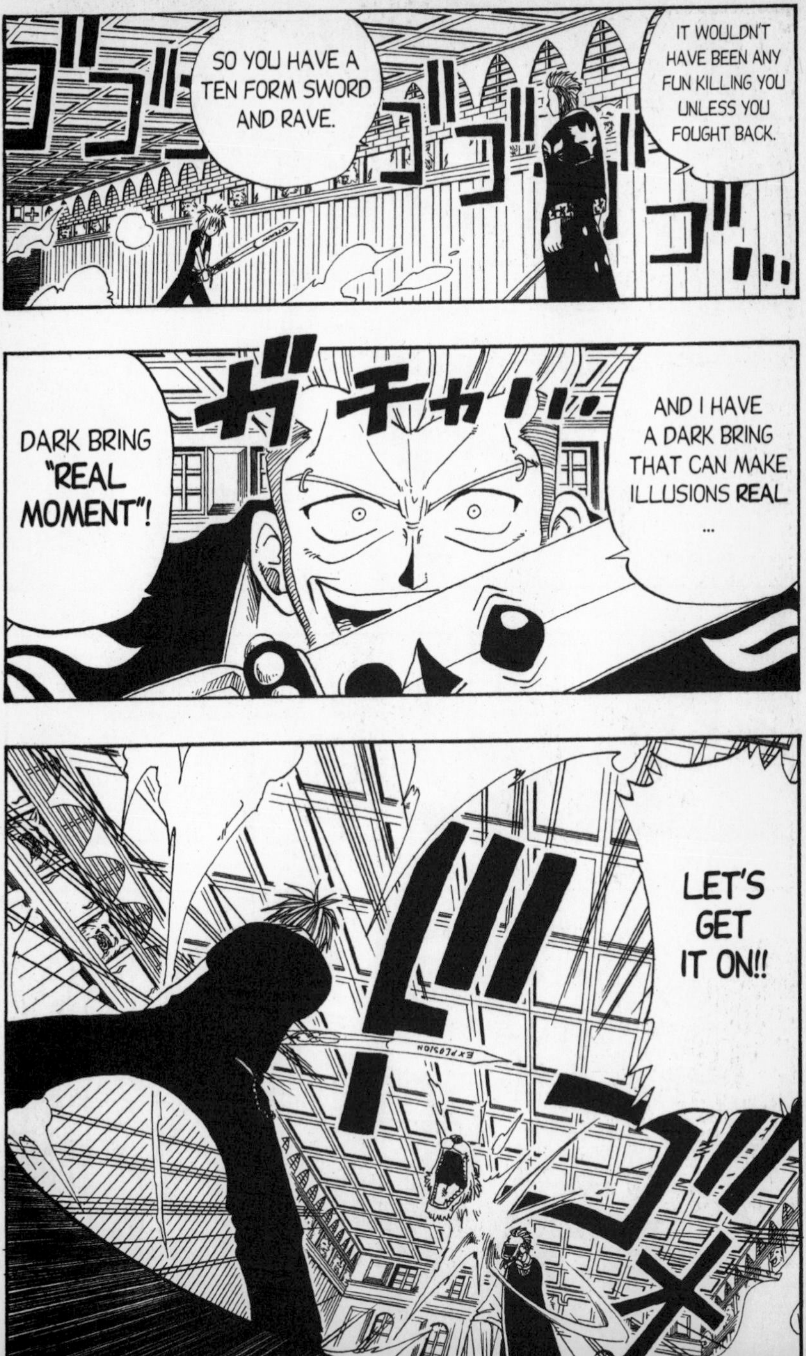
IT WOULDN'T HAVE BEEN ANY FUN KILLING YOU UNLESS YOU FOUGHT BACK.
ゴゴゴ
SO YOU HAVE A TEN FORM SWORD AND RAVE.
AND I HAVE A DARK BRING THAT CAN MAKE ILLUSIONS REAL ...
ガチャ
DARK BRING "REAL MOMENT"!
LET'S GET IT ON!!
ドン

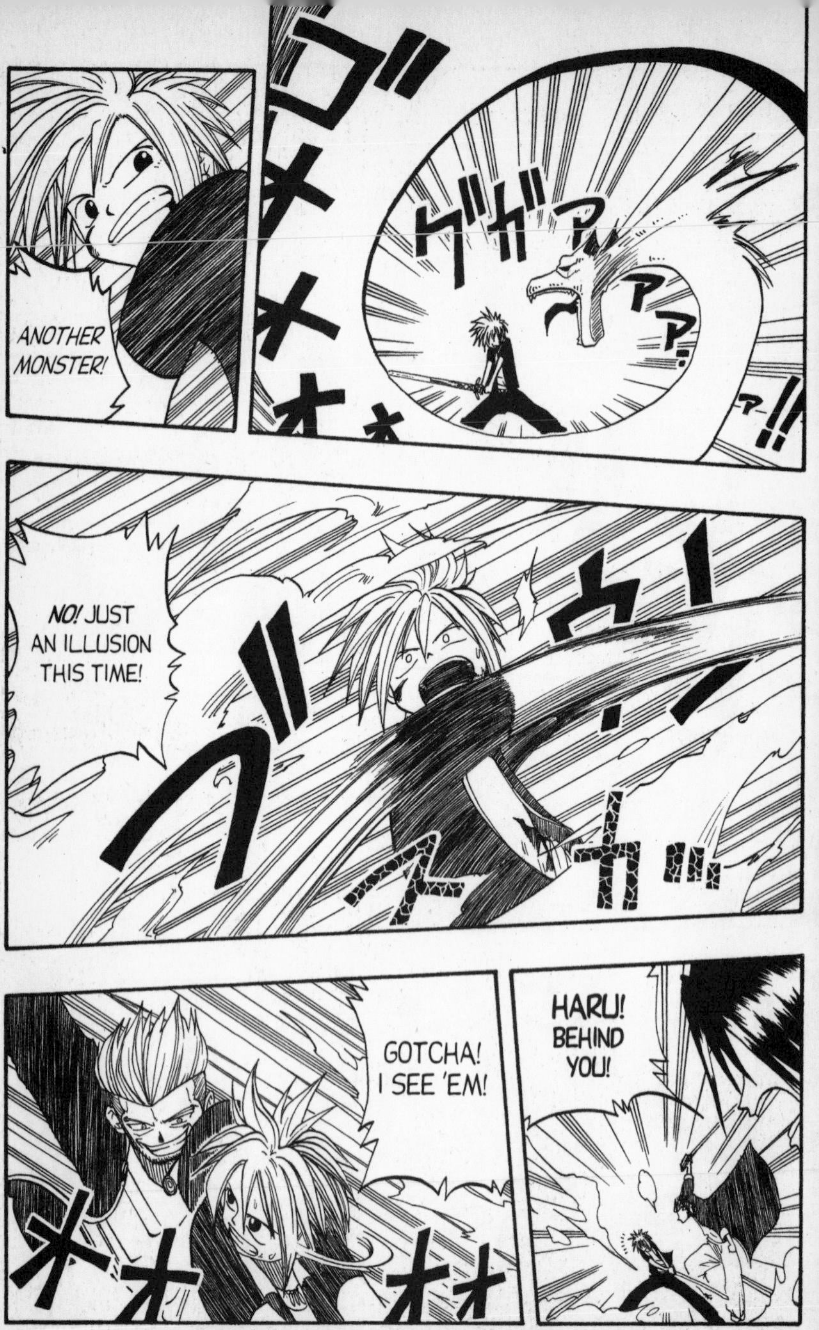
ANOTHER MONSTER!
NO! JUST AN ILLUSION THIS TIME!
HARU! BEHIND YOU!
GOTCHA! I SEE 'EM!

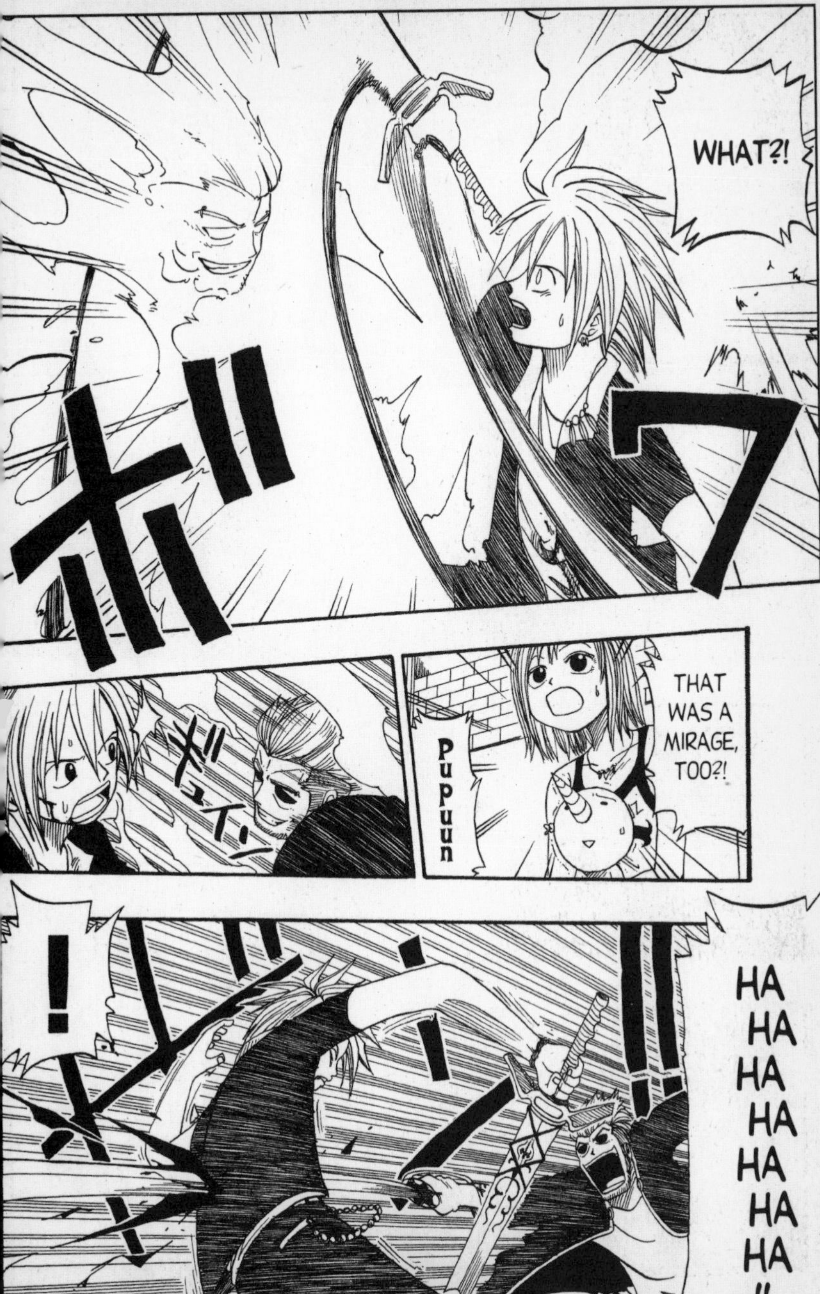
WHAT?!
THAT WAS A MIRAGE, TOO?!
Pupuun
HA HA HA HA HA HA HA HA HA!!
!

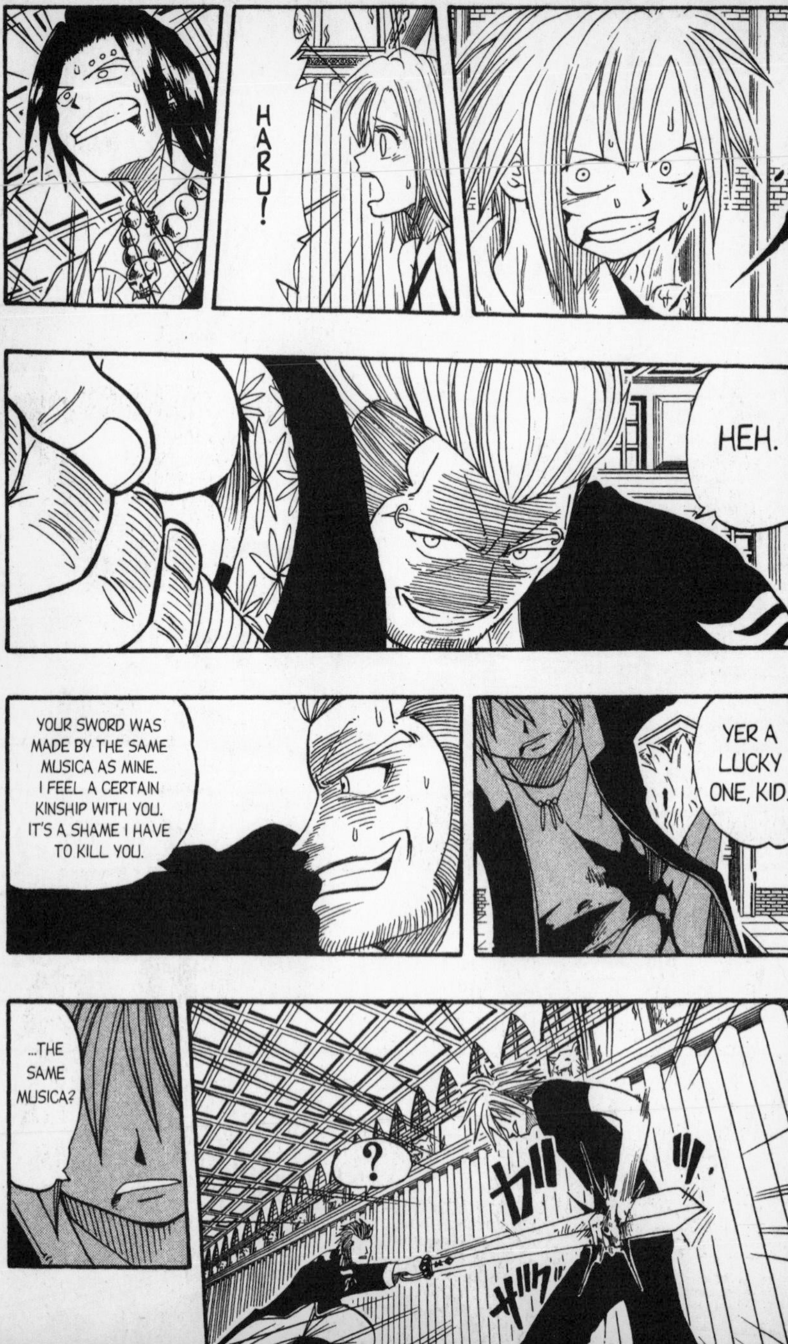
HARU!
HEH.
YER A LUCKY ONE, KID.
YOUR SWORD WAS MADE BY THE SAME MUSICA AS MINE. I FEEL A CERTAIN KINSHIP WITH YOU. IT'S A SHAME I HAVE TO KILL YOU.
?
...THE SAME MUSICA?

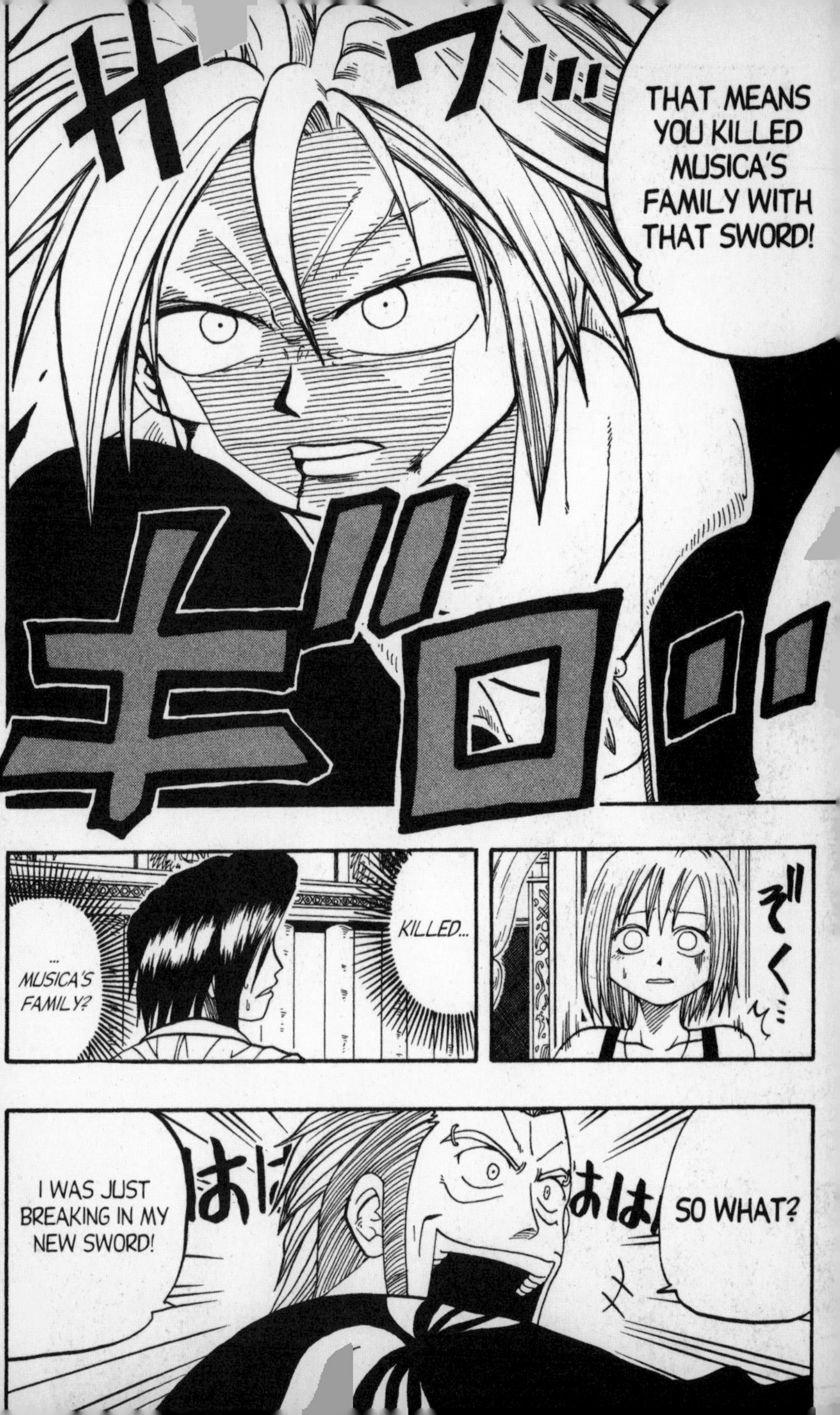
THAT MEANS YOU KILLED MUSICA'S FAMILY WITH THAT SWORD!
ギロッ
ぞく
KILLED...
... MUSICA'S FAMILY?
SO WHAT?
I WAS JUST BREAKING IN MY NEW SWORD!

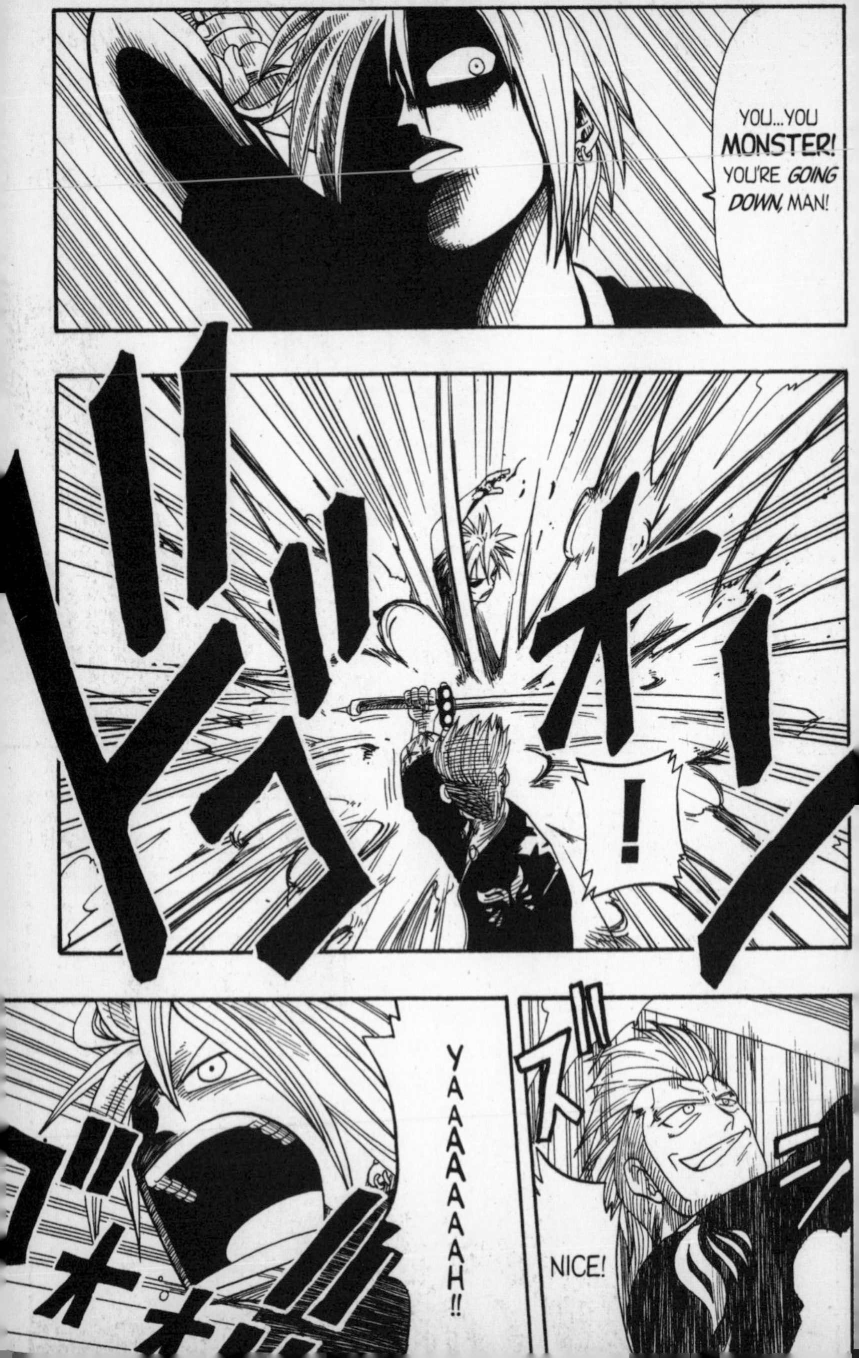

YOU...YOU **MONSTER!** YOU'RE *GOING DOWN,* MAN!
!
NICE!
YAAAAAAAH!!

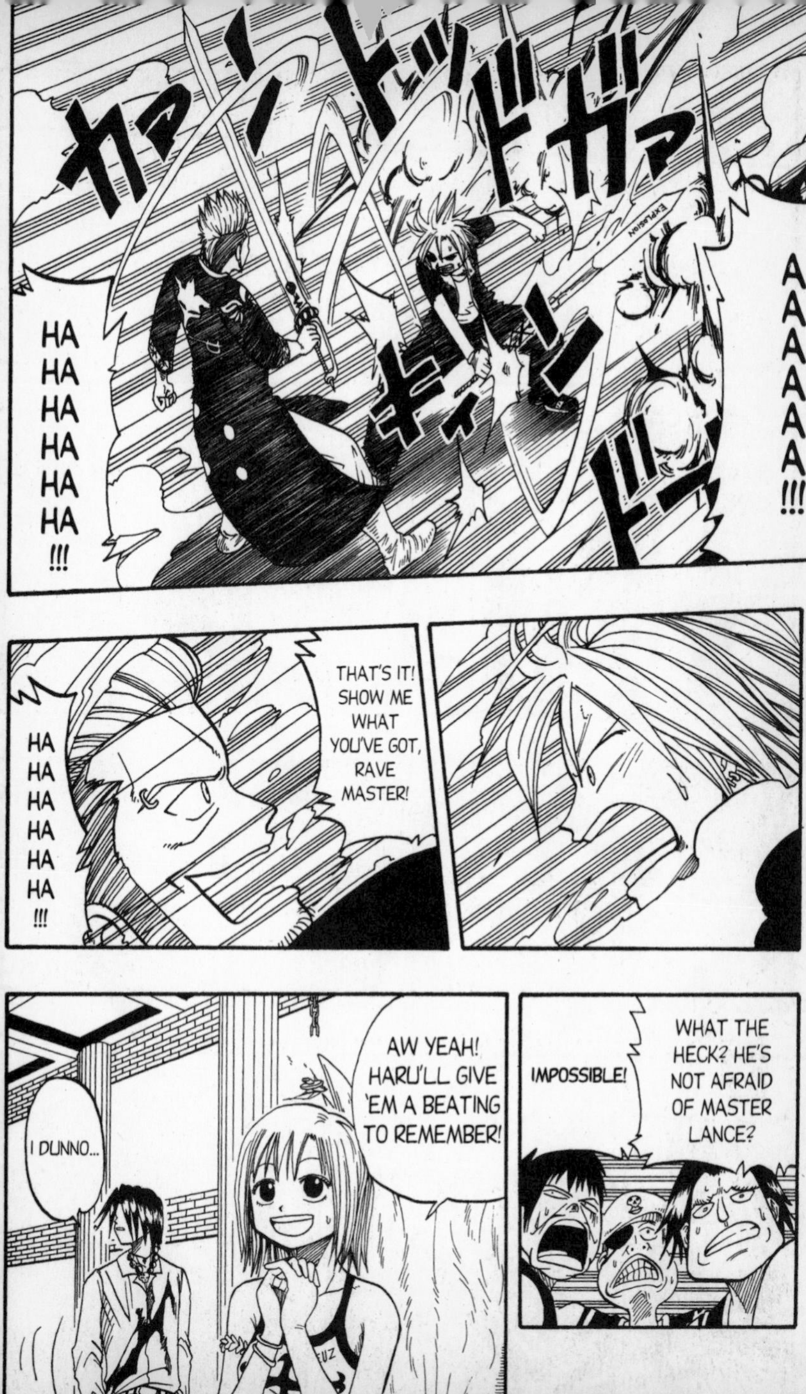
AAAAAAA!!!
EXPLOSION
HA HA HA HA HA HA!!!
THAT'S IT! SHOW ME WHAT YOU'VE GOT, RAVE MASTER!
HA HA HA HA HA HA!!!
WHAT THE HECK? HE'S NOT AFRAID OF MASTER LANCE?
IMPOSSIBLE!
AW YEAH! HARU'LL GIVE 'EM A BEATING TO REMEMBER!
I DUNNO...

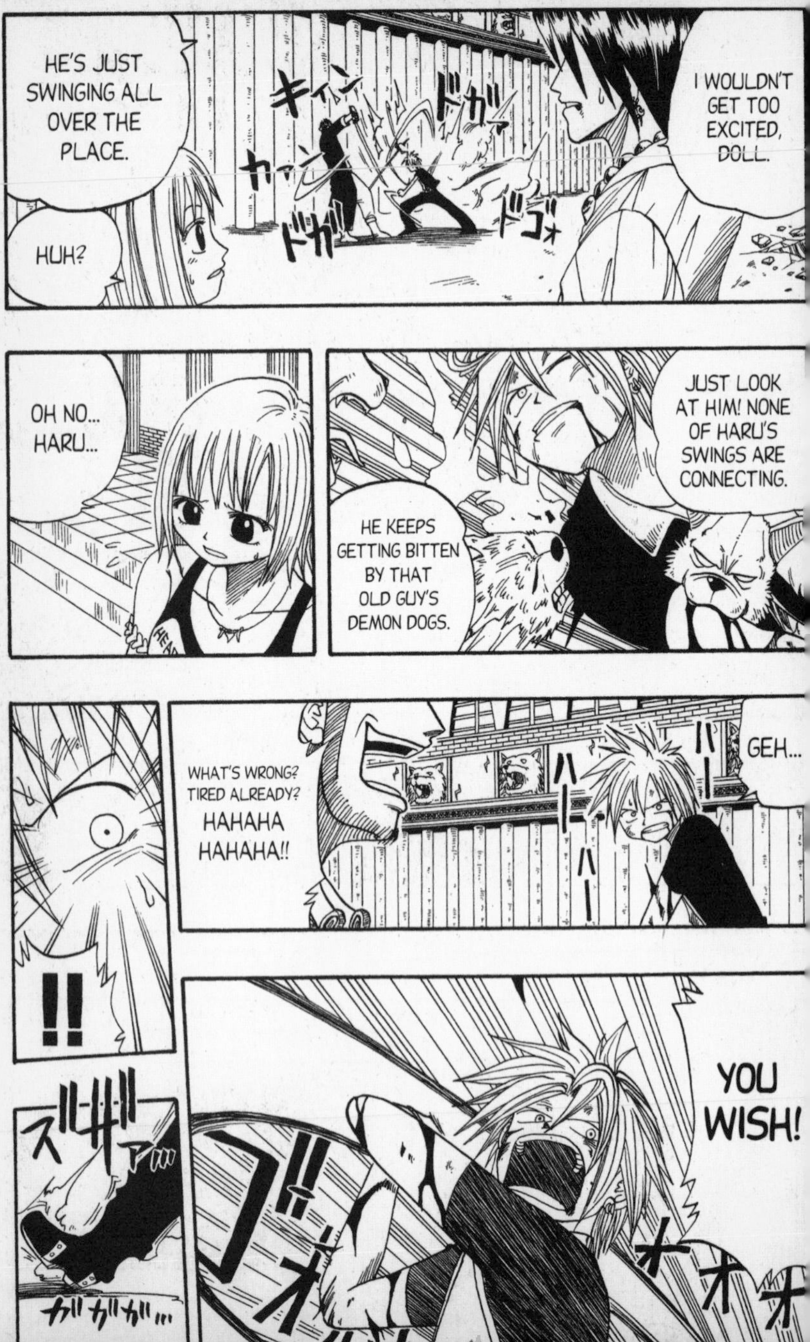
I WOULDN'T GET TOO EXCITED, DOLL.
HE'S JUST SWINGING ALL OVER THE PLACE.
HUH?
JUST LOOK AT HIM! NONE OF HARU'S SWINGS ARE CONNECTING.
HE KEEPS GETTING BITTEN BY THAT OLD GUY'S DEMON DOGS.
OH NO... HARU...
GEH...
WHAT'S WRONG? TIRED ALREADY? HAHAHA HAHAHA!!
!!
YOU WISH!
ガガガ…

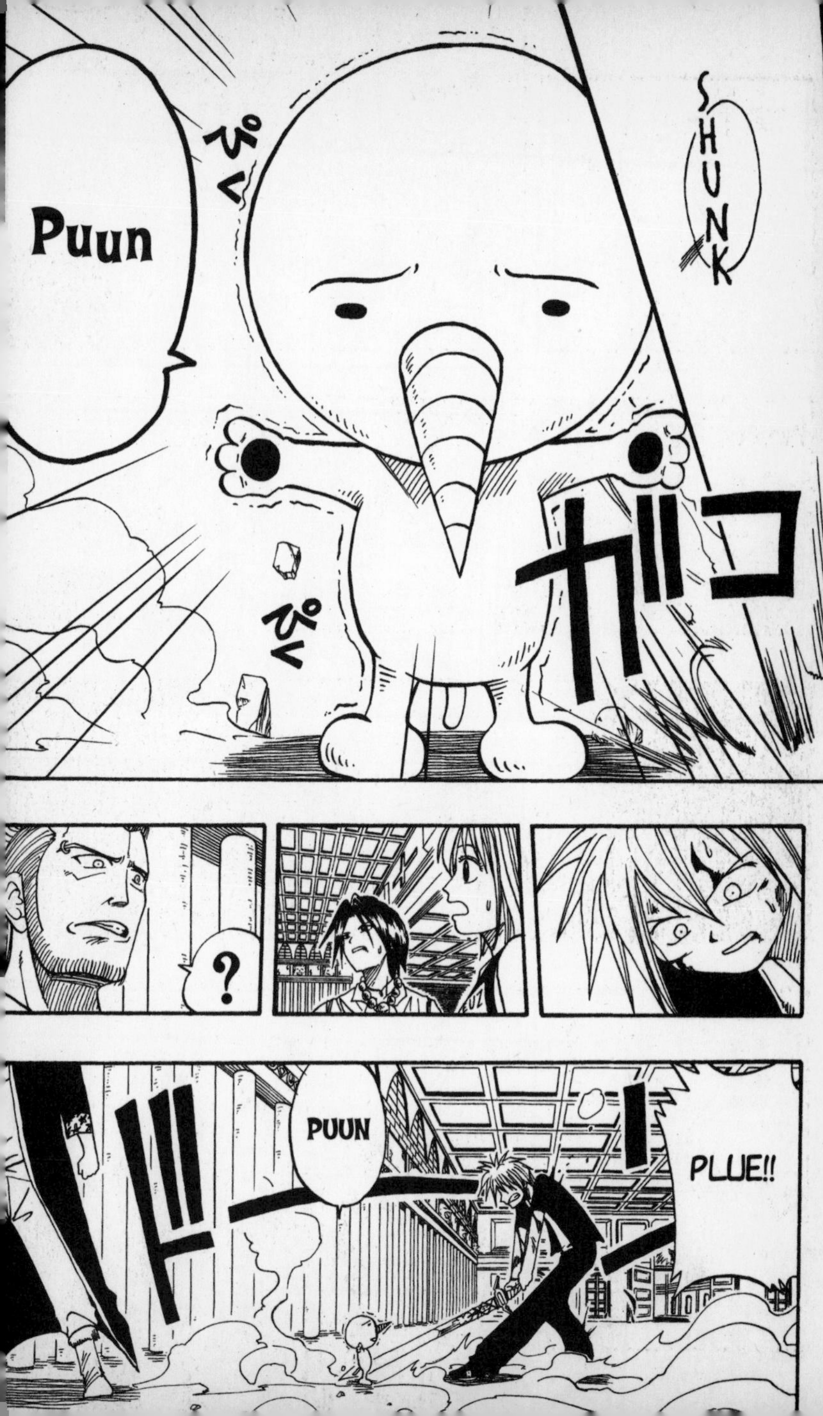
SHUNK
ガコ
ぴく
ぴく
Puun
?
PLUE!!
PUUN
ドー

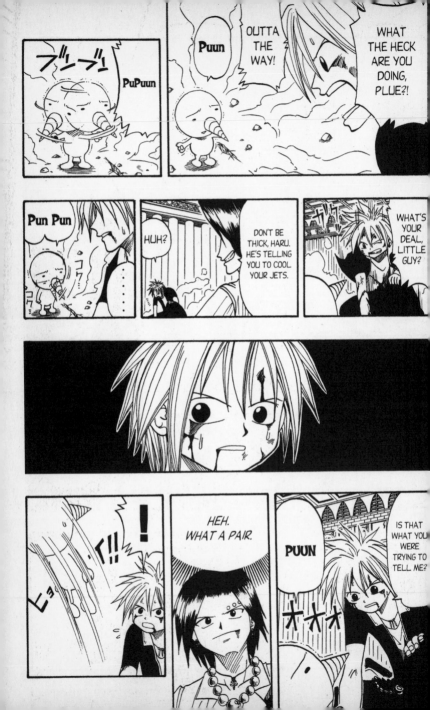

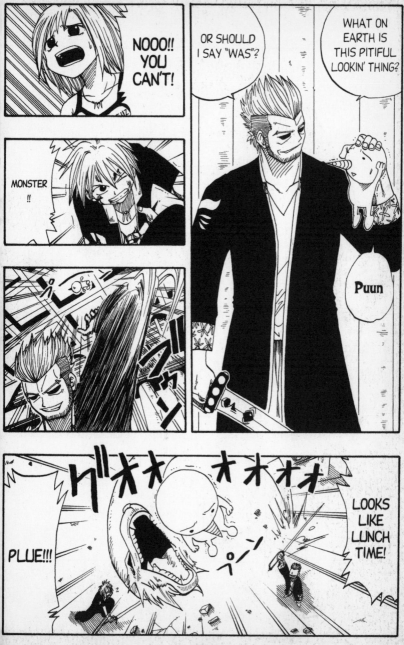

NOOO!! YOU CAN'T!

MONSTER !!

OR SHOULD I SAY "WAS"?

WHAT ON EARTH IS THIS PITIFUL LOOKIN' THING?

Puun

PLUE!!!

LOOKS LIKE LUNCH TIME!

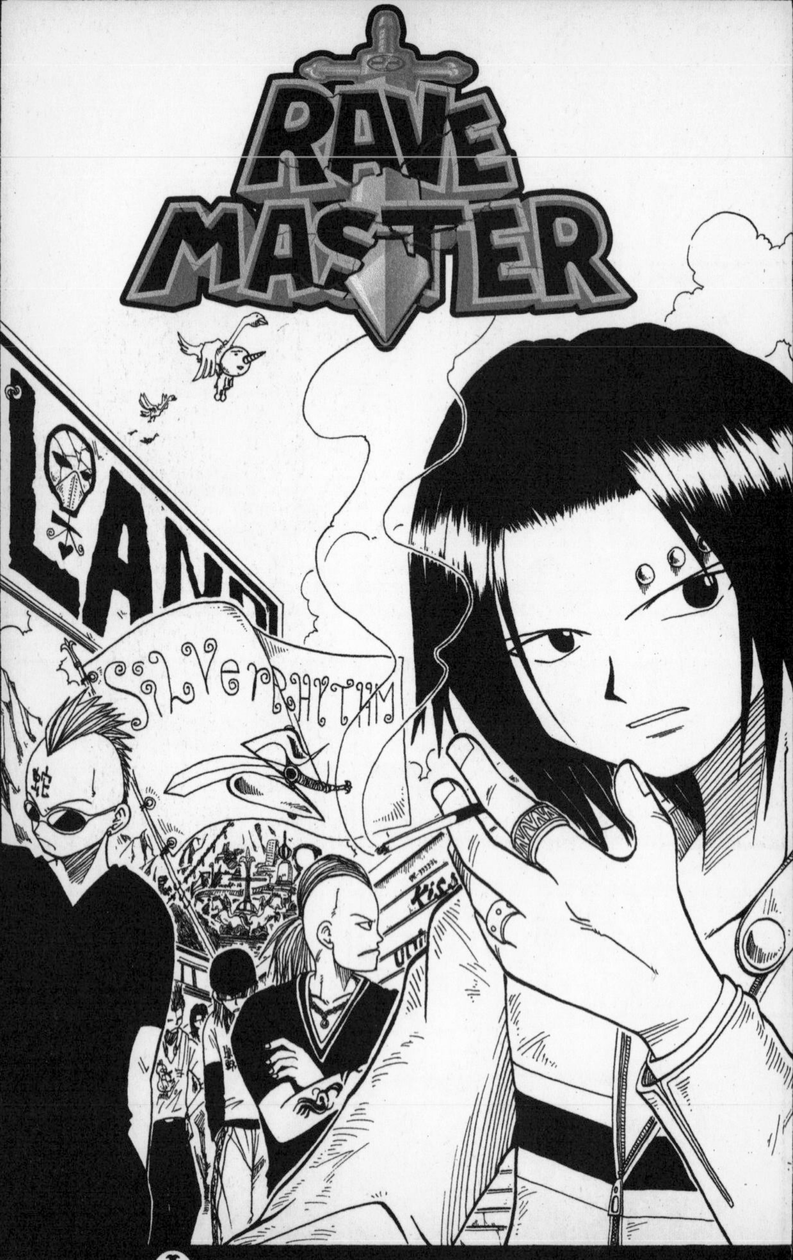
RAVE MASTER
SILVER RHYTHM

RAVE 15 ✠ SHOT TO THE HEART

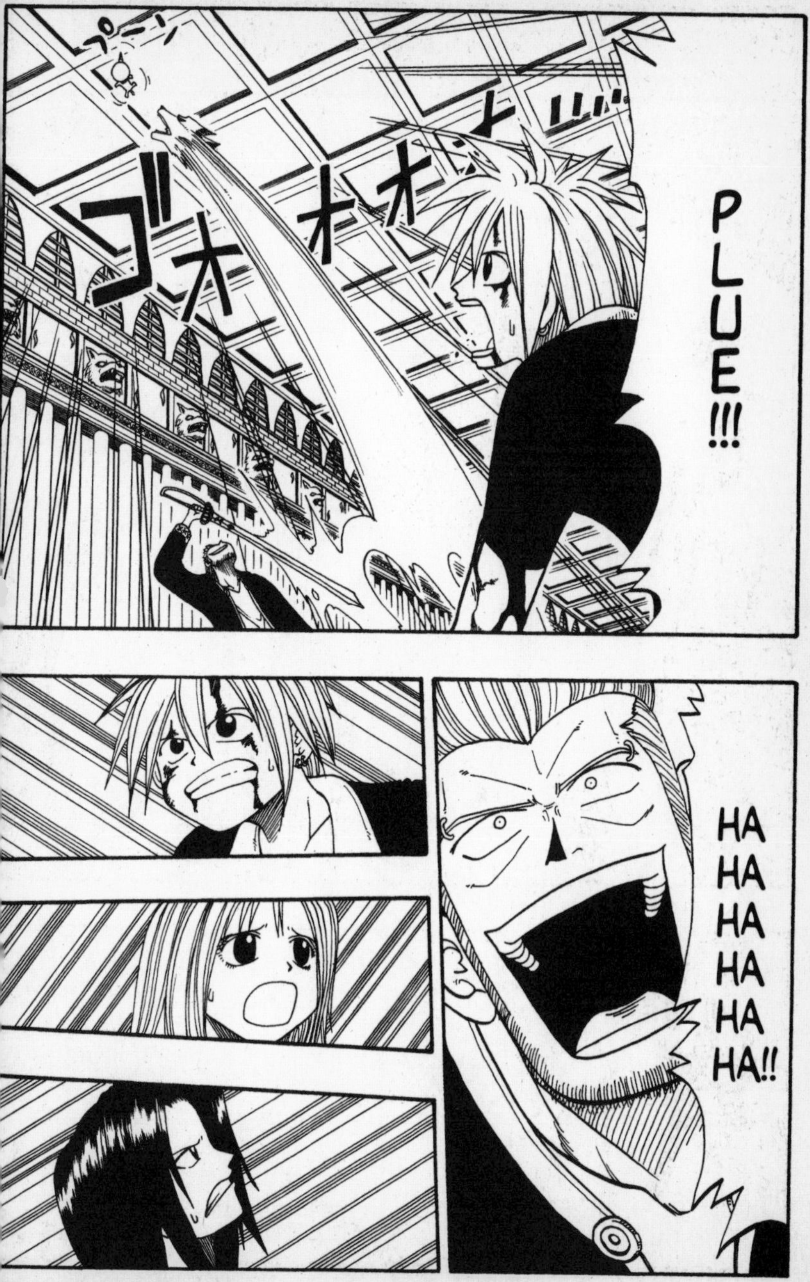
PLUE!!!
HA HA HA HA HA HA!!

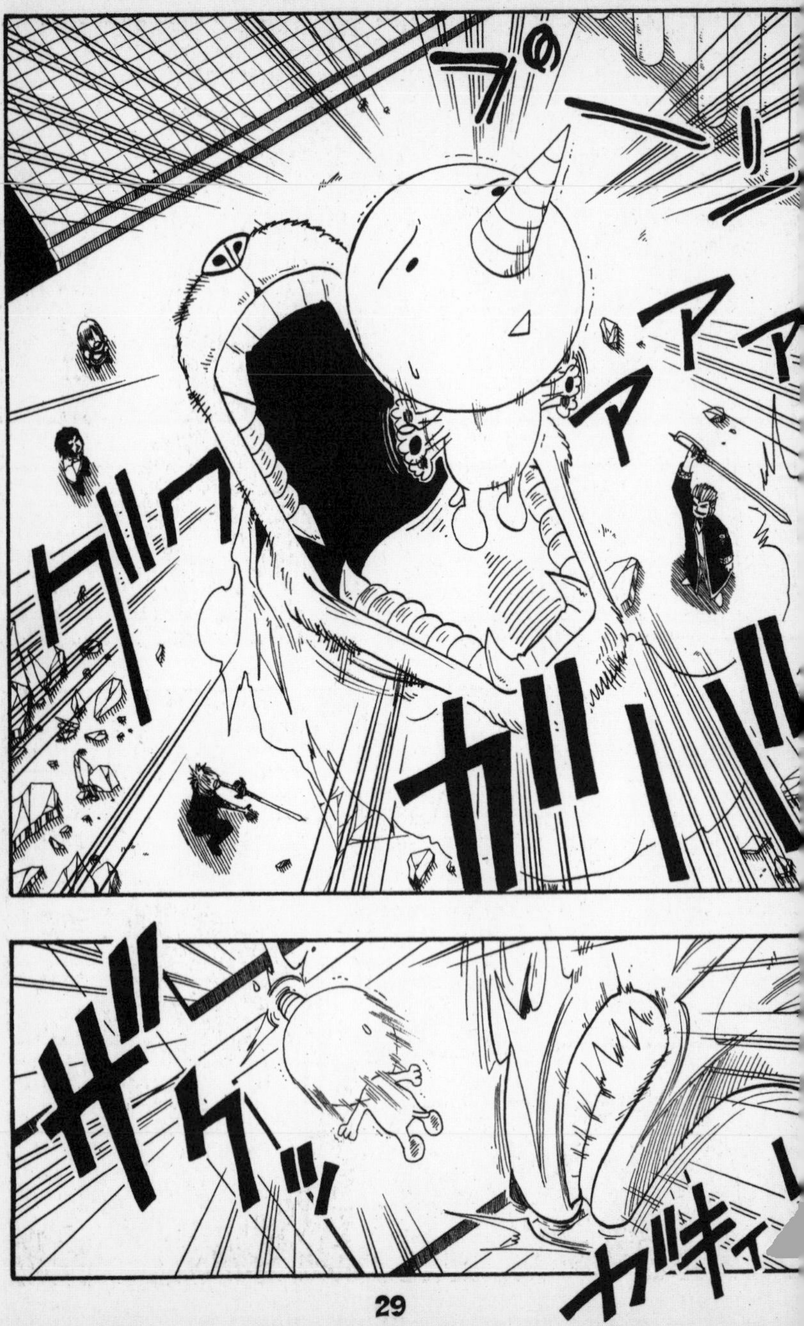
アアア
ガバ
グワ
ザグッ
ガキィ

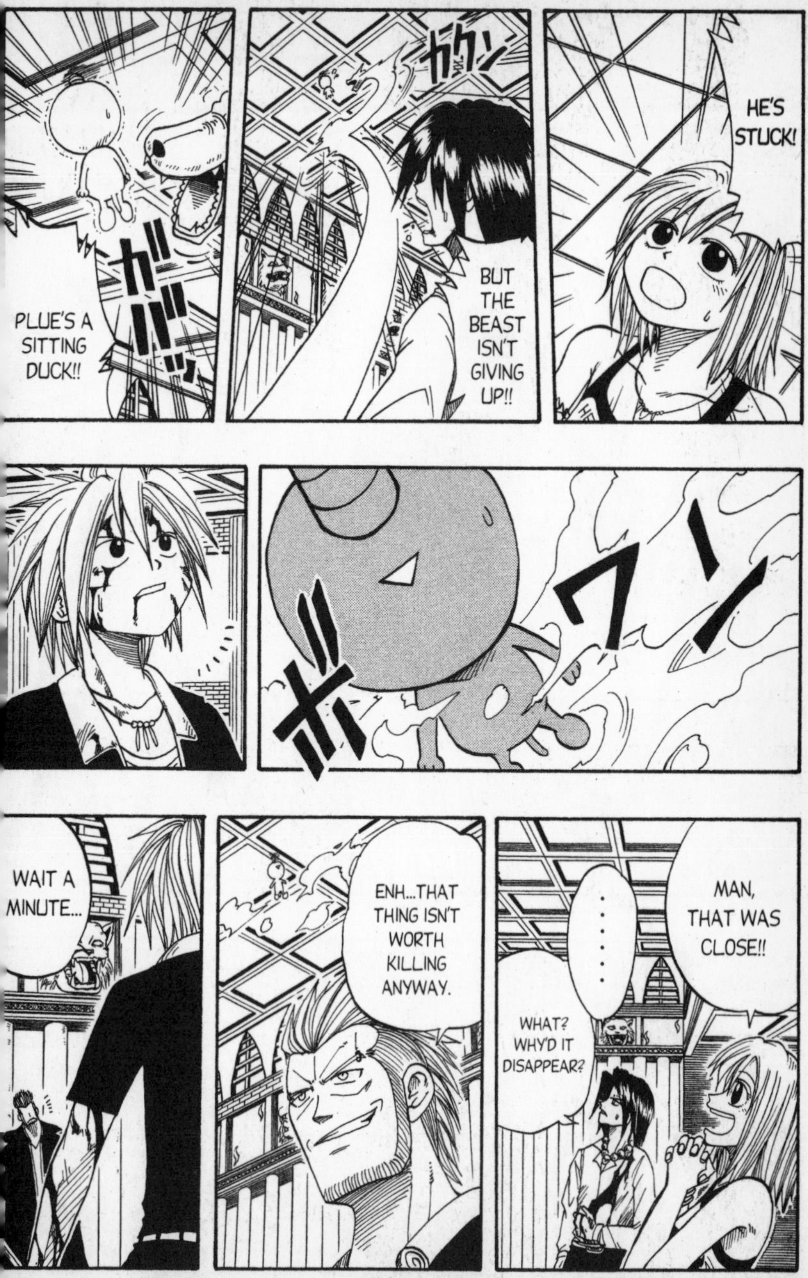
HE'S STUCK!
カクン
BUT THE BEAST ISN'T GIVING UP!!
PLUE'S A SITTING DUCK!!
ボワン
MAN, THAT WAS CLOSE!!
......
WHAT? WHY'D IT DISAPPEAR?
ENH...THAT THING ISN'T WORTH KILLING ANYWAY.
WAIT A MINUTE...

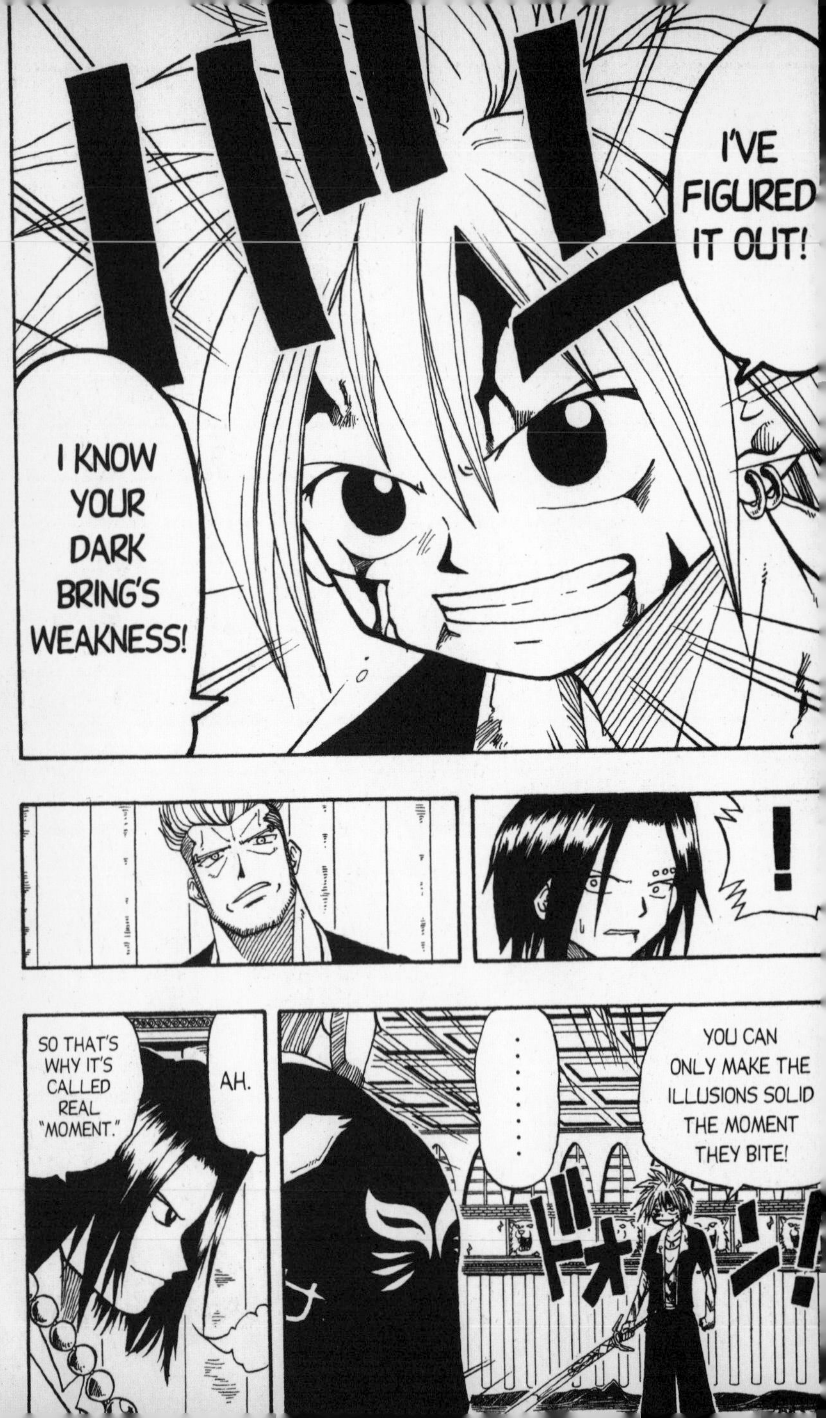
I'VE FIGURED IT OUT!
I KNOW YOUR DARK BRING'S WEAKNESS!
!
YOU CAN ONLY MAKE THE ILLUSIONS SOLID THE MOMENT THEY BITE!
......
ドオン!!
AH.
SO THAT'S WHY IT'S CALLED REAL "MOMENT."

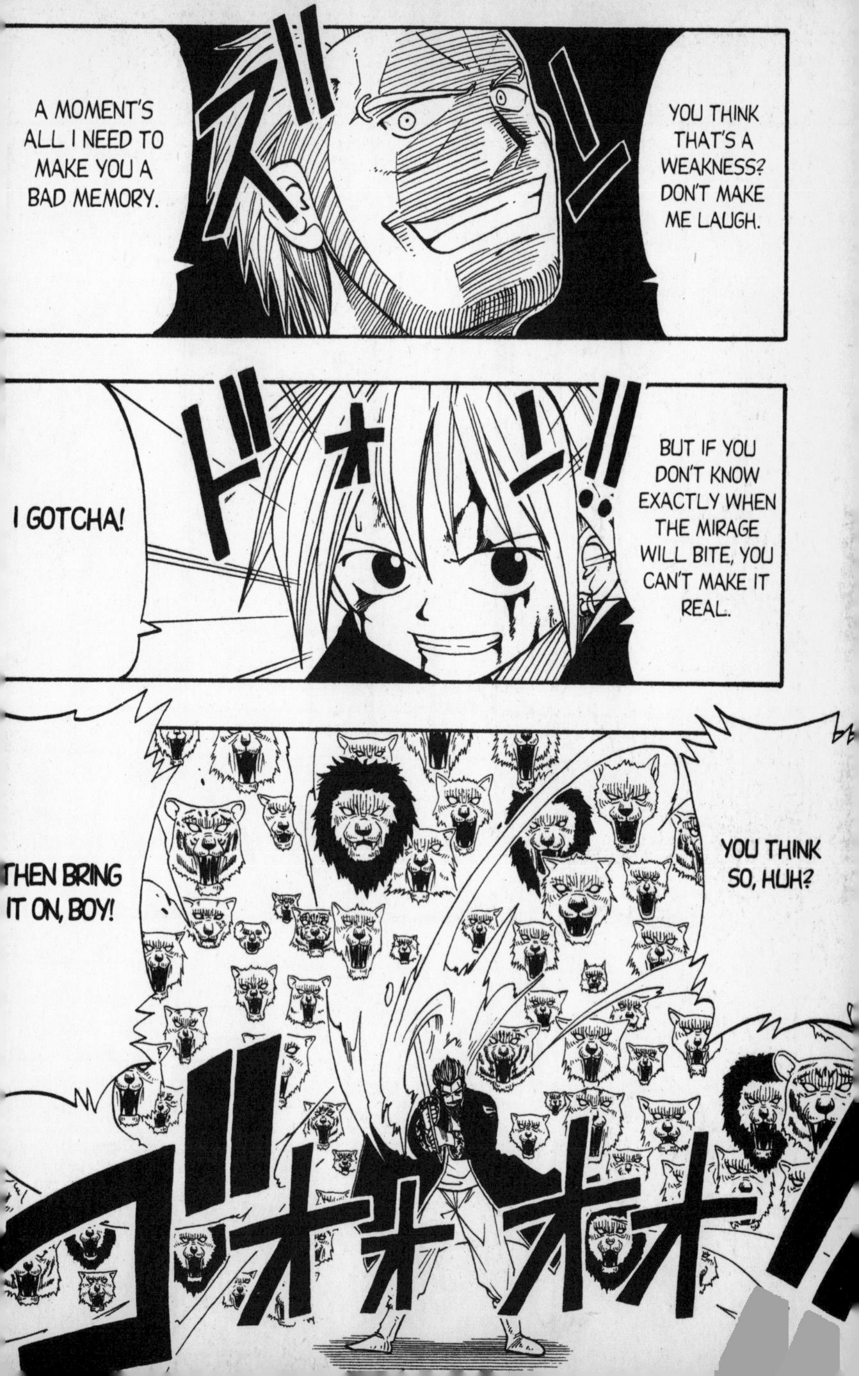
YOU THINK THAT'S A WEAKNESS? DON'T MAKE ME LAUGH.
ズン
A MOMENT'S ALL I NEED TO MAKE YOU A BAD MEMORY.
BUT IF YOU DON'T KNOW EXACTLY WHEN THE MIRAGE WILL BITE, YOU CAN'T MAKE IT REAL.
ドォーン!!
I GOTCHA!
YOU THINK SO, HUH?
THEN BRING IT ON, BOY!
ゴオオオ!!

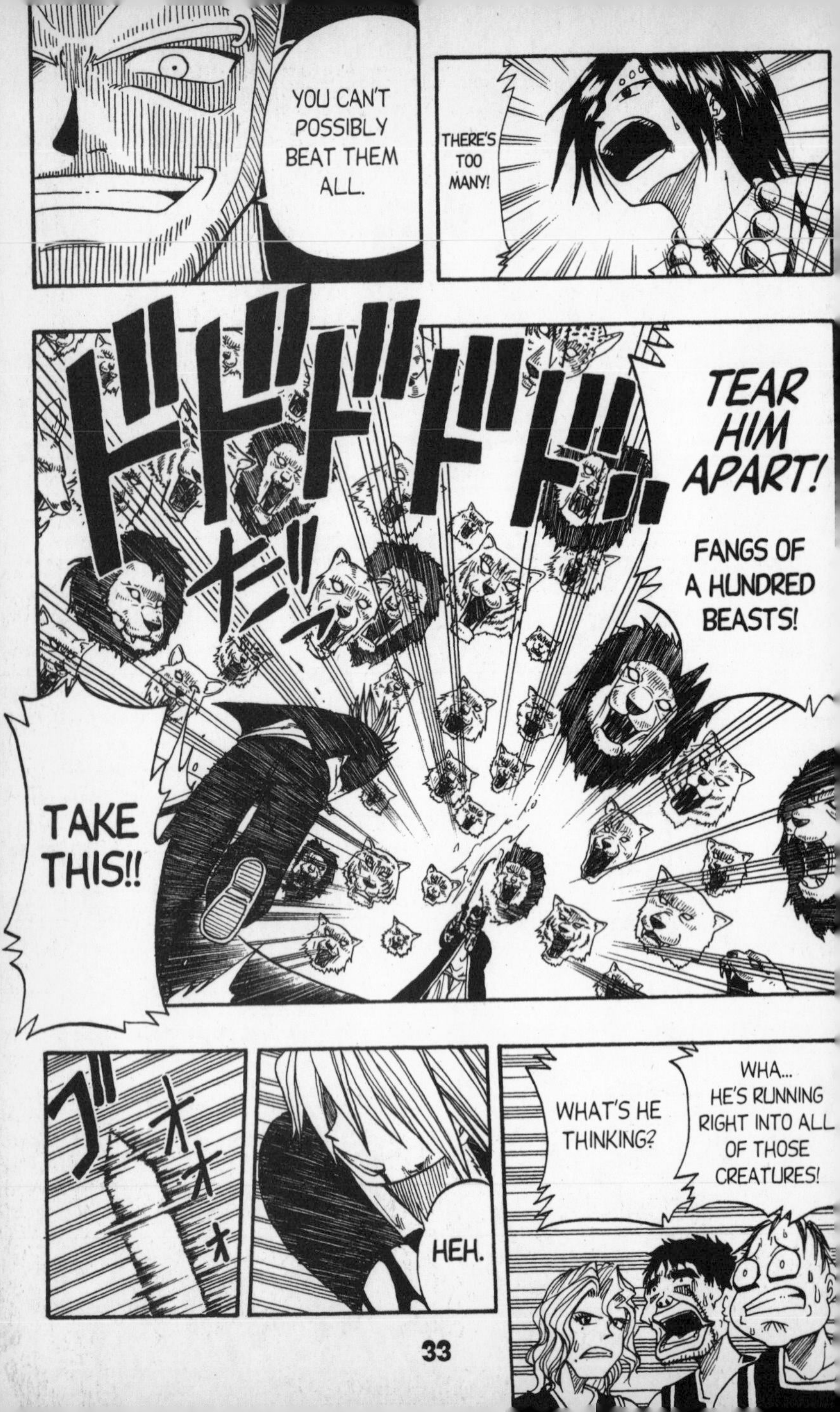
THERE'S TOO MANY!
YOU CAN'T POSSIBLY BEAT THEM ALL.
TEAR HIM APART!
FANGS OF A HUNDRED BEASTS!
TAKE THIS!!
WHA... HE'S RUNNING RIGHT INTO ALL OF THOSE CREATURES!
WHAT'S HE THINKING?
HEH.

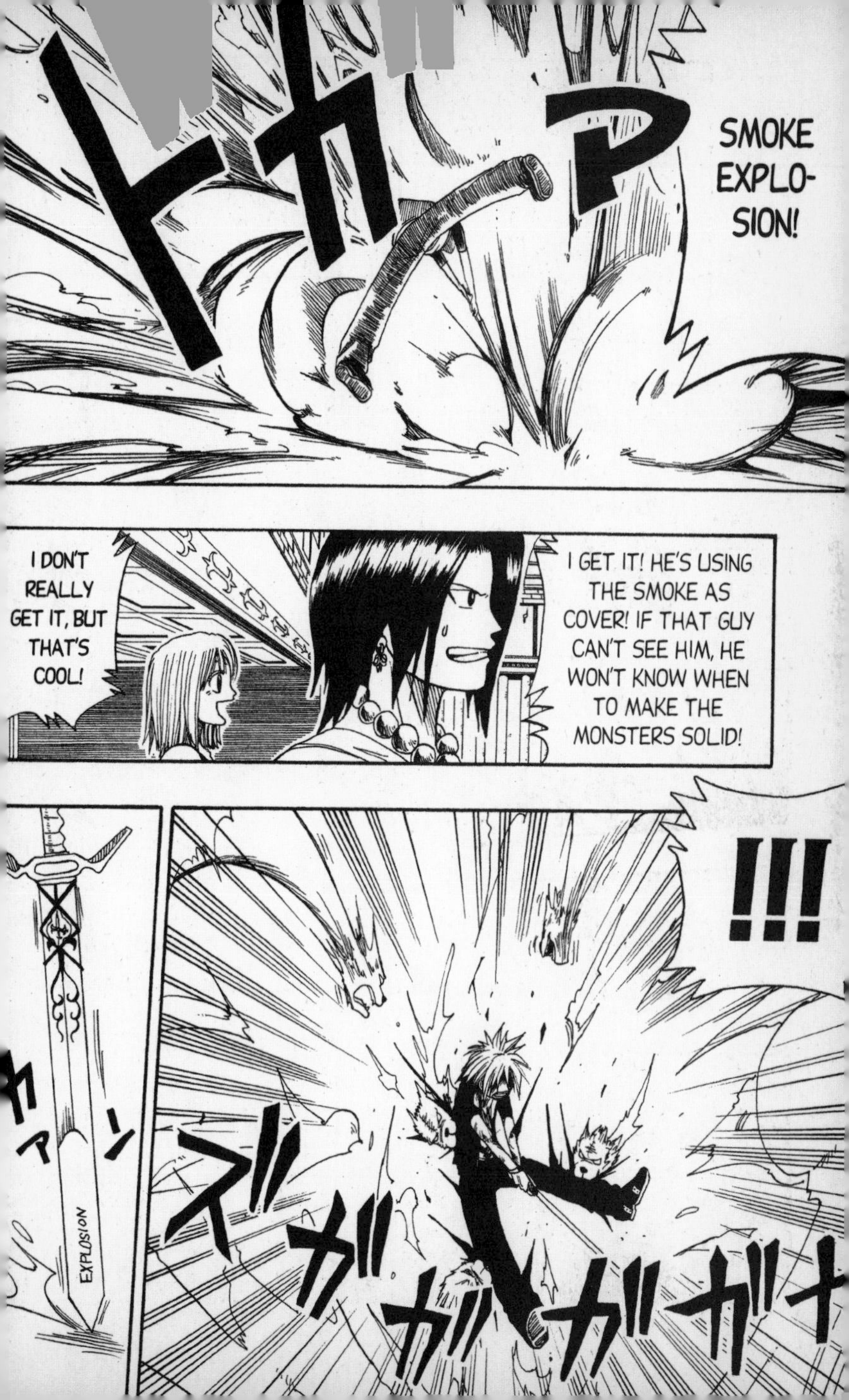
SMOKE EXPLOSION!
I GET IT! HE'S USING THE SMOKE AS COVER! IF THAT GUY CAN'T SEE HIM, HE WON'T KNOW WHEN TO MAKE THE MONSTERS SOLID!
I DON'T REALLY GET IT, BUT THAT'S COOL!
!!!
EXPLOSION

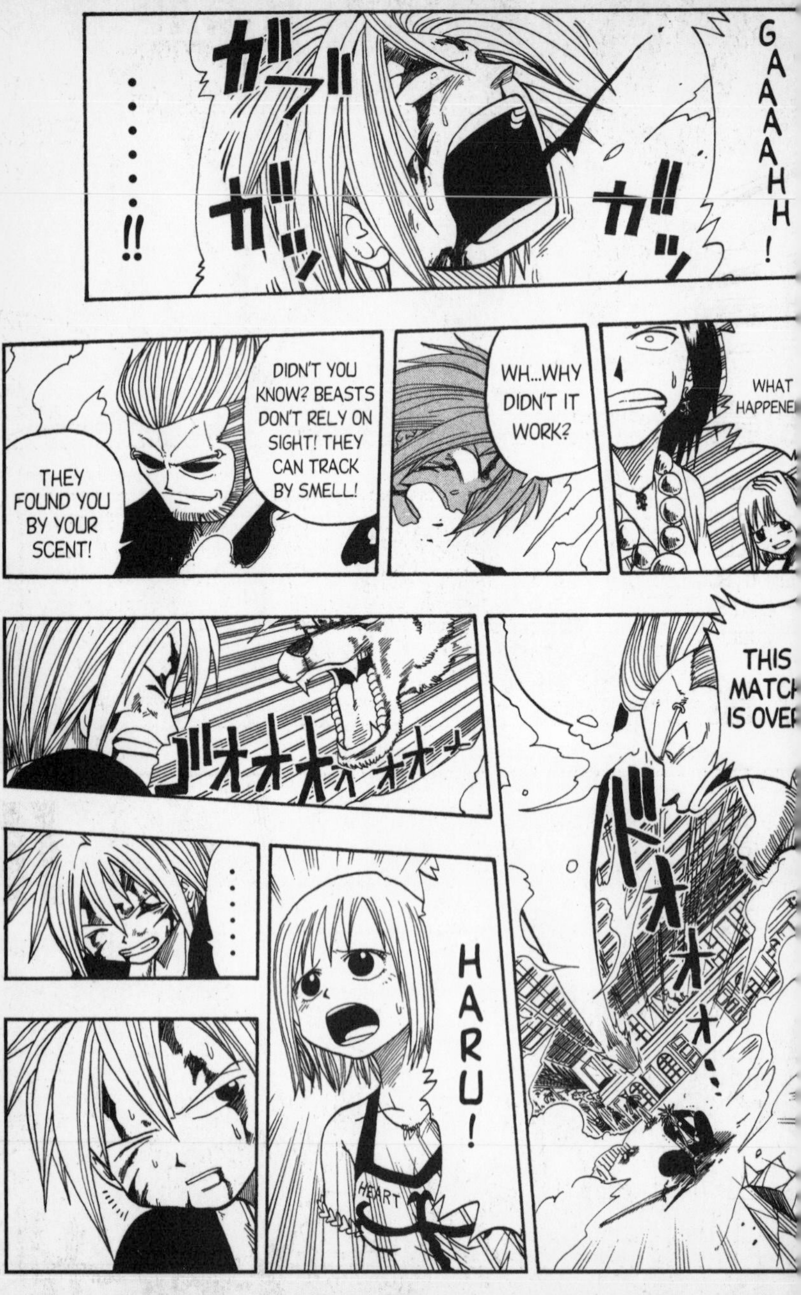
GAAAAHH!
ガッ
ガブッ
ガッ
......!!
WHAT HAPPENE
WH...WHY DIDN'T IT WORK?
DIDN'T YOU KNOW? BEASTS DON'T RELY ON SIGHT! THEY CAN TRACK BY SMELL!
THEY FOUND YOU BY YOUR SCENT!
THIS MATCH IS OVE
ドォオオ
ゴオオオォオオ
HARU!
HEART
......

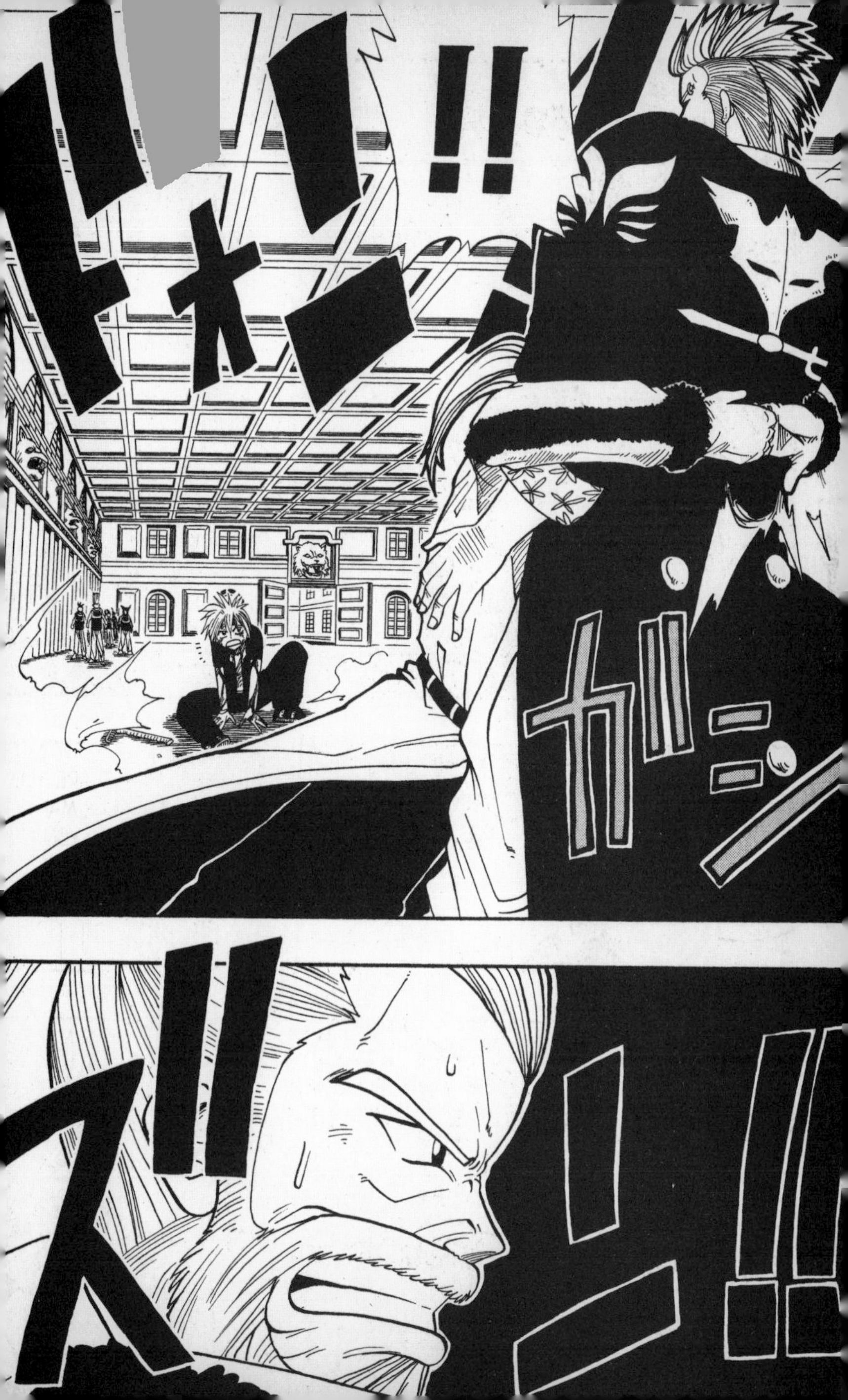
ドォーン!!

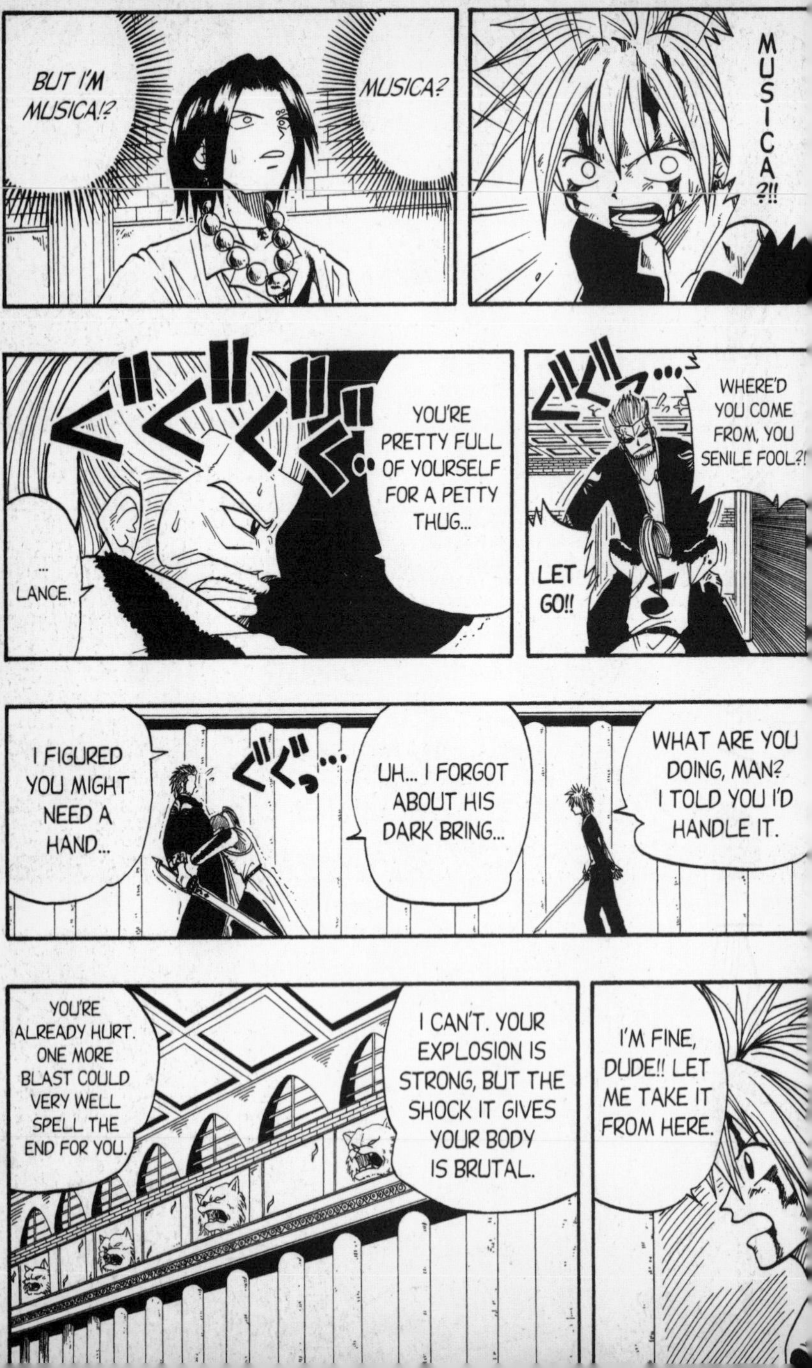
MUSICA?!!
MUSICA?
BUT I'M MUSICA!?
ぐぐっ…
WHERE'D YOU COME FROM, YOU SENILE FOOL?!
LET GO!!
ぐぐぐぐ…
YOU'RE PRETTY FULL OF YOURSELF FOR A PETTY THUG...
... LANCE.
WHAT ARE YOU DOING, MAN? I TOLD YOU I'D HANDLE IT.
UH... I FORGOT ABOUT HIS DARK BRING...
ぐぐっ…
I FIGURED YOU MIGHT NEED A HAND...
I'M FINE, DUDE!! LET ME TAKE IT FROM HERE.
I CAN'T. YOUR EXPLOSION IS STRONG, BUT THE SHOCK IT GIVES YOUR BODY IS BRUTAL.
YOU'RE ALREADY HURT. ONE MORE BLAST COULD VERY WELL SPELL THE END FOR YOU.

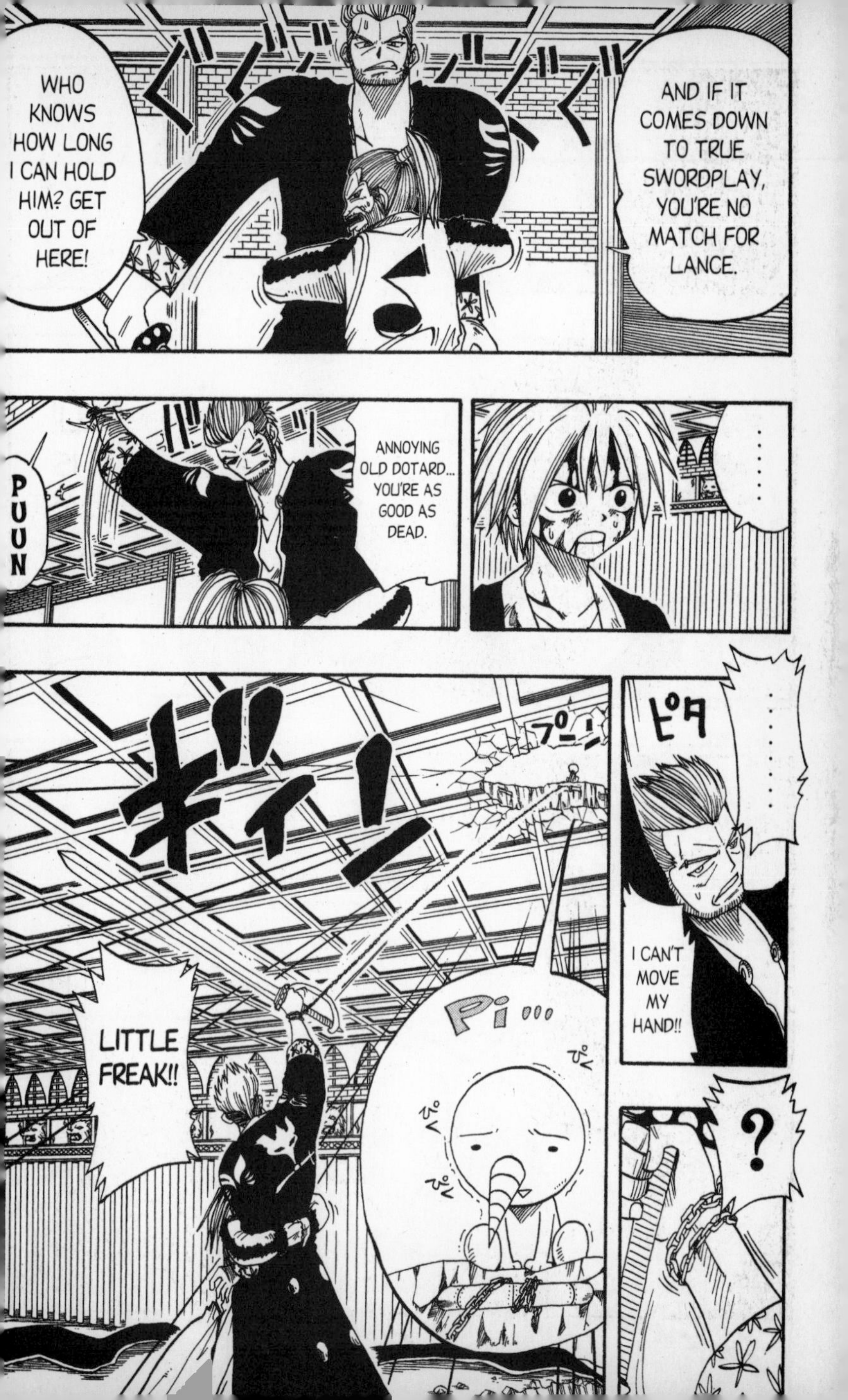
AND IF IT COMES DOWN TO TRUE SWORDPLAY, YOU'RE NO MATCH FOR LANCE.
WHO KNOWS HOW LONG I CAN HOLD HIM? GET OUT OF HERE!
......
ANNOYING OLD DOTARD... YOU'RE AS GOOD AS DEAD.
PUUN
ピタ
......
I CAN'T MOVE MY HAND!!
?
Pi ...
LITTLE FREAK!!

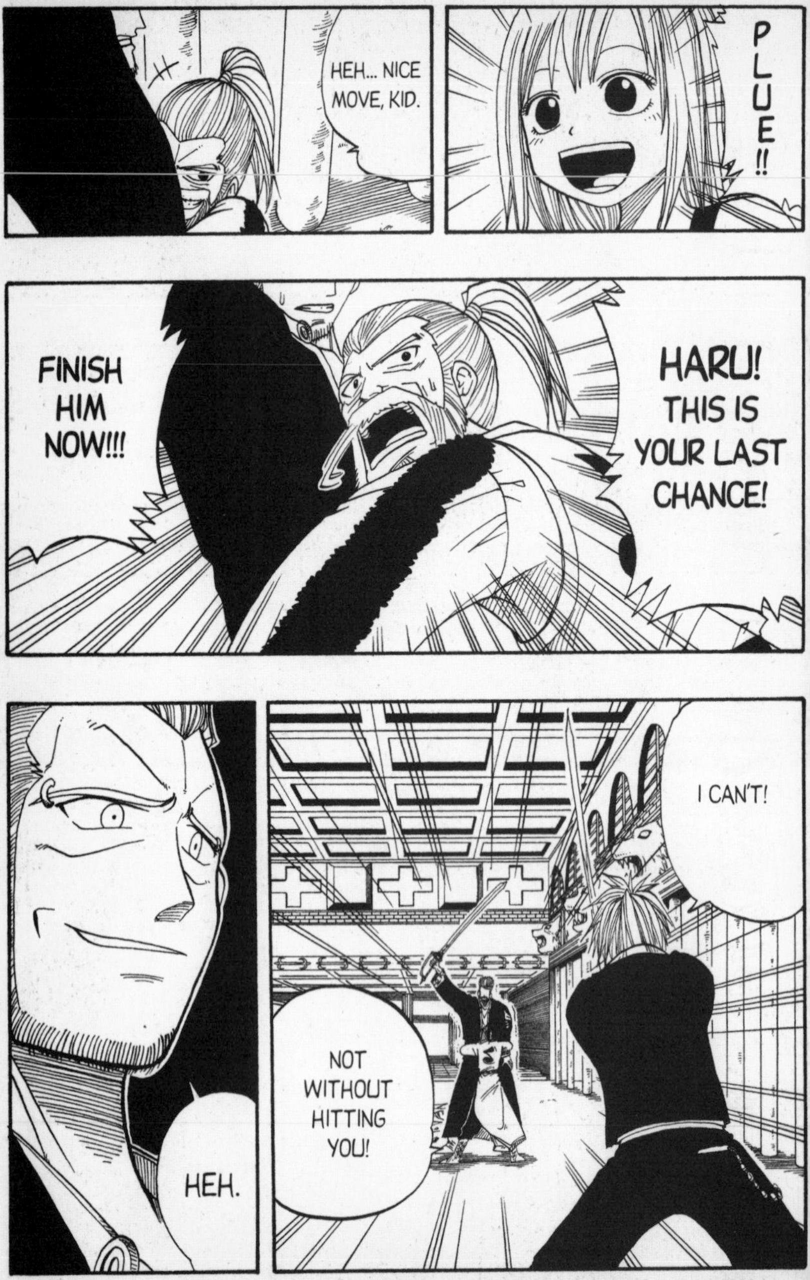
PLUE!!
HEH... NICE MOVE, KID.
HARU! THIS IS YOUR LAST CHANCE!
FINISH HIM NOW!!!
I CAN'T!
NOT WITHOUT HITTING YOU!
HEH.

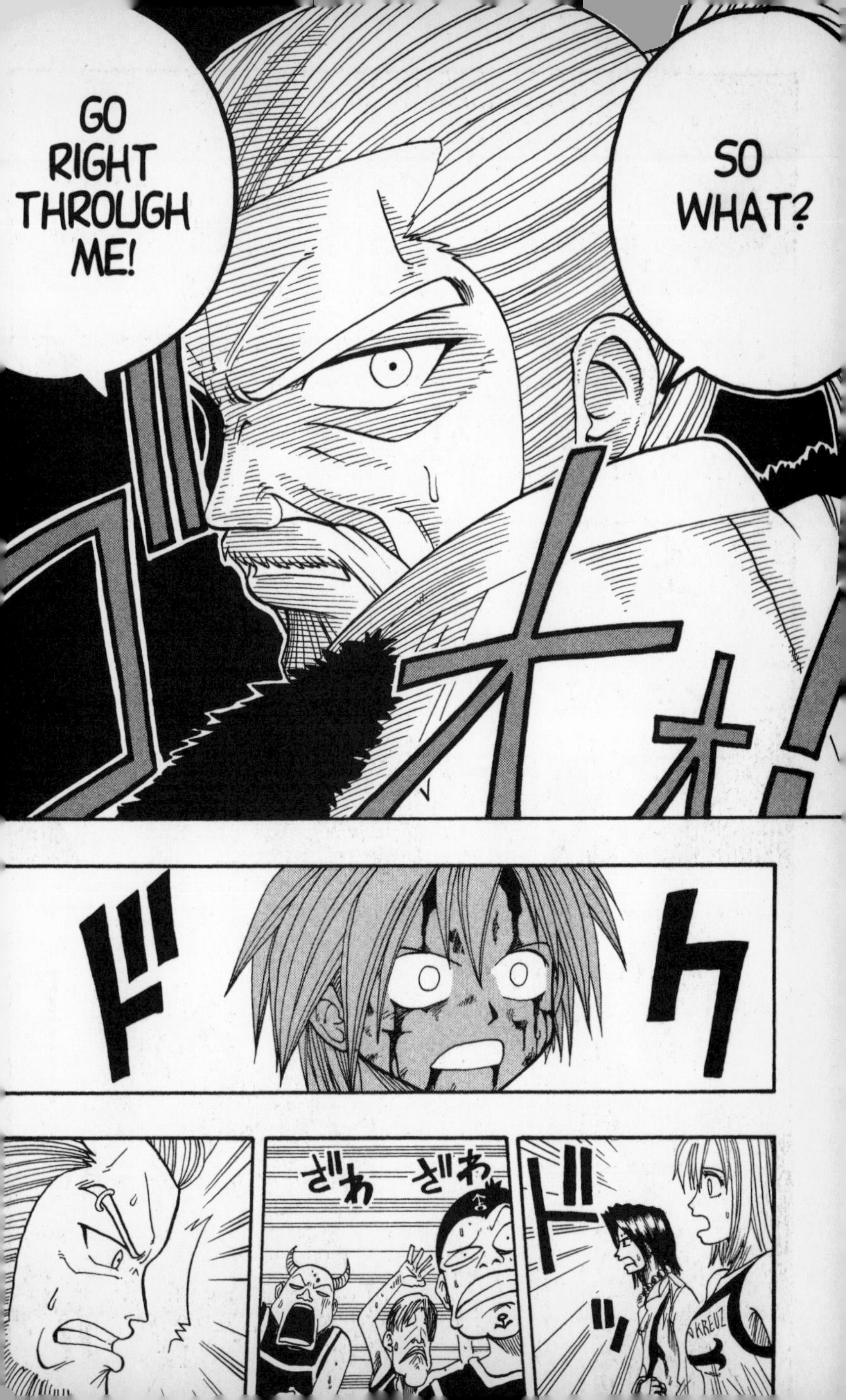
SO WHAT?
GO RIGHT THROUGH ME!
ゴオォ!
ドク
ドドッ
KREUZ
ざわ ざわ

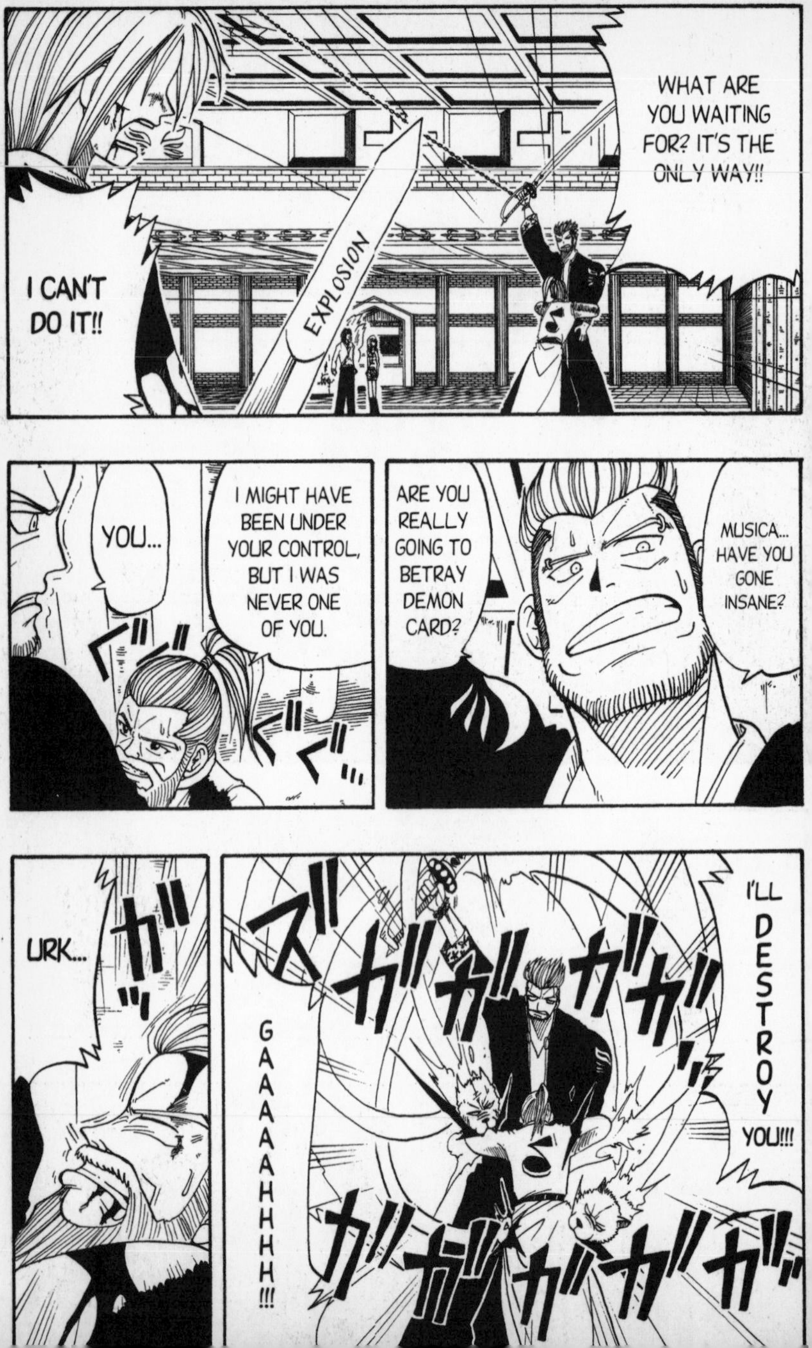
WHAT ARE YOU WAITING FOR? IT'S THE ONLY WAY!!
EXPLOSION
I CAN'T DO IT!!
MUSICA... HAVE YOU GONE INSANE?
ARE YOU REALLY GOING TO BETRAY DEMON CARD?
I MIGHT HAVE BEEN UNDER YOUR CONTROL, BUT I WAS NEVER ONE OF YOU.
YOU...
I'LL DESTROY YOU!!!
GAAAAAHHHH!!!
URK...

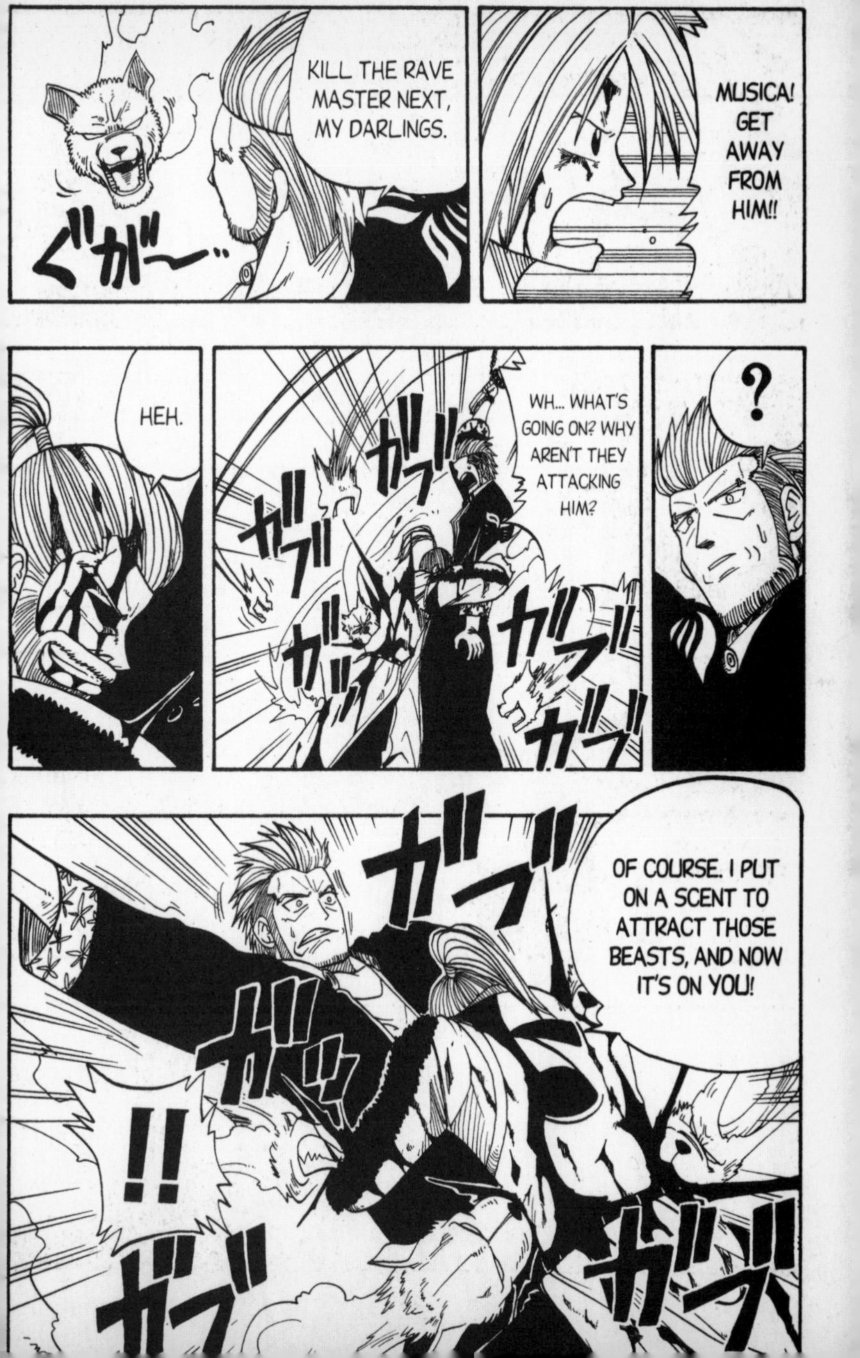

MUSICA! GET AWAY FROM HIM!!
KILL THE RAVE MASTER NEXT, MY DARLINGS.
?
WH... WHAT'S GOING ON? WHY AREN'T THEY ATTACKING HIM?
ガブ
ガッ
HEH.
OF COURSE. I PUT ON A SCENT TO ATTRACT THOSE BEASTS, AND NOW IT'S ON YOU!
ガブ
ガッ
!!

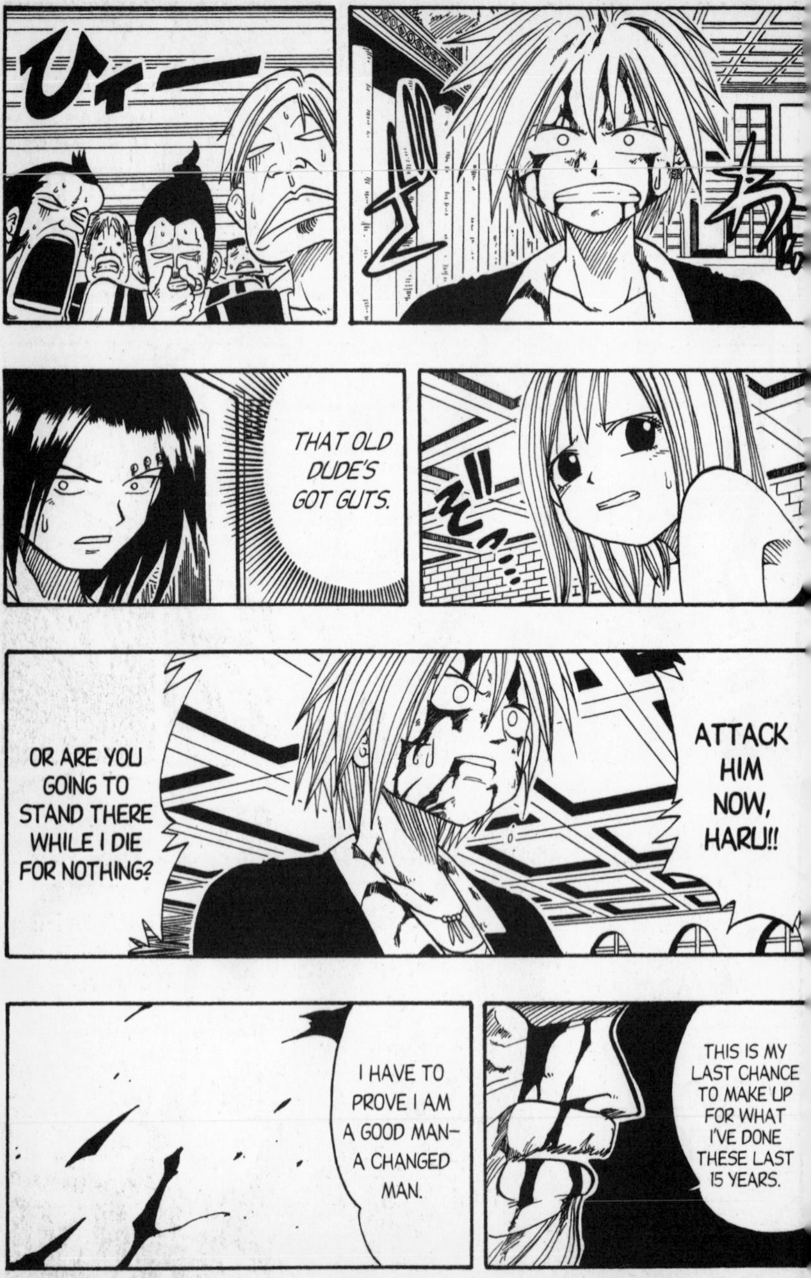
ひィーー
THAT OLD DUDE'S GOT GUTS.
ATTACK HIM NOW, HARU!!
OR ARE YOU GOING TO STAND THERE WHILE I DIE FOR NOTHING?
THIS IS MY LAST CHANCE TO MAKE UP FOR WHAT I'VE DONE THESE LAST 15 YEARS.
I HAVE TO PROVE I AM A GOOD MAN– A CHANGED MAN.

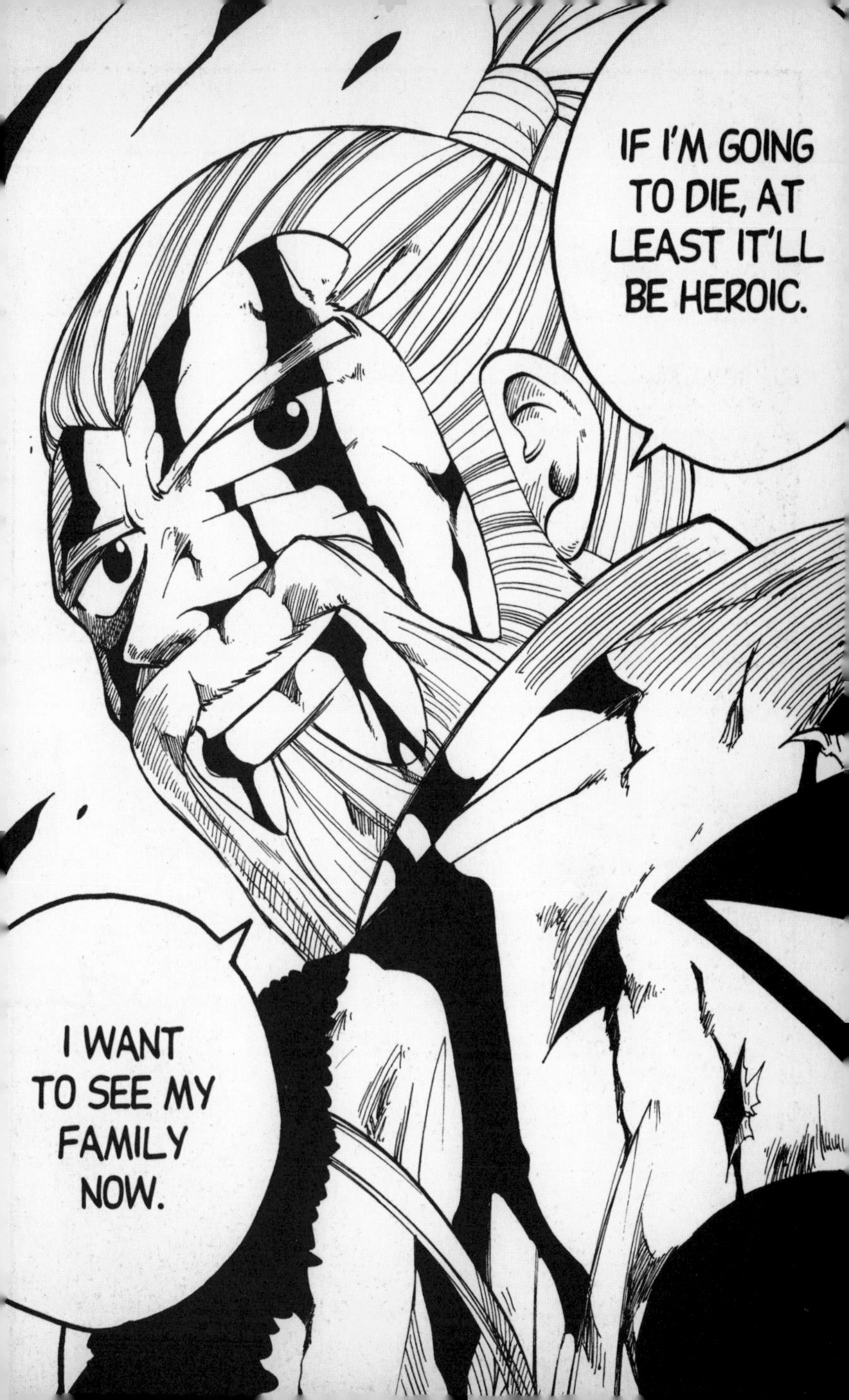
IF I'M GOING TO DIE, AT LEAST IT'LL BE HEROIC.
I WANT TO SEE MY FAMILY NOW.

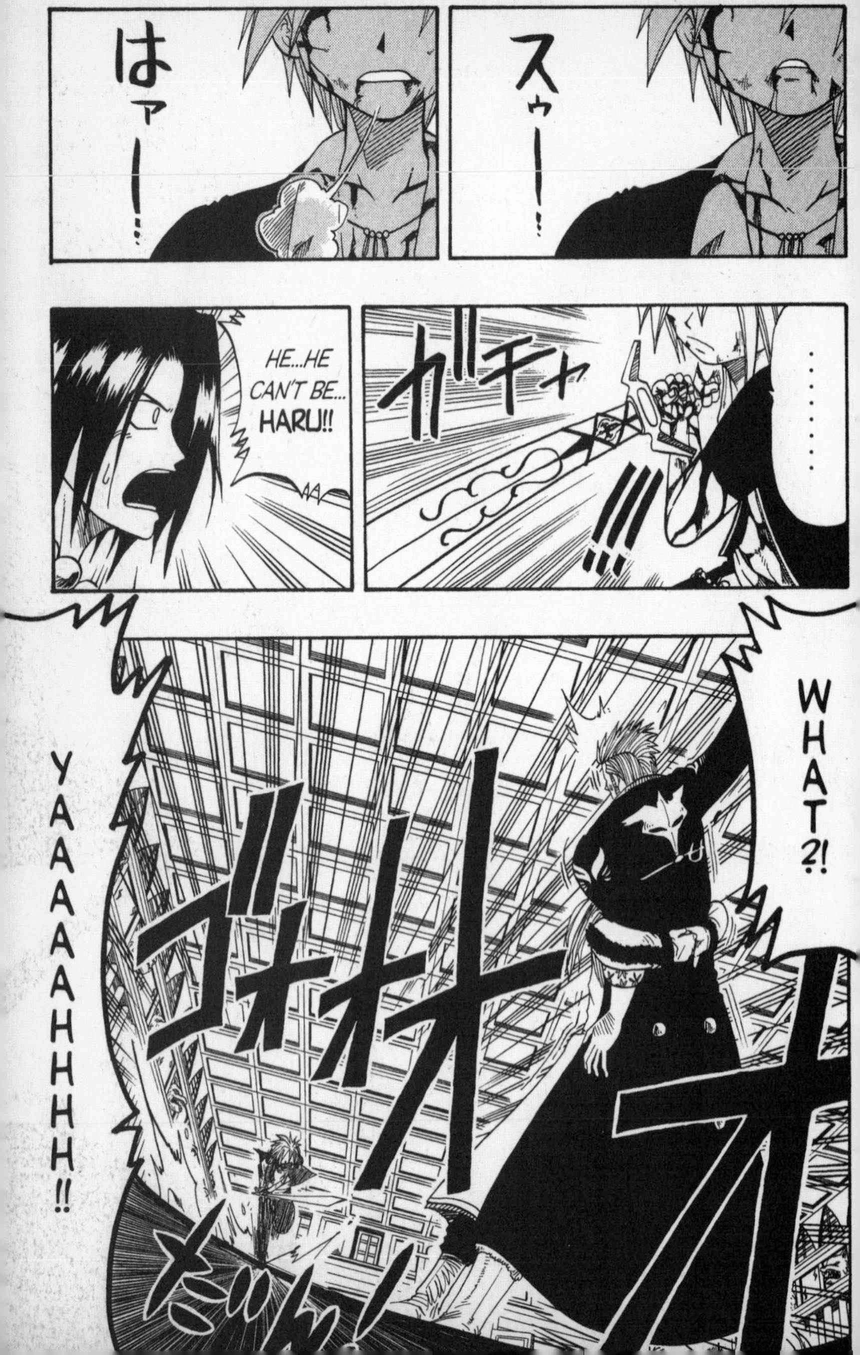
スゥー…!
はァー…!
ガチャ
……
HE...HE CAN'T BE... HARU!!
WHAT?!
ゴオオ
YAAAAAHHHH!!

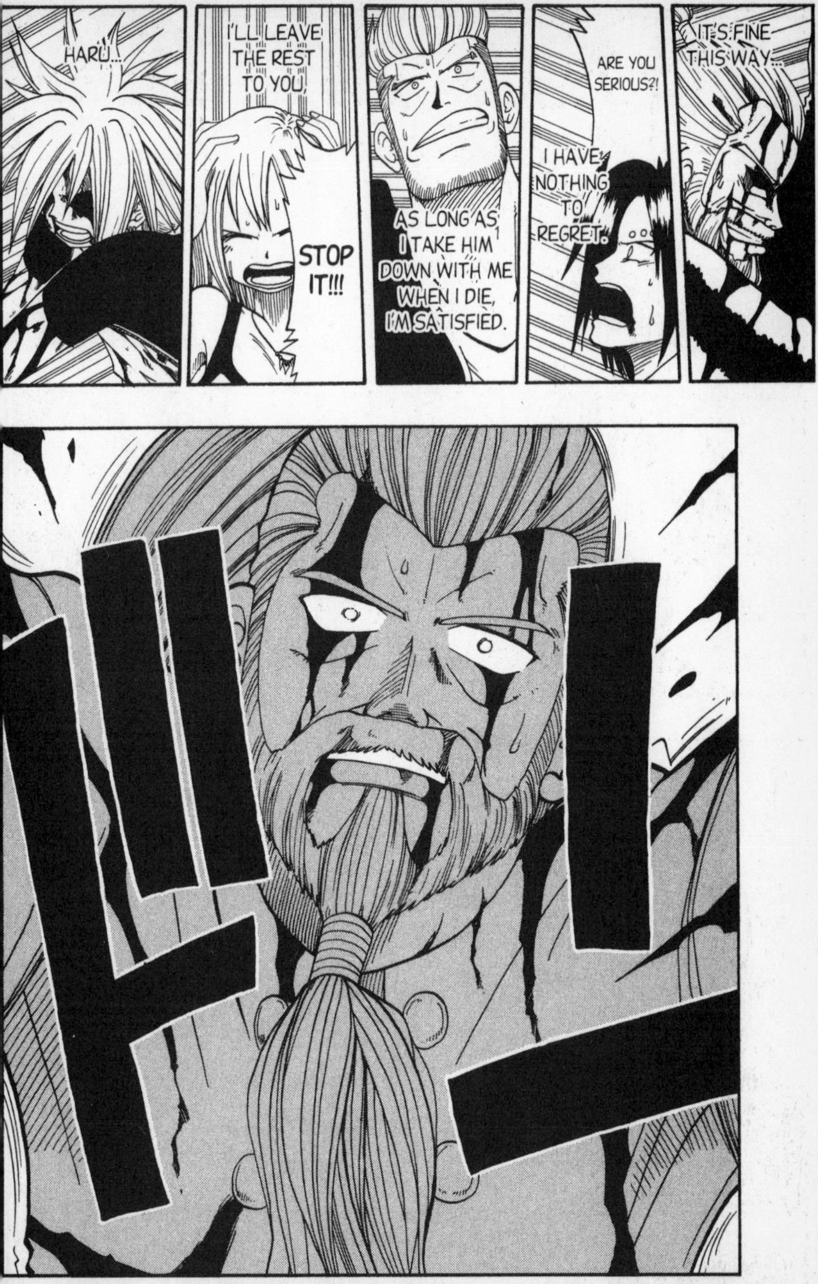
IT'S FINE THIS WAY...
ARE YOU SERIOUS?!
I HAVE NOTHING TO REGRET.
AS LONG AS I TAKE HIM DOWN WITH ME WHEN I DIE, I'M SATISFIED.
I'LL LEAVE THE REST TO YOU,
STOP IT!!!
HARU...

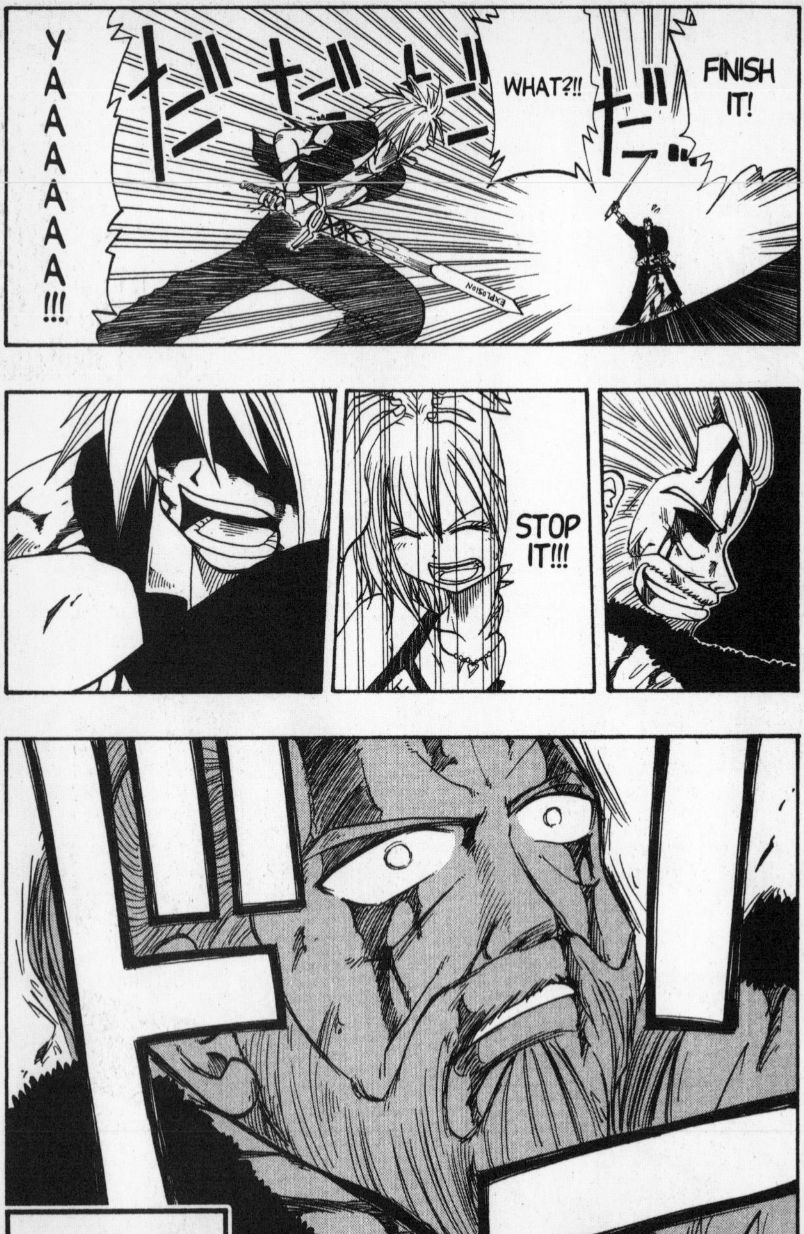
FINISH IT!
WHAT?!!
YAAAAAAAAA!!!
EXPLOSION
STOP IT!!!

RAVE

RAVE 16 ✚ FEEL THE BURN

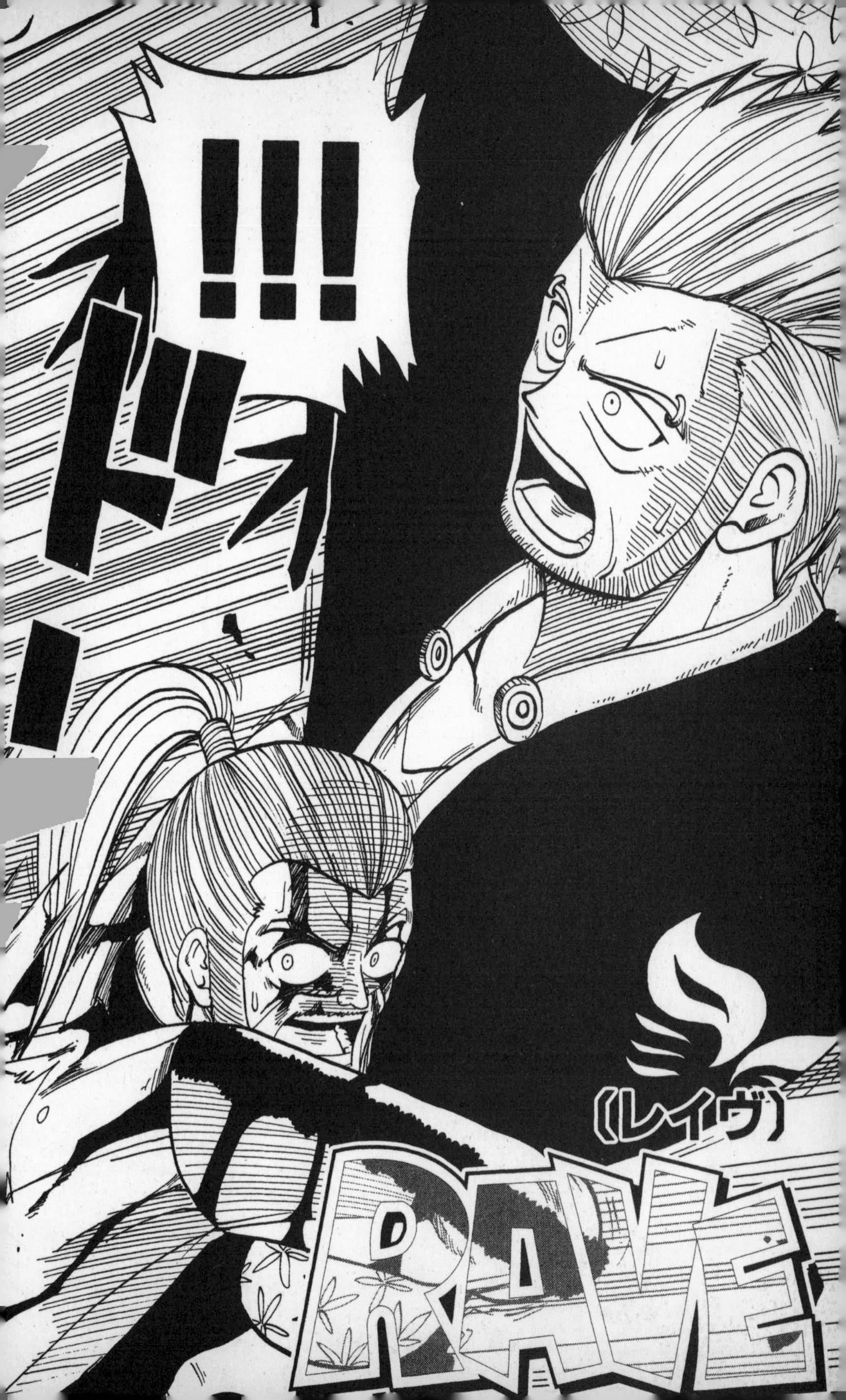
!!!
ドッ
(レイヴ)
RAVE

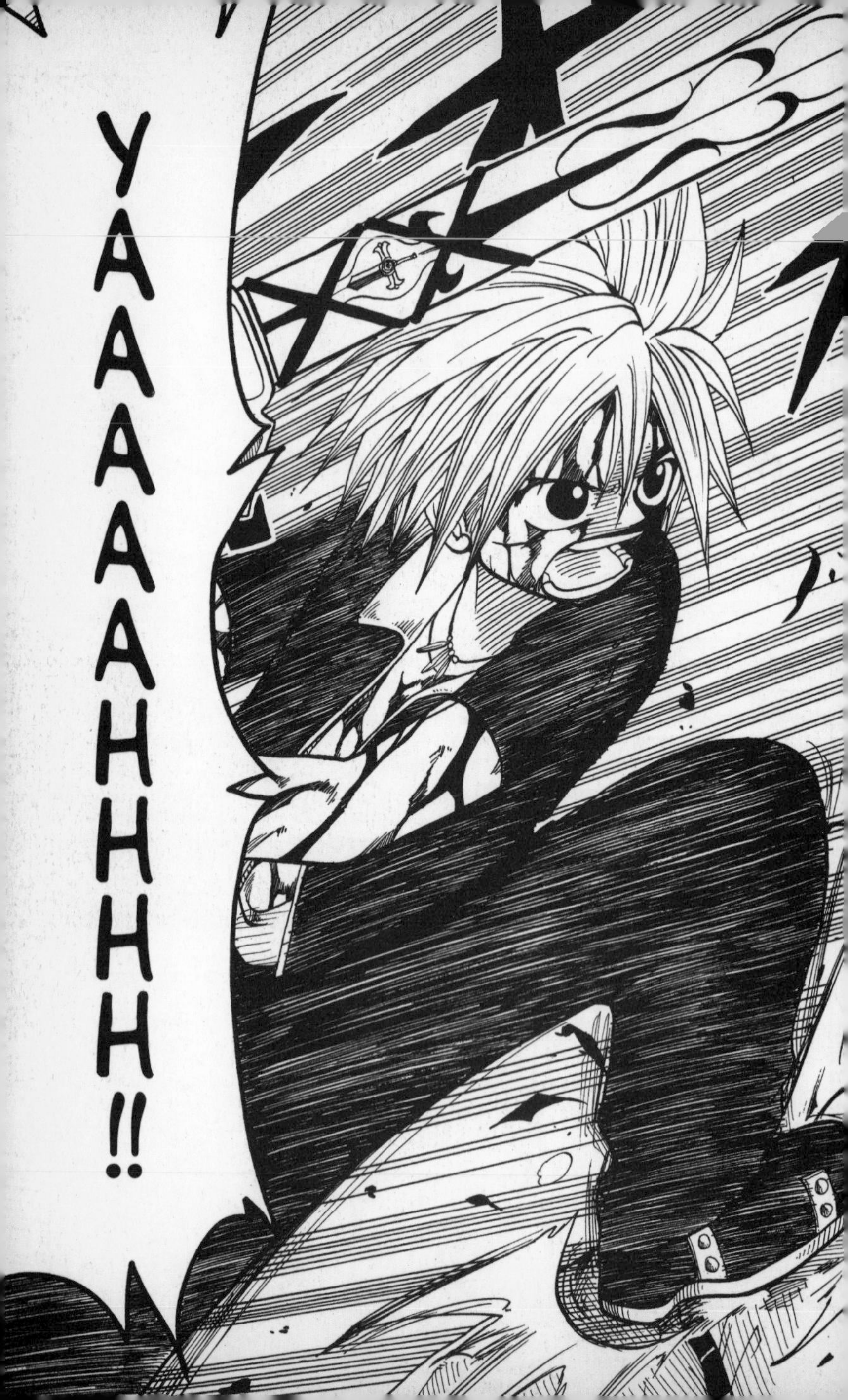
YAAAAAAHHHH!!

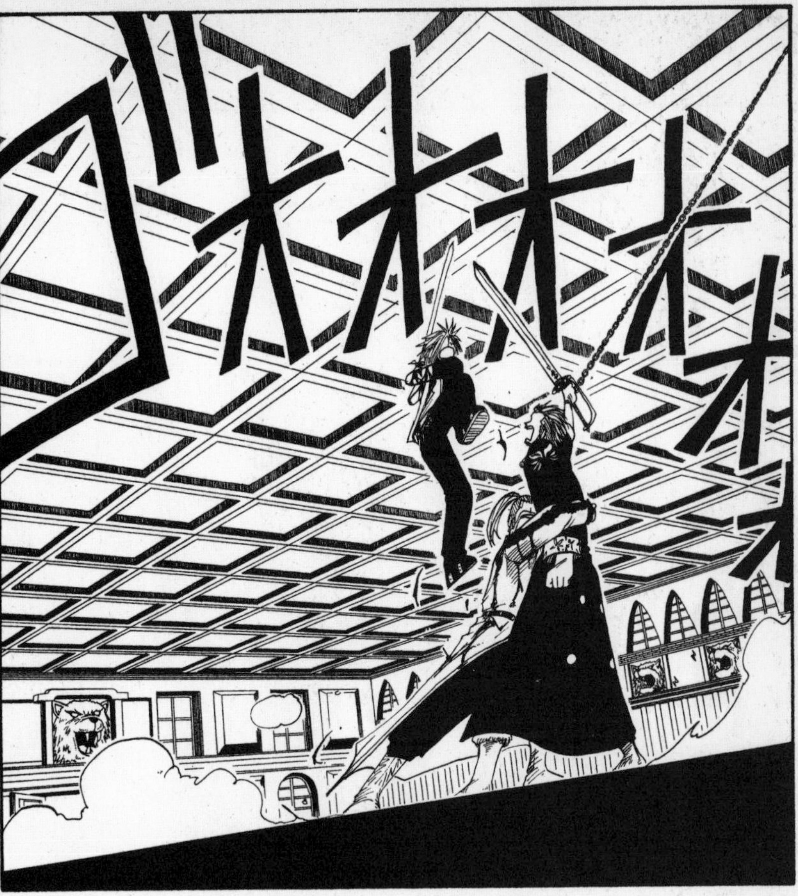

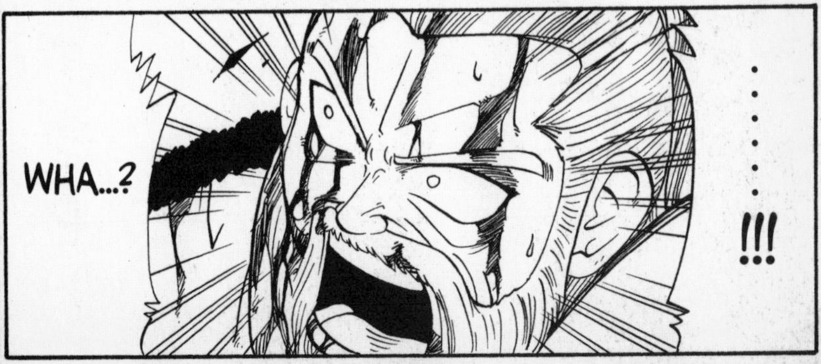
......!!!
WHA...?

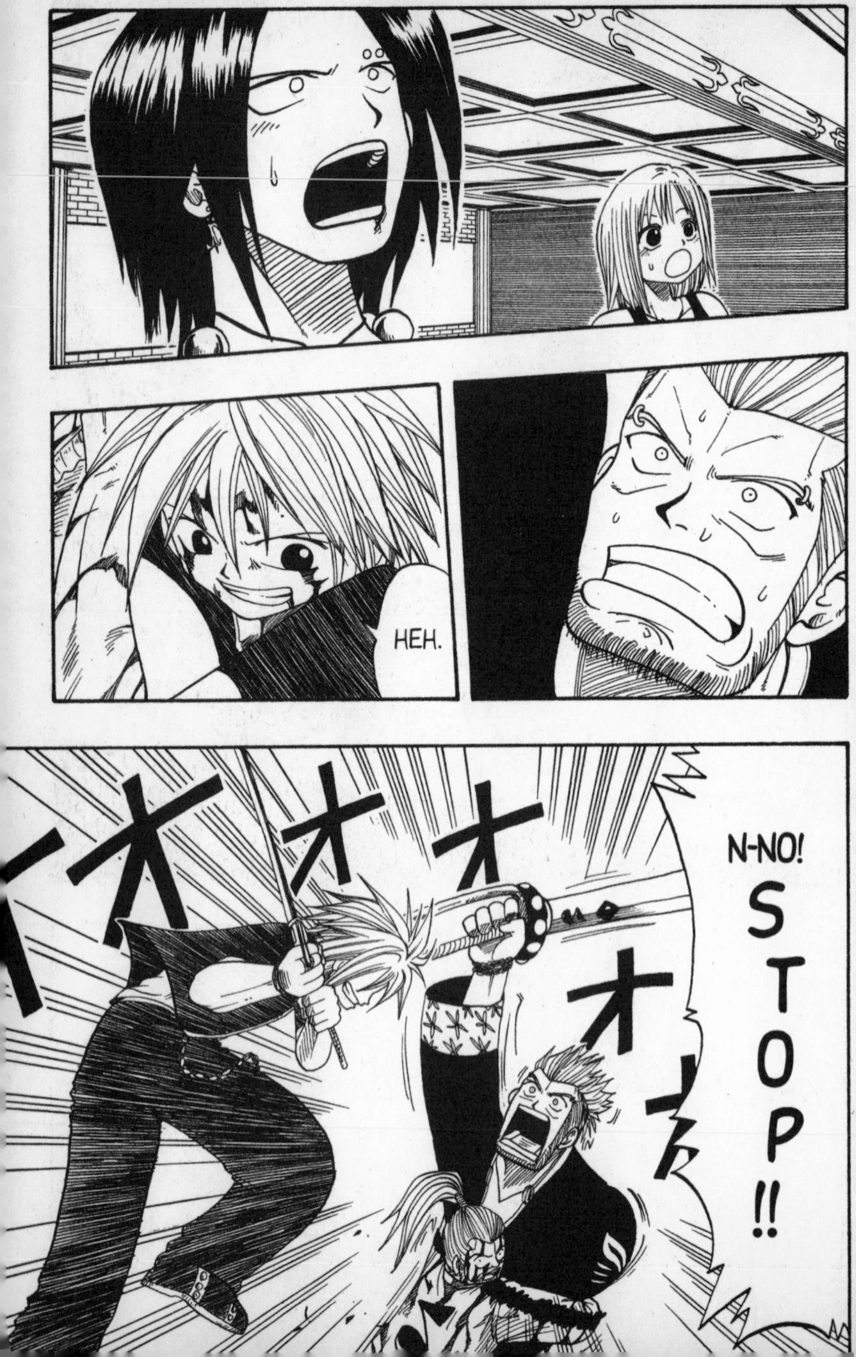
HEH.
N-NO!
STOP!!

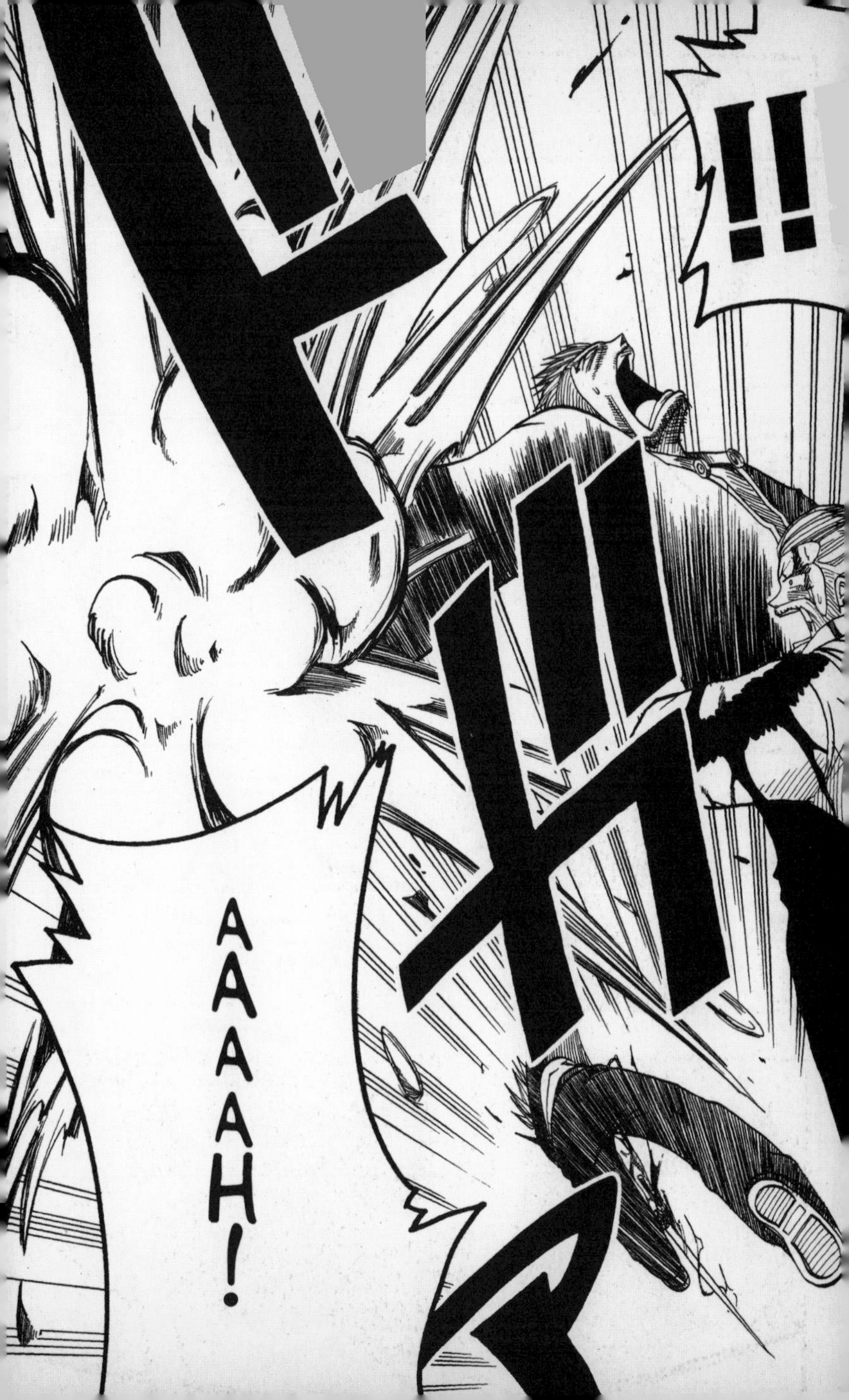
!!
AAAAH!

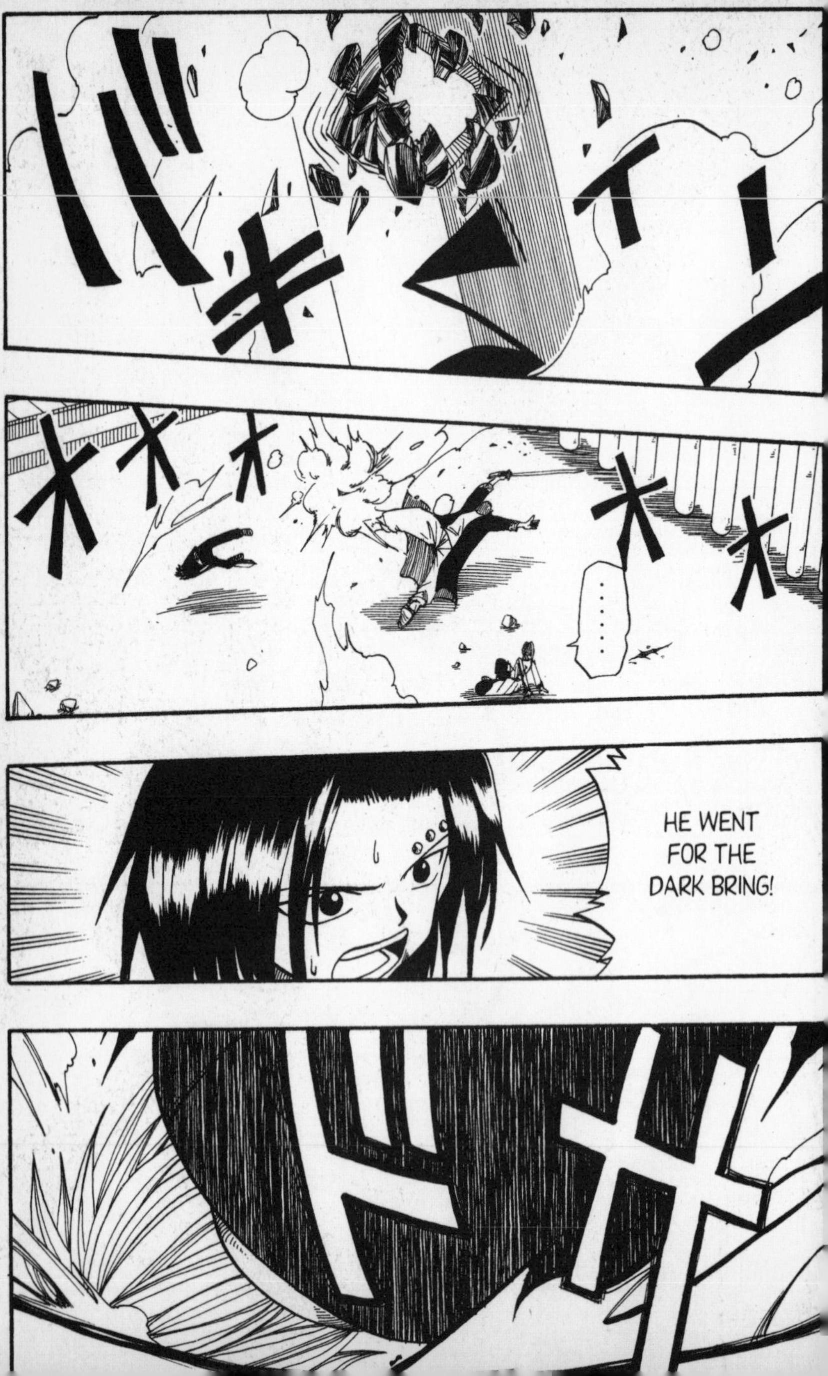

......
HE WENT FOR THE DARK BRING!

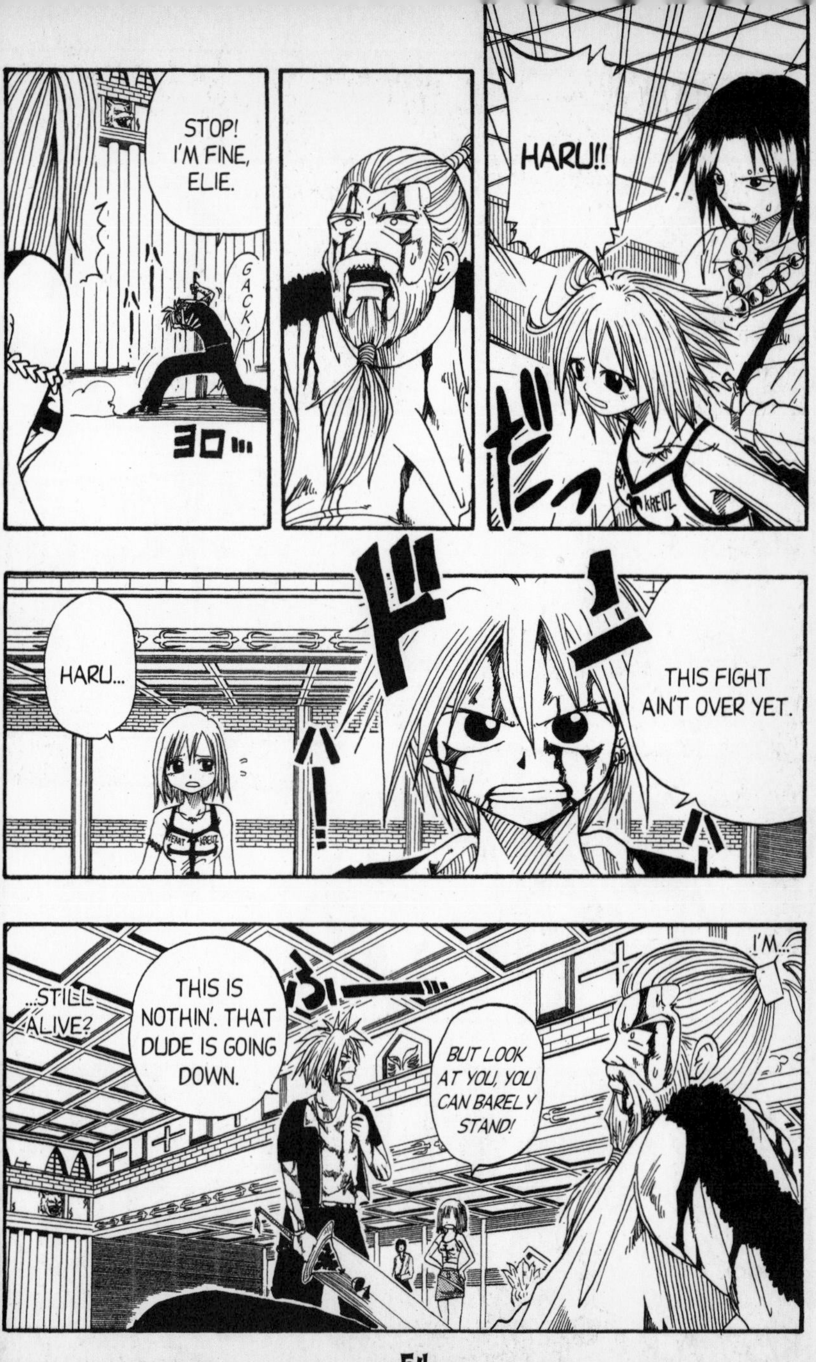
HARU!!
だっ
STOP! I'M FINE, ELIE.
GACK
ヨロ
THIS FIGHT AIN'T OVER YET.
HARU...
I'M...
BUT LOOK AT YOU, YOU CAN BARELY STAND!
THIS IS NOTHIN'. THAT DUDE IS GOING DOWN.
...STILL ALIVE?

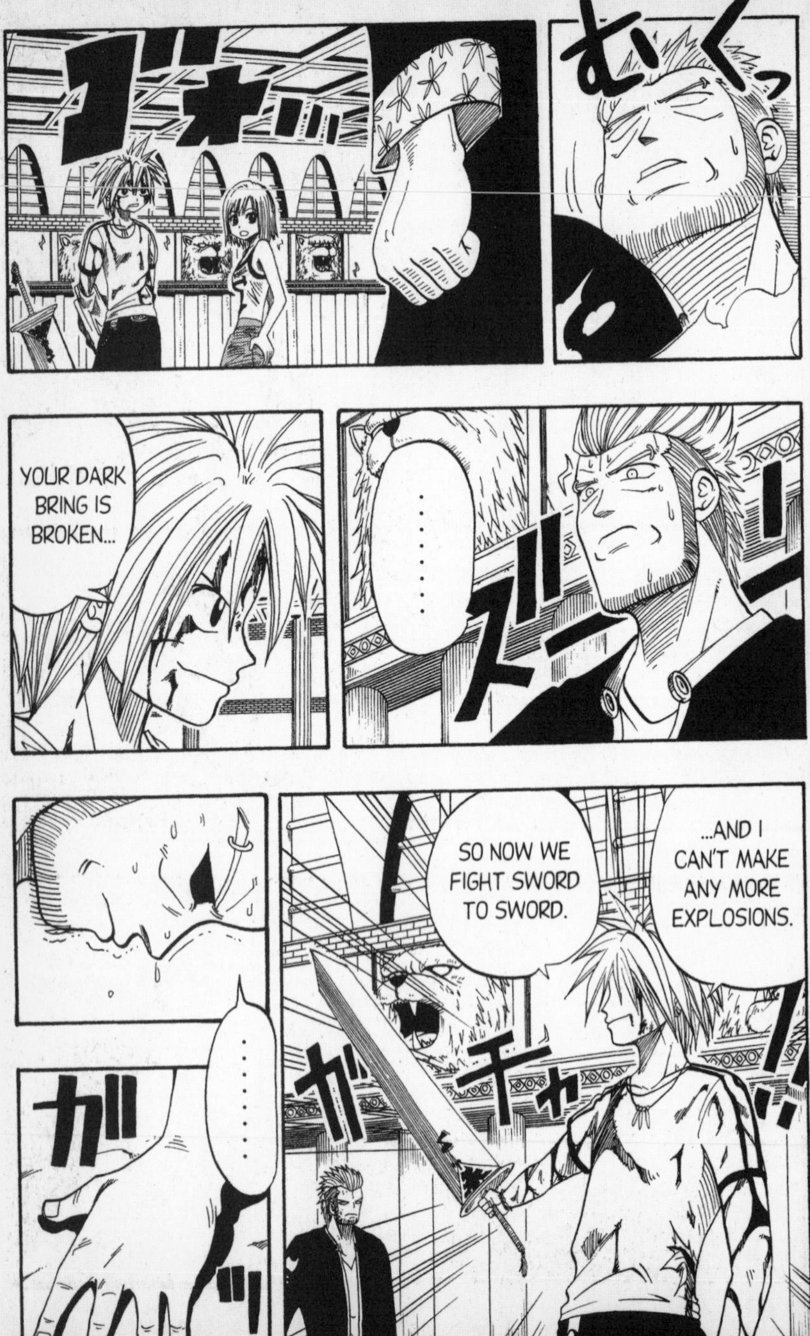
むくっ
ズーー
......
YOUR DARK BRING IS BROKEN...
...AND I CAN'T MAKE ANY MORE EXPLOSIONS.
SO NOW WE FIGHT SWORD TO SWORD.
ガチャ!!
......
ガッ

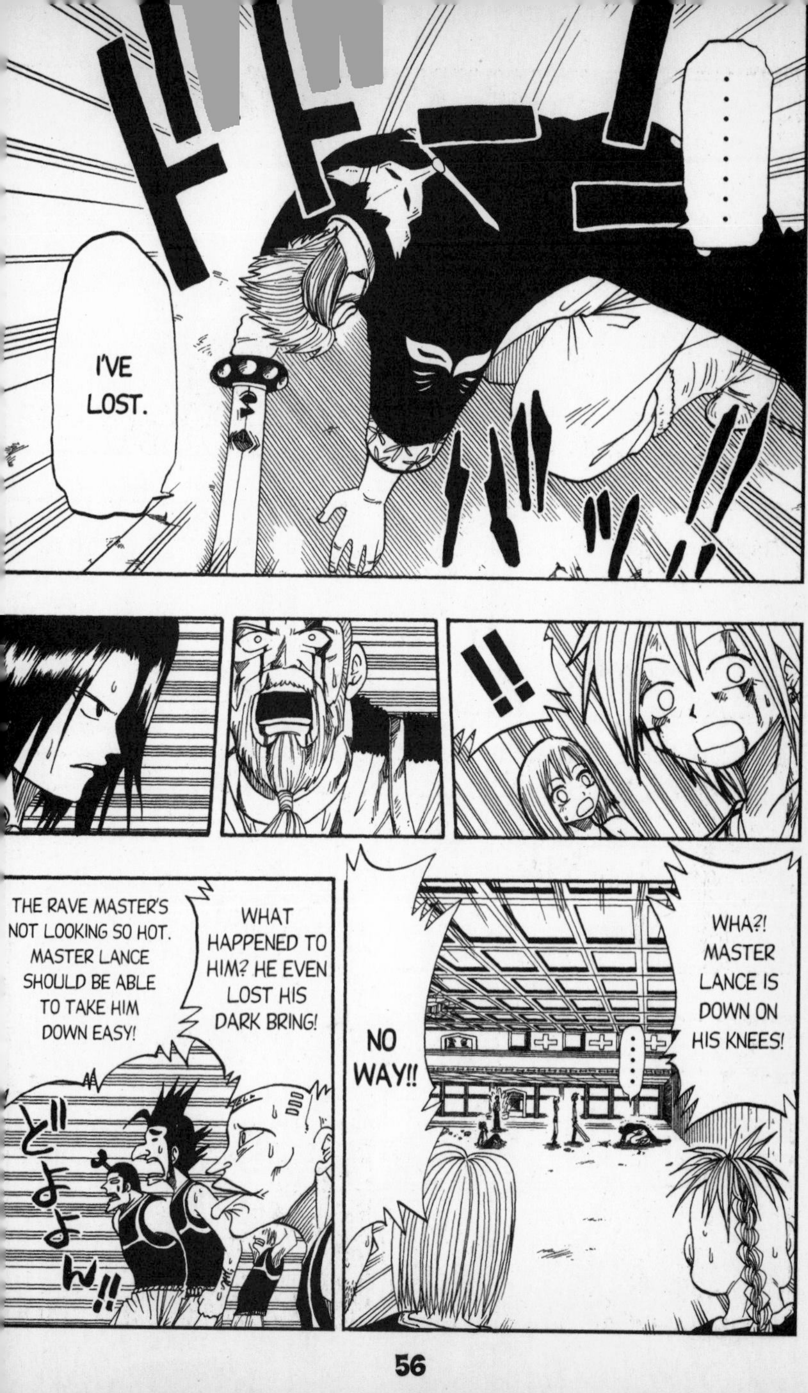
......
I'VE LOST.
!!
WHA?! MASTER LANCE IS DOWN ON HIS KNEES!
......
NO WAY!!
WHAT HAPPENED TO HIM? HE EVEN LOST HIS DARK BRING!
THE RAVE MASTER'S NOT LOOKING SO HOT. MASTER LANCE SHOULD BE ABLE TO TAKE HIM DOWN EASY!
どよよん!!

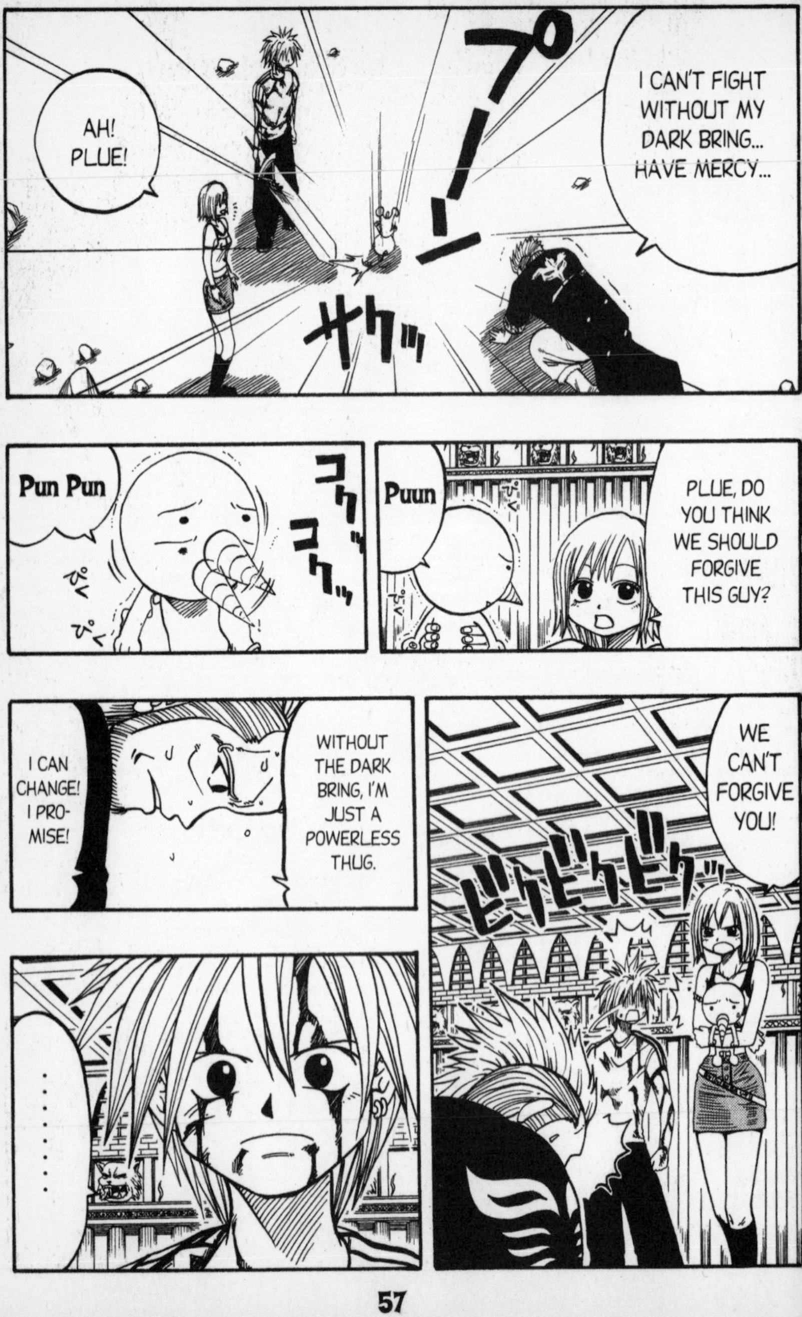
I CAN'T FIGHT WITHOUT MY DARK BRING... HAVE MERCY...
AH! PLUE!
PLUE, DO YOU THINK WE SHOULD FORGIVE THIS GUY?
Puun
Pun Pun
WE CAN'T FORGIVE YOU!
WITHOUT THE DARK BRING, I'M JUST A POWERLESS THUG.
I CAN CHANGE! I PRO-MISE!
....

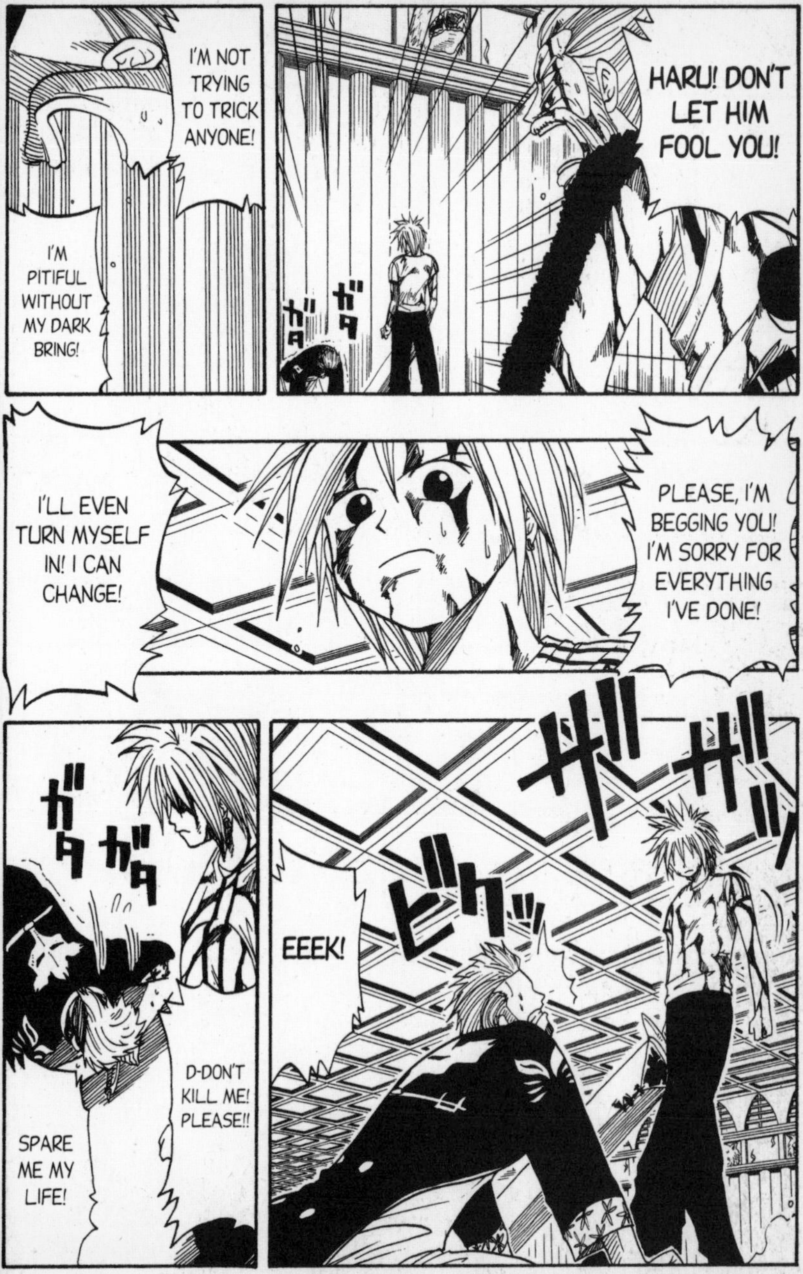
HARU! DON'T LET HIM FOOL YOU!
ガタ
ガタ
I'M NOT TRYING TO TRICK ANYONE!
I'M PITIFUL WITHOUT MY DARK BRING!
PLEASE, I'M BEGGING YOU! I'M SORRY FOR EVERYTHING I'VE DONE!
I'LL EVEN TURN MYSELF IN! I CAN CHANGE!
ザッ
ザッ
ビクッ
EEEK!
ガタ
ガタ
D-DON'T KILL ME! PLEASE!!
SPARE ME MY LIFE!

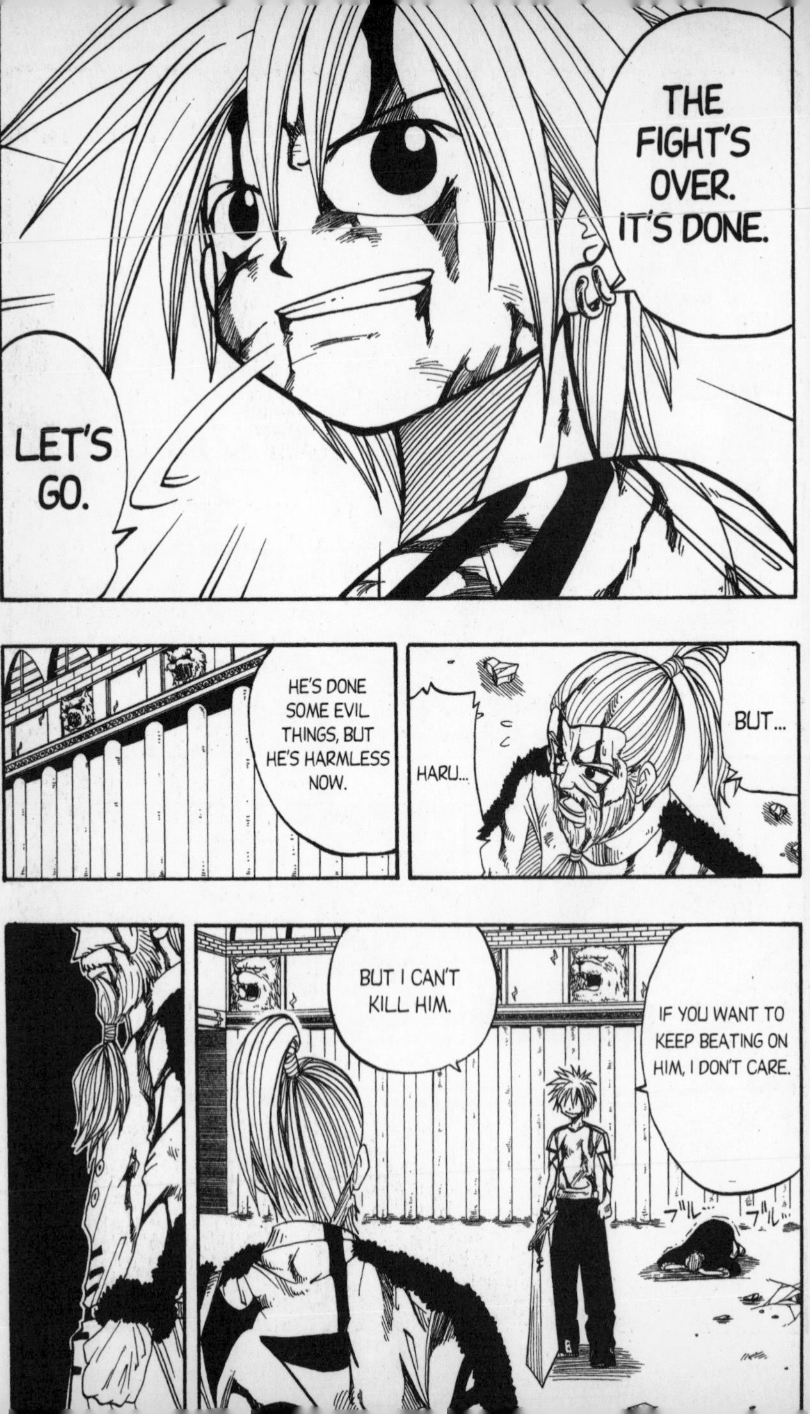
THE FIGHT'S OVER. IT'S DONE.
LET'S GO.
BUT...
HARU...
HE'S DONE SOME EVIL THINGS, BUT HE'S HARMLESS NOW.
IF YOU WANT TO KEEP BEATING ON HIM, I DON'T CARE.
BUT I CAN'T KILL HIM.
ブル…
ブル…

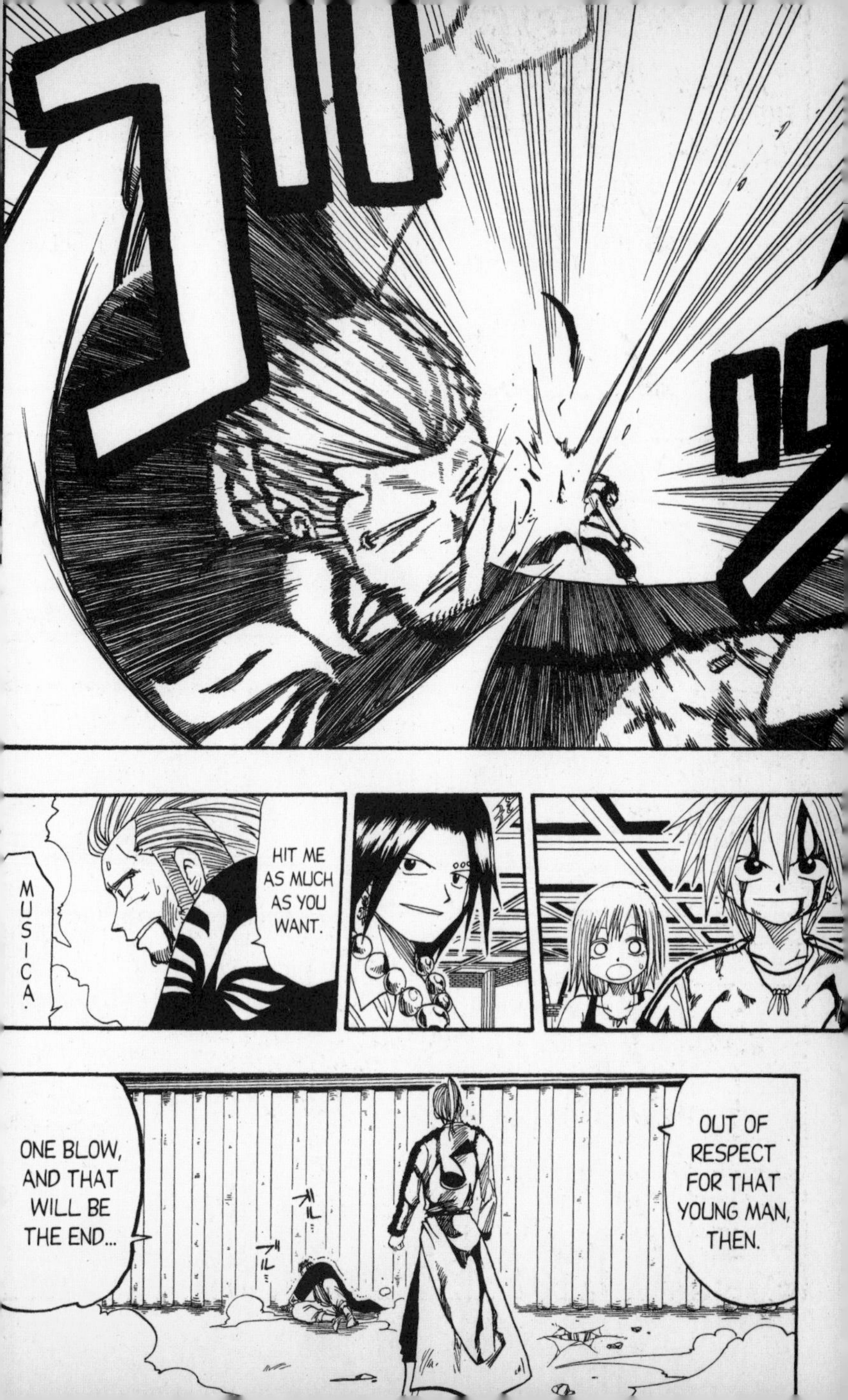

HIT ME AS MUCH AS YOU WANT.
MUSICA.
OUT OF RESPECT FOR THAT YOUNG MAN, THEN.
ブル
ブル
ONE BLOW, AND THAT WILL BE THE END...

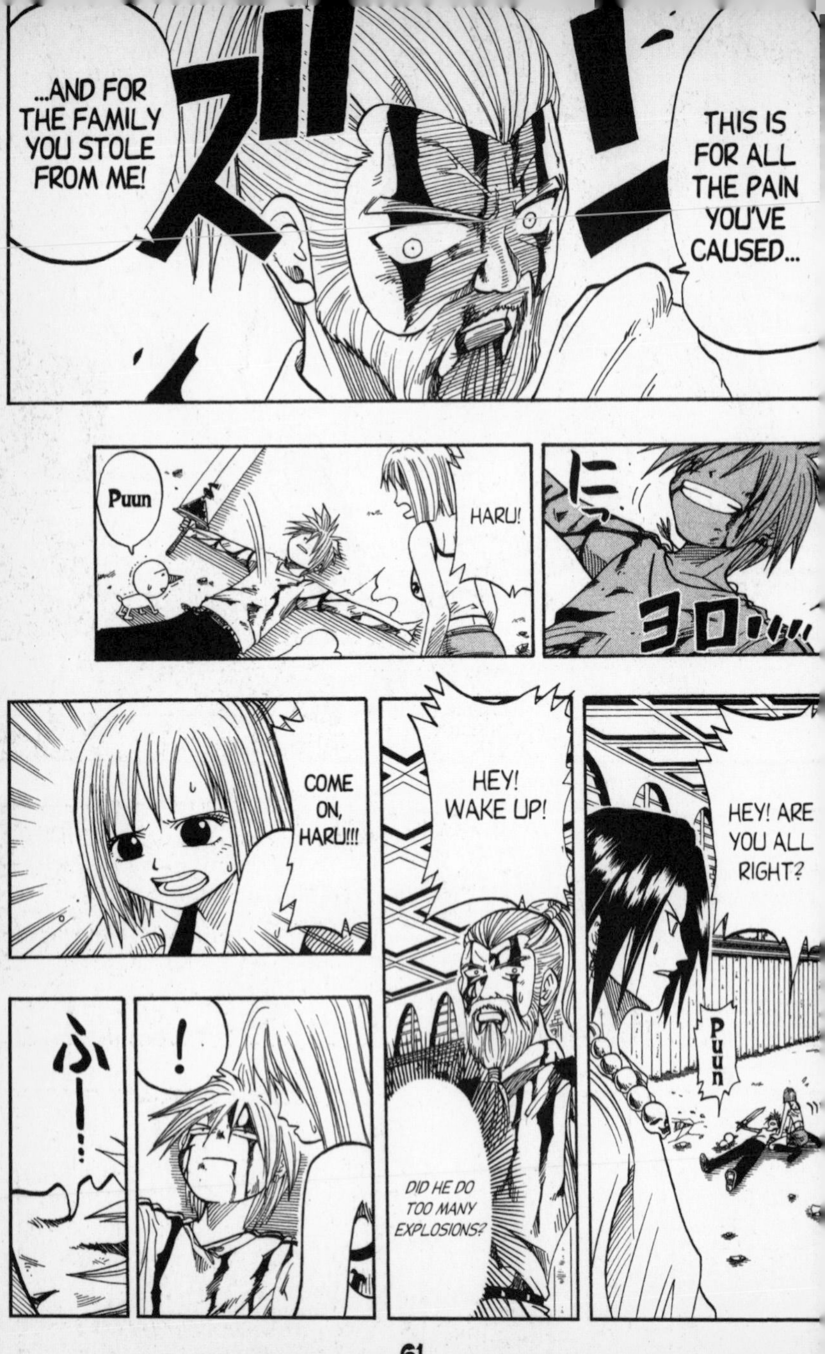
THIS IS FOR ALL THE PAIN YOU'VE CAUSED...
...AND FOR THE FAMILY YOU STOLE FROM ME!
にっ
ヨロ
HARU!
Puun
HEY! ARE YOU ALL RIGHT?
Puun
HEY! WAKE UP!
DID HE DO TOO MANY EXPLOSIONS?
COME ON, HARU!!!
!
ふー

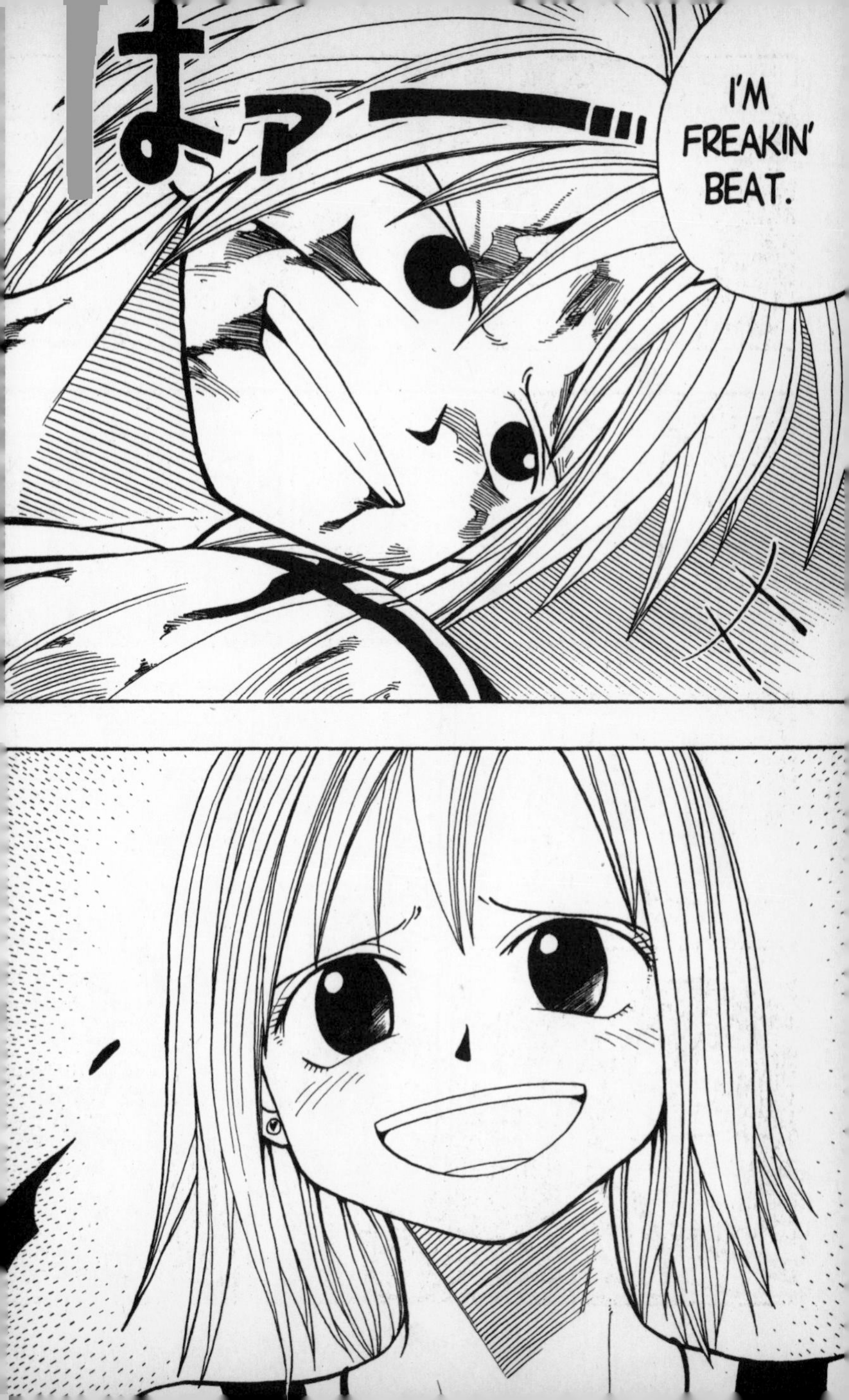
はァーーー…
I'M FREAKIN' BEAT.

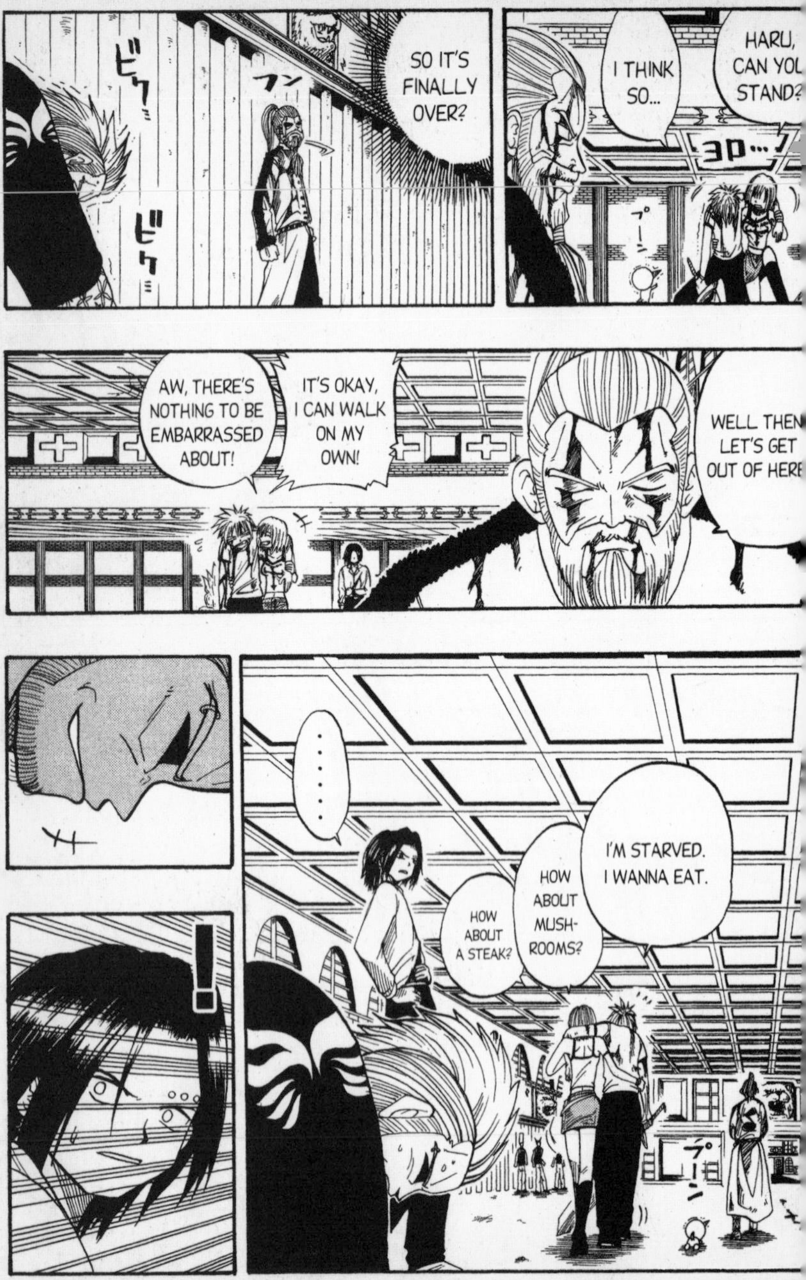
HARU, CAN YOU STAND?
I THINK SO...
ヨロ…
プーン
SO IT'S FINALLY OVER?
フン
ビクッ
ビクッ
WELL THEN LET'S GET OUT OF HERE
IT'S OKAY, I CAN WALK ON MY OWN!
AW, THERE'S NOTHING TO BE EMBARRASSED ABOUT!
I'M STARVED. I WANNA EAT.
HOW ABOUT MUSH-ROOMS?
HOW ABOUT A STEAK?
......
プーン
!

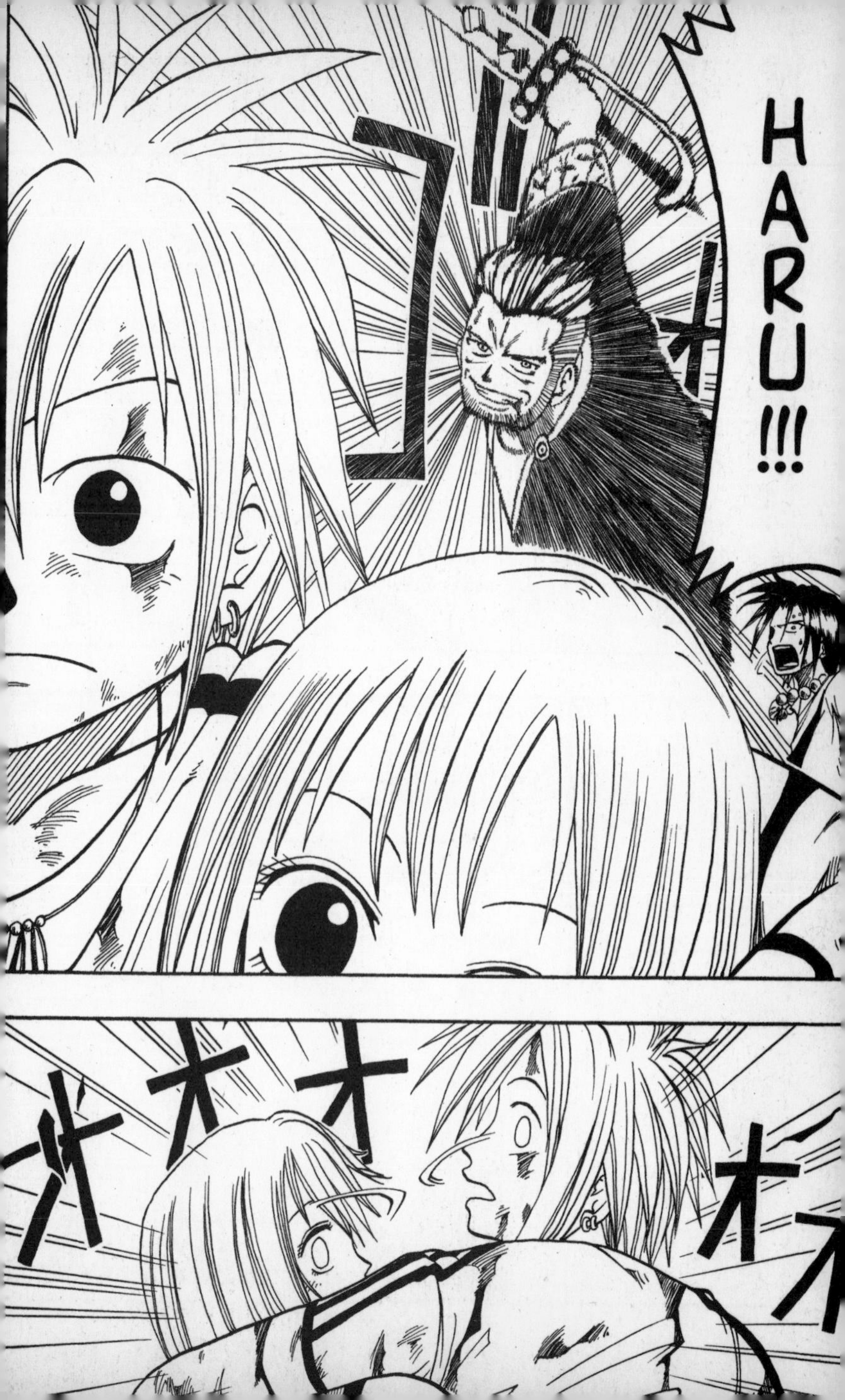
HARU!!!
ゴオ

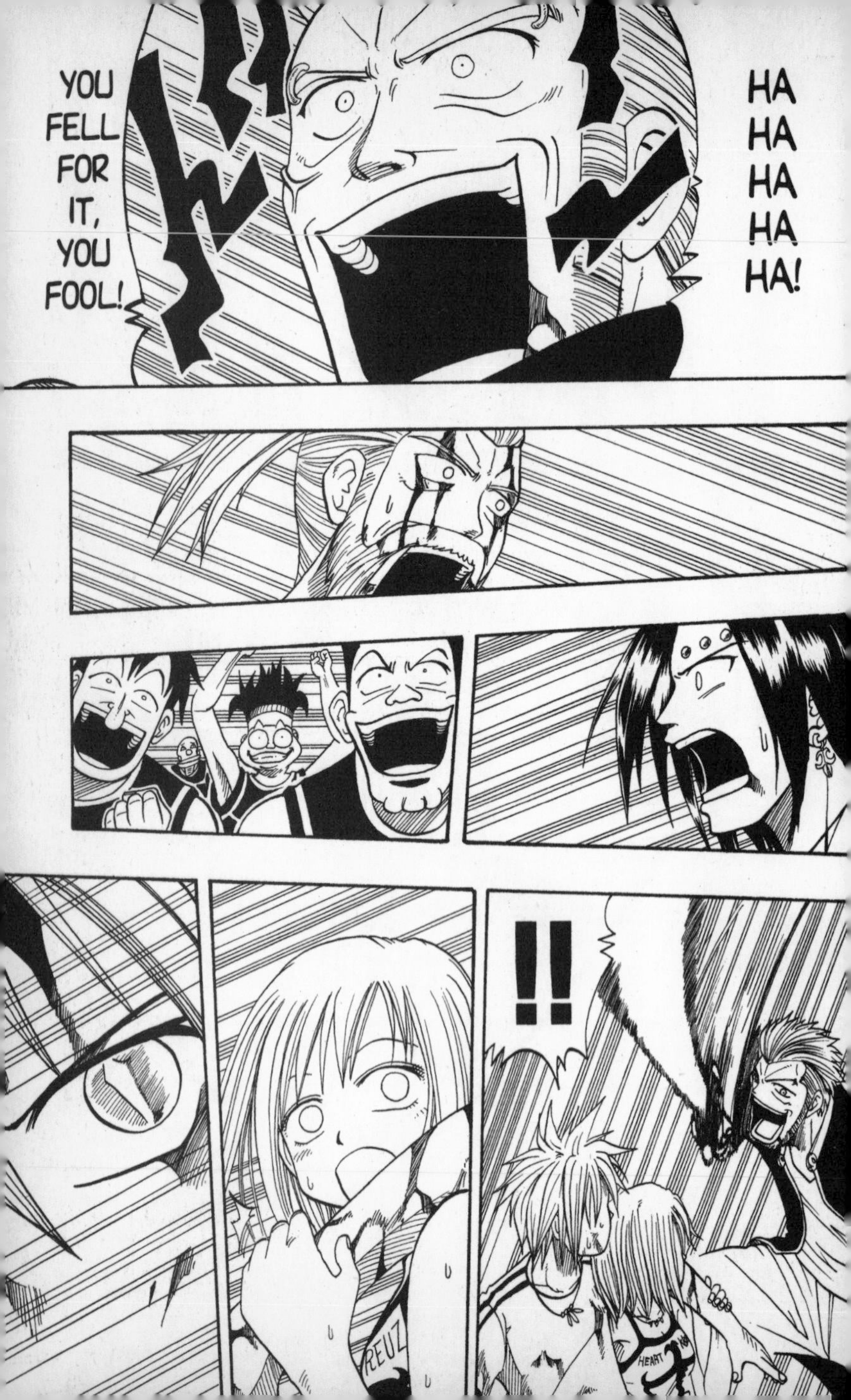
HA HA HA HA HA!
YOU FELL FOR IT, YOU FOOL!
!!
REUZ
HEART

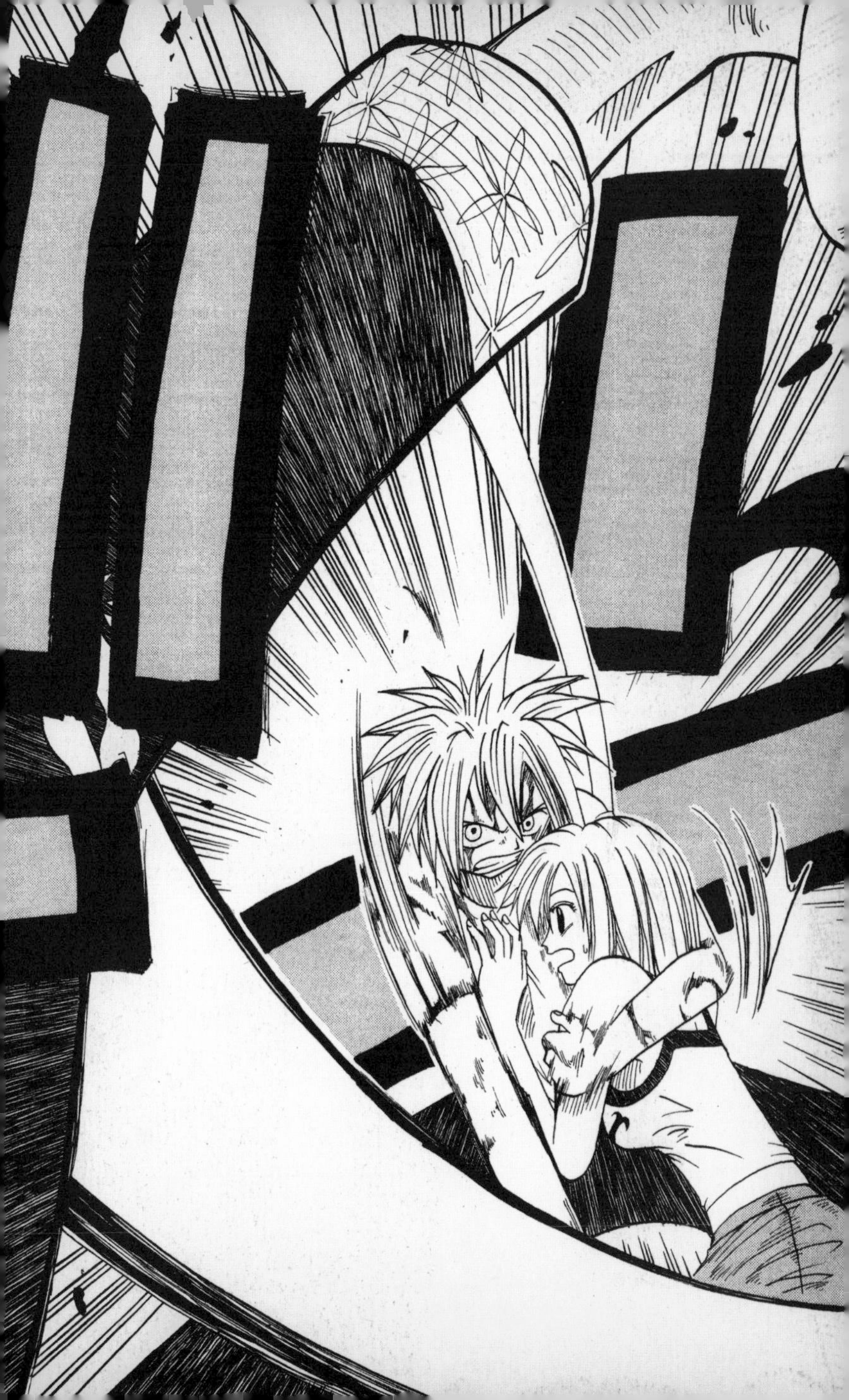

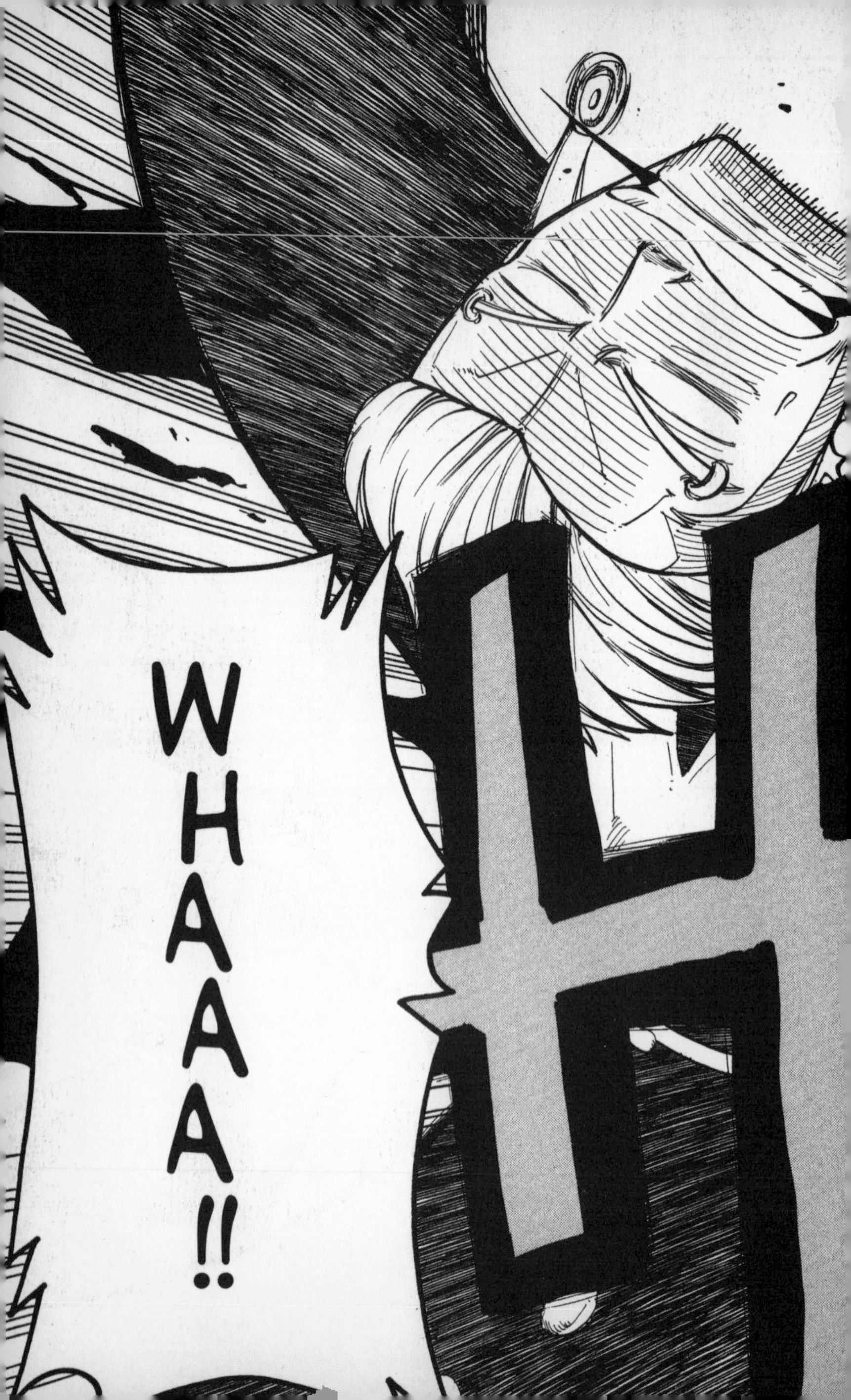
WHAAA!!

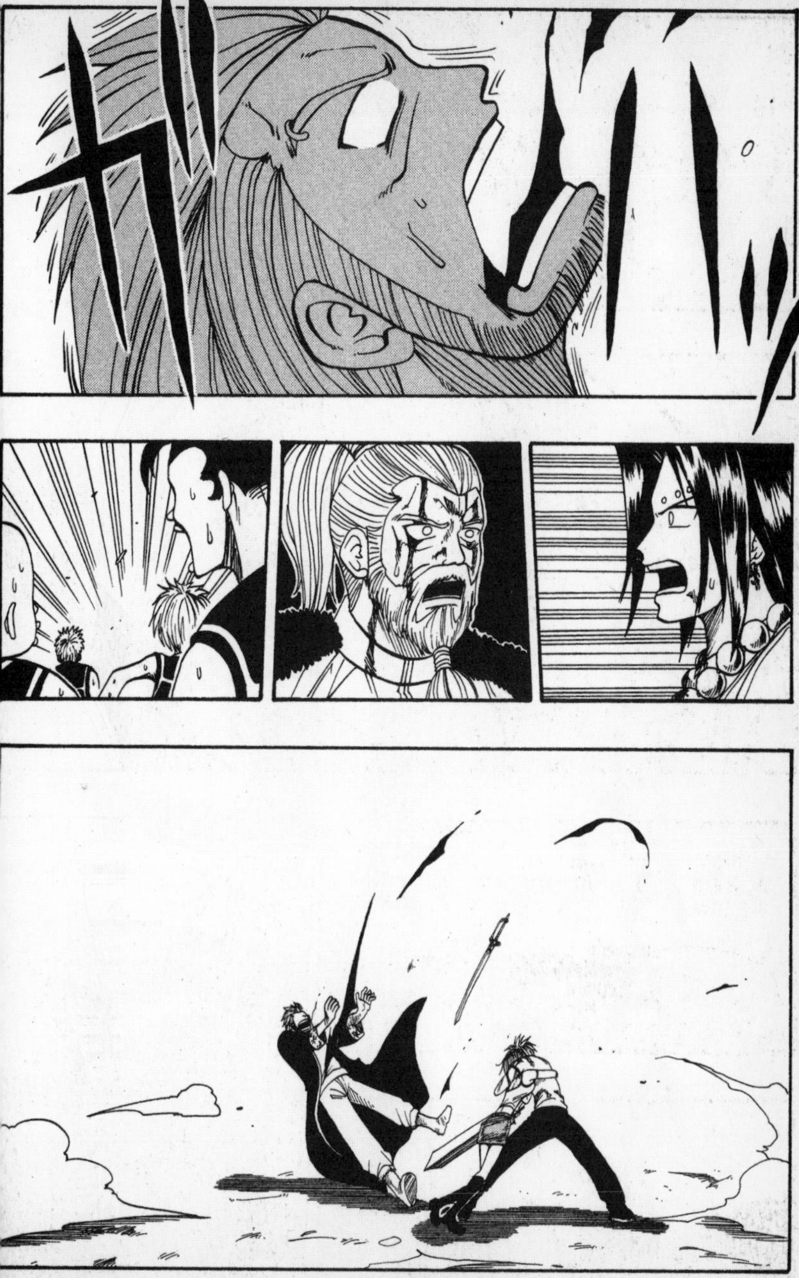

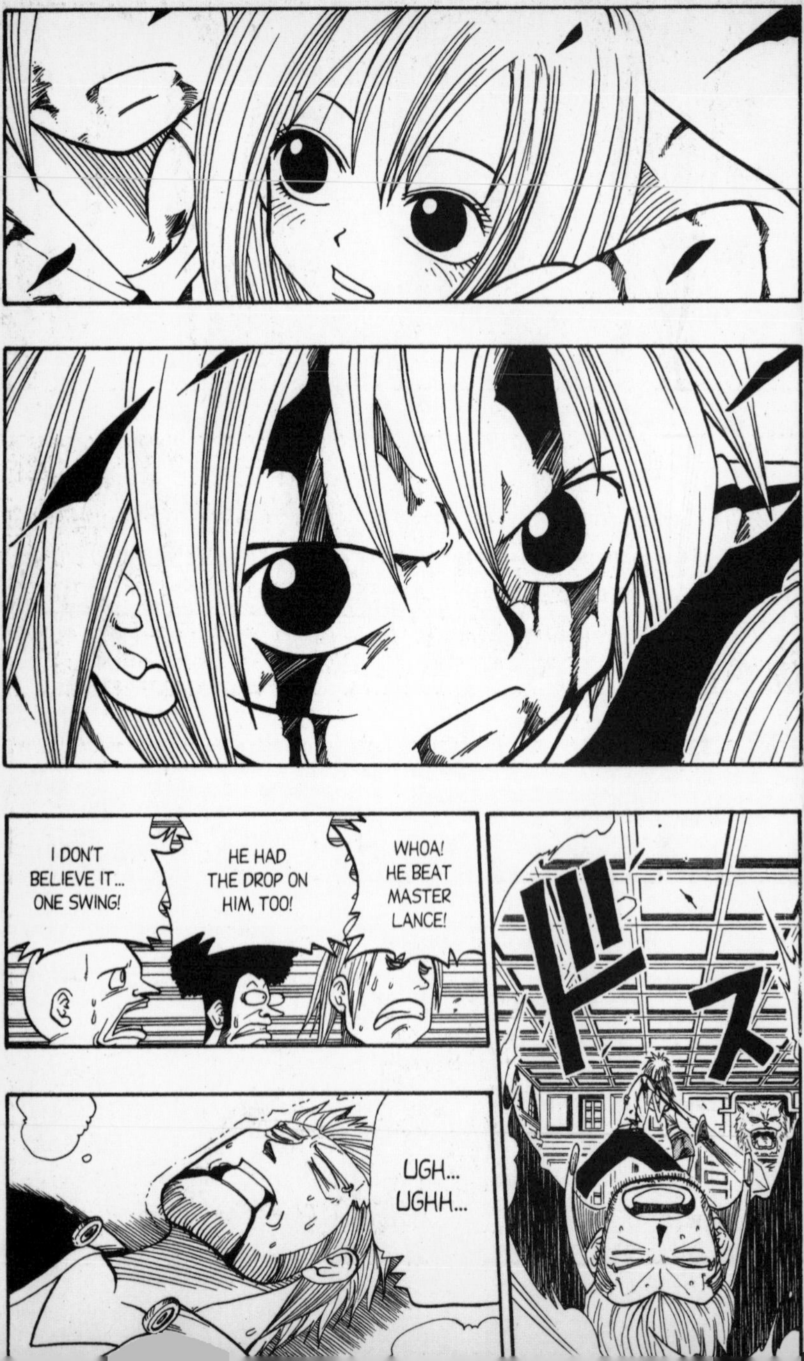
ドス
WHOA! HE BEAT MASTER LANCE!
HE HAD THE DROP ON HIM, TOO!
I DON'T BELIEVE IT... ONE SWING!
UGH... UGHH...

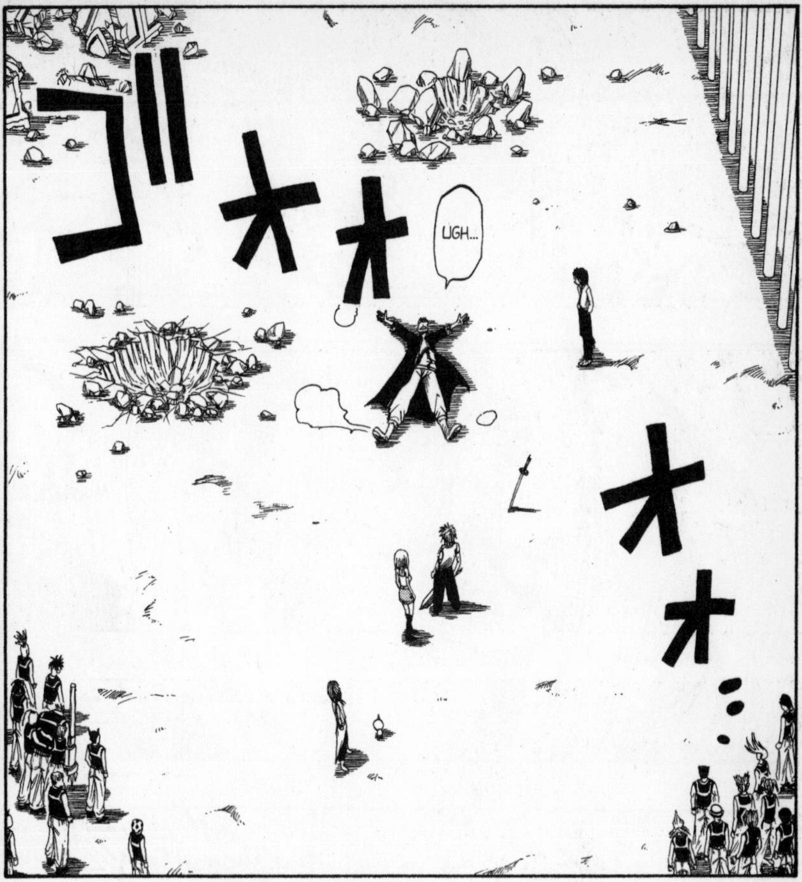
ゴオオオオ…
UGH...

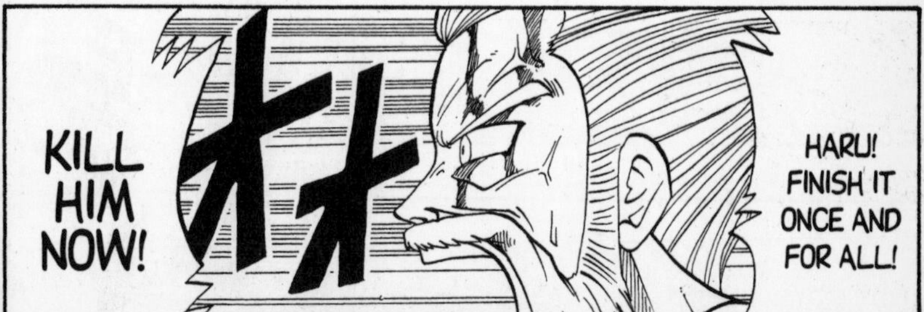
HARU! FINISH IT ONCE AND FOR ALL!
オオ
KILL HIM NOW!

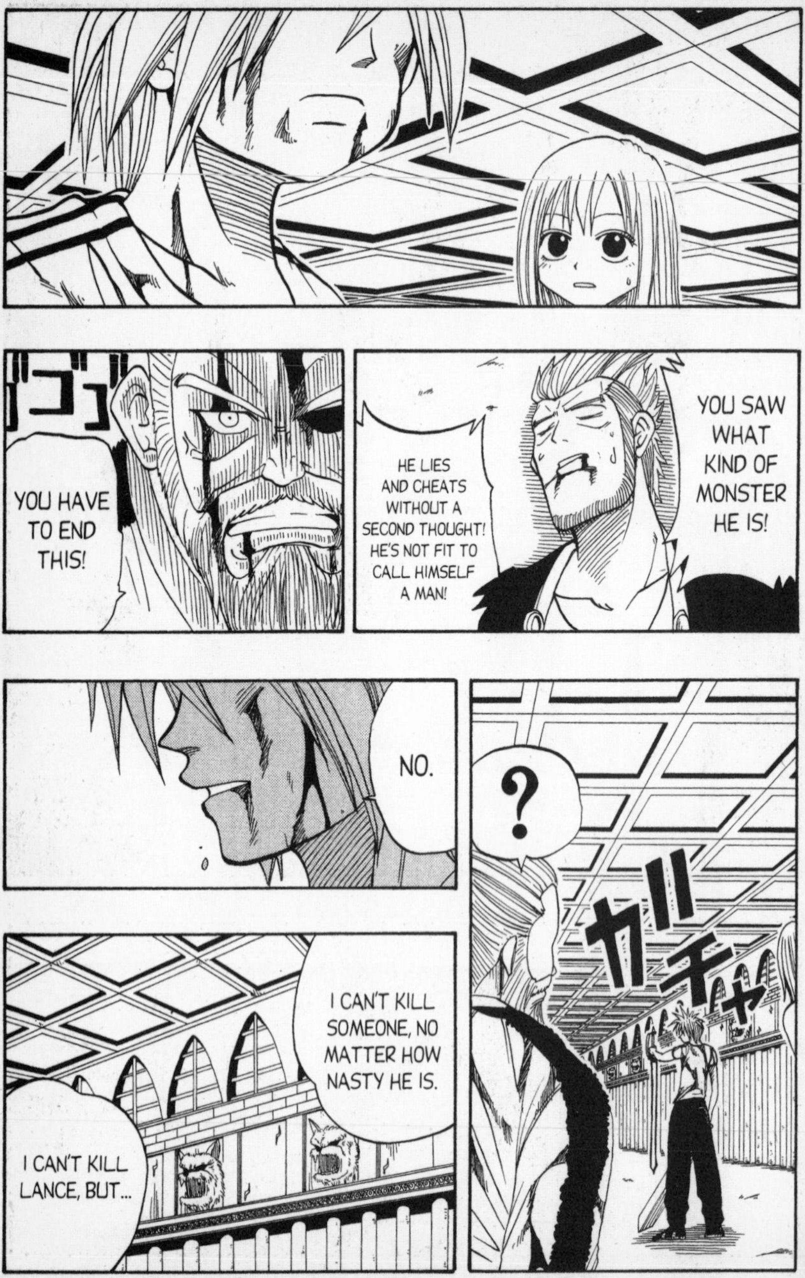
YOU SAW WHAT KIND OF MONSTER HE IS!
HE LIES AND CHEATS WITHOUT A SECOND THOUGHT! HE'S NOT FIT TO CALL HIMSELF A MAN!
YOU HAVE TO END THIS!
?
ガチャ
NO.
I CAN'T KILL SOMEONE, NO MATTER HOW NASTY HE IS.
I CAN'T KILL LANCE, BUT...

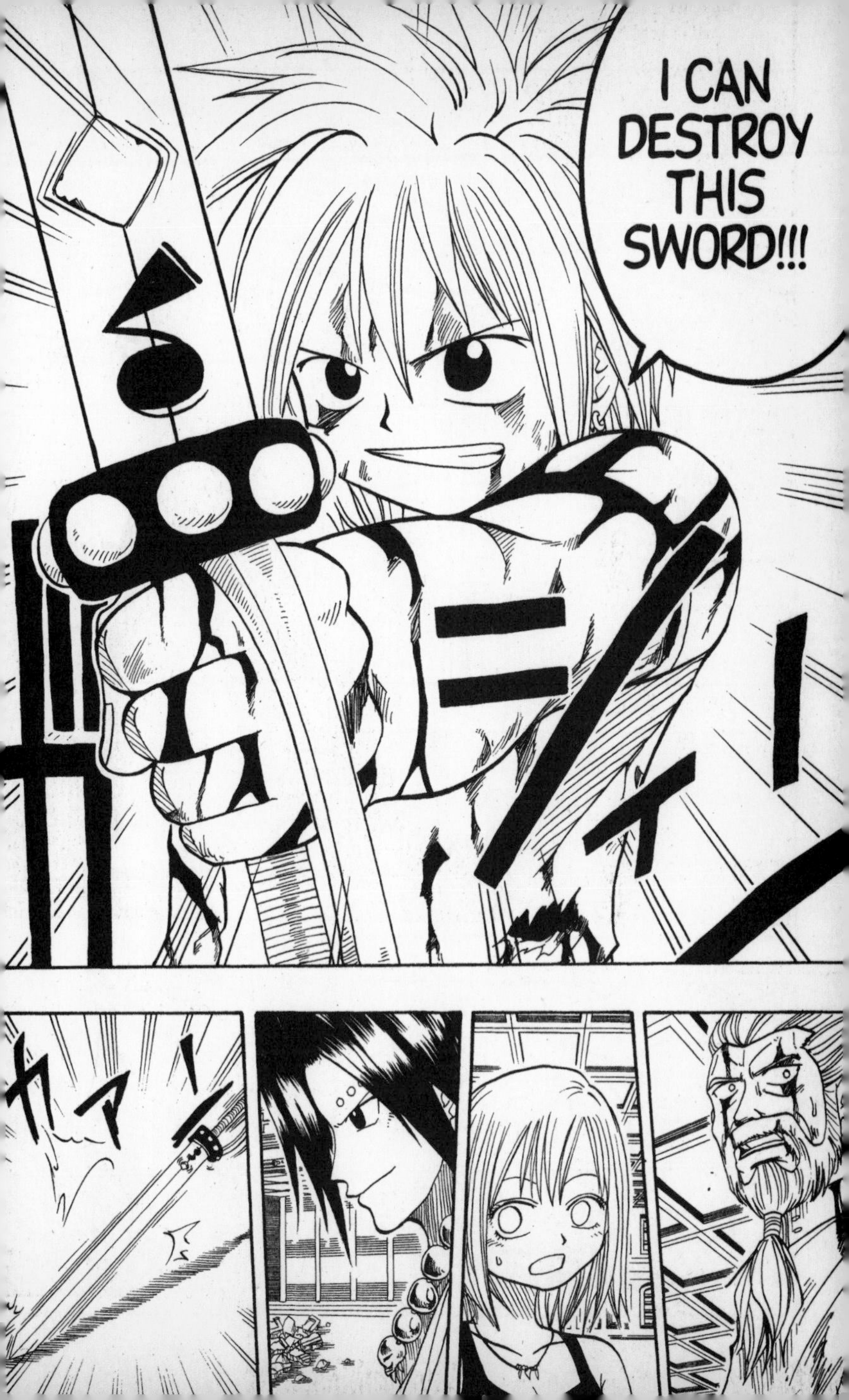
I CAN DESTROY THIS SWORD!!!

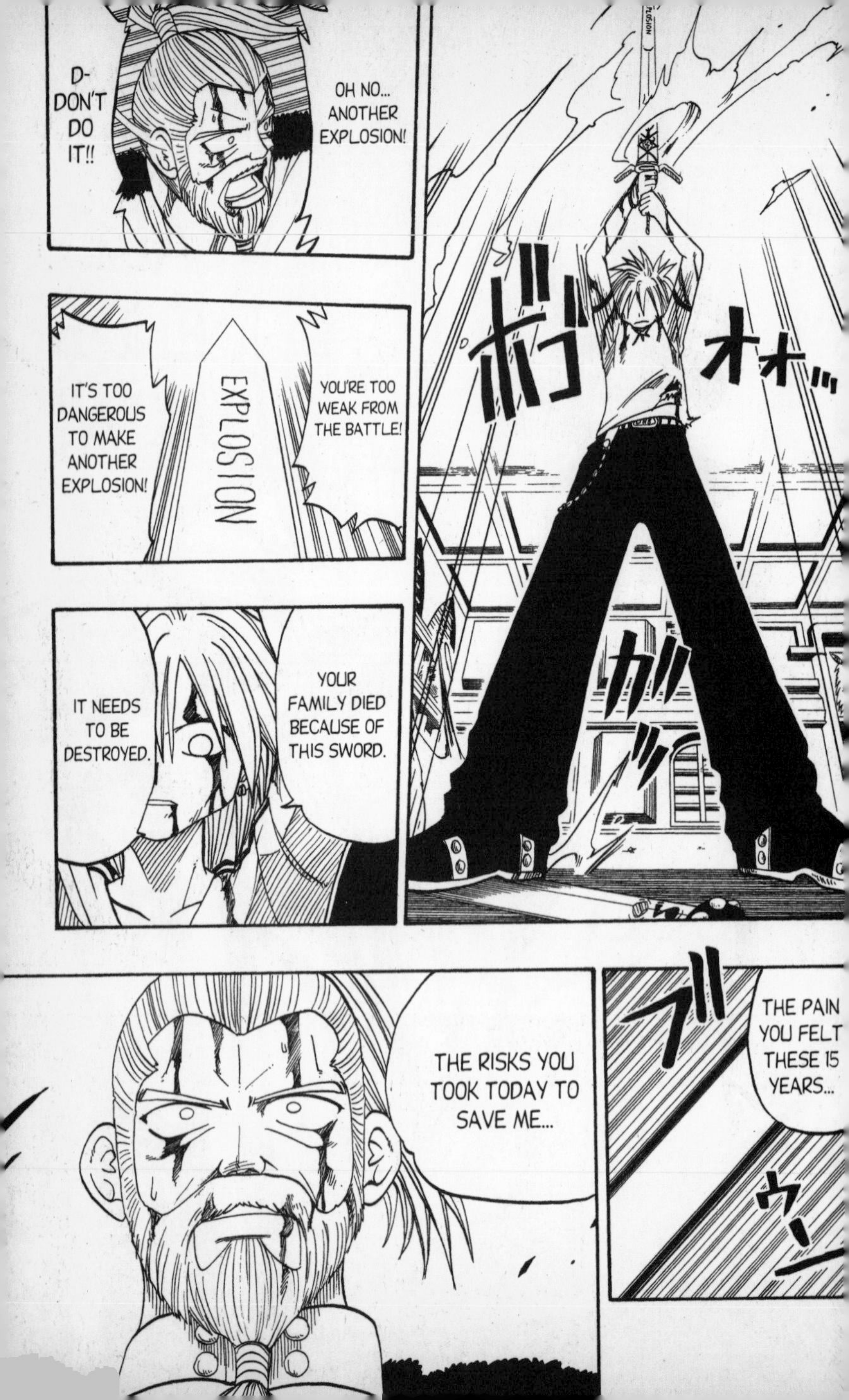
ボゴオオッ
ガッ
OH NO... ANOTHER EXPLOSION!
D- DON'T DO IT!!
YOU'RE TOO WEAK FROM THE BATTLE!
EXPLOSION
IT'S TOO DANGEROUS TO MAKE ANOTHER EXPLOSION!
YOUR FAMILY DIED BECAUSE OF THIS SWORD.
IT NEEDS TO BE DESTROYED.
ブ
THE PAIN YOU FELT THESE 15 YEARS...
ウー
THE RISKS YOU TOOK TODAY TO SAVE ME...

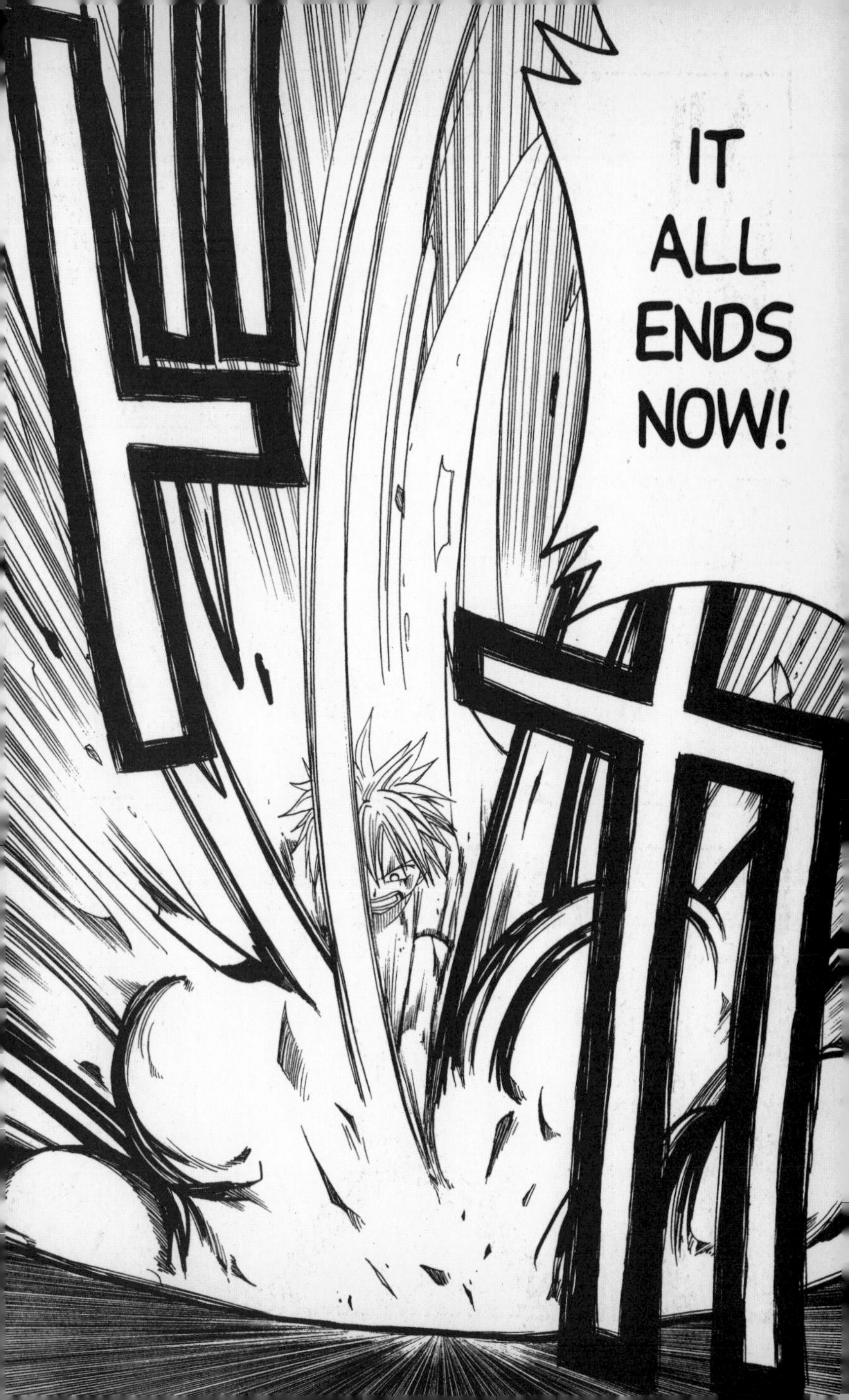
IT ALL ENDS NOW!

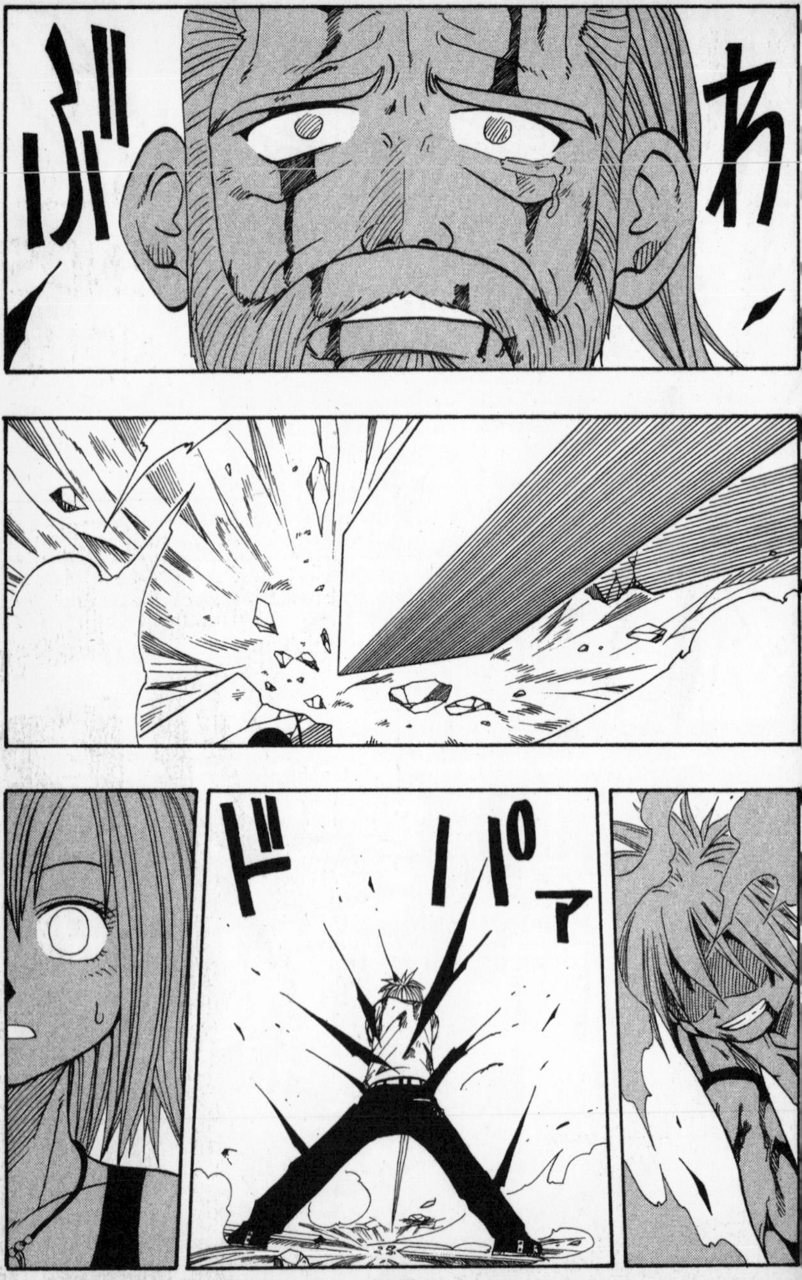
ぶわ
ドパア

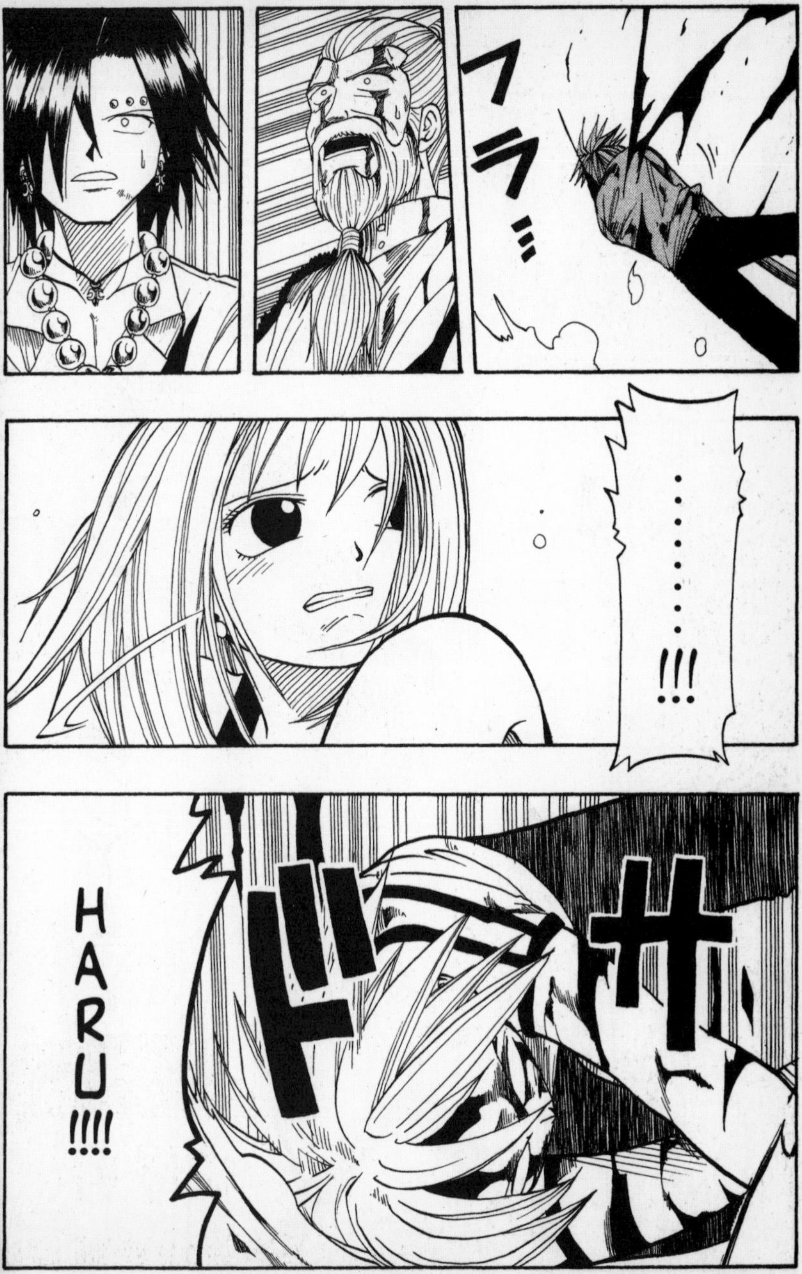
フラ…
......!!!
ドサ
HARU!!!!

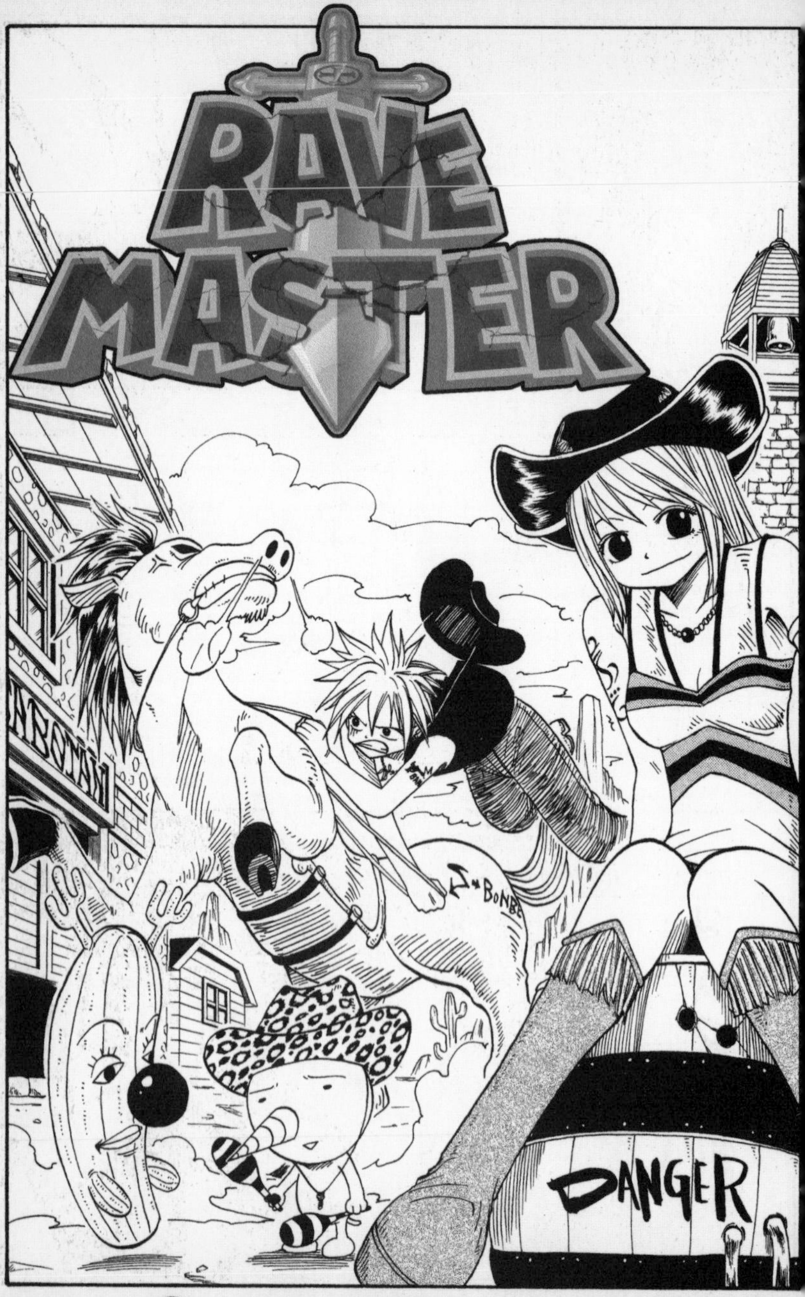
RAVE MASTER
BONBE
DANGER

RAVE 17 SWEET DREAMS & BITTER KISSES

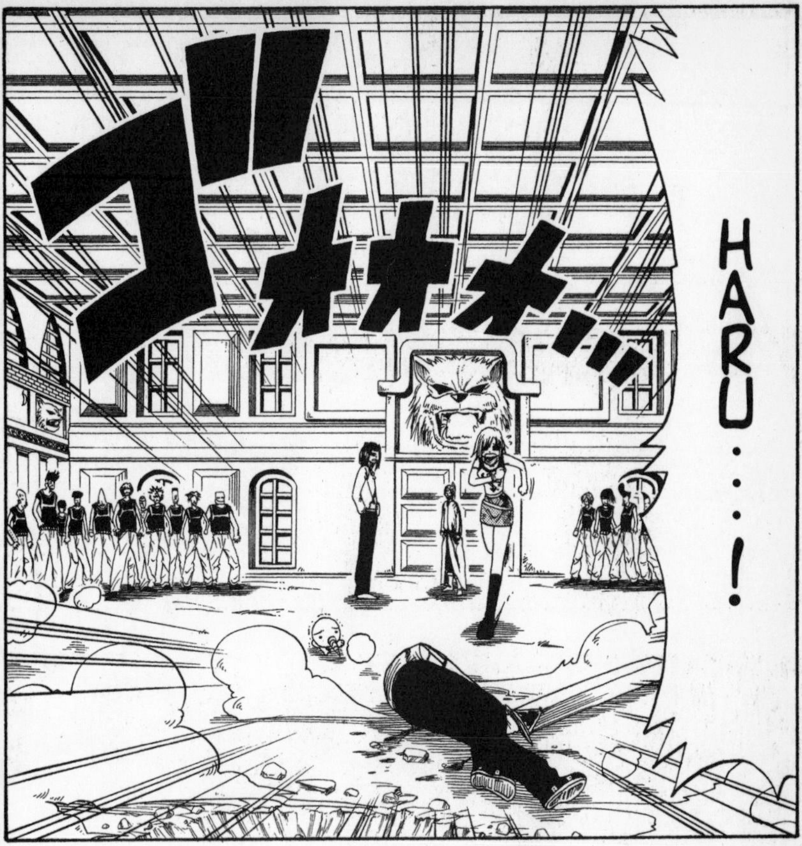
HARU...!
ゴオオオ…

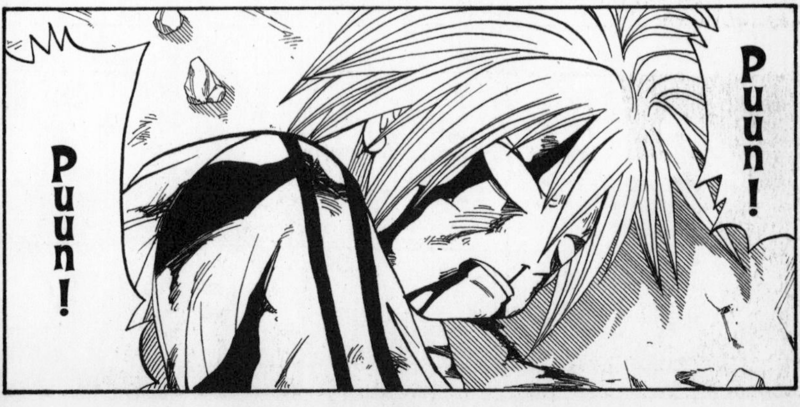
Puun!
Puun!

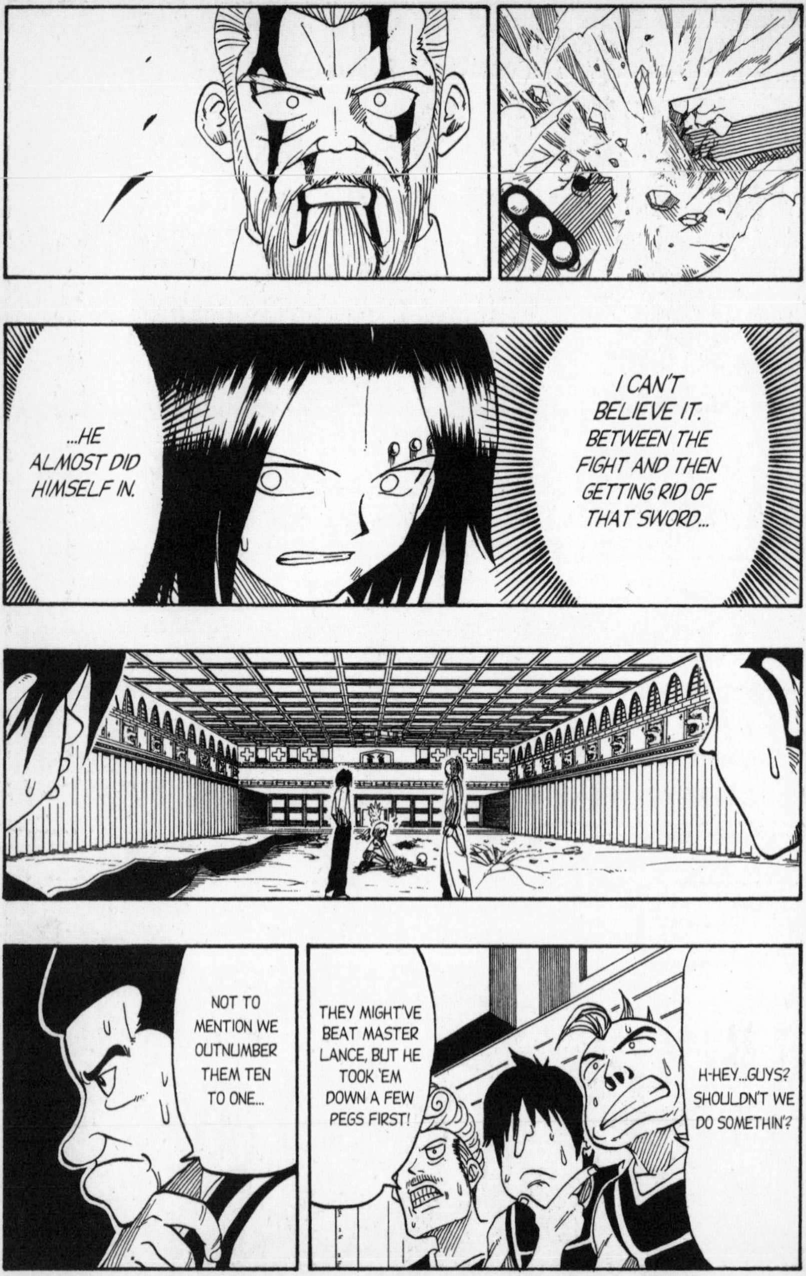
I CAN'T BELIEVE IT. BETWEEN THE FIGHT AND THEN GETTING RID OF THAT SWORD...
...HE ALMOST DID HIMSELF IN.
H-HEY...GUYS? SHOULDN'T WE DO SOMETHIN'?
THEY MIGHT'VE BEAT MASTER LANCE, BUT HE TOOK 'EM DOWN A FEW PEGS FIRST!
NOT TO MENTION WE OUTNUMBER THEM TEN TO ONE...

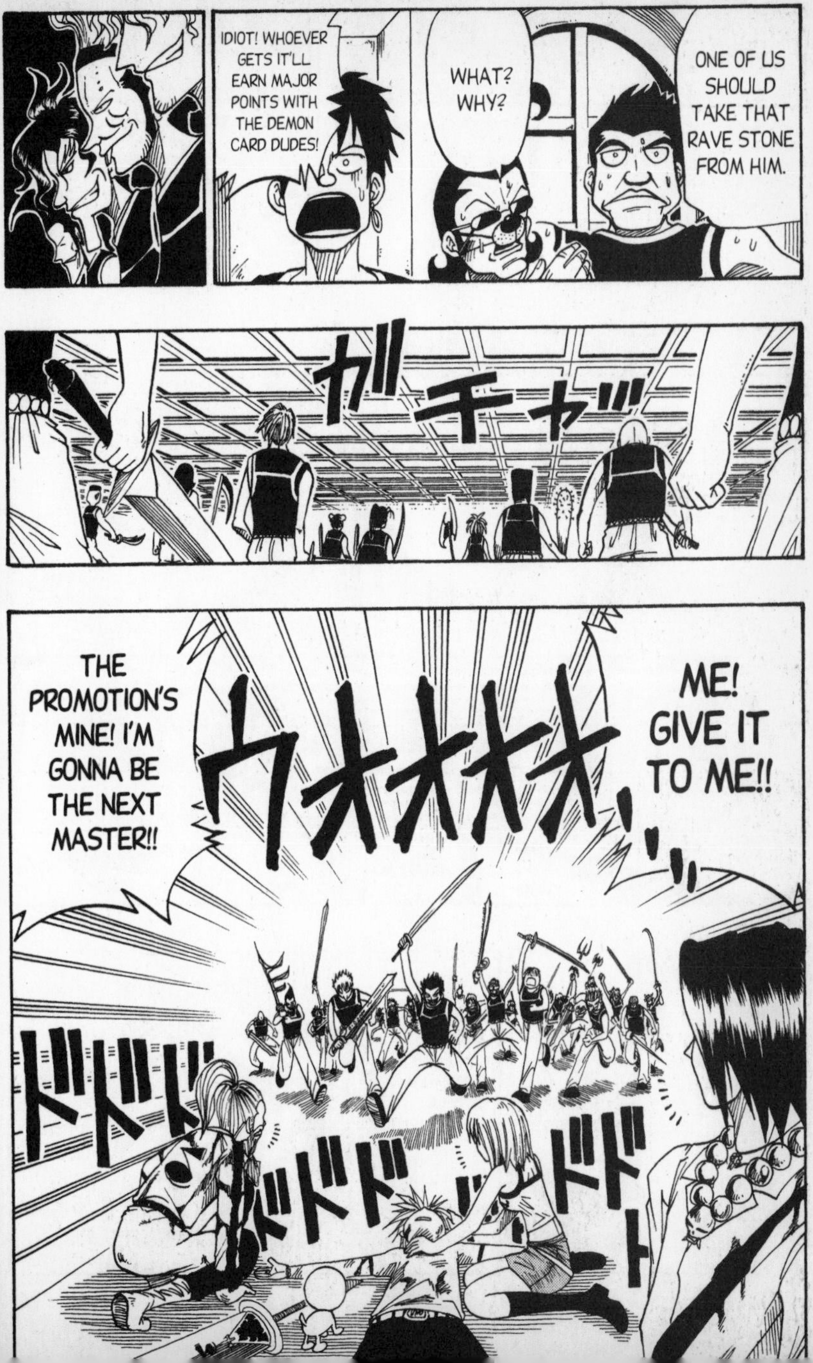
ONE OF US SHOULD TAKE THAT RAVE STONE FROM HIM.
WHAT? WHY?
IDIOT! WHOEVER GETS IT'LL EARN MAJOR POINTS WITH THE DEMON CARD DUDES!
ME! GIVE IT TO ME!!
ウオオオオ
THE PROMOTION'S MINE! I'M GONNA BE THE NEXT MASTER!!

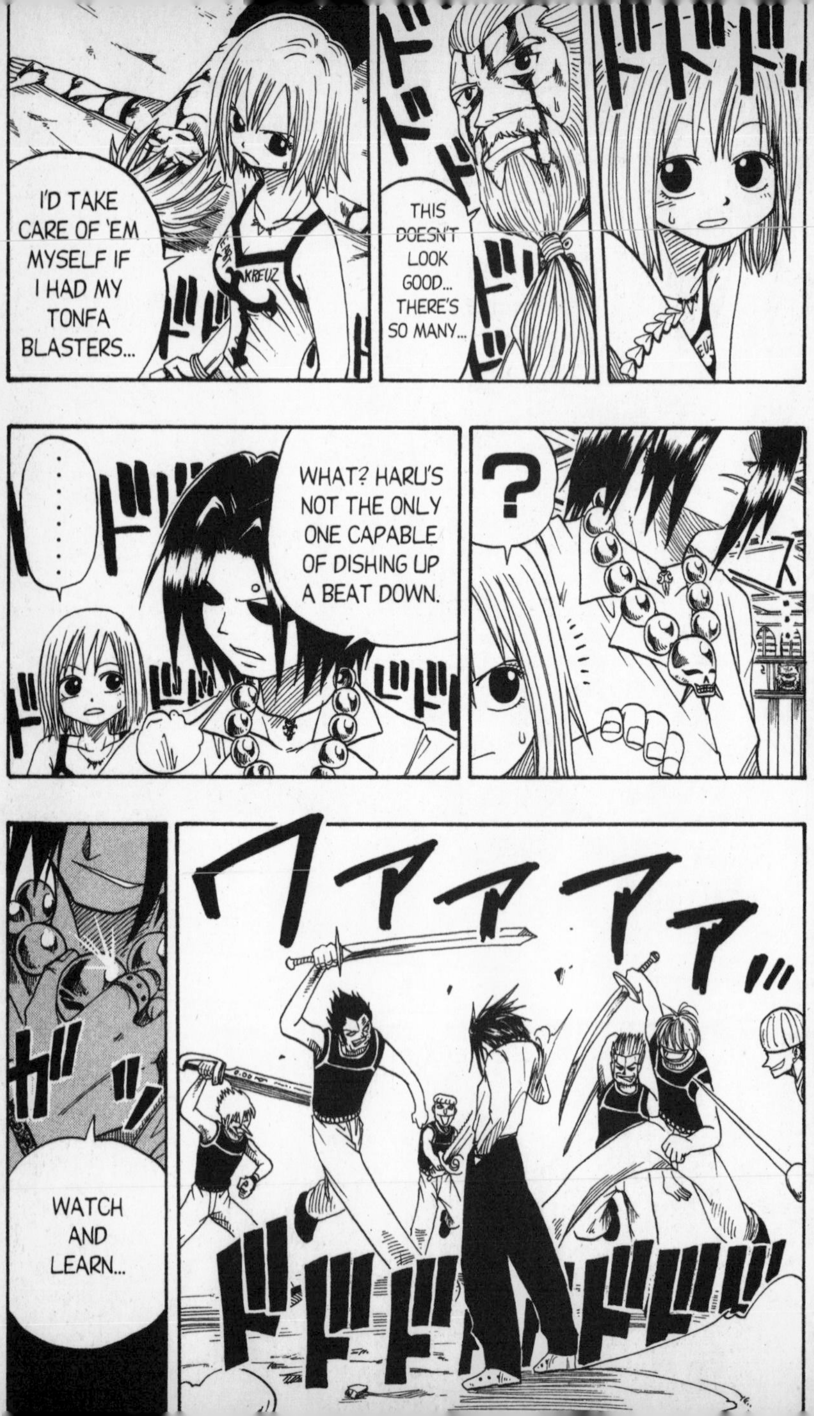
ドドド
THIS DOESN'T LOOK GOOD... THERE'S SO MANY...
I'D TAKE CARE OF 'EM MYSELF IF I HAD MY TONFA BLASTERS...
?
WHAT? HARU'S NOT THE ONLY ONE CAPABLE OF DISHING UP A BEAT DOWN.
......
ワアアアッ
ドドドドドド
ガッ
WATCH AND LEARN...

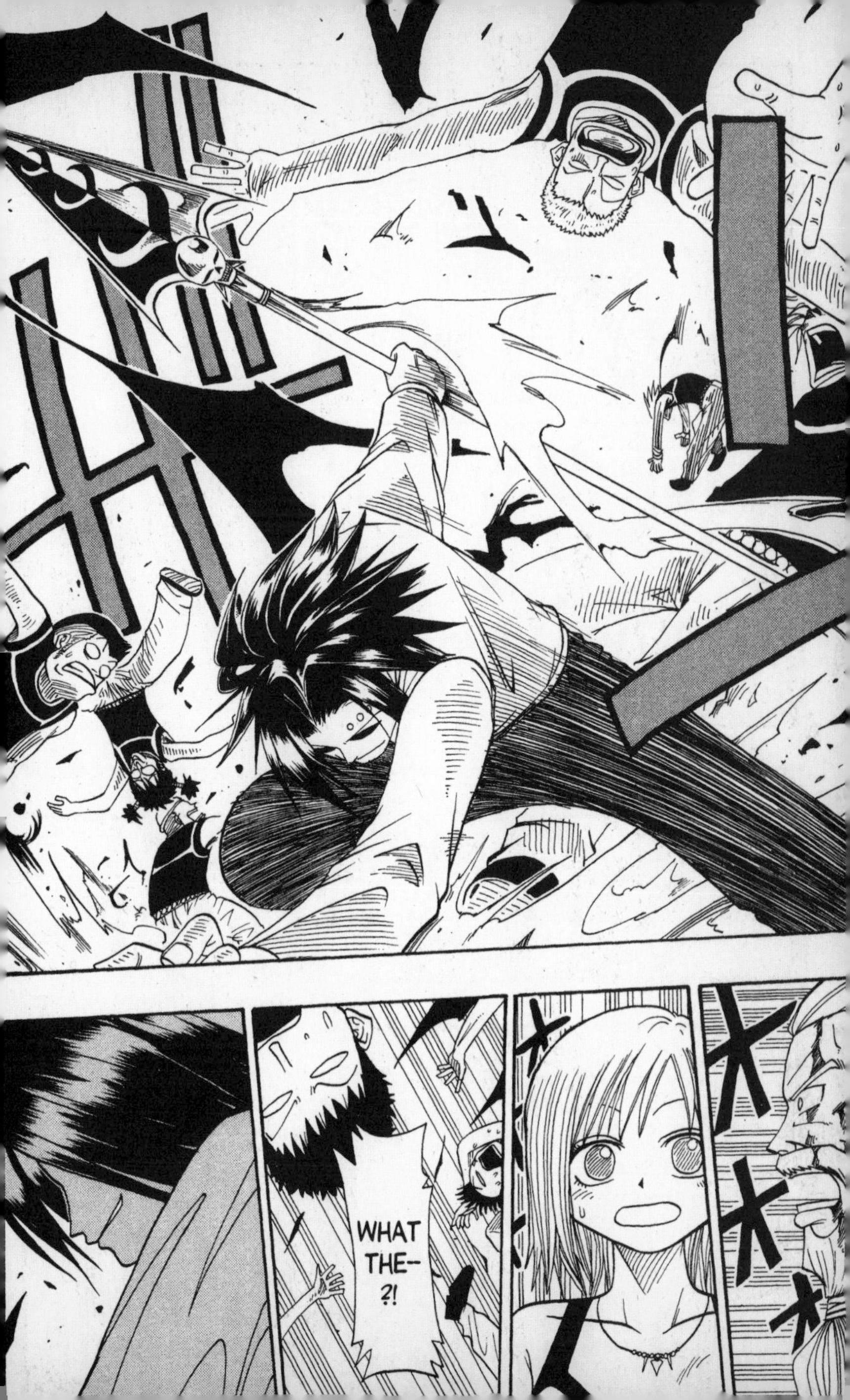
WHAT THE-?!

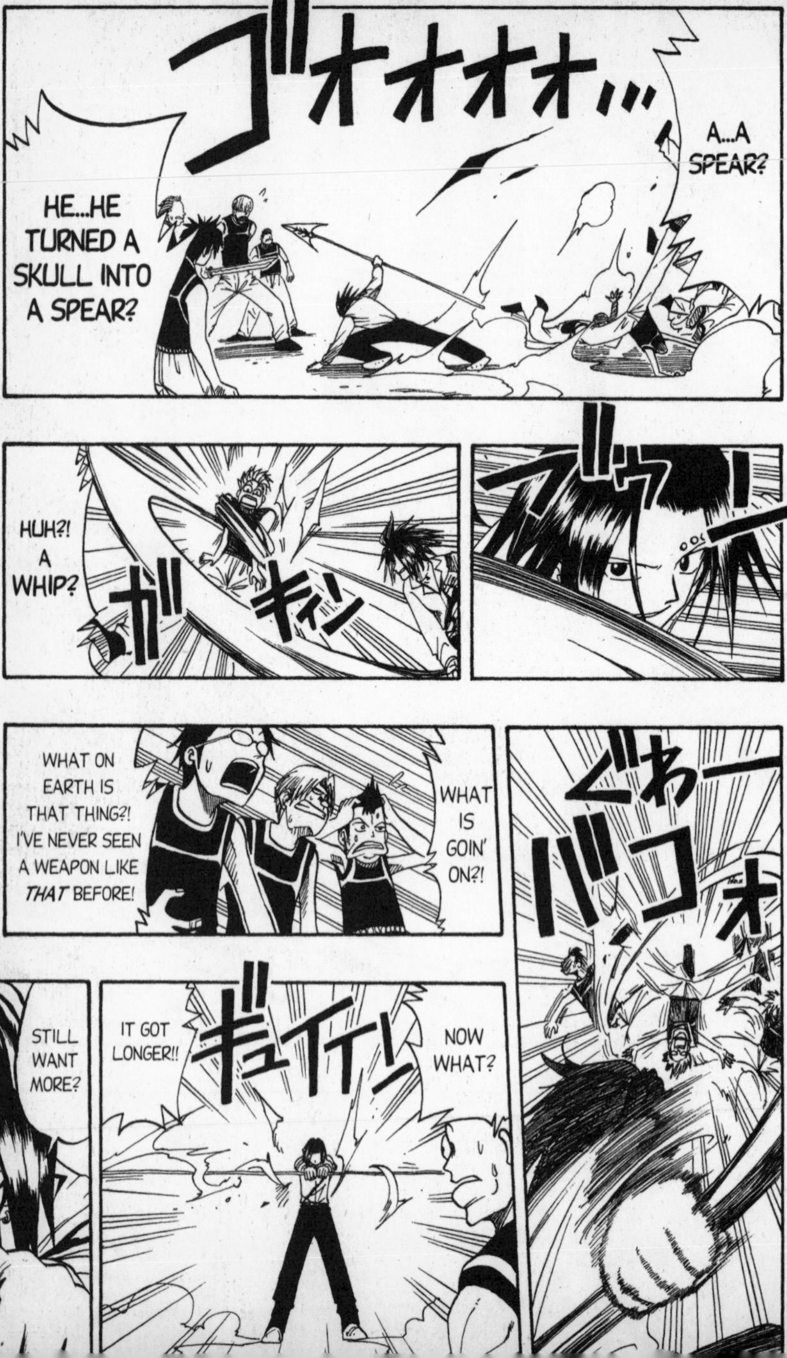
ゴオオオオッ
A...A SPEAR?
HE...HE TURNED A SKULL INTO A SPEAR?
ブゥン
ガキィン
HUH?! A WHIP?
ぐぁー
バコォ
WHAT IS GOIN' ON?!
WHAT ON EARTH IS THAT THING?! I'VE NEVER SEEN A WEAPON LIKE *THAT* BEFORE!
NOW WHAT?
ギュイイン
IT GOT LONGER!!
STILL WANT MORE?

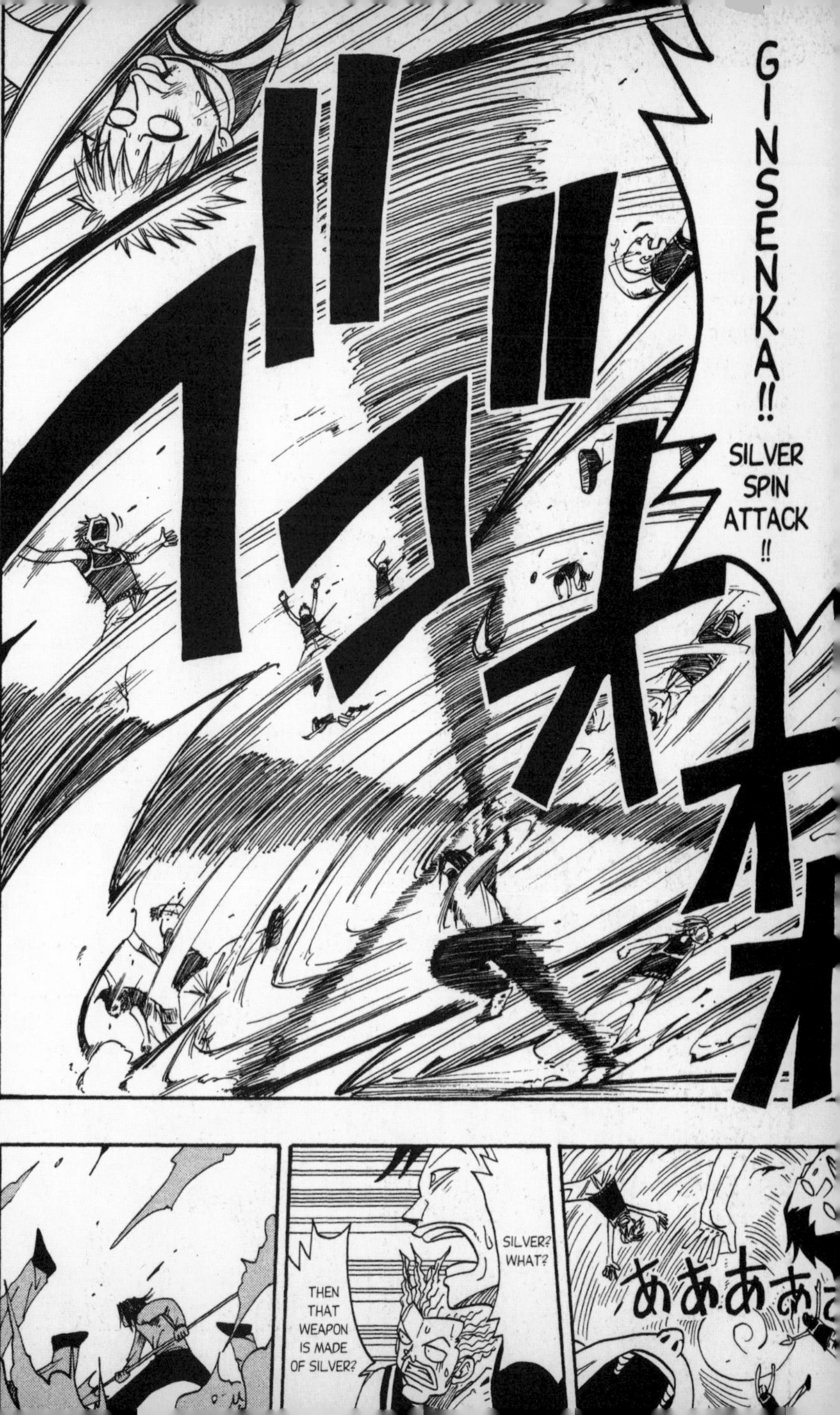
GINSENKA!!
SILVER SPIN ATTACK !!
ああああ
SILVER? WHAT?
THEN THAT WEAPON IS MADE OF SILVER?

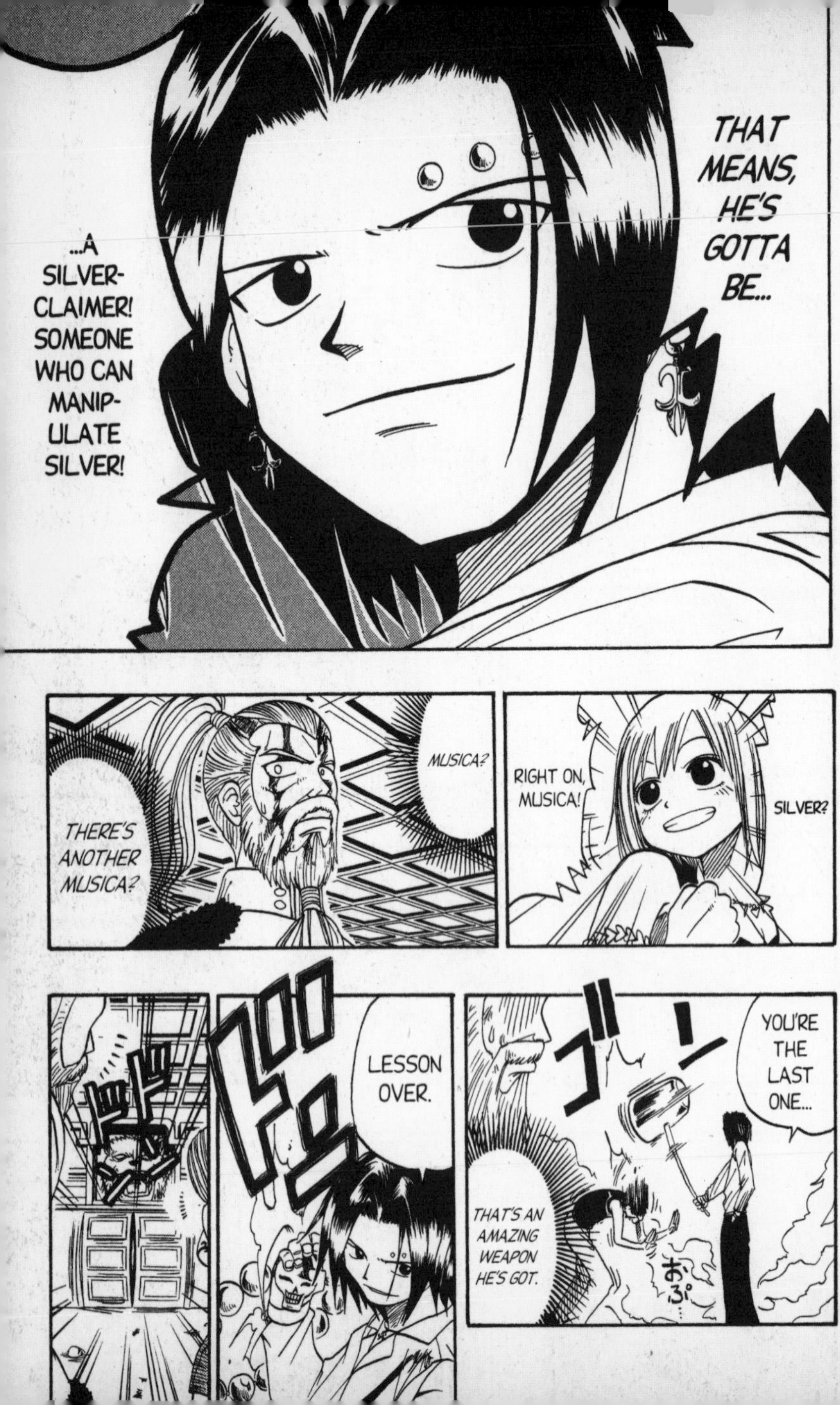
THAT MEANS, HE'S GOTTA BE...
...A SILVER-CLAIMER! SOMEONE WHO CAN MANIP-ULATE SILVER!
SILVER?
RIGHT ON, MUSICA!
MUSICA?
THERE'S ANOTHER MUSICA?
YOU'RE THE LAST ONE...
THAT'S AN AMAZING WEAPON HE'S GOT.
おぷ…
LESSON OVER.

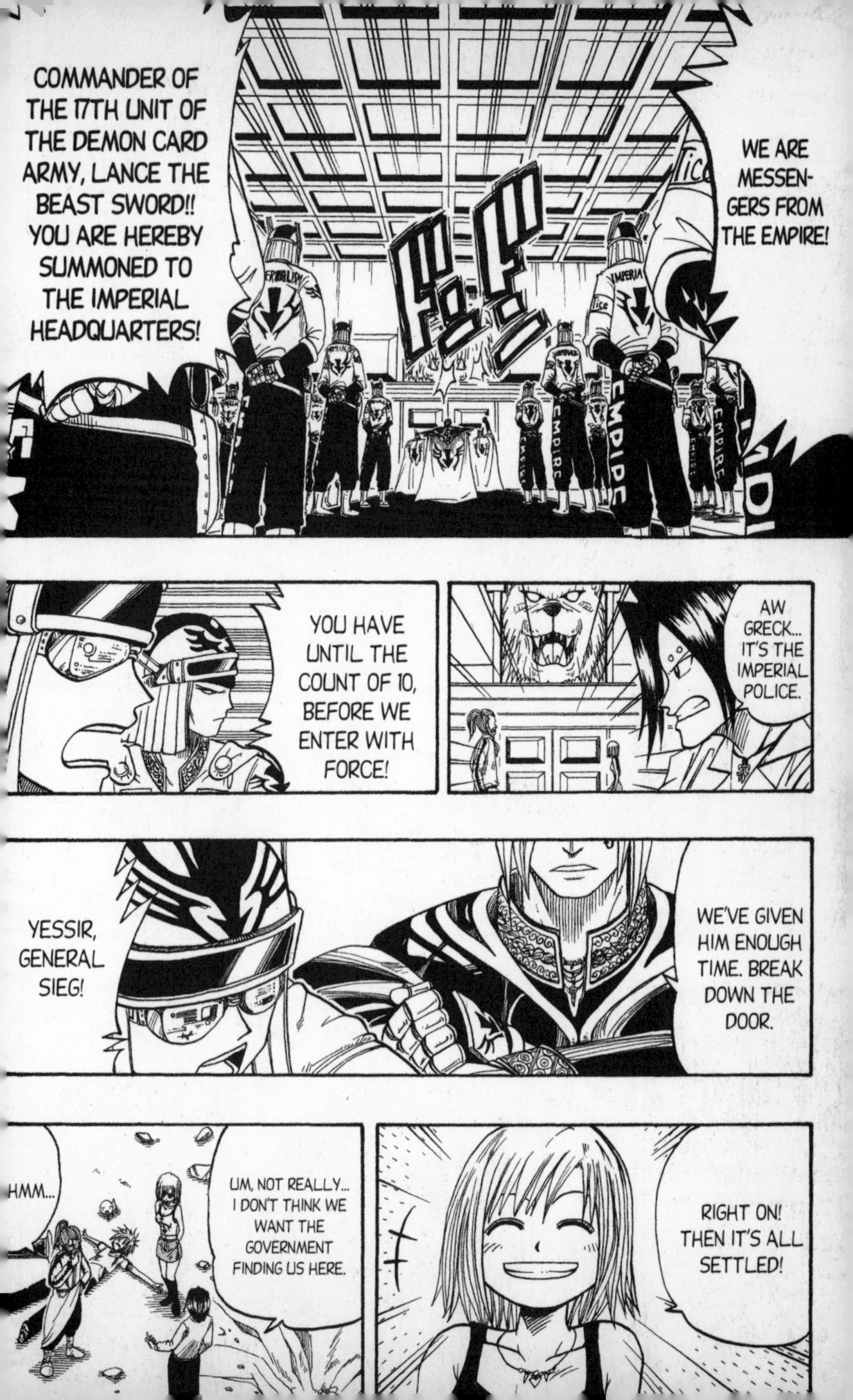
WE ARE MESSENGERS FROM THE EMPIRE!
COMMANDER OF THE 17TH UNIT OF THE DEMON CARD ARMY, LANCE THE BEAST SWORD!! YOU ARE HEREBY SUMMONED TO THE IMPERIAL HEADQUARTERS!
AW GRECK... IT'S THE IMPERIAL POLICE.
YOU HAVE UNTIL THE COUNT OF 10, BEFORE WE ENTER WITH FORCE!
WE'VE GIVEN HIM ENOUGH TIME. BREAK DOWN THE DOOR.
YESSIR, GENERAL SIEG!
RIGHT ON! THEN IT'S ALL SETTLED!
UM, NOT REALLY... I DON'T THINK WE WANT THE GOVERNMENT FINDING US HERE.
HMM...

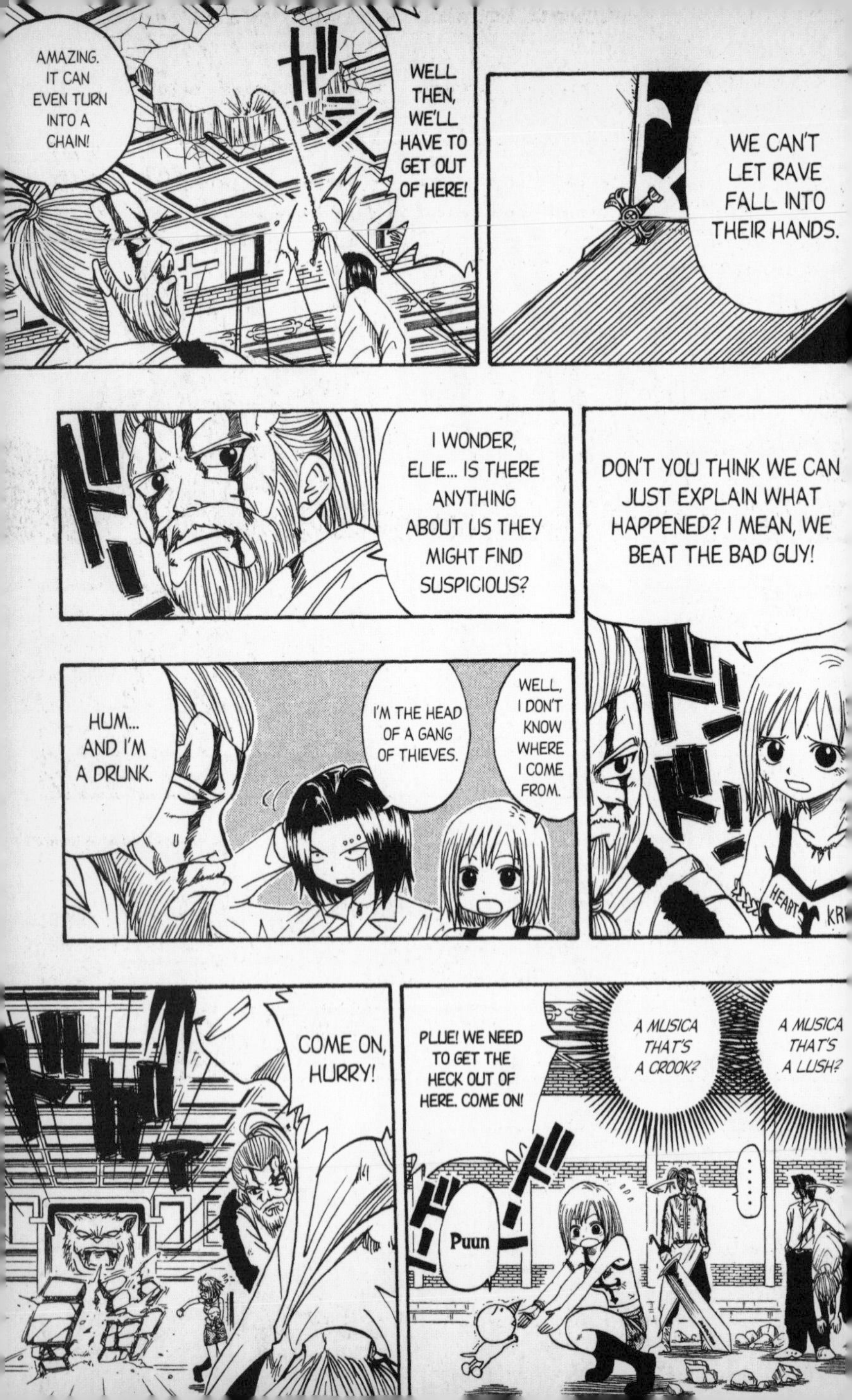
WE CAN'T LET RAVE FALL INTO THEIR HANDS.
WELL THEN, WE'LL HAVE TO GET OUT OF HERE!
AMAZING. IT CAN EVEN TURN INTO A CHAIN!
DON'T YOU THINK WE CAN JUST EXPLAIN WHAT HAPPENED? I MEAN, WE BEAT THE BAD GUY!
I WONDER, ELIE... IS THERE ANYTHING ABOUT US THEY MIGHT FIND SUSPICIOUS?
WELL, I DON'T KNOW WHERE I COME FROM.
I'M THE HEAD OF A GANG OF THIEVES.
HUM... AND I'M A DRUNK.
A MUSICA THAT'S A LUSH?
A MUSICA THAT'S A CROOK?
....
PLUE! WE NEED TO GET THE HECK OUT OF HERE. COME ON!
Puun
COME ON, HURRY!

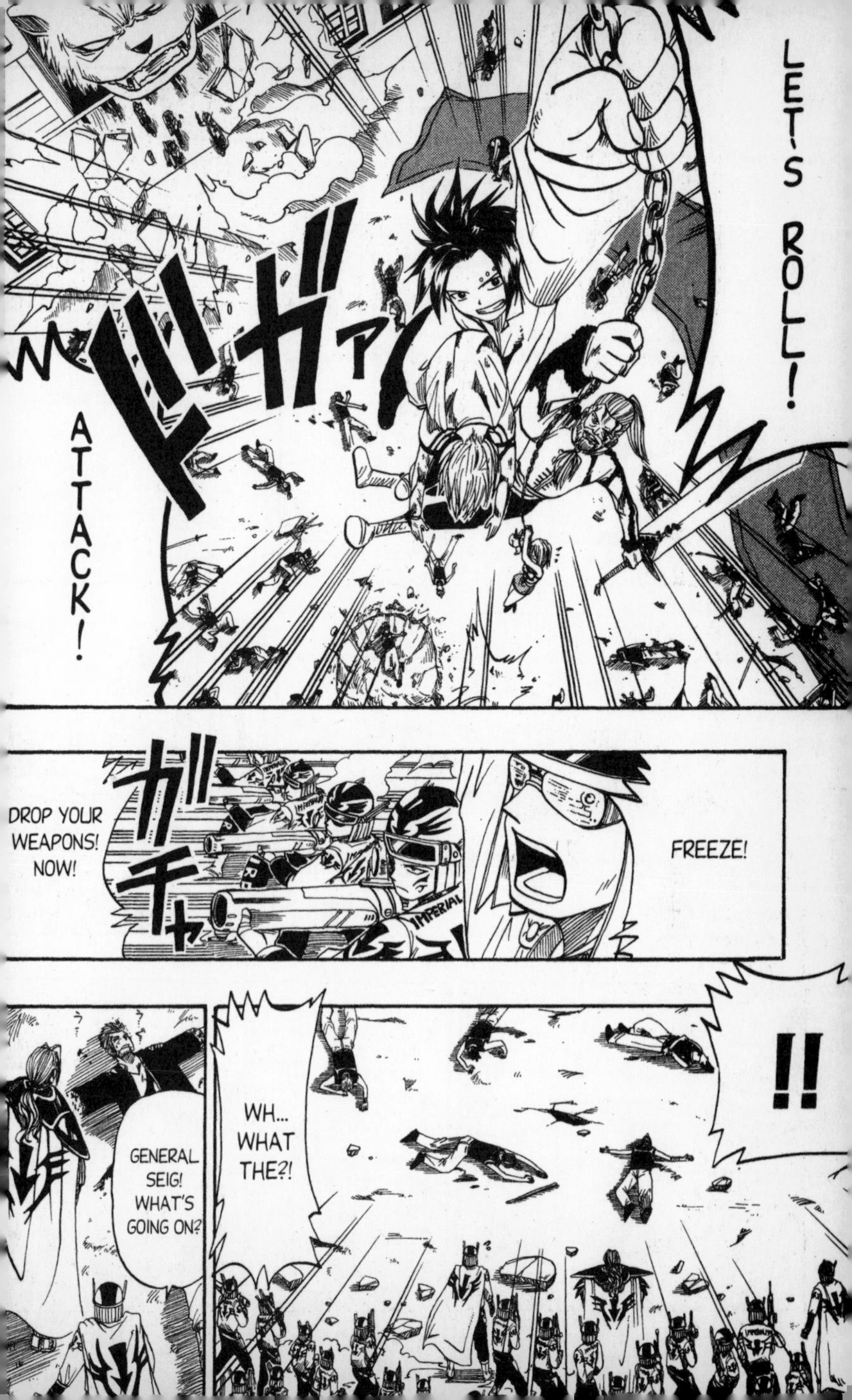
LET'S ROLL!
ドガァ
ATTACK!
FREEZE!
ガチャ
DROP YOUR WEAPONS! NOW!
!!
WH... WHAT THE?!
GENERAL SEIG! WHAT'S GOING ON?

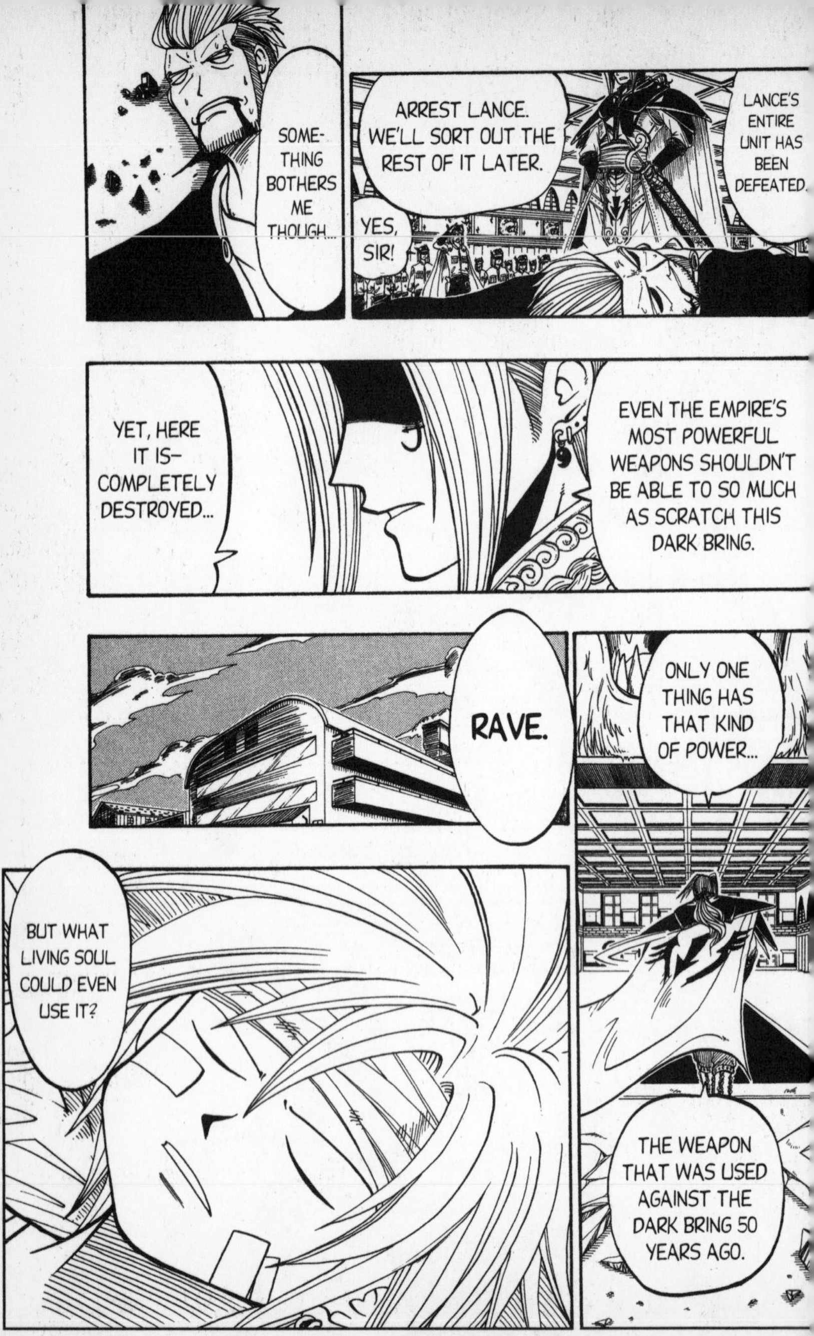
LANCE'S ENTIRE UNIT HAS BEEN DEFEATED.
ARREST LANCE. WE'LL SORT OUT THE REST OF IT LATER.
YES, SIR!
SOMETHING BOTHERS ME THOUGH...
EVEN THE EMPIRE'S MOST POWERFUL WEAPONS SHOULDN'T BE ABLE TO SO MUCH AS SCRATCH THIS DARK BRING.
YET, HERE IT IS—COMPLETELY DESTROYED...
ONLY ONE THING HAS THAT KIND OF POWER...
RAVE.
THE WEAPON THAT WAS USED AGAINST THE DARK BRING 50 YEARS AGO.
BUT WHAT LIVING SOUL COULD EVEN USE IT?

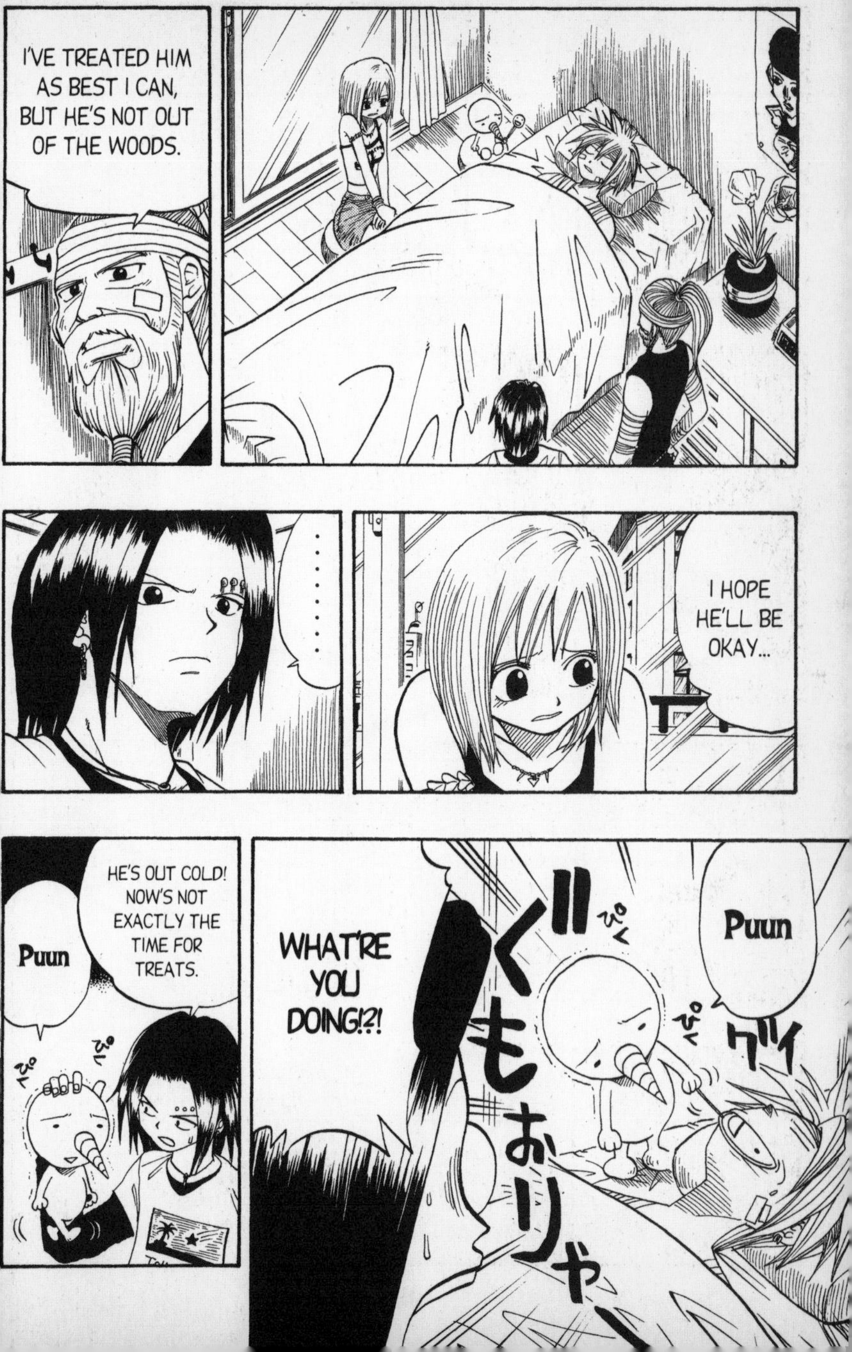
I'VE TREATED HIM AS BEST I CAN, BUT HE'S NOT OUT OF THE WOODS.
I HOPE HE'LL BE OKAY...
....
Puun
グイ
ぴく
くもぉりゃ〜
WHAT'RE YOU DOING!?!
HE'S OUT COLD! NOW'S NOT EXACTLY THE TIME FOR TREATS.
Puun
ぴく

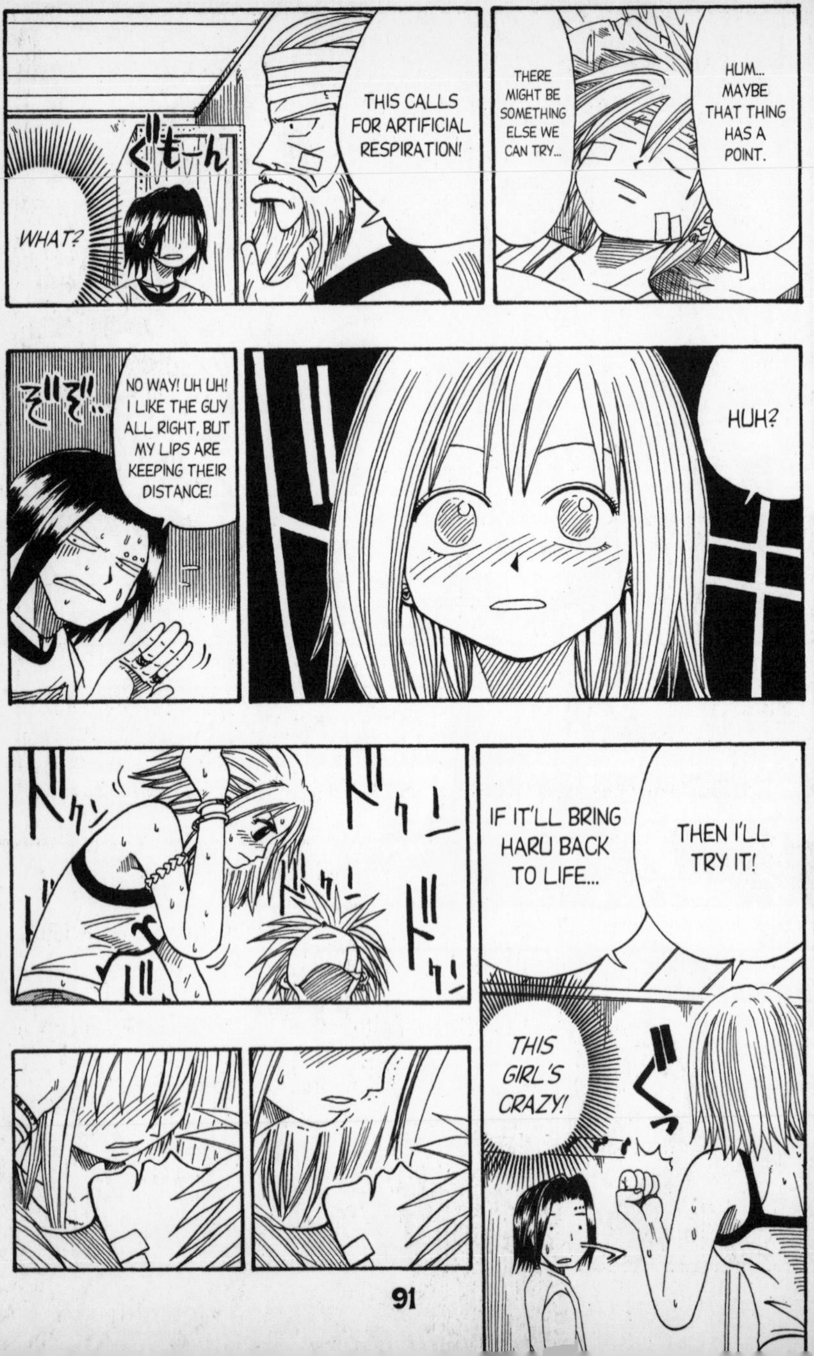
HUM... MAYBE THAT THING HAS A POINT.
THERE MIGHT BE SOMETHING ELSE WE CAN TRY...
THIS CALLS FOR ARTIFICIAL RESPIRATION!
ぐもーん
WHAT?
HUH?
NO WAY! UH UH! I LIKE THE GUY ALL RIGHT, BUT MY LIPS ARE KEEPING THEIR DISTANCE!
ぞぞ..
IF IT'LL BRING HARU BACK TO LIFE...
THEN I'LL TRY IT!
THIS GIRL'S CRAZY!
ぐっ
ドクン
ドクン
ドクン
ドクン

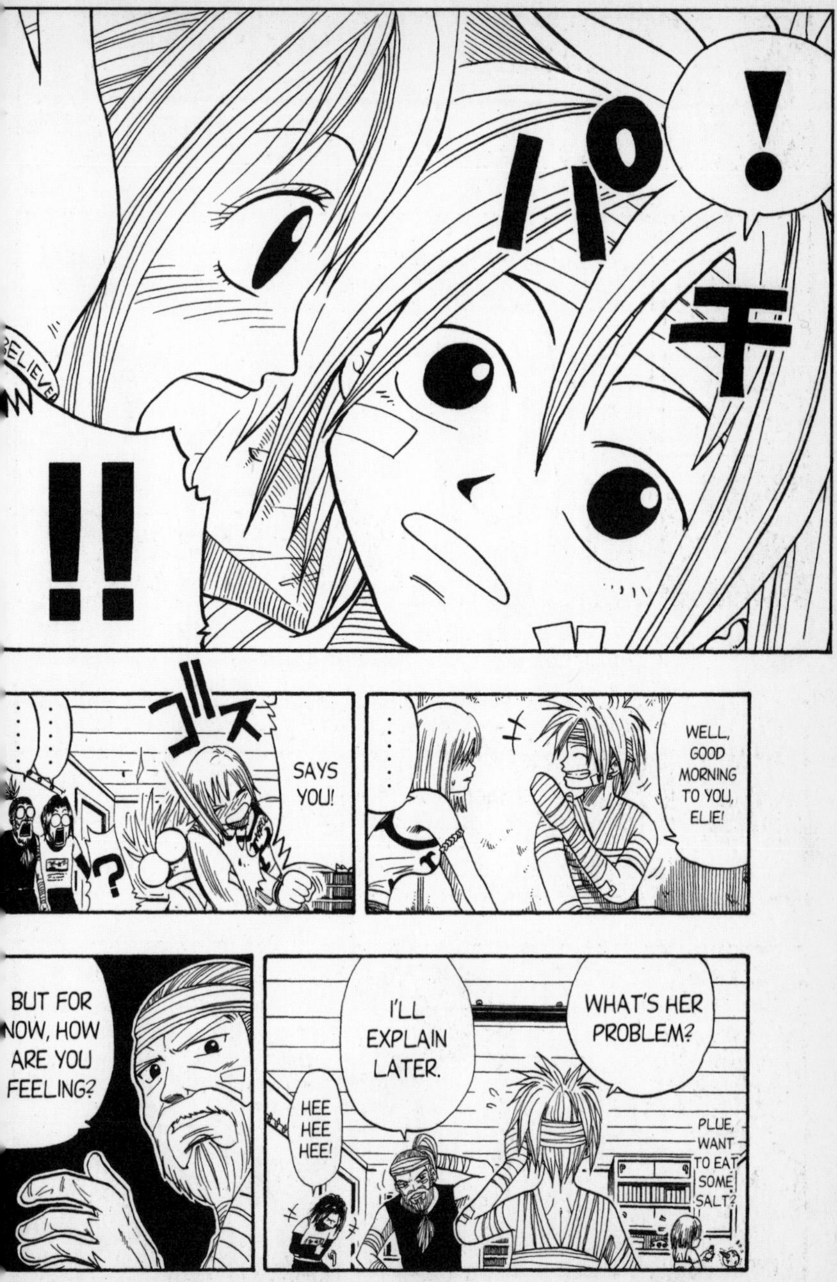
!
パチ
BELIEVE
!!
WELL, GOOD MORNING TO YOU, ELIE!
......
SAYS YOU!
ゴス
......
......
?
WHAT'S HER PROBLEM?
I'LL EXPLAIN LATER.
PLUE, WANT TO EAT SOME SALT?
HEE HEE HEE!
BUT FOR NOW, HOW ARE YOU FEELING?

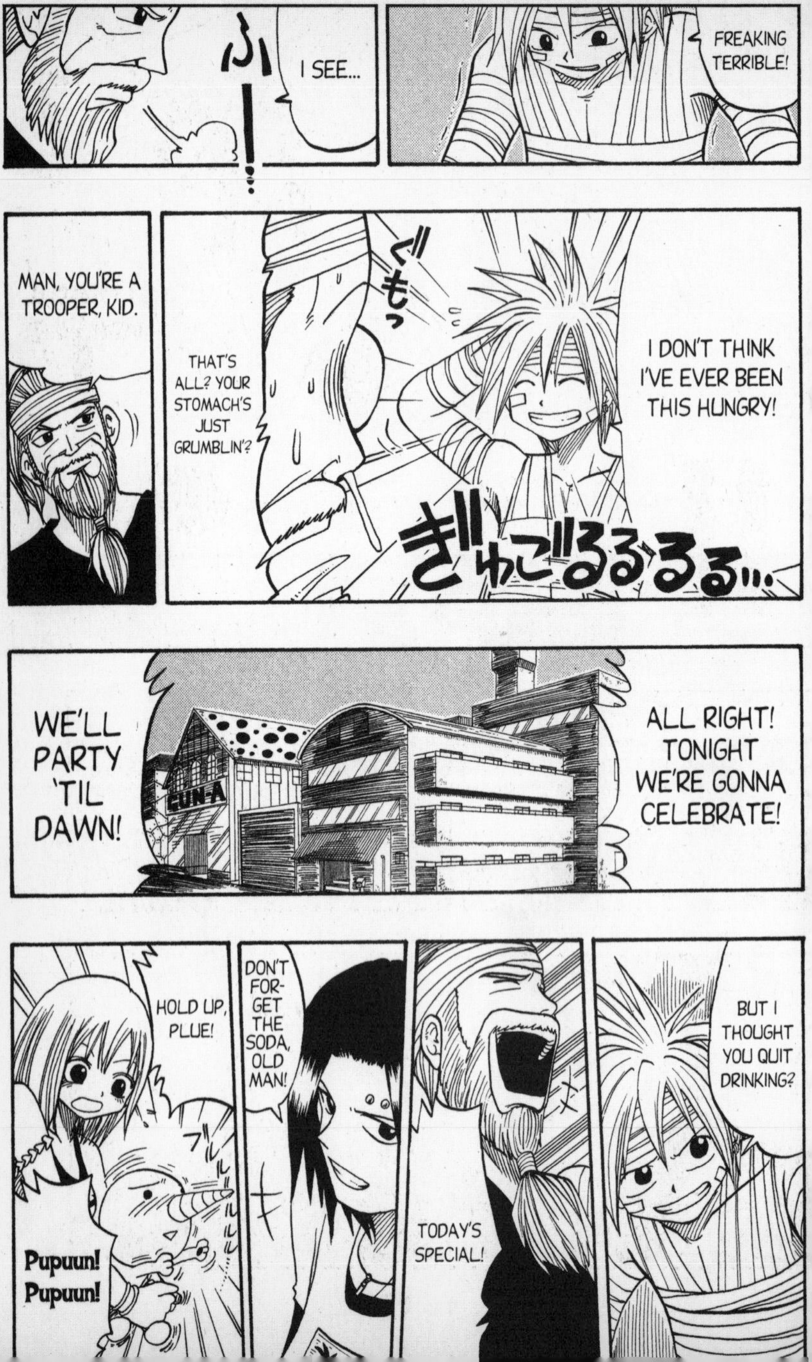
FREAKING TERRIBLE!
I SEE...
ふーー!
I DON'T THINK I'VE EVER BEEN THIS HUNGRY!
ぐもっ
THAT'S ALL? YOUR STOMACH'S JUST GRUMBLIN'?
ぎゅごるるるる...
MAN, YOU'RE A TROOPER, KID.
ALL RIGHT! TONIGHT WE'RE GONNA CELEBRATE!
GUN-A
WE'LL PARTY 'TIL DAWN!
BUT I THOUGHT YOU QUIT DRINKING?
TODAY'S SPECIAL!
DON'T FOR-GET THE SODA, OLD MAN!
HOLD UP, PLUE!
Pupuun! Pupuun!

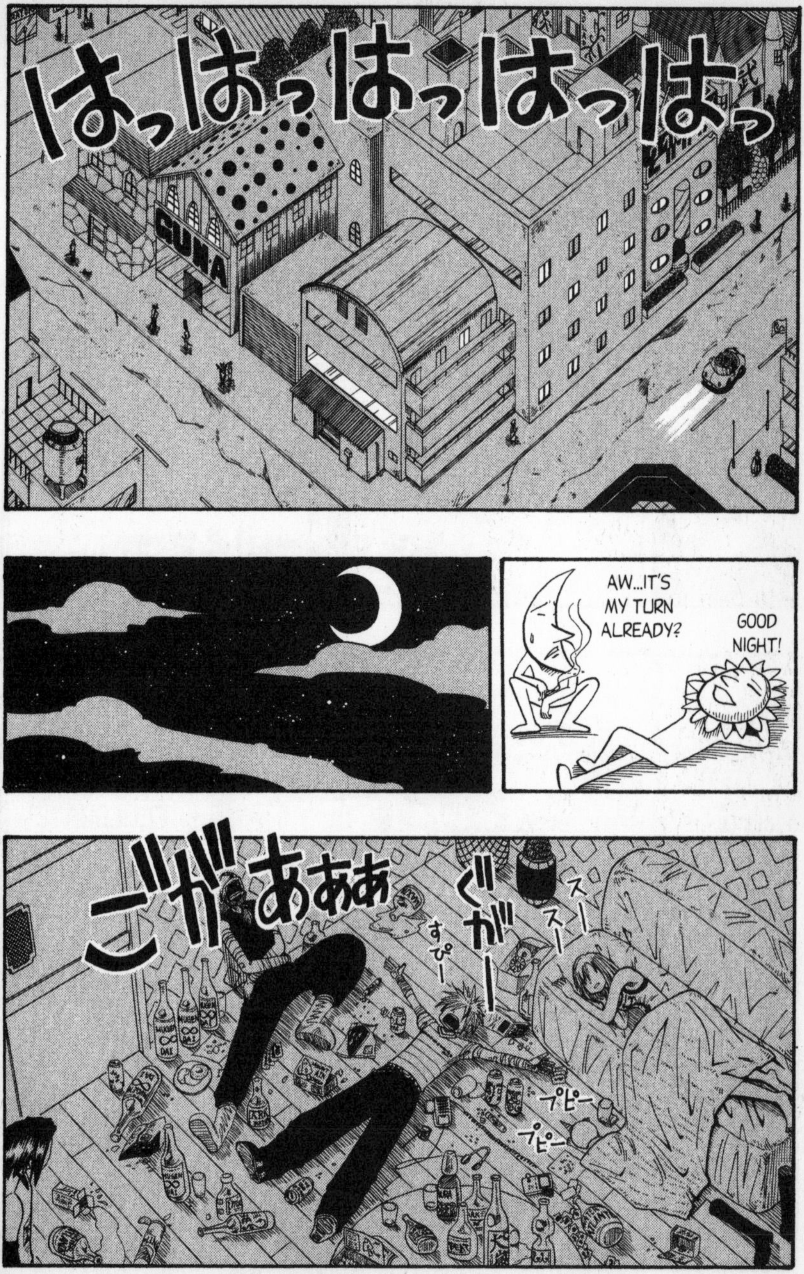
はっはっはっはっはっ
GUNA
AW...IT'S MY TURN ALREADY?
GOOD NIGHT!
スースー
ぐがーー
すぴー
ごがあああ
プピー
プピー

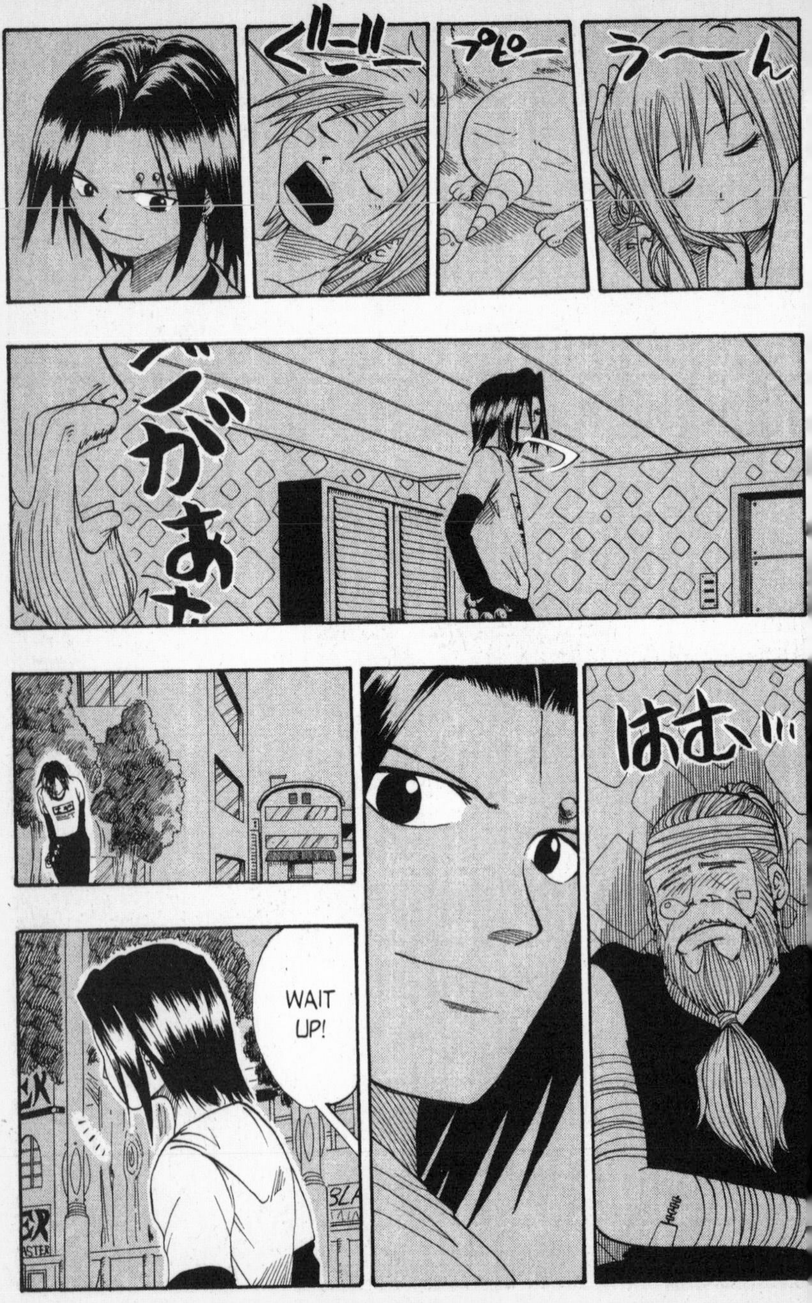

うーん
プピー
はむぃ
WAIT UP!

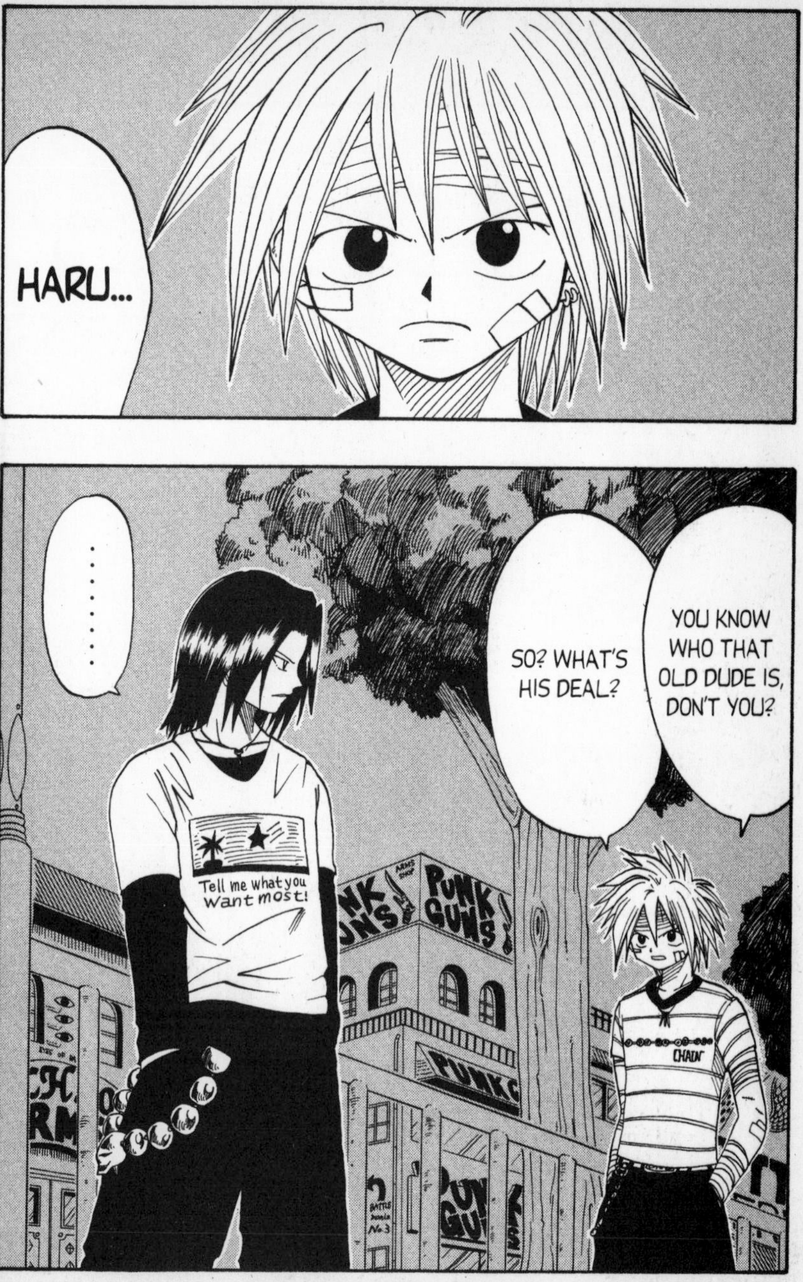
HARU...
YOU KNOW WHO THAT OLD DUDE IS, DON'T YOU?
SO? WHAT'S HIS DEAL?
....
Tell me what you want most!
ARMS SHOP
PUNK GUNS
CHAIN

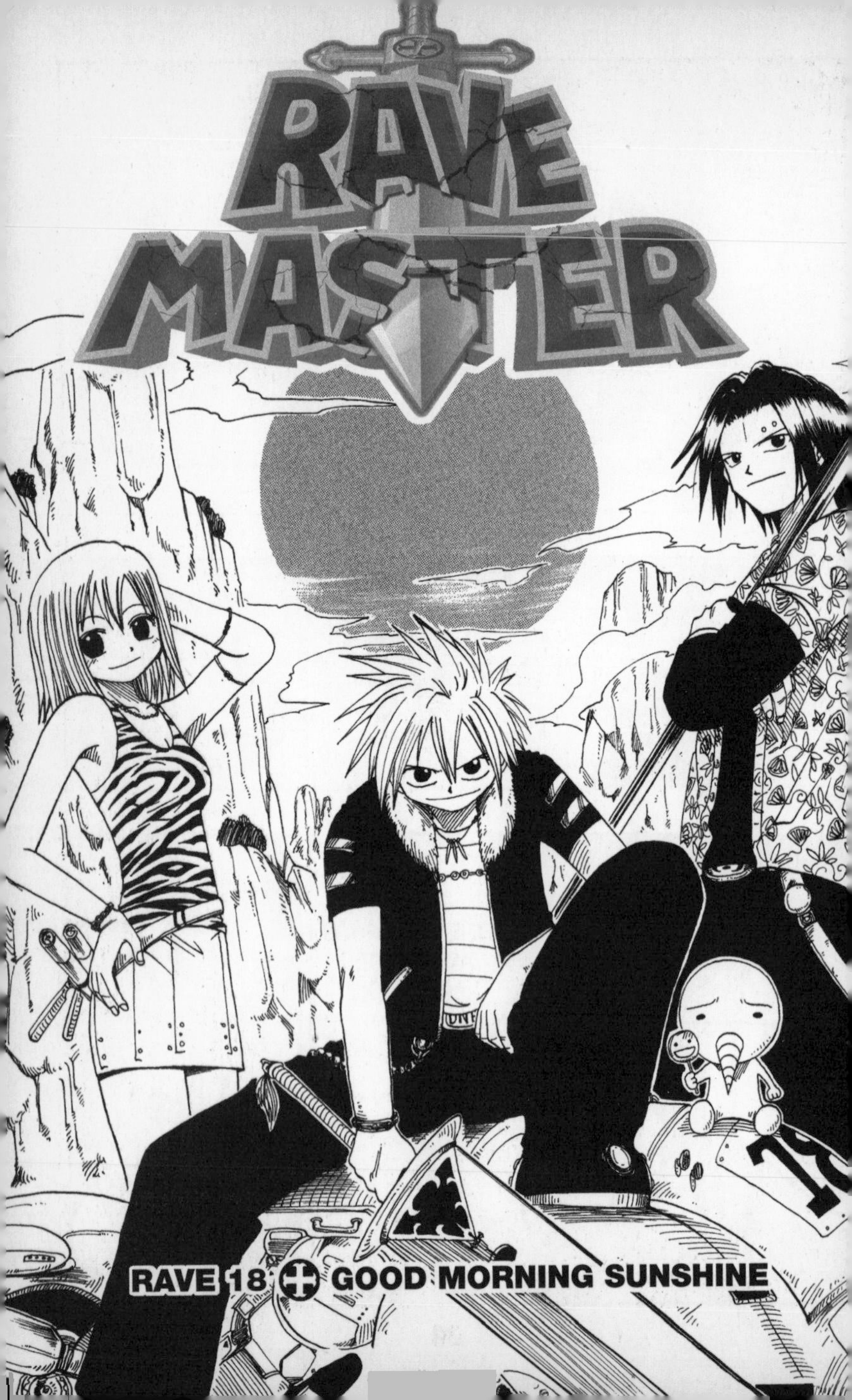
RAVE MASTER
RAVE 18 GOOD MORNING SUNSHINE

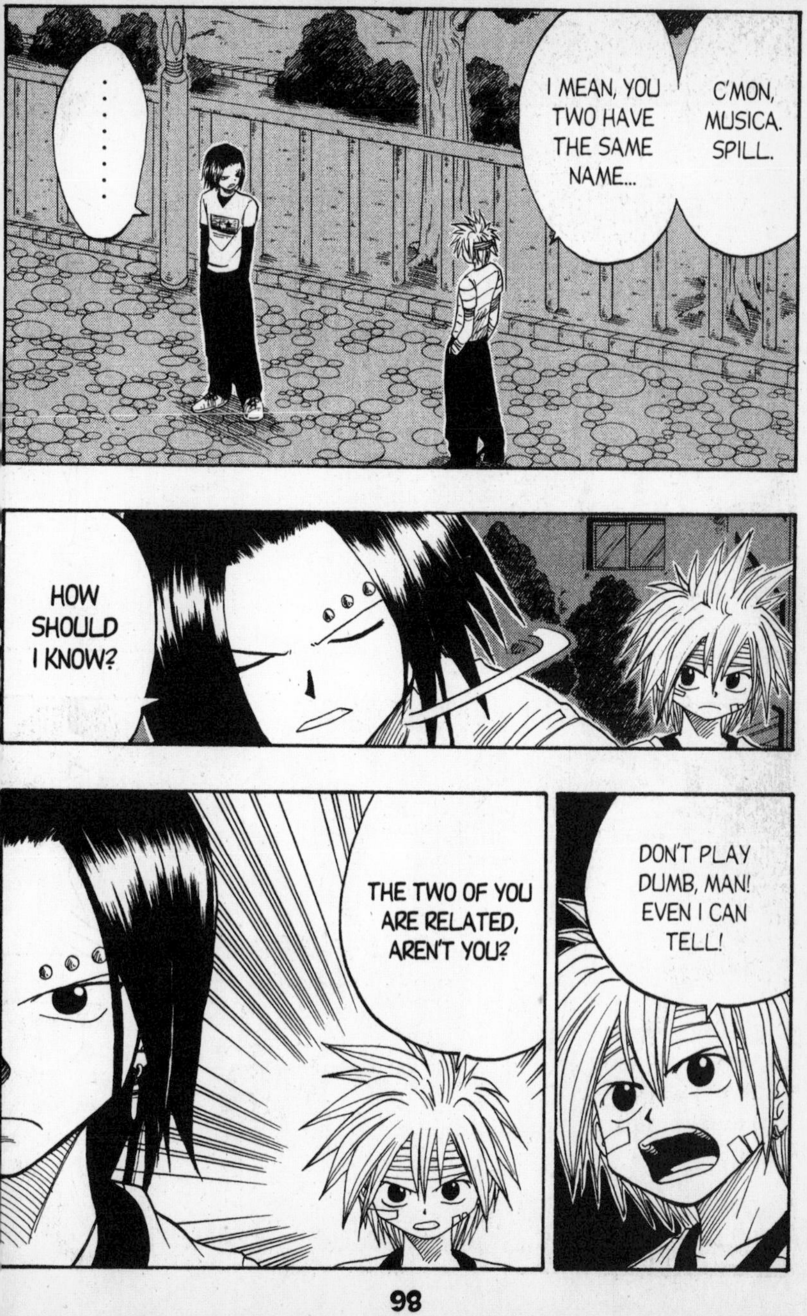
C'MON, MUSICA. SPILL.
I MEAN, YOU TWO HAVE THE SAME NAME...
......
HOW SHOULD I KNOW?
DON'T PLAY DUMB, MAN! EVEN I CAN TELL!
THE TWO OF YOU ARE RELATED, AREN'T YOU?

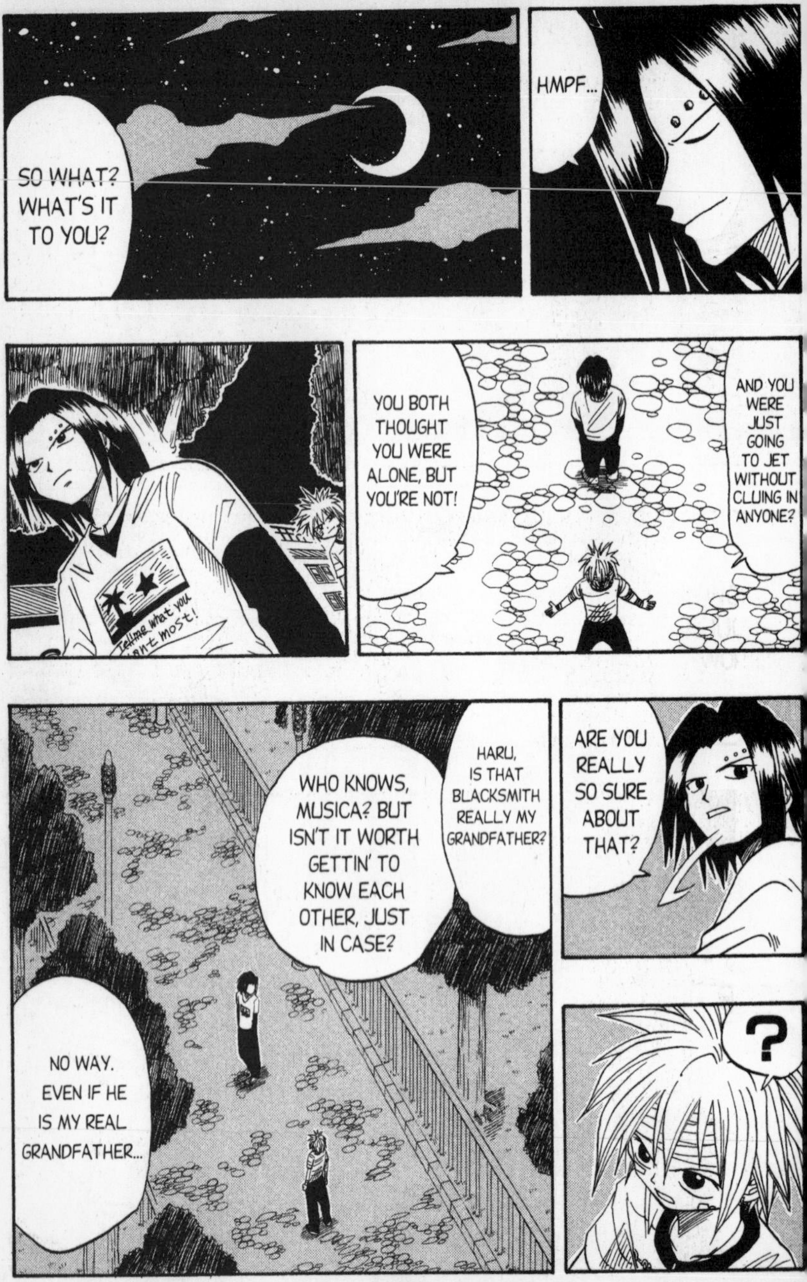
HMPF...
SO WHAT? WHAT'S IT TO YOU?
AND YOU WERE JUST GOING TO JET WITHOUT CLUING IN ANYONE?
YOU BOTH THOUGHT YOU WERE ALONE, BUT YOU'RE NOT!
ARE YOU REALLY SO SURE ABOUT THAT?
?
HARU, IS THAT BLACKSMITH REALLY MY GRANDFATHER?
WHO KNOWS, MUSICA? BUT ISN'T IT WORTH GETTIN' TO KNOW EACH OTHER, JUST IN CASE?
NO WAY. EVEN IF HE IS MY REAL GRANDFATHER...

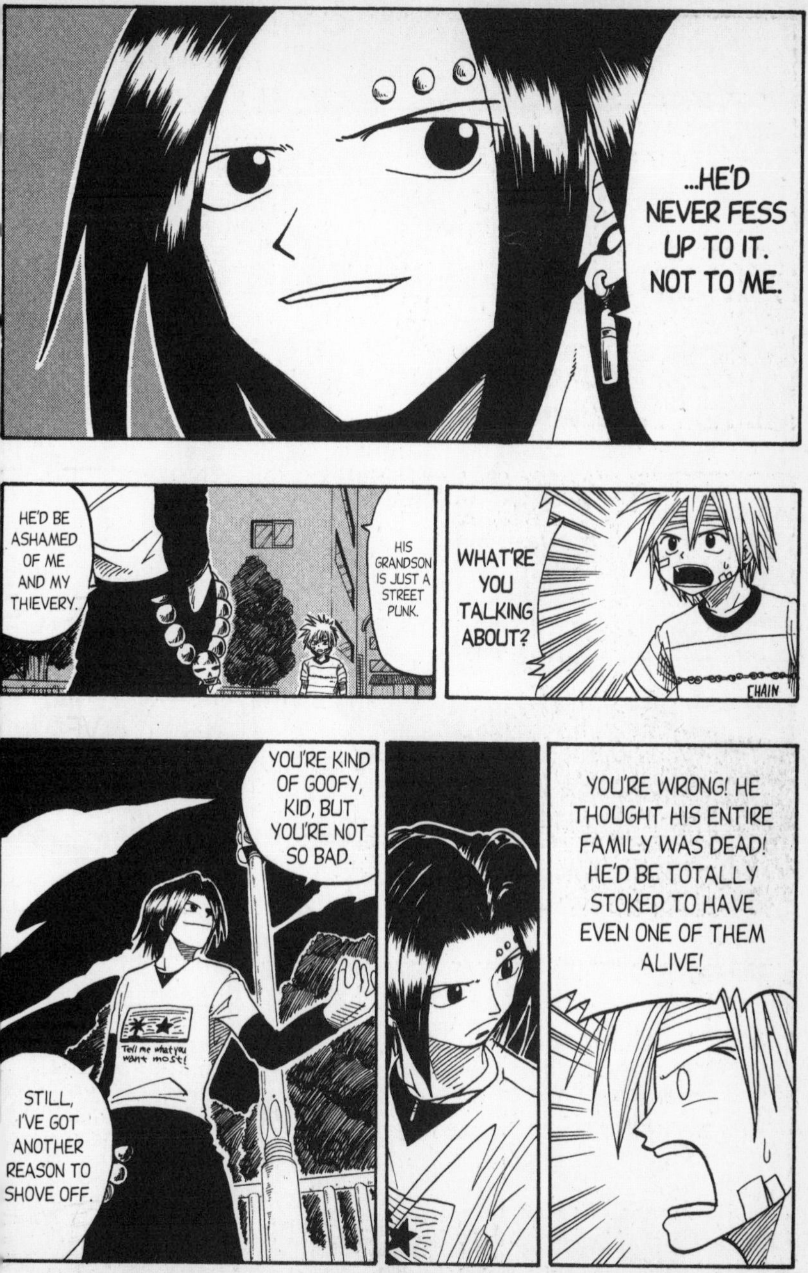
...HE'D NEVER FESS UP TO IT. NOT TO ME.
WHAT'RE YOU TALKING ABOUT?
CHAIN
HE'D BE ASHAMED OF ME AND MY THIEVERY.
HIS GRANDSON IS JUST A STREET PUNK.
YOU'RE WRONG! HE THOUGHT HIS ENTIRE FAMILY WAS DEAD! HE'D BE TOTALLY STOKED TO HAVE EVEN ONE OF THEM ALIVE!
YOU'RE KIND OF GOOFY, KID, BUT YOU'RE NOT SO BAD.
Tell me what you want most!
STILL, I'VE GOT ANOTHER REASON TO SHOVE OFF.

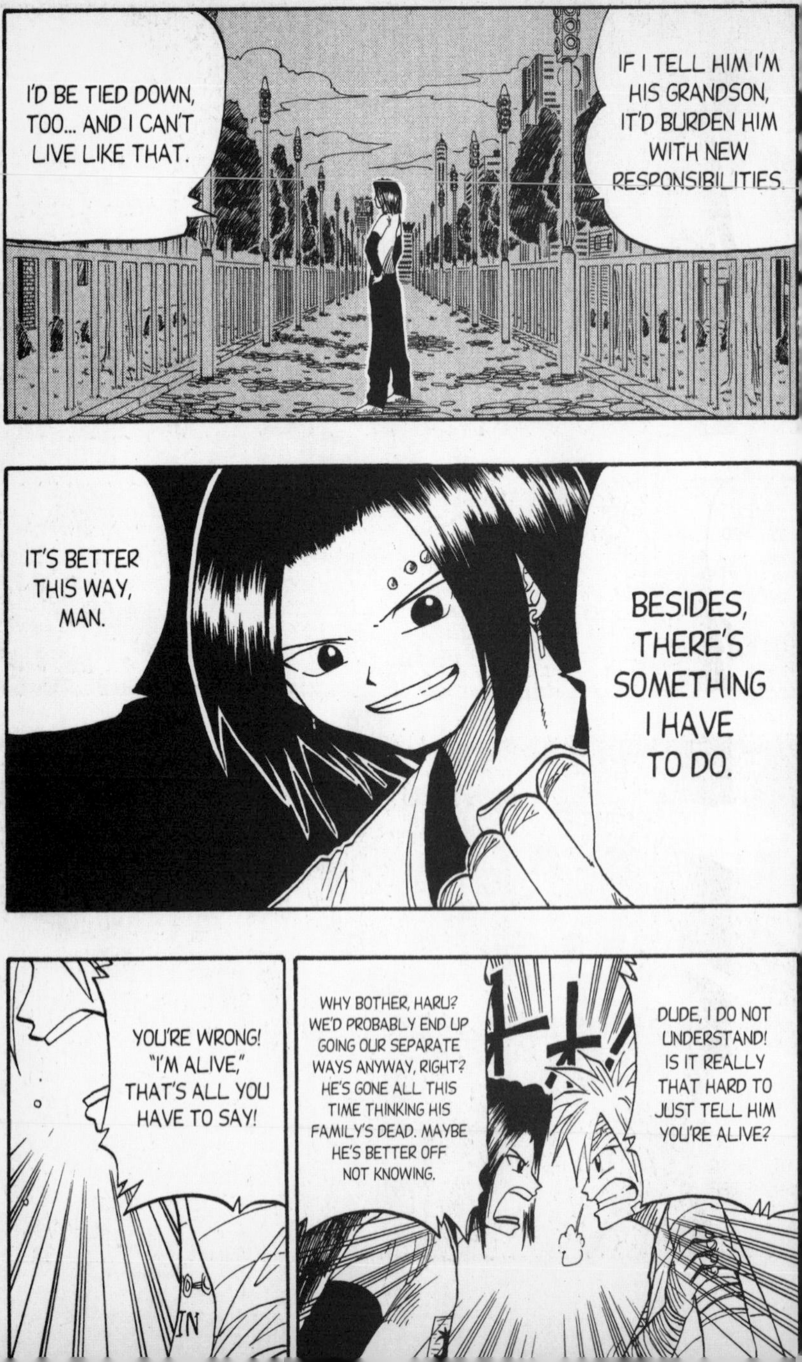

IF I TELL HIM I'M HIS GRANDSON, IT'D BURDEN HIM WITH NEW RESPONSIBILITIES.
I'D BE TIED DOWN, TOO... AND I CAN'T LIVE LIKE THAT.
IT'S BETTER THIS WAY, MAN.
BESIDES, THERE'S SOMETHING I HAVE TO DO.
DUDE, I DO NOT UNDERSTAND! IS IT REALLY THAT HARD TO JUST TELL HIM YOU'RE ALIVE?
WHY BOTHER, HARU? WE'D PROBABLY END UP GOING OUR SEPARATE WAYS ANYWAY, RIGHT? HE'S GONE ALL THIS TIME THINKING HIS FAMILY'S DEAD. MAYBE HE'S BETTER OFF NOT KNOWING.
YOU'RE WRONG! "I'M ALIVE," THAT'S ALL YOU HAVE TO SAY!

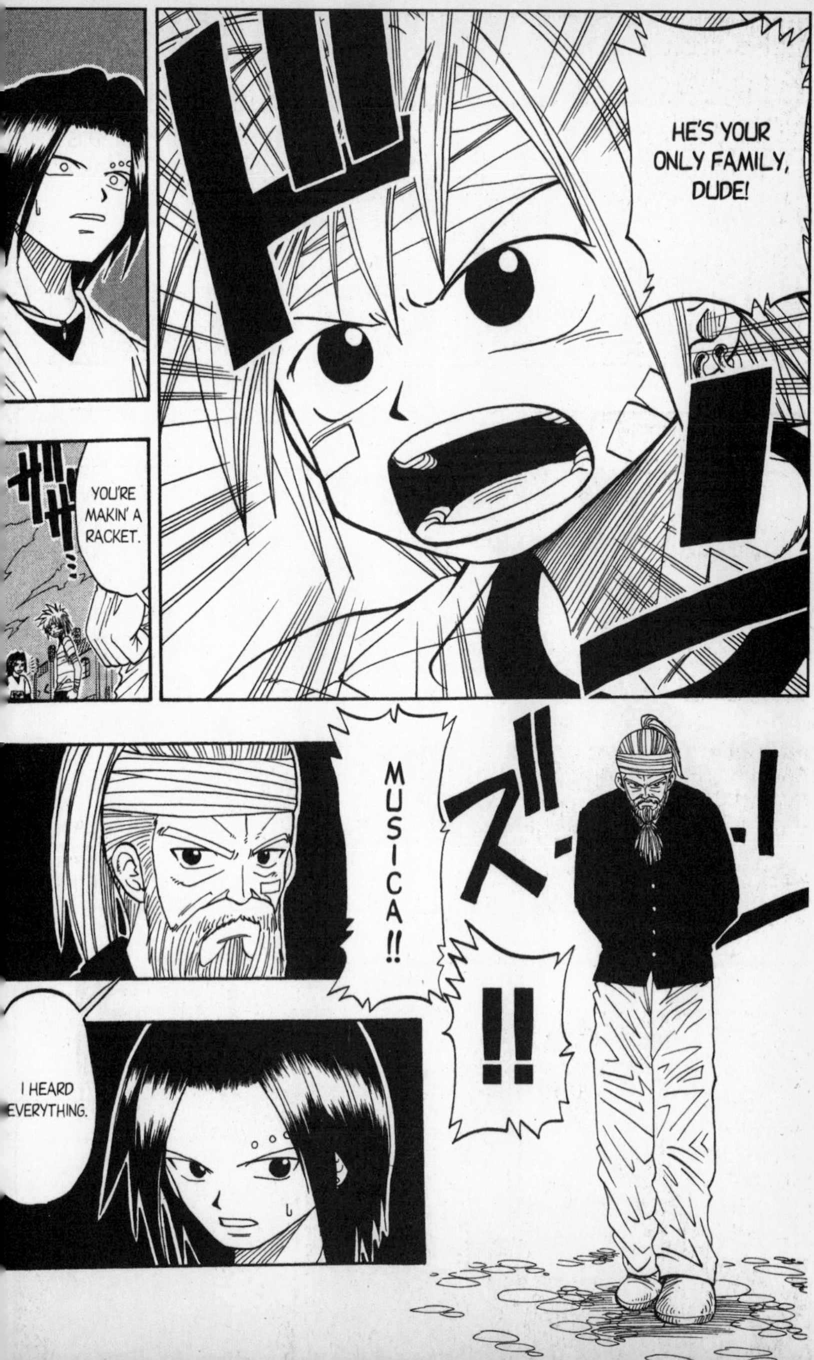
HE'S YOUR ONLY FAMILY, DUDE!
YOU'RE MAKIN' A RACKET.
MUSICA!!
!!
I HEARD EVERYTHING.

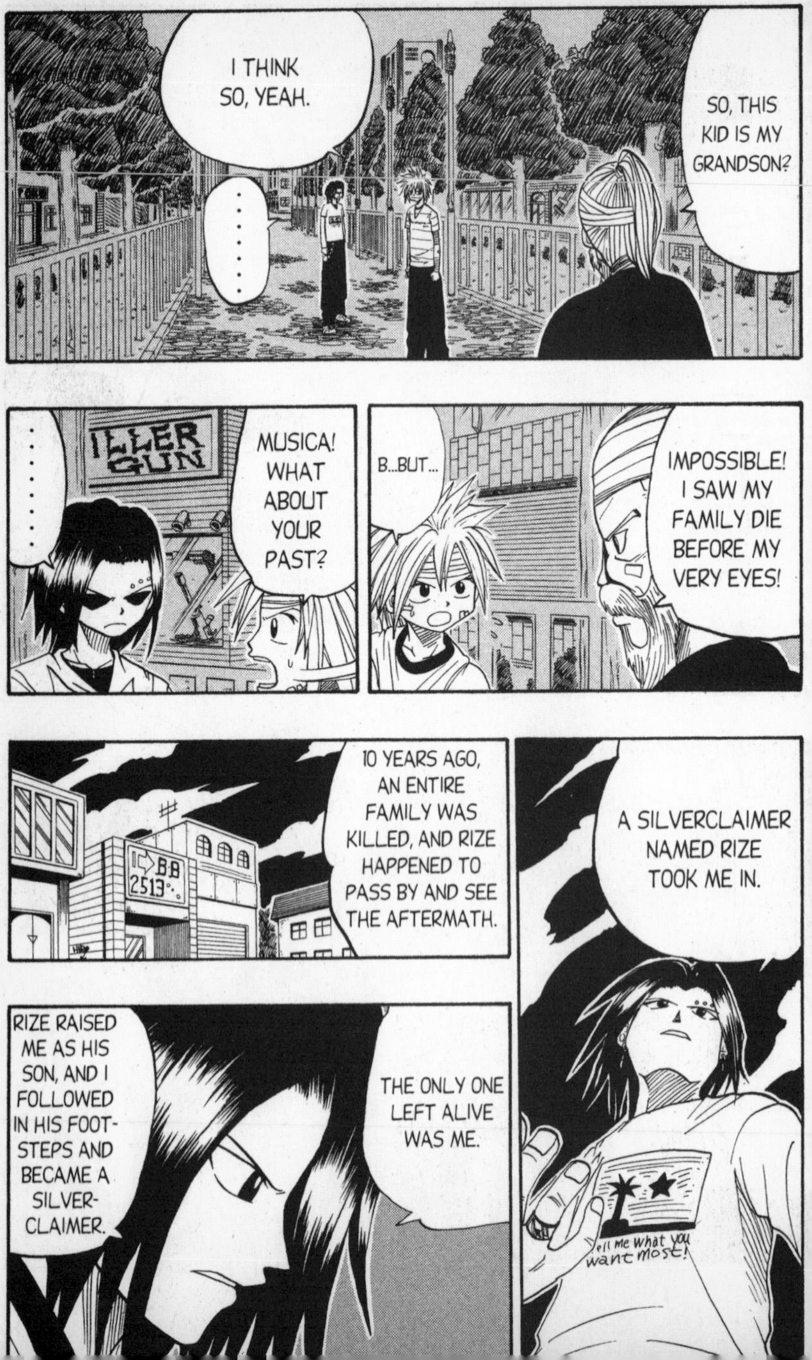
SO, THIS KID IS MY GRANDSON?
I THINK SO, YEAH.
......
IMPOSSIBLE! I SAW MY FAMILY DIE BEFORE MY VERY EYES!
B...BUT...
MUSICA! WHAT ABOUT YOUR PAST?
ILLER GUN
......
A SILVERCLAIMER NAMED RIZE TOOK ME IN.
ell me what you want most!
10 YEARS AGO, AN ENTIRE FAMILY WAS KILLED, AND RIZE HAPPENED TO PASS BY AND SEE THE AFTERMATH.
B.B 2513
THE ONLY ONE LEFT ALIVE WAS ME.
RIZE RAISED ME AS HIS SON, AND I FOLLOWED IN HIS FOOT-STEPS AND BECAME A SILVER-CLAIMER.

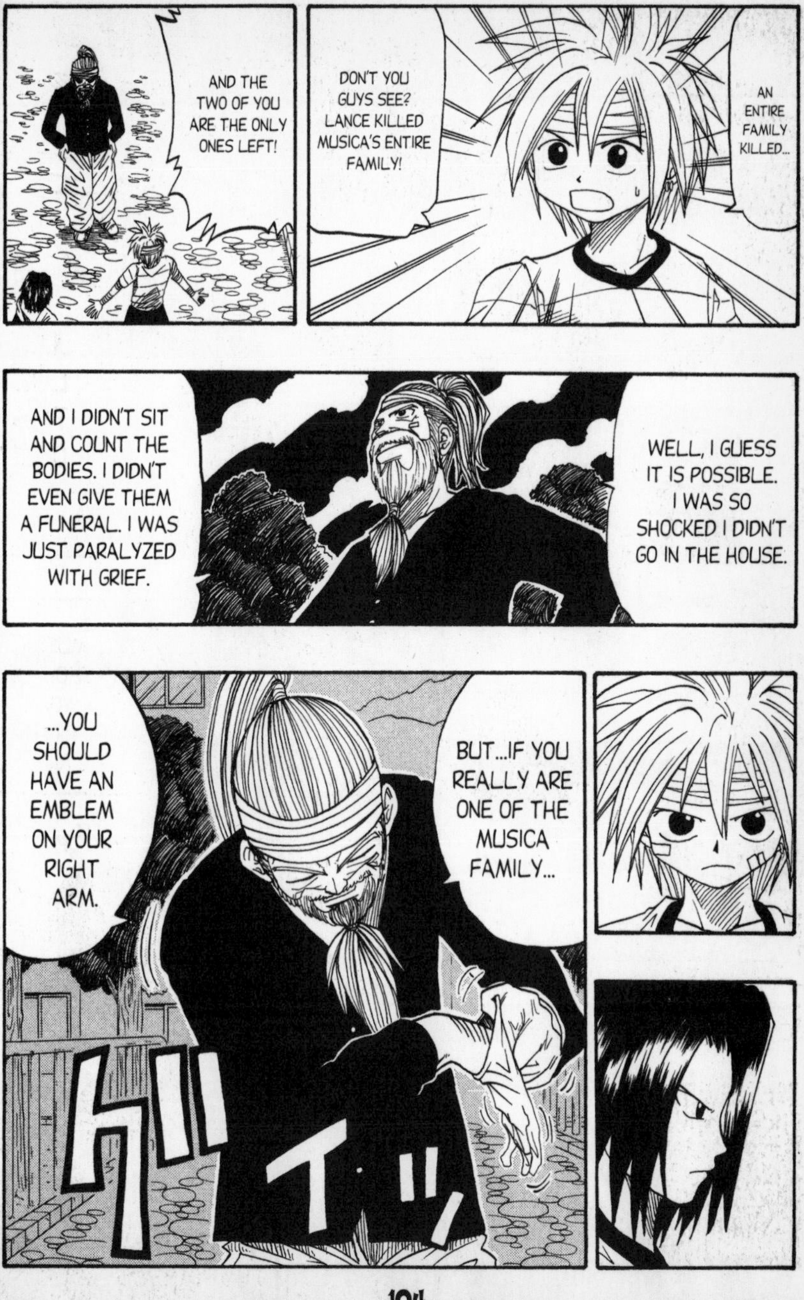

AN ENTIRE FAMILY KILLED...
DON'T YOU GUYS SEE? LANCE KILLED MUSICA'S ENTIRE FAMILY!
AND THE TWO OF YOU ARE THE ONLY ONES LEFT!
WELL, I GUESS IT IS POSSIBLE. I WAS SO SHOCKED I DIDN'T GO IN THE HOUSE.
AND I DIDN'T SIT AND COUNT THE BODIES. I DIDN'T EVEN GIVE THEM A FUNERAL. I WAS JUST PARALYZED WITH GRIEF.
BUT...IF YOU REALLY ARE ONE OF THE MUSICA FAMILY...
...YOU SHOULD HAVE AN EMBLEM ON YOUR RIGHT ARM.

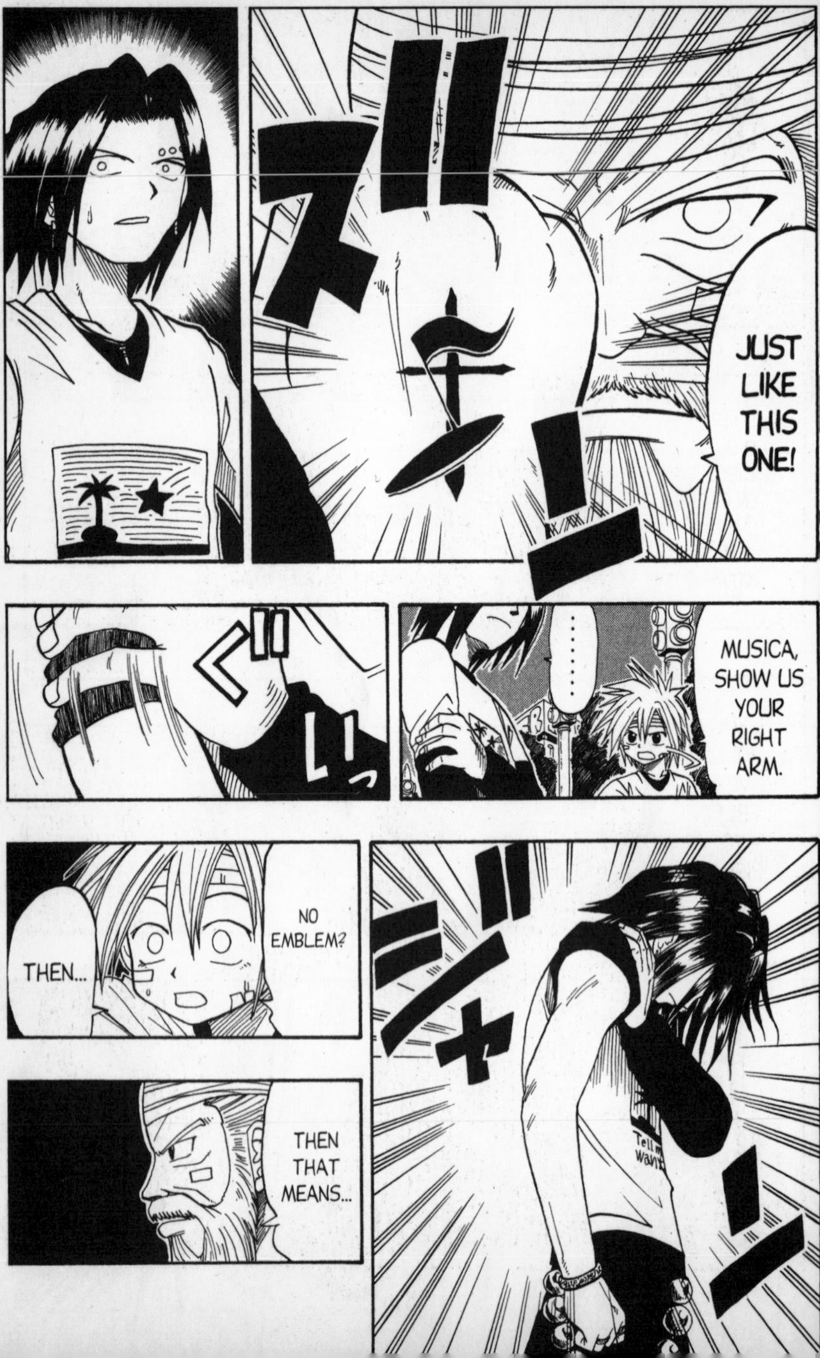
JUST LIKE THIS ONE!
MUSICA, SHOW US YOUR RIGHT ARM.
....
NO EMBLEM?
THEN...
THEN THAT MEANS...

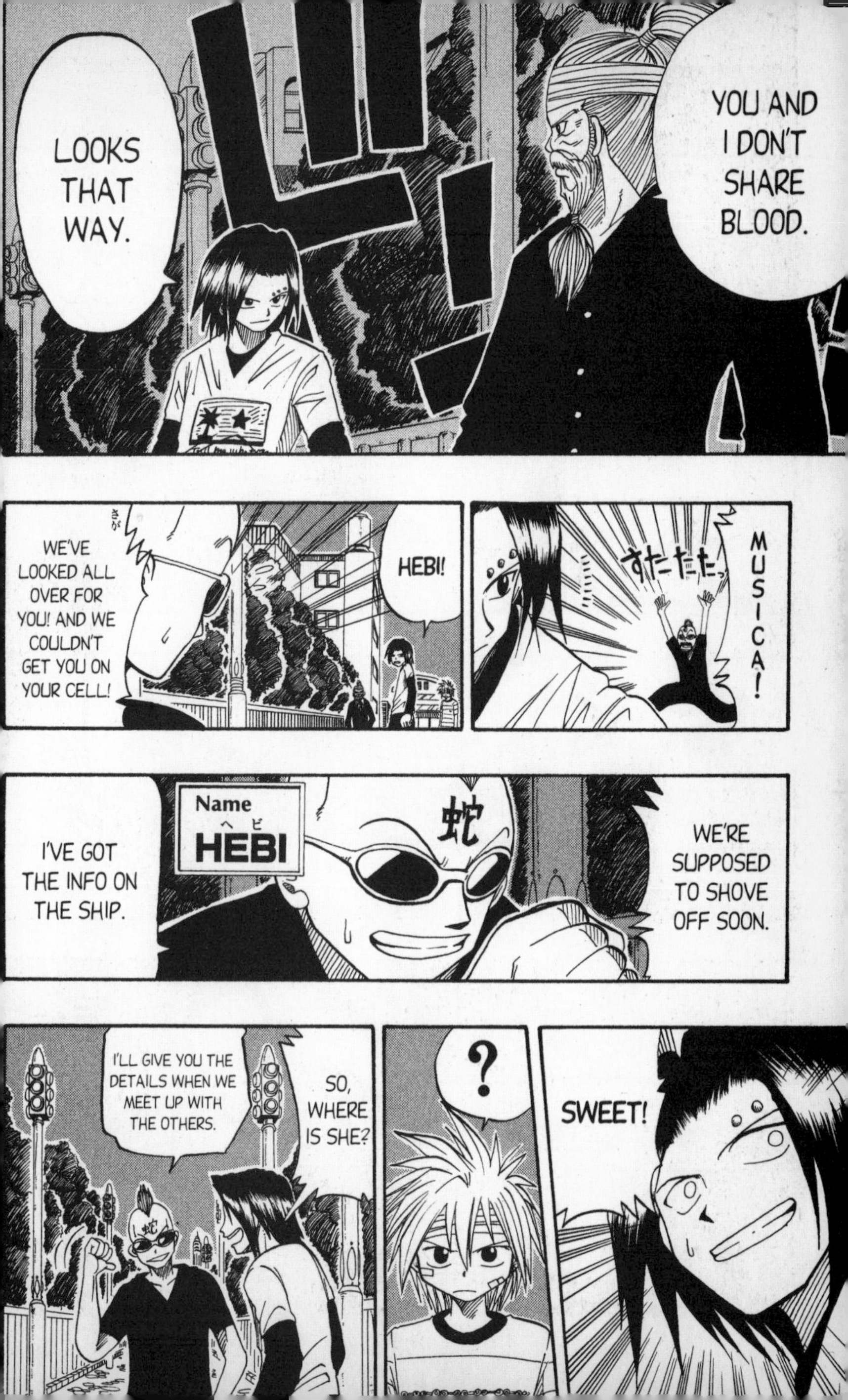
YOU AND I DON'T SHARE BLOOD.
LOOKS THAT WAY.
MUSICA!
すたたたっ
HEBI!
さが
WE'VE LOOKED ALL OVER FOR YOU! AND WE COULDN'T GET YOU ON YOUR CELL!
WE'RE SUPPOSED TO SHOVE OFF SOON.
蛇
Name
へび
HEBI
I'VE GOT THE INFO ON THE SHIP.
SWEET!
?
I'LL GIVE YOU THE DETAILS WHEN WE MEET UP WITH THE OTHERS.
SO, WHERE IS SHE?

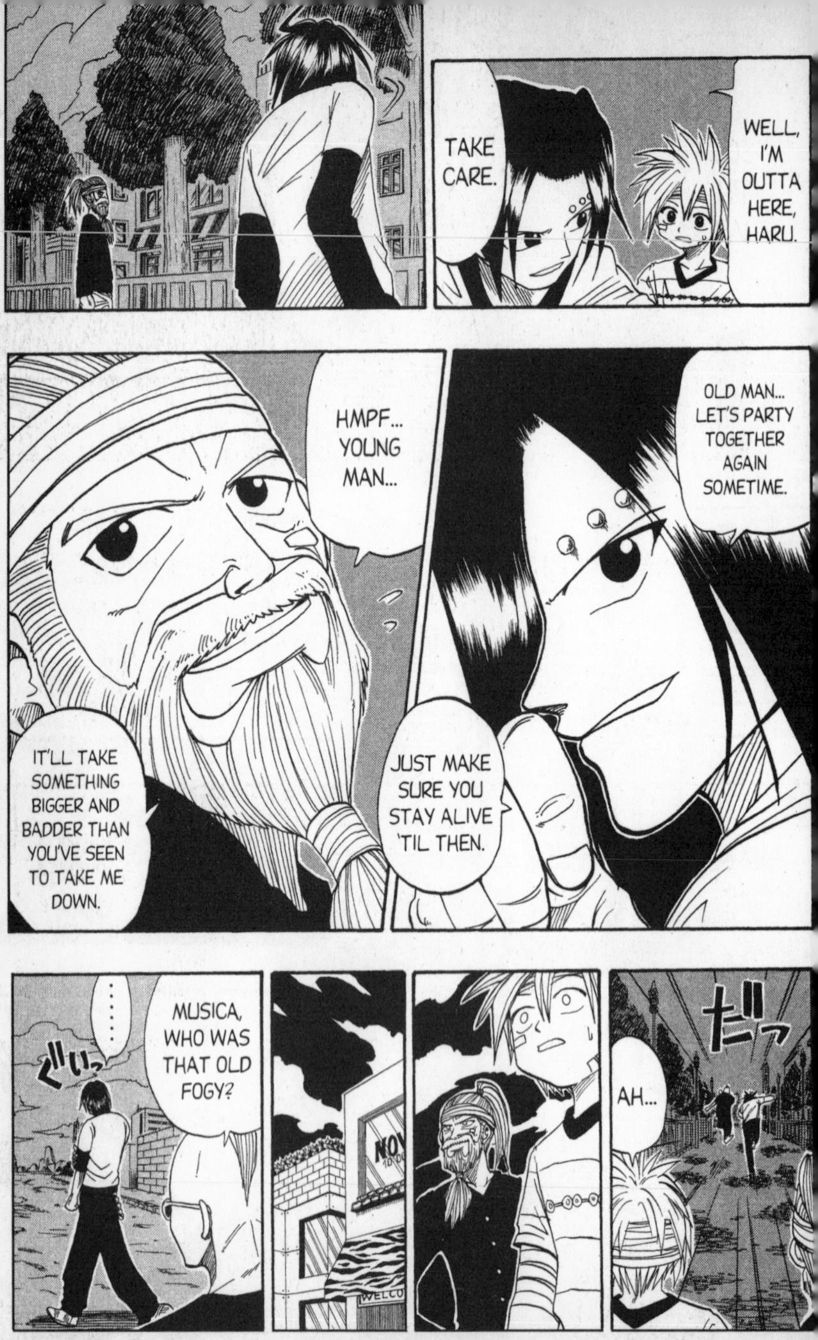
WELL, I'M OUTTA HERE, HARU.
TAKE CARE.
OLD MAN... LET'S PARTY TOGETHER AGAIN SOMETIME.
JUST MAKE SURE YOU STAY ALIVE 'TIL THEN.
HMPF... YOUNG MAN...
IT'LL TAKE SOMETHING BIGGER AND BADDER THAN YOU'VE SEEN TO TAKE ME DOWN.
だっ
AH...
MUSICA, WHO WAS THAT OLD FOGY?
......
ぐいっ

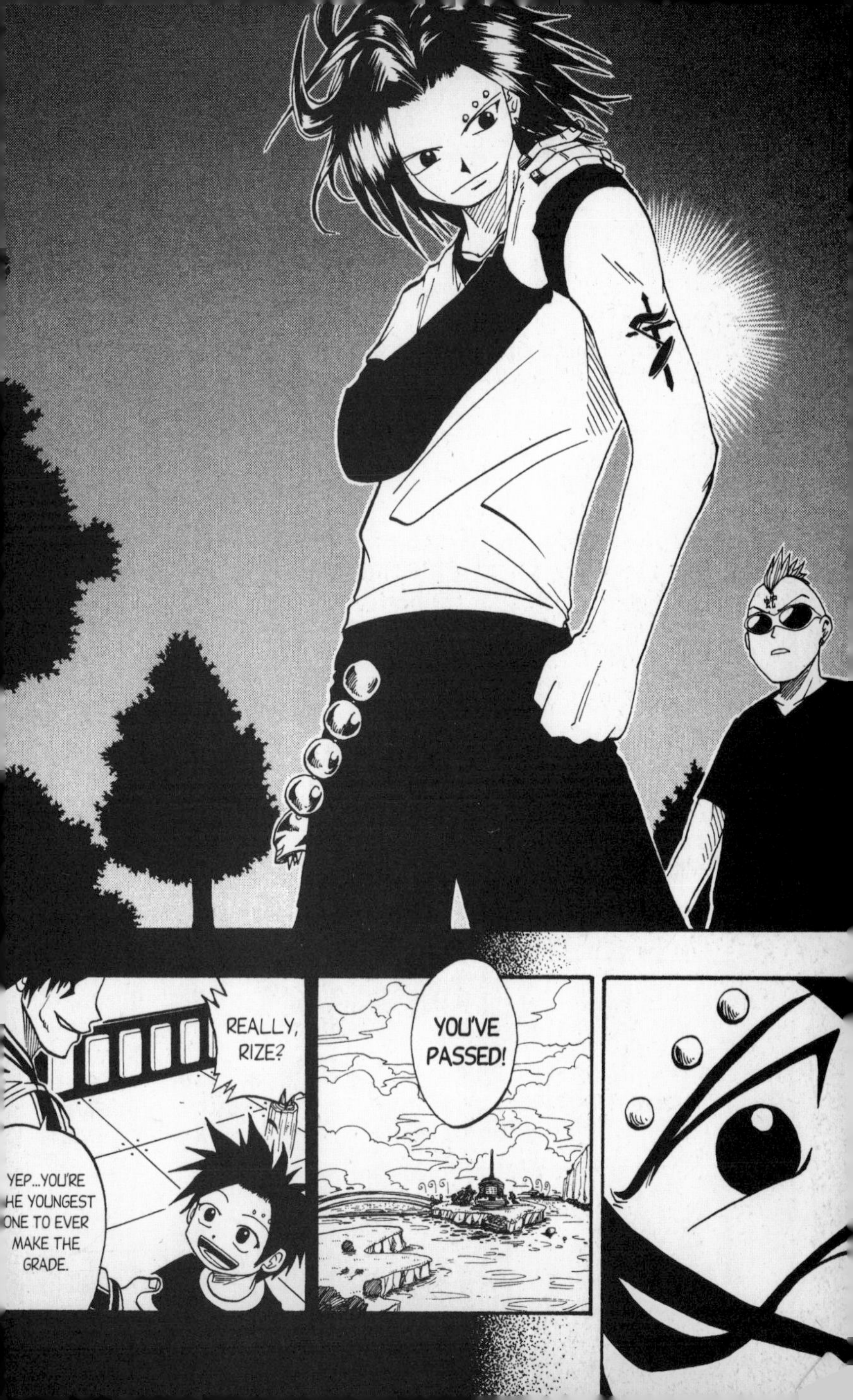
YOU'VE PASSED!
REALLY, RIZE?
YEP...YOU'RE HE YOUNGEST ONE TO EVER MAKE THE GRADE.

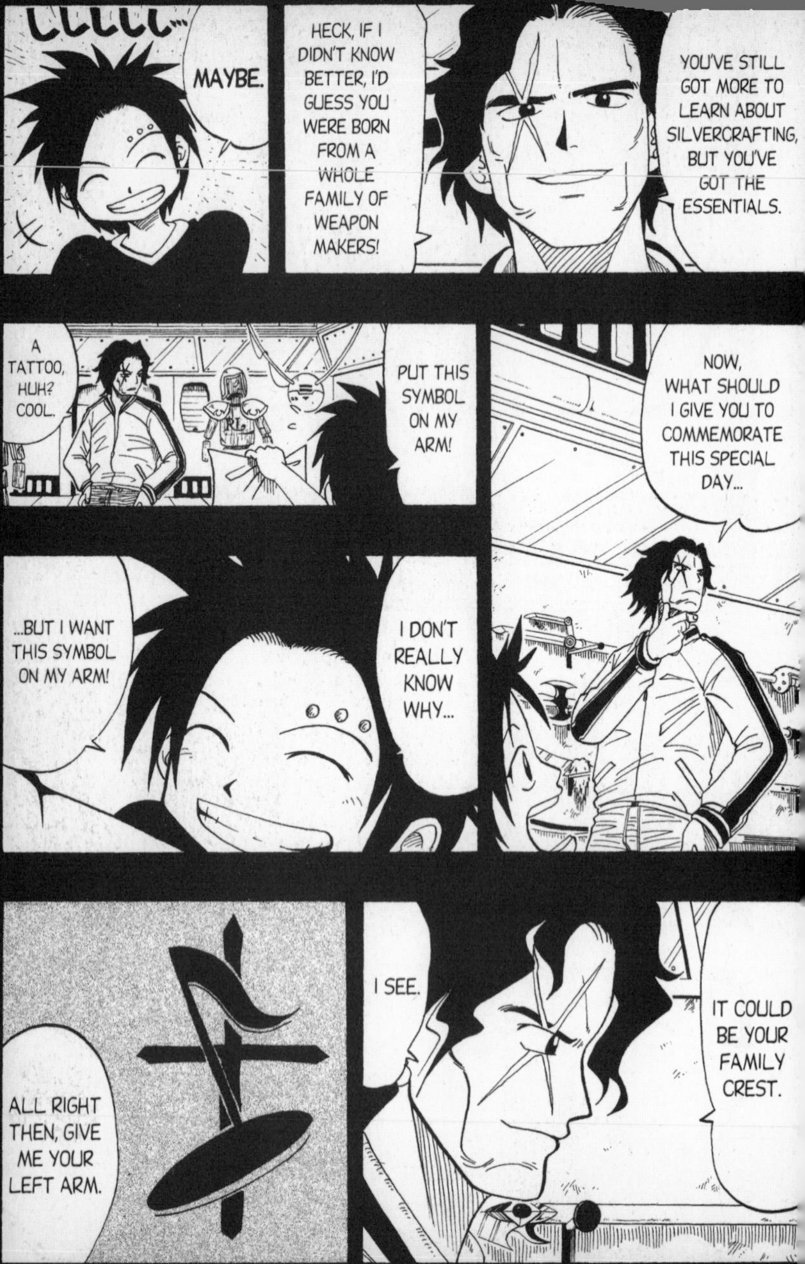
YOU'VE STILL GOT MORE TO LEARN ABOUT SILVERCRAFTING, BUT YOU'VE GOT THE ESSENTIALS.
HECK, IF I DIDN'T KNOW BETTER, I'D GUESS YOU WERE BORN FROM A WHOLE FAMILY OF WEAPON MAKERS!
LLLLL...
MAYBE.
NOW, WHAT SHOULD I GIVE YOU TO COMMEMORATE THIS SPECIAL DAY...
PUT THIS SYMBOL ON MY ARM!
A TATTOO, HUH? COOL.
I DON'T REALLY KNOW WHY...
...BUT I WANT THIS SYMBOL ON MY ARM!
IT COULD BE YOUR FAMILY CREST.
I SEE.
ALL RIGHT THEN, GIVE ME YOUR LEFT ARM.

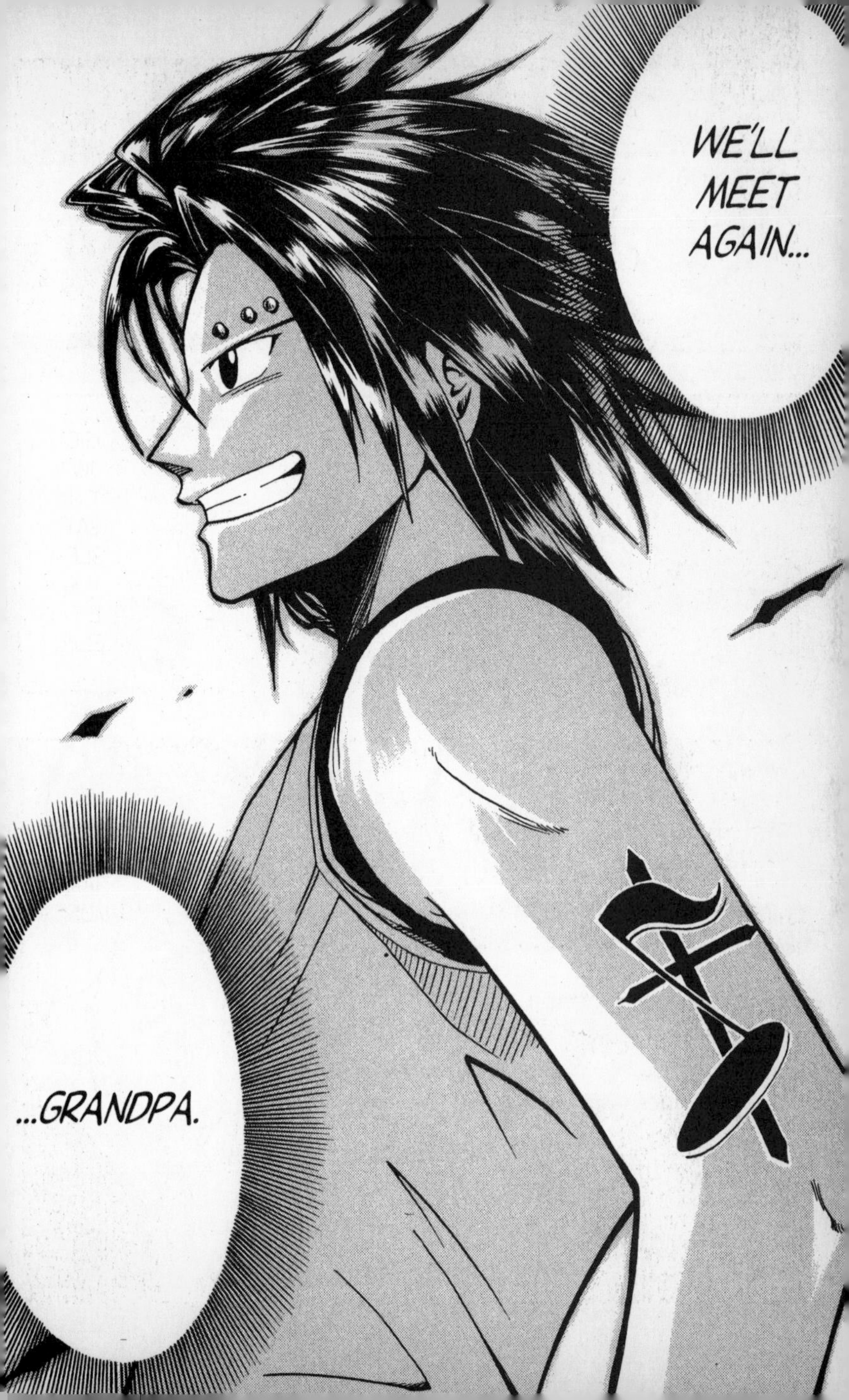
WE'LL MEET AGAIN...
...GRANDPA.

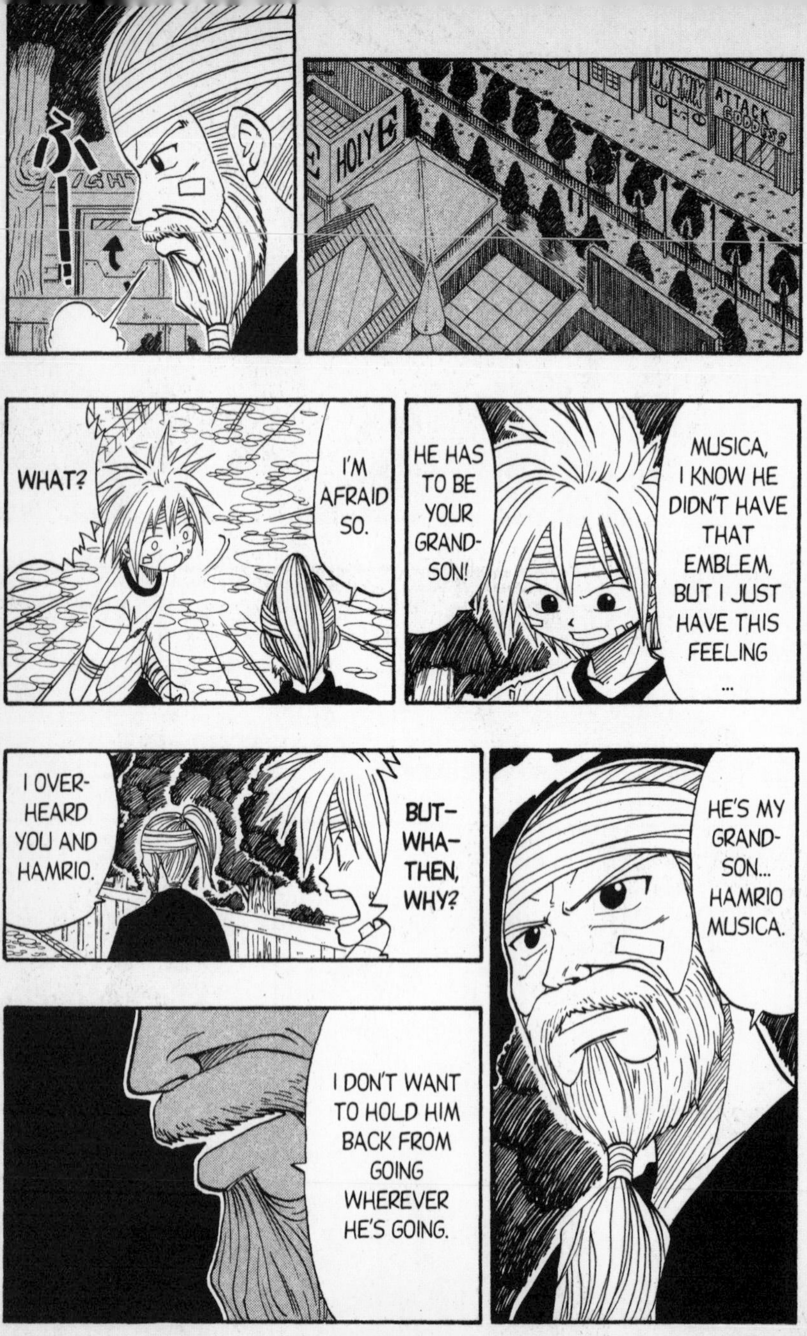
HOLY
ATTACK GODDESS
ふー!
MUSICA, I KNOW HE DIDN'T HAVE THAT EMBLEM, BUT I JUST HAVE THIS FEELING ...
HE HAS TO BE YOUR GRANDSON!
I'M AFRAID SO.
WHAT?
HE'S MY GRANDSON... HAMRIO MUSICA.
BUT— WHA— THEN, WHY?
I OVERHEARD YOU AND HAMRIO.
I DON'T WANT TO HOLD HIM BACK FROM GOING WHEREVER HE'S GOING.

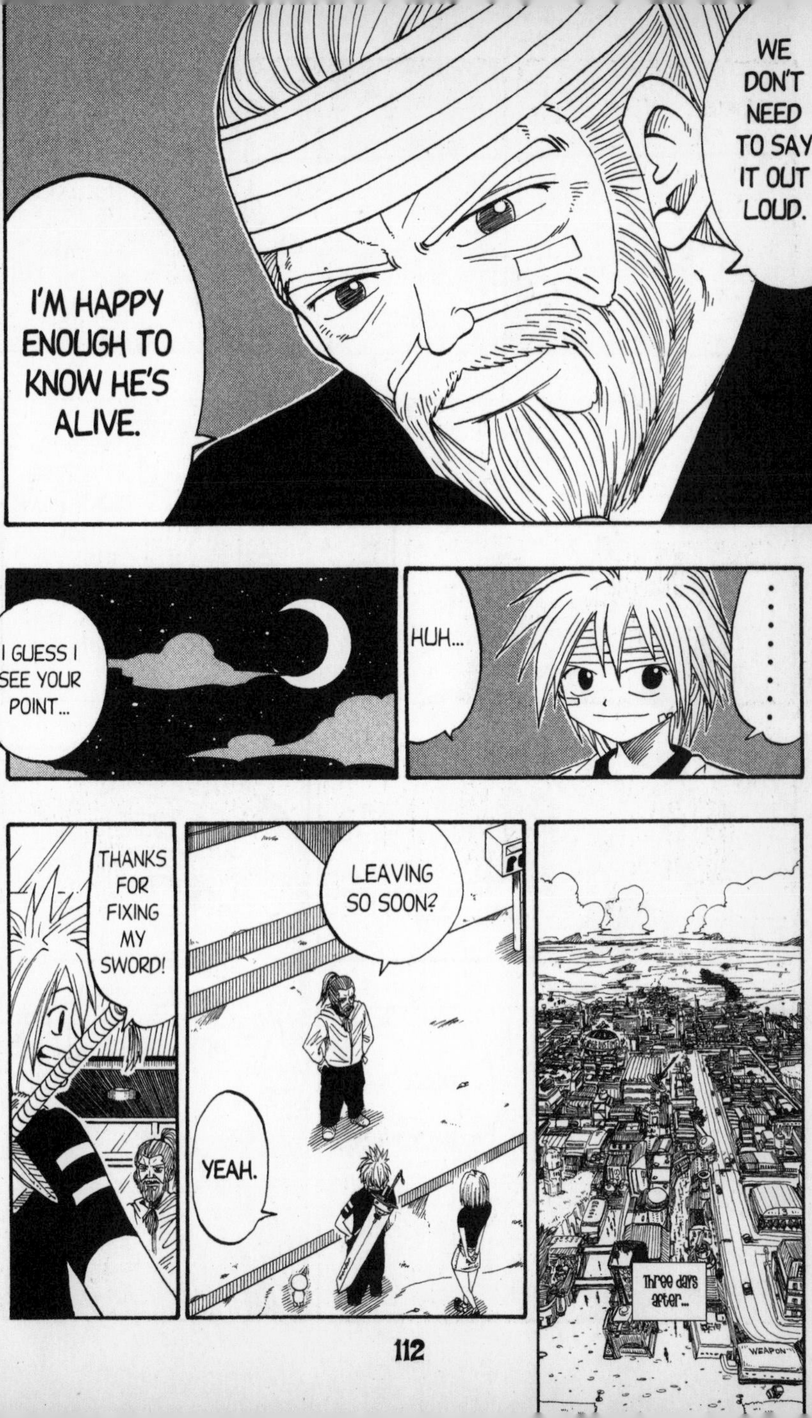
WE DON'T NEED TO SAY IT OUT LOUD.
I'M HAPPY ENOUGH TO KNOW HE'S ALIVE.
......
HUH...
I GUESS I SEE YOUR POINT...
Three days after...
WEAPON
LEAVING SO SOON?
YEAH.
THANKS FOR FIXING MY SWORD!

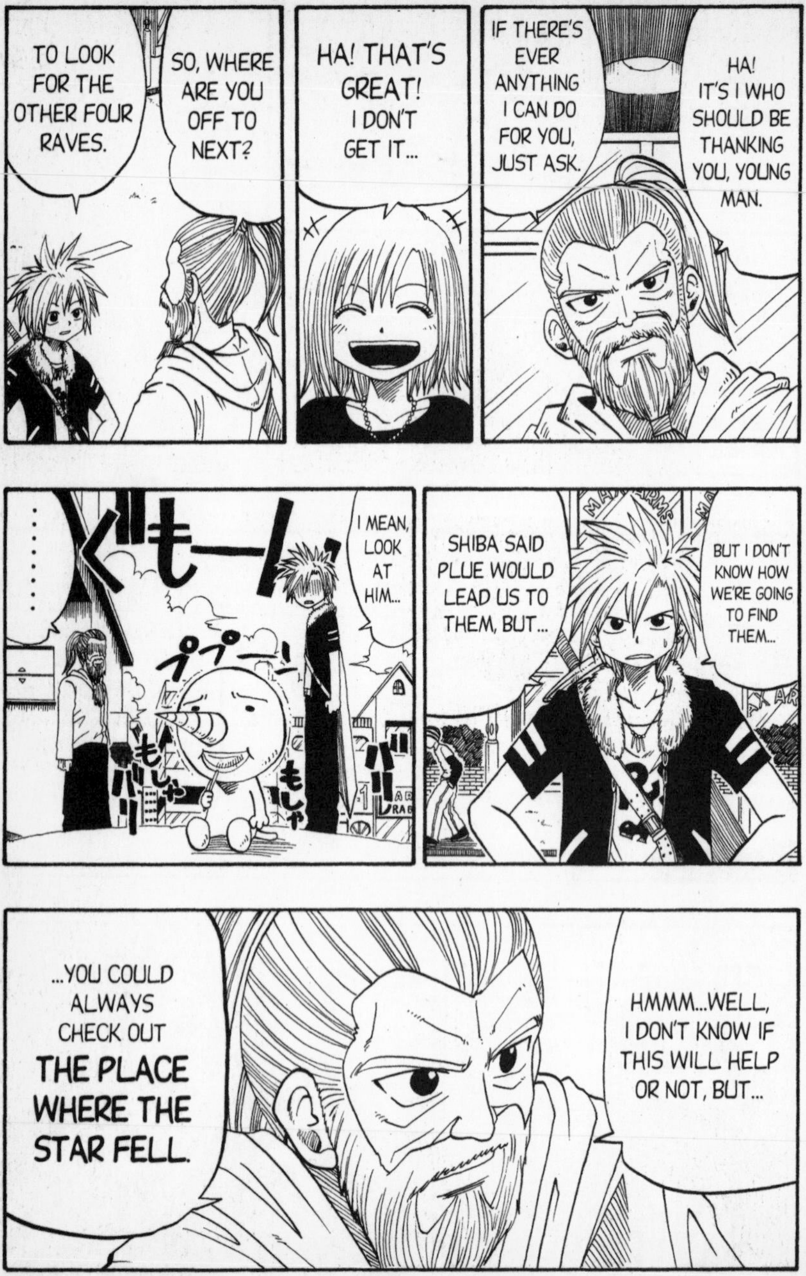
HA! IT'S I WHO SHOULD BE THANKING YOU, YOUNG MAN.
IF THERE'S EVER ANYTHING I CAN DO FOR YOU, JUST ASK.
HA! THAT'S GREAT! I DON'T GET IT...
SO, WHERE ARE YOU OFF TO NEXT?
TO LOOK FOR THE OTHER FOUR RAVES.
BUT I DON'T KNOW HOW WE'RE GOING TO FIND THEM...
SHIBA SAID PLUE WOULD LEAD US TO THEM, BUT...
I MEAN, LOOK AT HIM...
もしゃ
......
HMMM...WELL, I DON'T KNOW IF THIS WILL HELP OR NOT, BUT...
...YOU COULD ALWAYS CHECK OUT **THE PLACE WHERE THE STAR FELL.**

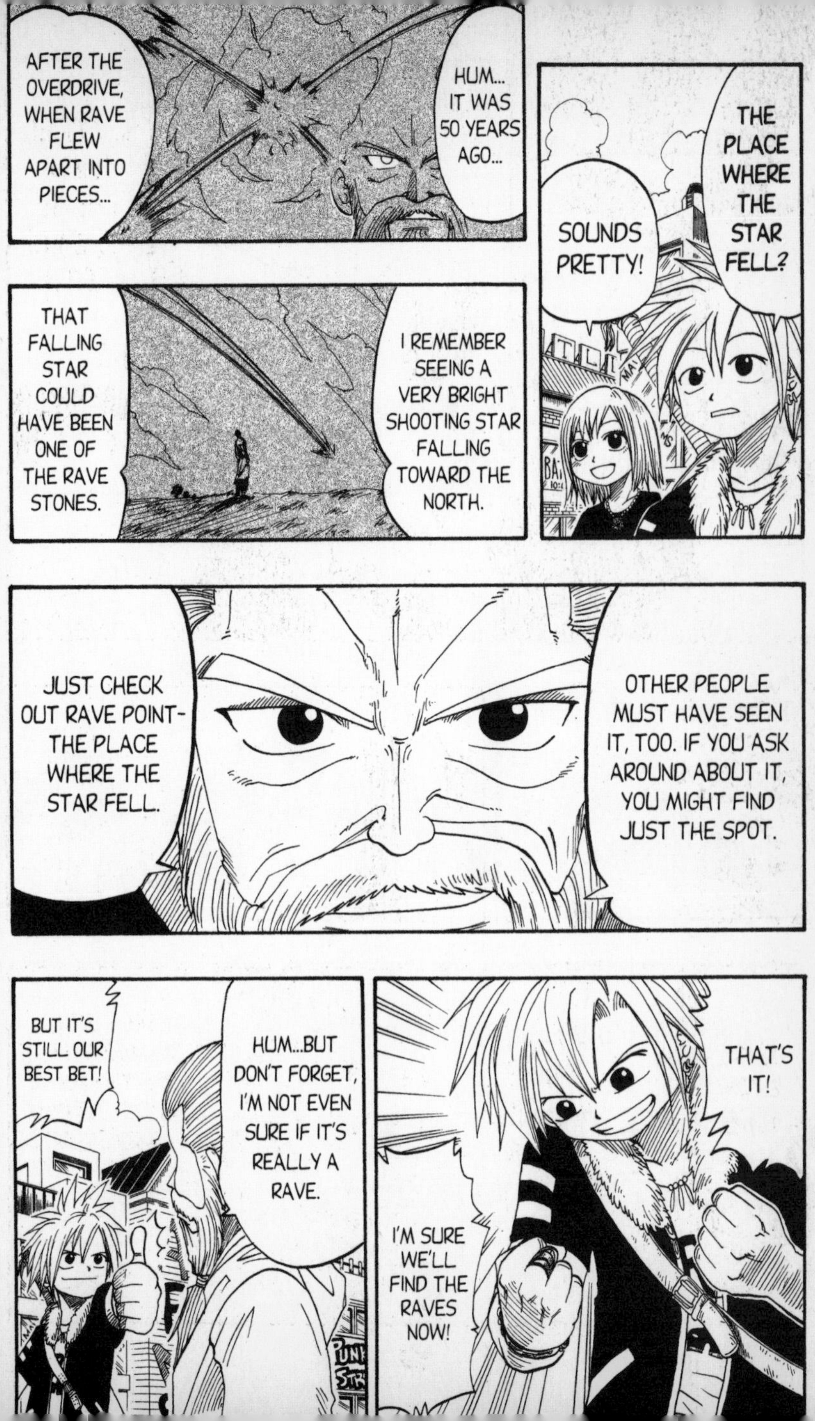
THE PLACE WHERE THE STAR FELL?
SOUNDS PRETTY!
HUM... IT WAS 50 YEARS AGO...
AFTER THE OVERDRIVE, WHEN RAVE FLEW APART INTO PIECES...
I REMEMBER SEEING A VERY BRIGHT SHOOTING STAR FALLING TOWARD THE NORTH.
THAT FALLING STAR COULD HAVE BEEN ONE OF THE RAVE STONES.
OTHER PEOPLE MUST HAVE SEEN IT, TOO. IF YOU ASK AROUND ABOUT IT, YOU MIGHT FIND JUST THE SPOT.
JUST CHECK OUT RAVE POINT- THE PLACE WHERE THE STAR FELL.
THAT'S IT!
I'M SURE WE'LL FIND THE RAVES NOW!
HUM...BUT DON'T FORGET, I'M NOT EVEN SURE IF IT'S REALLY A RAVE.
BUT IT'S STILL OUR BEST BET!

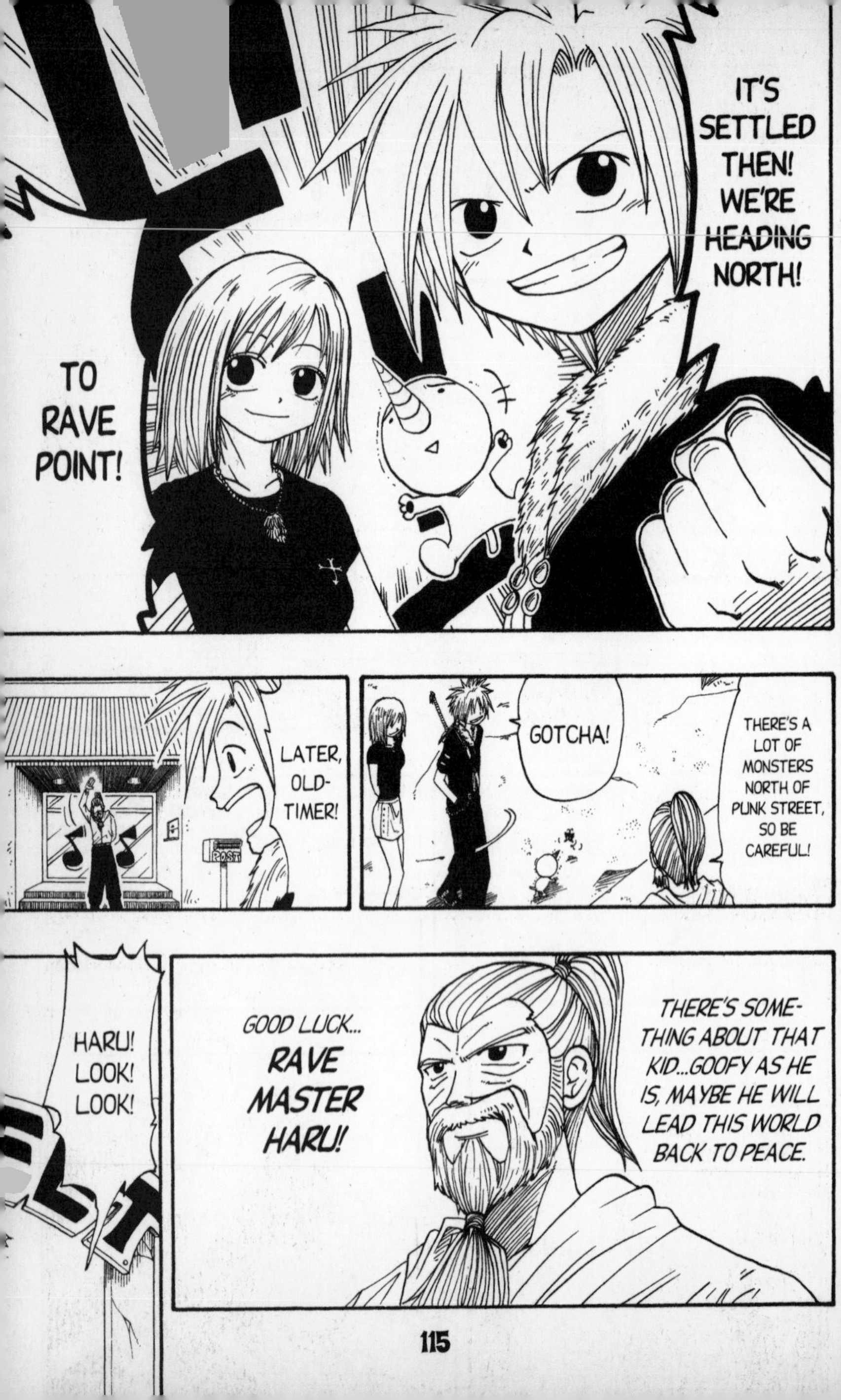
IT'S SETTLED THEN! WE'RE HEADING NORTH!
TO RAVE POINT!
THERE'S A LOT OF MONSTERS NORTH OF PUNK STREET, SO BE CAREFUL!
GOTCHA!
LATER, OLD-TIMER!
THERE'S SOME-THING ABOUT THAT KID...GOOFY AS HE IS, MAYBE HE WILL LEAD THIS WORLD BACK TO PEACE.
GOOD LUCK... RAVE MASTER HARU!
HARU! LOOK! LOOK!

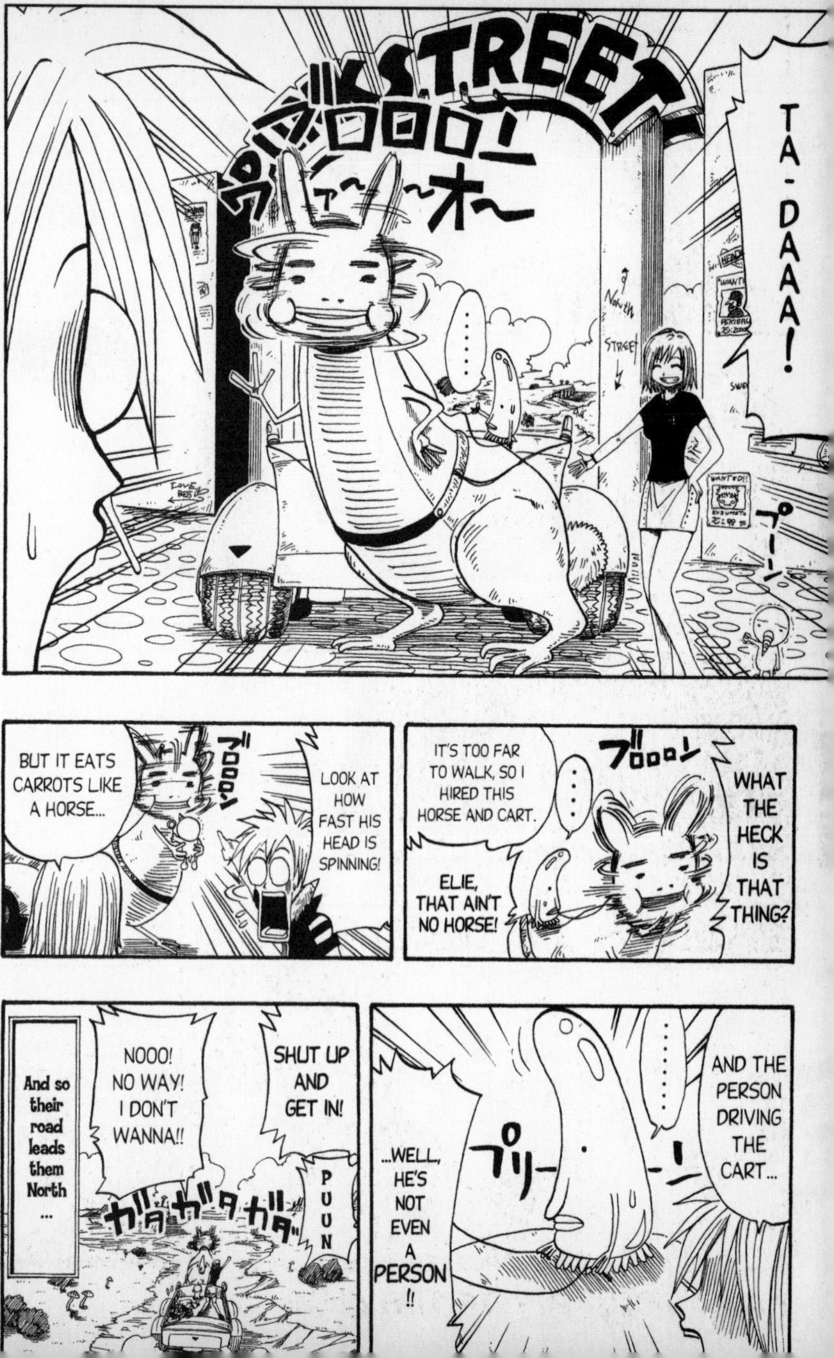
TA-DAAA!
STREET
North STREET
WHAT THE HECK IS THAT THING?
ブロロロン
IT'S TOO FAR TO WALK, SO I HIRED THIS HORSE AND CART.
...
ELIE, THAT AIN'T NO HORSE!
LOOK AT HOW FAST HIS HEAD IS SPINNING!
BUT IT EATS CARROTS LIKE A HORSE...
AND THE PERSON DRIVING THE CART...
......
プリー
...WELL, HE'S NOT EVEN A PERSON!!
SHUT UP AND GET IN!
NOOO! NO WAY! I DON'T WANNA!!
PUUN
And so their road leads them North ...

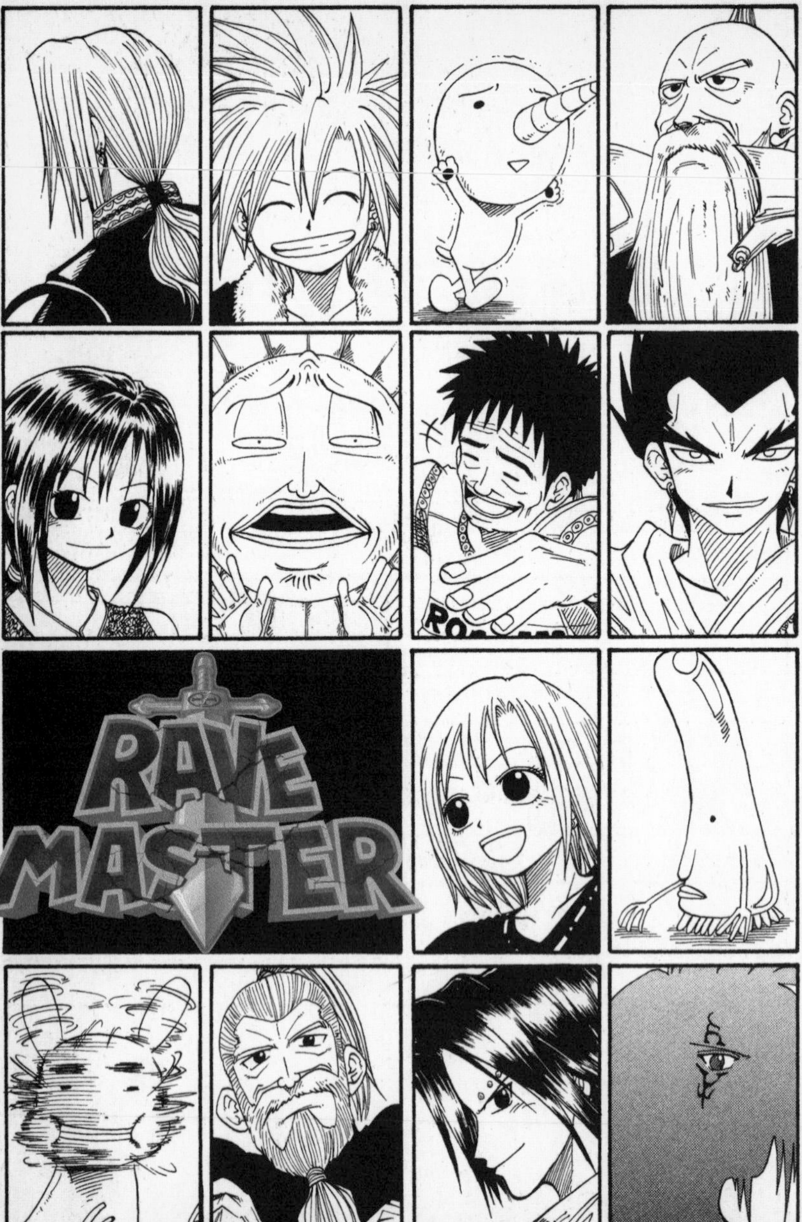
RAVE
MASTER

RAVE 19 ✠ OUT OF THE PLUE

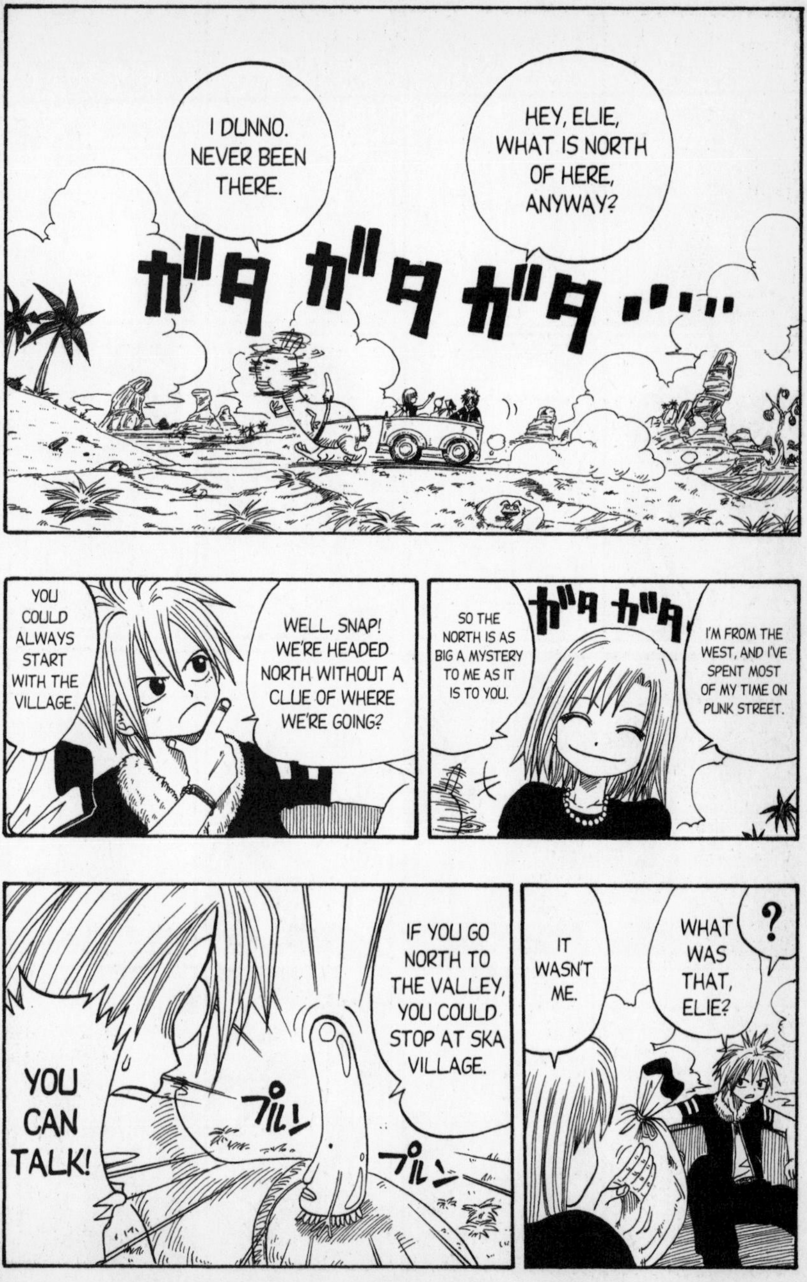
HEY, ELIE, WHAT IS NORTH OF HERE, ANYWAY?
I DUNNO. NEVER BEEN THERE.
ガタガタガタ…
I'M FROM THE WEST, AND I'VE SPENT MOST OF MY TIME ON PUNK STREET.
ガタガタ
SO THE NORTH IS AS BIG A MYSTERY TO ME AS IT IS TO YOU.
WELL, SNAP! WE'RE HEADED NORTH WITHOUT A CLUE OF WHERE WE'RE GOING?
YOU COULD ALWAYS START WITH THE VILLAGE.
?
WHAT WAS THAT, ELIE?
IT WASN'T ME.
IF YOU GO NORTH TO THE VALLEY, YOU COULD STOP AT SKA VILLAGE.
プルン
プルン
YOU CAN TALK!

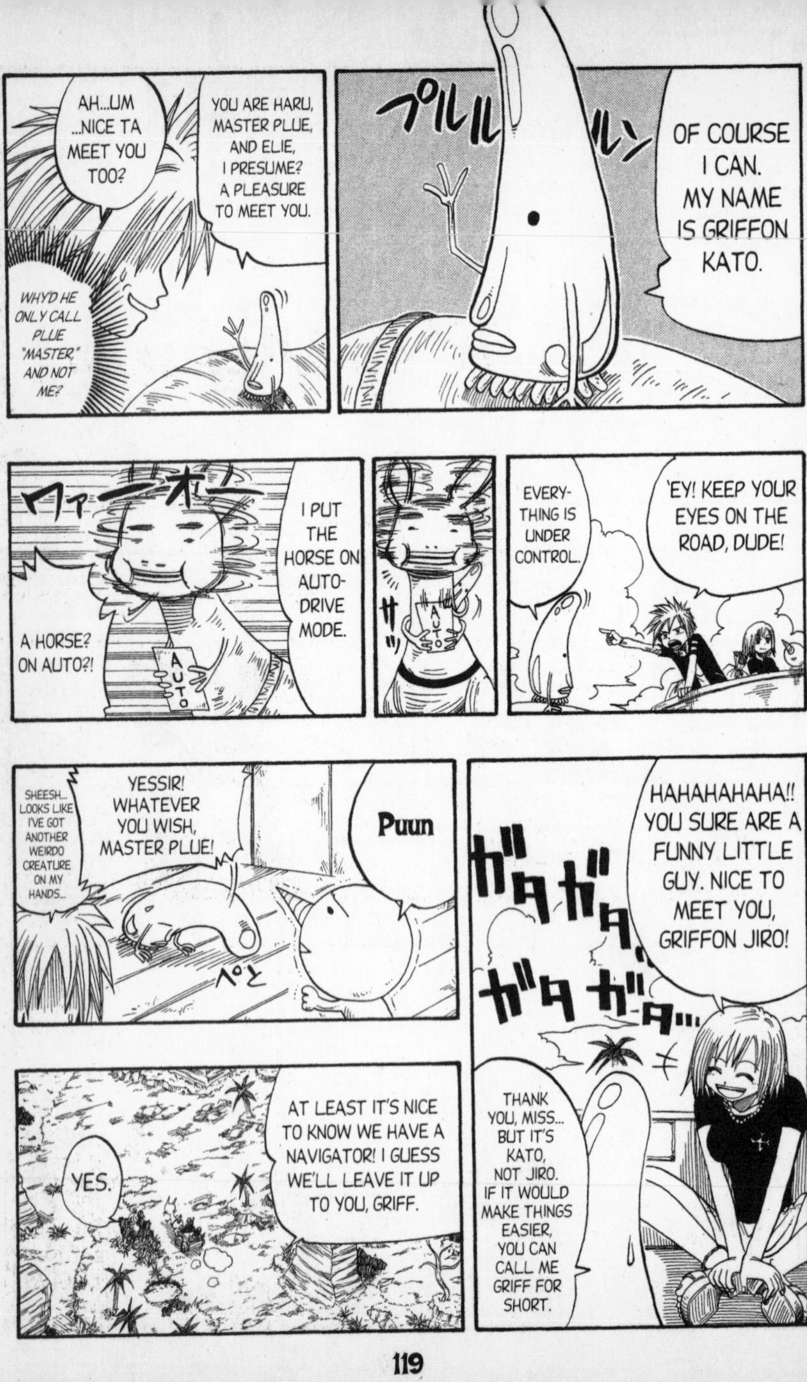
プルルルン
OF COURSE I CAN. MY NAME IS GRIFFON KATO.
YOU ARE HARU, MASTER PLUE, AND ELIE, I PRESUME? A PLEASURE TO MEET YOU.
AH...UM ...NICE TA MEET YOU TOO?
WHY'D HE ONLY CALL PLUE "MASTER," AND NOT ME?
'EY! KEEP YOUR EYES ON THE ROAD, DUDE!
EVERY-THING IS UNDER CONTROL.
サッ
AUTO
ワァーオー
I PUT THE HORSE ON AUTO-DRIVE MODE.
A HORSE? ON AUTO?!
AUTO
HAHAHAHAHA!! YOU SURE ARE A FUNNY LITTLE GUY. NICE TO MEET YOU, GRIFFON JIRO!
ガタガタ, ガタガタ...
THANK YOU, MISS... BUT IT'S KATO, NOT JIRO. IF IT WOULD MAKE THINGS EASIER, YOU CAN CALL ME GRIFF FOR SHORT.
Puun
YESSIR! WHATEVER YOU WISH, MASTER PLUE!
SHEESH... LOOKS LIKE I'VE GOT ANOTHER WEIRDO CREATURE ON MY HANDS...
ペと
AT LEAST IT'S NICE TO KNOW WE HAVE A NAVIGATOR! I GUESS WE'LL LEAVE IT UP TO YOU, GRIFF.
YES.

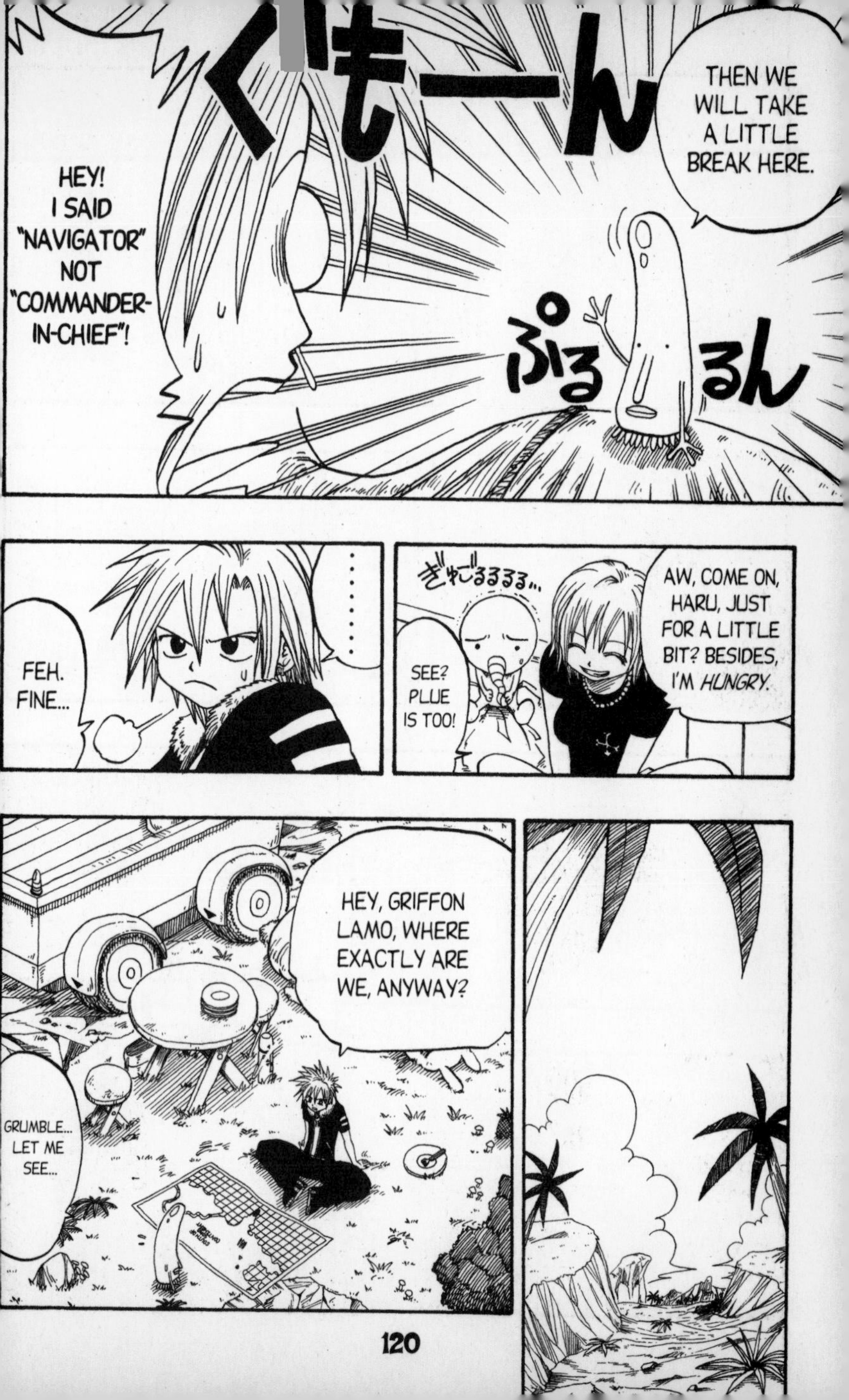
くもーん
THEN WE WILL TAKE A LITTLE BREAK HERE.
ぷるるん
HEY! I SAID "NAVIGATOR" NOT "COMMANDER-IN-CHIEF"!
AW, COME ON, HARU, JUST FOR A LITTLE BIT? BESIDES, I'M *HUNGRY.*
ぎゅごるるるる...
SEE? PLUE IS TOO!
......
FEH. FINE...
HEY, GRIFFON LAMO, WHERE EXACTLY ARE WE, ANYWAY?
GRUMBLE... LET ME SEE...

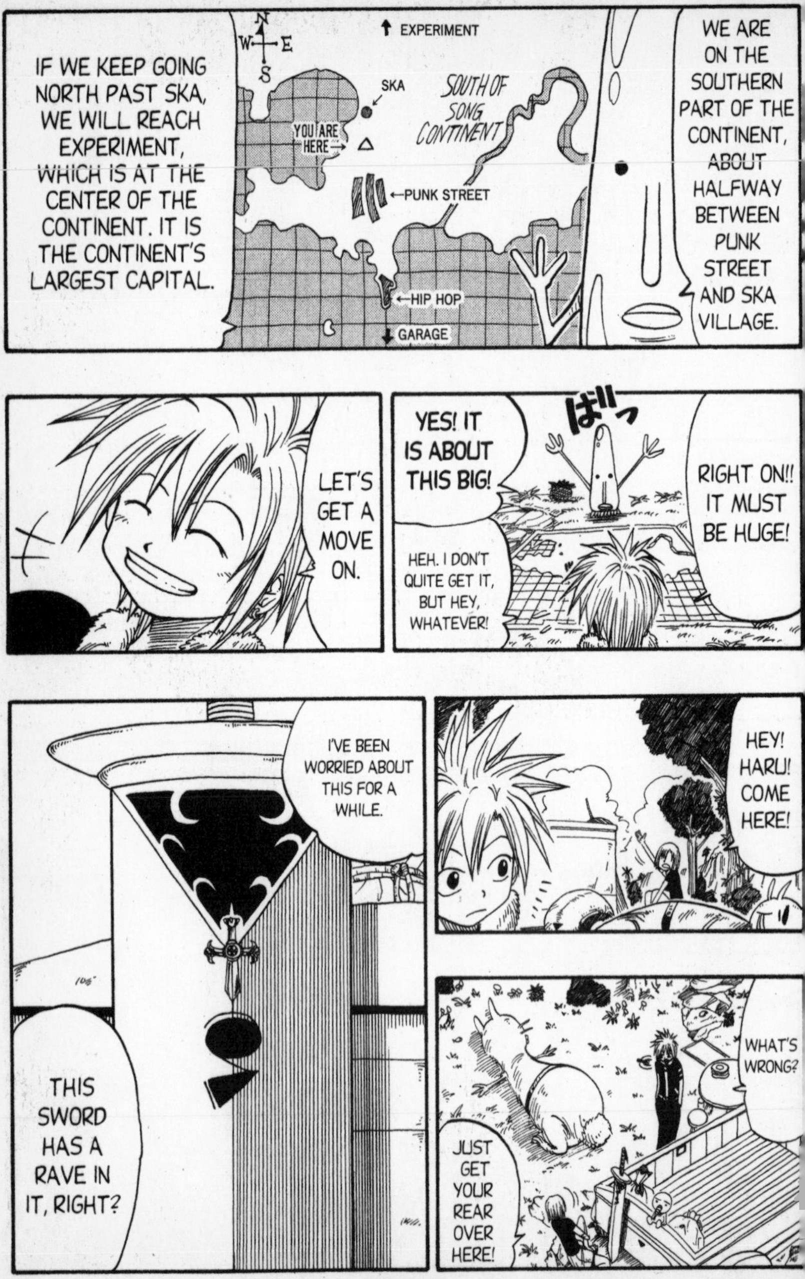
WE ARE ON THE SOUTHERN PART OF THE CONTINENT, ABOUT HALFWAY BETWEEN PUNK STREET AND SKA VILLAGE.
N
W
E
S
EXPERIMENT
SKA
SOUTH OF SONG CONTINENT
YOU ARE HERE
PUNK STREET
HIP HOP
GARAGE
IF WE KEEP GOING NORTH PAST SKA, WE WILL REACH EXPERIMENT, WHICH IS AT THE CENTER OF THE CONTINENT. IT IS THE CONTINENT'S LARGEST CAPITAL.
RIGHT ON!! IT MUST BE HUGE!
ばっ
YES! IT IS ABOUT THIS BIG!
HEH. I DON'T QUITE GET IT, BUT HEY, WHATEVER!
LET'S GET A MOVE ON.
HEY! HARU! COME HERE!
WHAT'S WRONG?
JUST GET YOUR REAR OVER HERE!
I'VE BEEN WORRIED ABOUT THIS FOR A WHILE.
THIS SWORD HAS A RAVE IN IT, RIGHT?

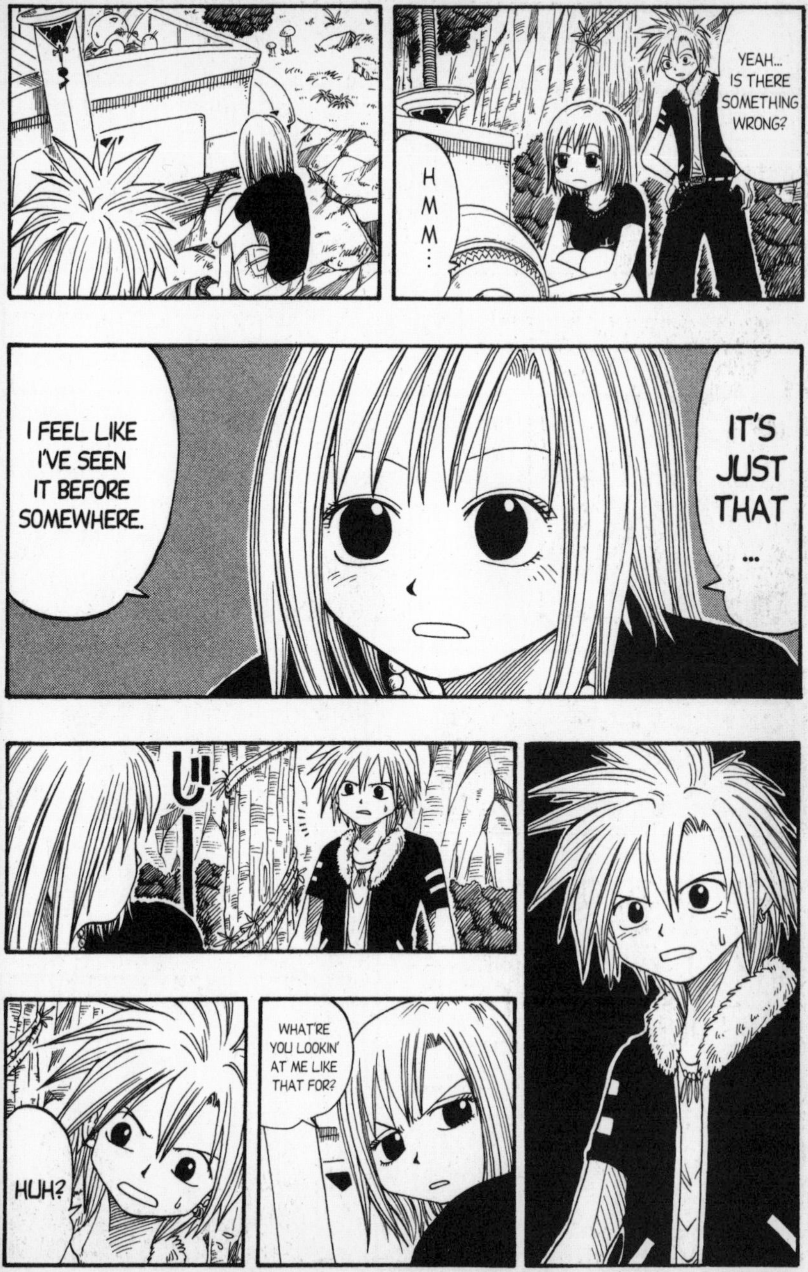
YEAH... IS THERE SOMETHING WRONG?
HMM...
IT'S JUST THAT...
I FEEL LIKE I'VE SEEN IT BEFORE SOMEWHERE.
じー
WHAT'RE YOU LOOKIN' AT ME LIKE THAT FOR?
HUH?

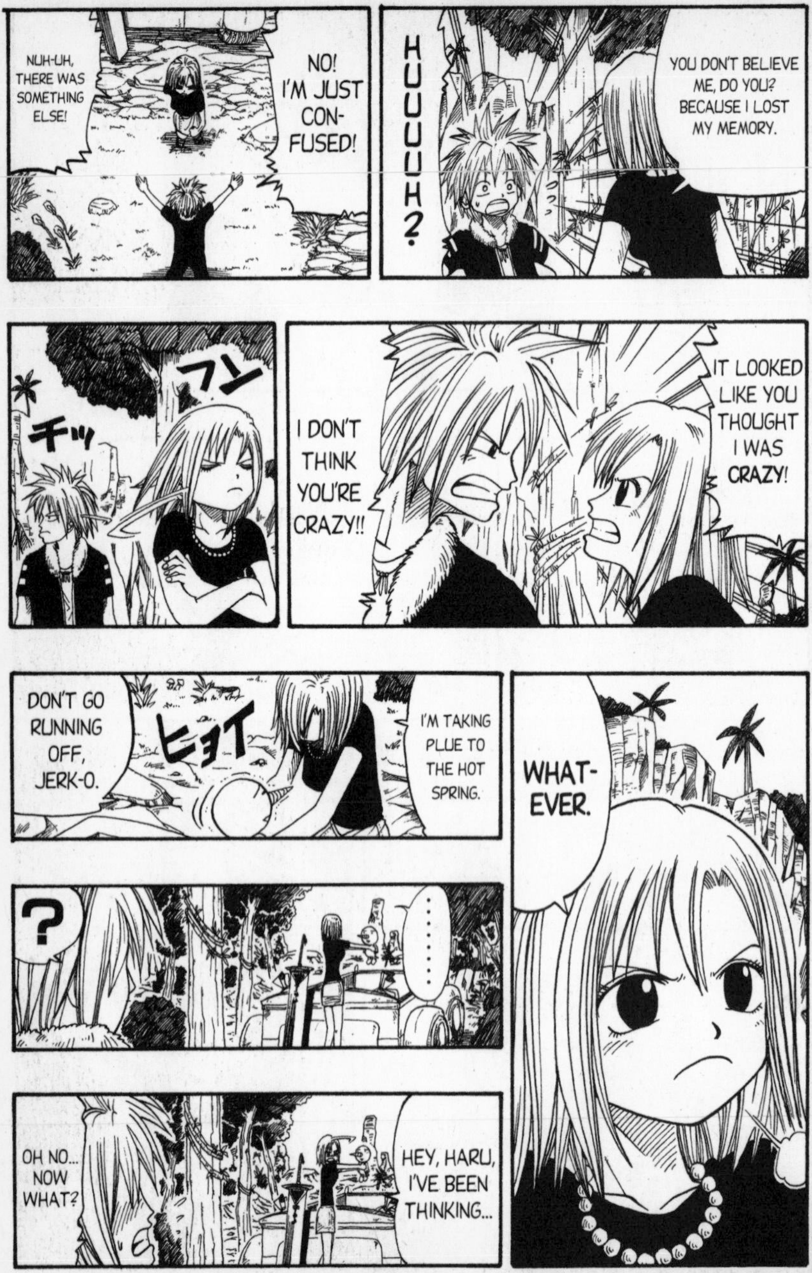
YOU DON'T BELIEVE ME, DO YOU? BECAUSE I LOST MY MEMORY.
HUUUUH?
NO! I'M JUST CON-FUSED!
NUH-UH, THERE WAS SOMETHING ELSE!
IT LOOKED LIKE YOU THOUGHT I WAS CRAZY!
I DON'T THINK YOU'RE CRAZY!!
フン
チッ
WHAT-EVER.
I'M TAKING PLUE TO THE HOT SPRING.
ヒョイ
DON'T GO RUNNING OFF, JERK-O.
....
?
HEY, HARU, I'VE BEEN THINKING...
OH NO... NOW WHAT?

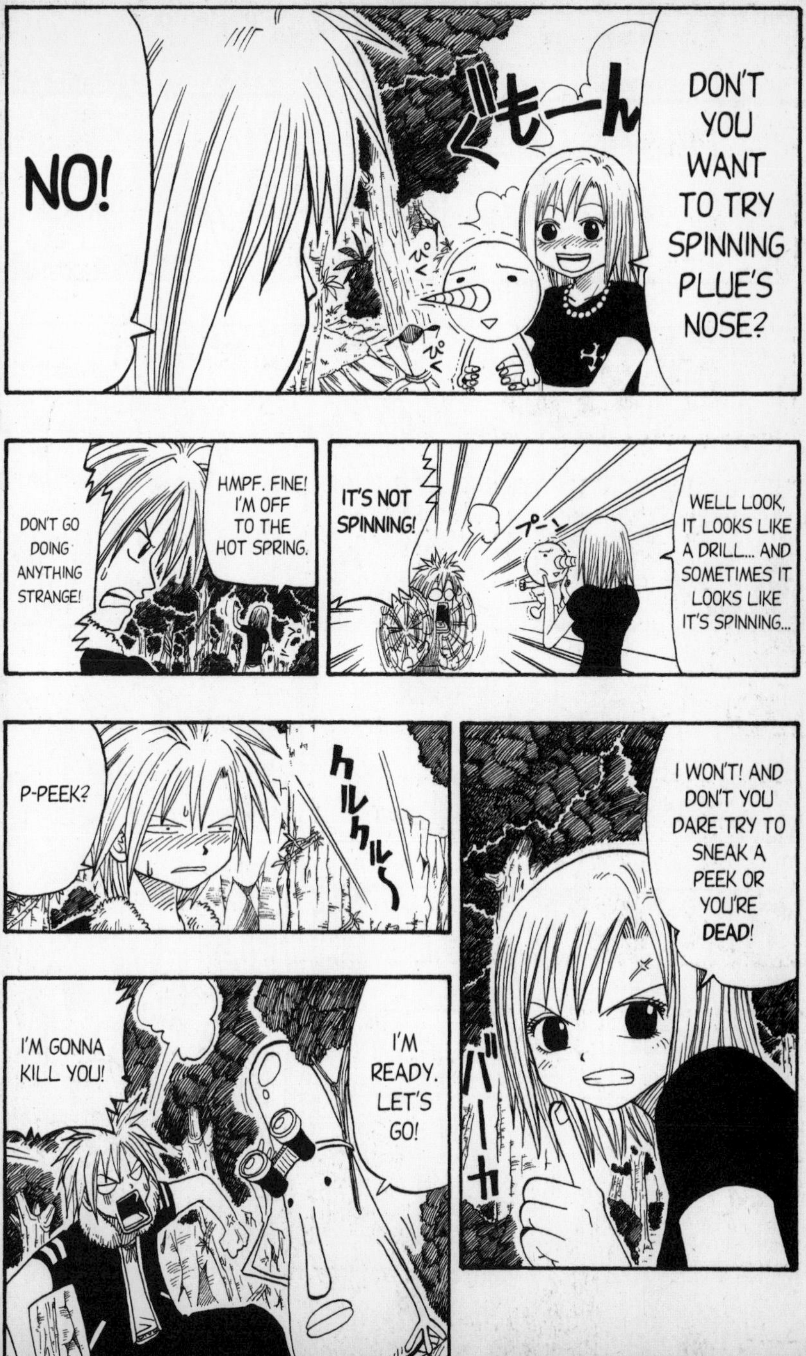
DON'T YOU WANT TO TRY SPINNING PLUE'S NOSE?
ぐもーん
ぴく
ぴく
NO!
WELL LOOK, IT LOOKS LIKE A DRILL... AND SOMETIMES IT LOOKS LIKE IT'S SPINNING...
プ〜ン
IT'S NOT SPINNING!
HMPF. FINE! I'M OFF TO THE HOT SPRING.
DON'T GO DOING ANYTHING STRANGE!
I WON'T! AND DON'T YOU DARE TRY TO SNEAK A PEEK OR YOU'RE **DEAD**!
バーカ
クルクル〜
P-PEEK?
I'M READY. LET'S GO!
I'M GONNA KILL YOU!

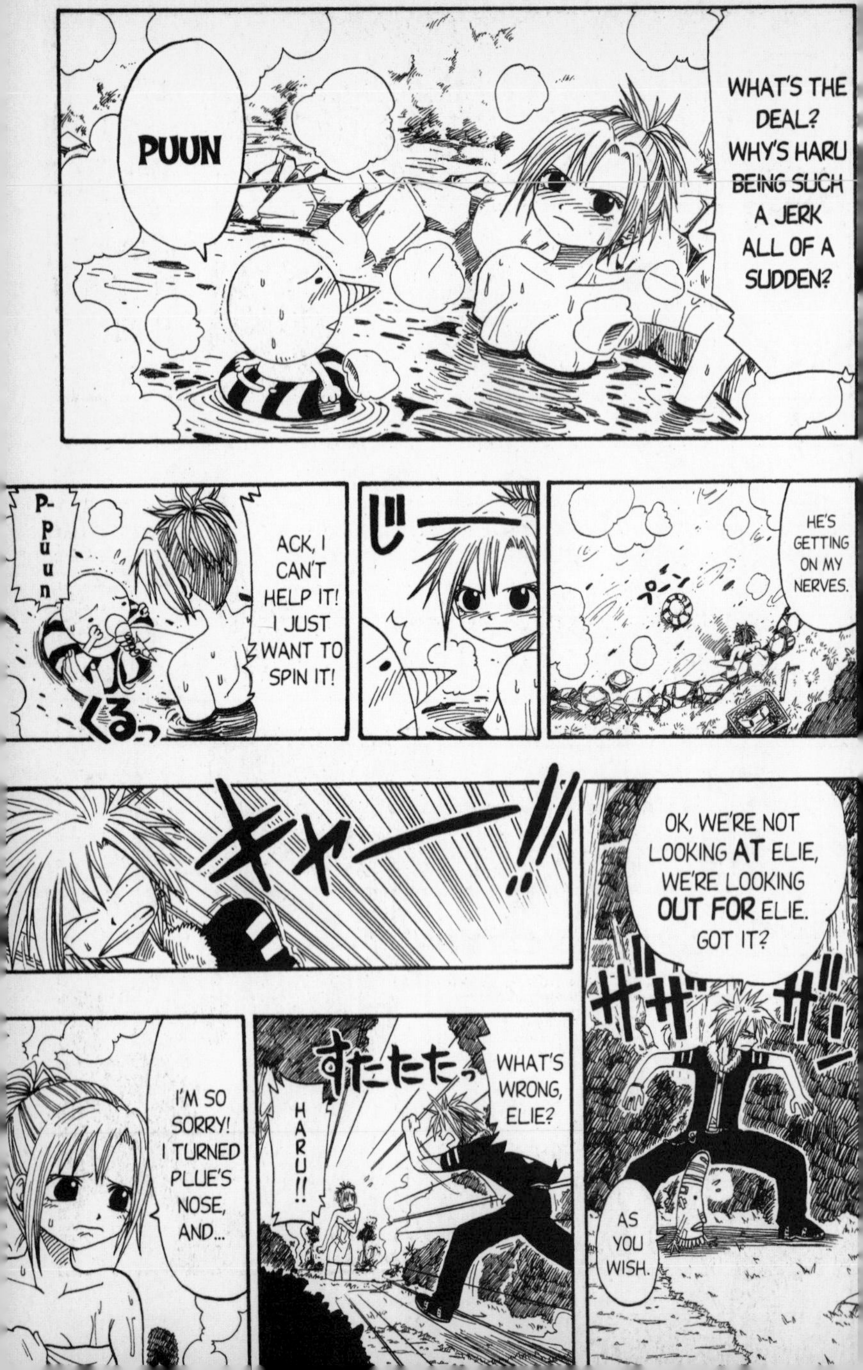
WHAT'S THE DEAL? WHY'S HARU BEING SUCH A JERK ALL OF A SUDDEN?
PUUN
HE'S GETTING ON MY NERVES.
じーー
ACK, I CAN'T HELP IT! I JUST WANT TO SPIN IT!
P-puun
くるっ
OK, WE'RE NOT LOOKING **AT** ELIE, WE'RE LOOKING **OUT FOR** ELIE. GOT IT?
ザザ
ザ!
AS YOU WISH.
キャー!!
すたたたっ
WHAT'S WRONG, ELIE?
HARU!!
I'M SO SORRY! I TURNED PLUE'S NOSE, AND...

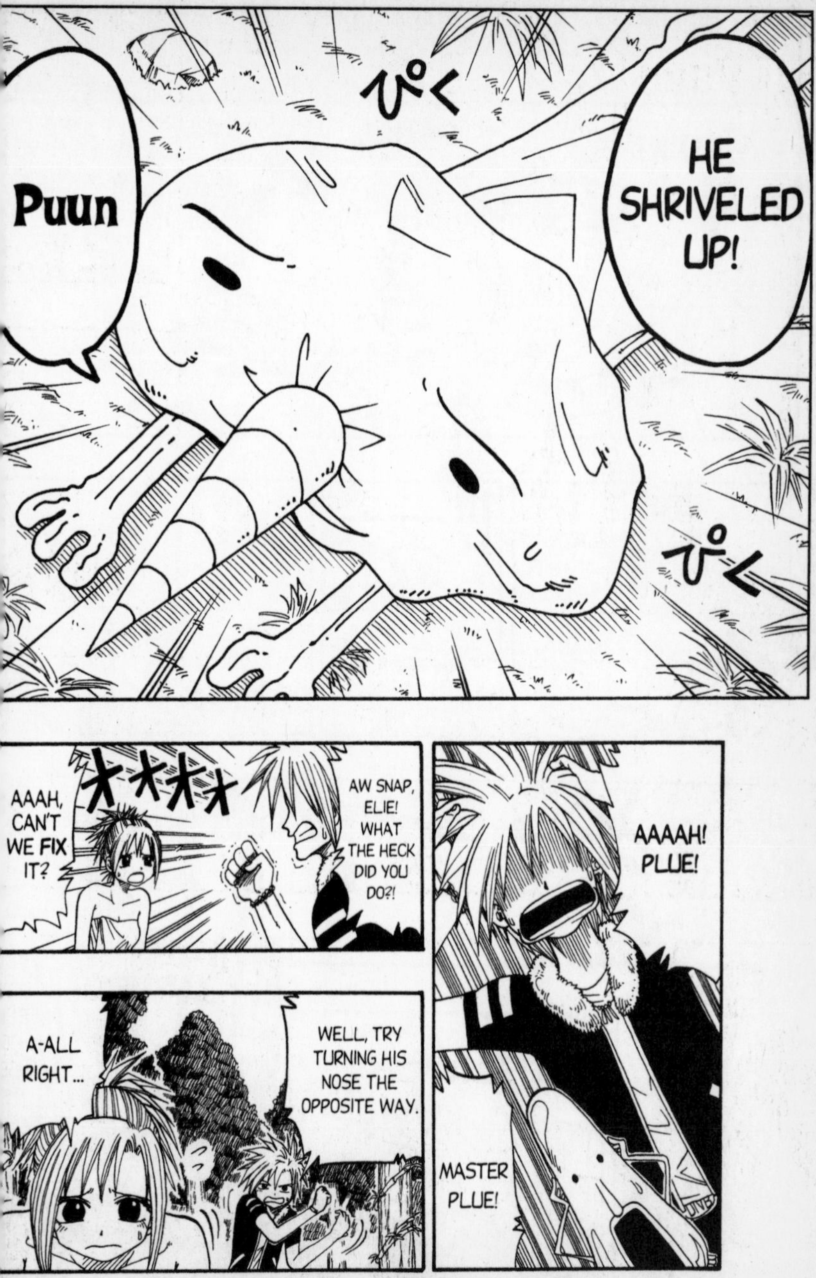
HE SHRIVELED UP!
ぴく
Puun
ぴく
AAAAH! PLUE!
MASTER PLUE!
AW SNAP, ELIE! WHAT THE HECK DID YOU DO?!
AAAH, CAN'T WE FIX IT?
WELL, TRY TURNING HIS NOSE THE OPPOSITE WAY.
A-ALL RIGHT...

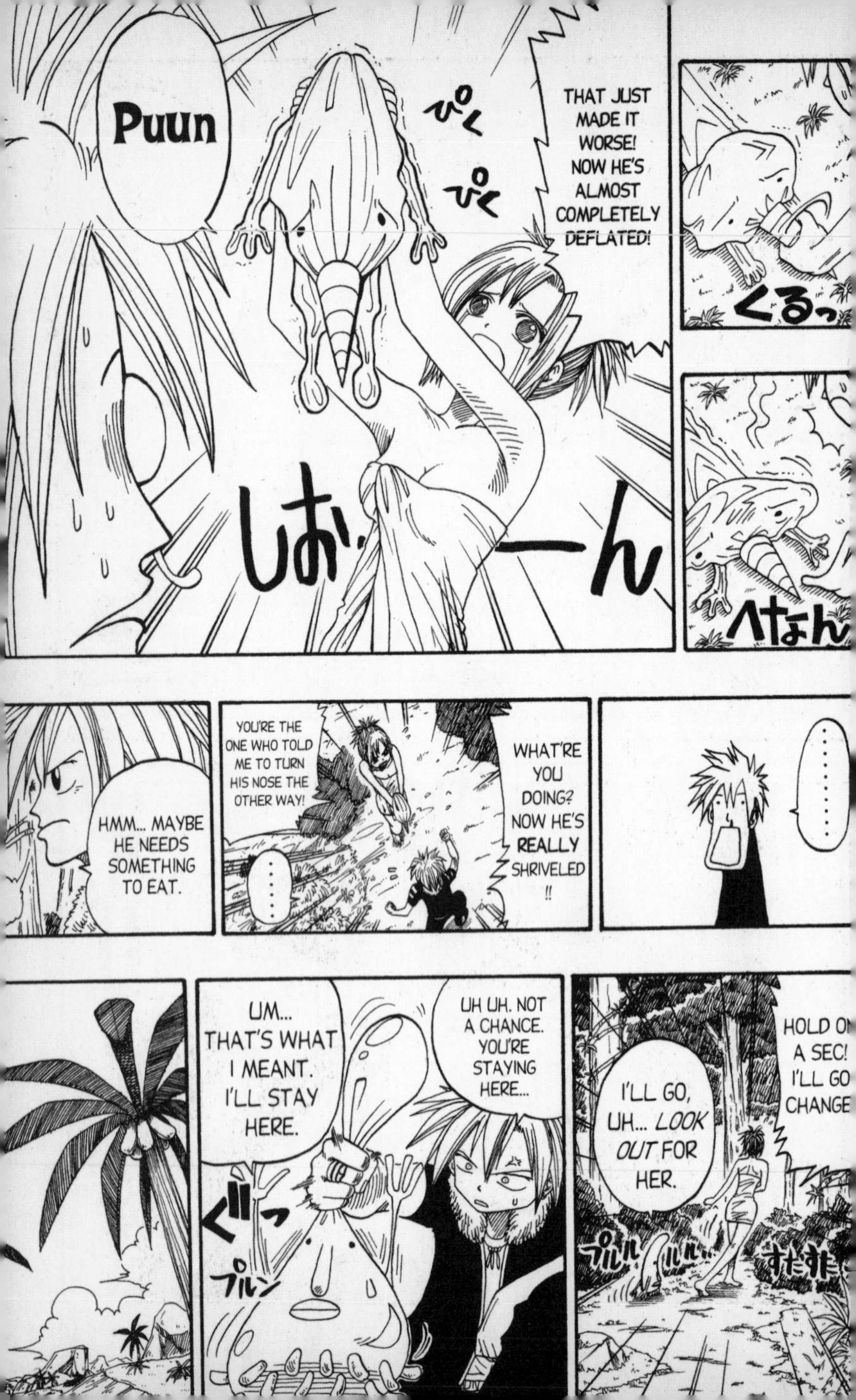
くるっ
へなん
THAT JUST MADE IT WORSE! NOW HE'S ALMOST COMPLETELY DEFLATED!
ぴく
ぴく
Puun
しおーん
......
WHAT'RE YOU DOING? NOW HE'S REALLY SHRIVELED !!
YOU'RE THE ONE WHO TOLD ME TO TURN HIS NOSE THE OTHER WAY!
......
HMM... MAYBE HE NEEDS SOMETHING TO EAT.
HOLD ON A SEC! I'LL GO CHANGE
I'LL GO, UH... *LOOK OUT* FOR HER.
すたすた
プルルルル...
UH UH. NOT A CHANCE. YOU'RE STAYING HERE...
UM... THAT'S WHAT I MEANT. I'LL STAY HERE.
ぐいっ
プルン

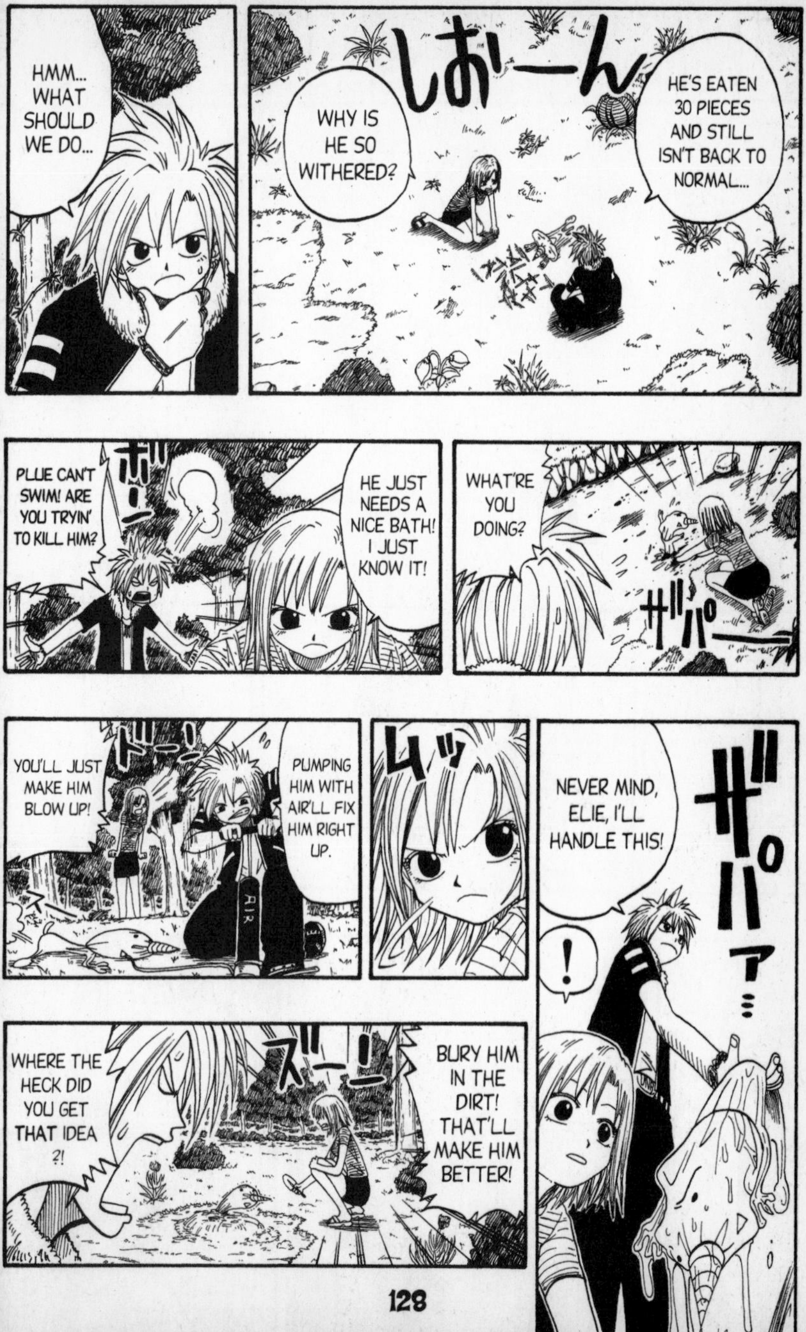
しおーん
HE'S EATEN 30 PIECES AND STILL ISN'T BACK TO NORMAL...
WHY IS HE SO WITHERED?
HMM... WHAT SHOULD WE DO...
WHAT'RE YOU DOING?
ザパー
HE JUST NEEDS A NICE BATH! I JUST KNOW IT!
PLUE CAN'T SWIM! ARE YOU TRYIN' TO KILL HIM?
ザパァ
NEVER MIND, ELIE, I'LL HANDLE THIS!
!
ムッ
PUMPING HIM WITH AIR'LL FIX HIM RIGHT UP.
YOU'LL JUST MAKE HIM BLOW UP!
BURY HIM IN THE DIRT! THAT'LL MAKE HIM BETTER!
WHERE THE HECK DID YOU GET THAT IDEA?!

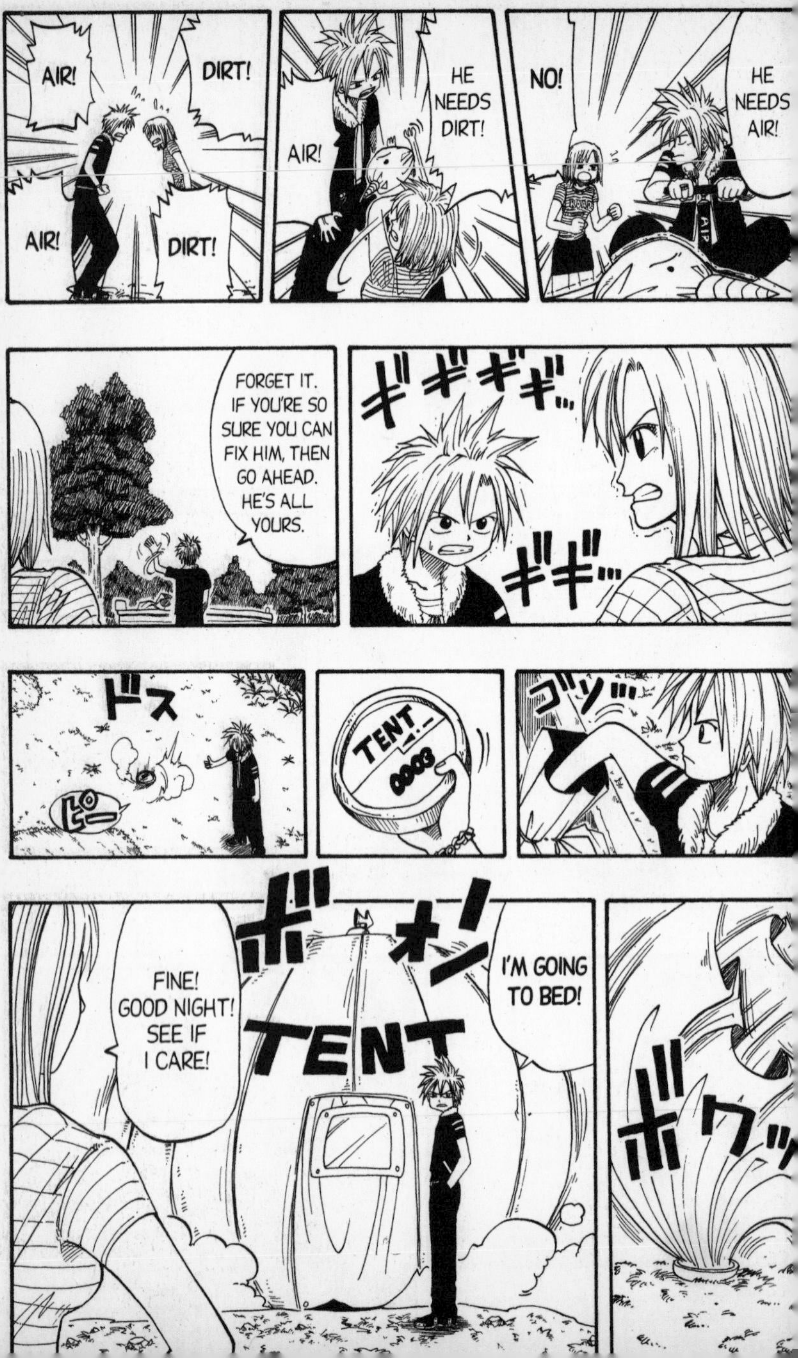
HE NEEDS AIR!
NO!
HE NEEDS DIRT!
AIR!
DIRT!
AIR!
DIRT!
AIR!
ギギギギ…
ギギ…
FORGET IT. IF YOU'RE SO SURE YOU CAN FIX HIM, THEN GO AHEAD. HE'S ALL YOURS.
ゴッ…
TENT
0003
ドス
ピー
ボワッ
ボオン
TENT
I'M GOING TO BED!
FINE! GOOD NIGHT! SEE IF I CARE!

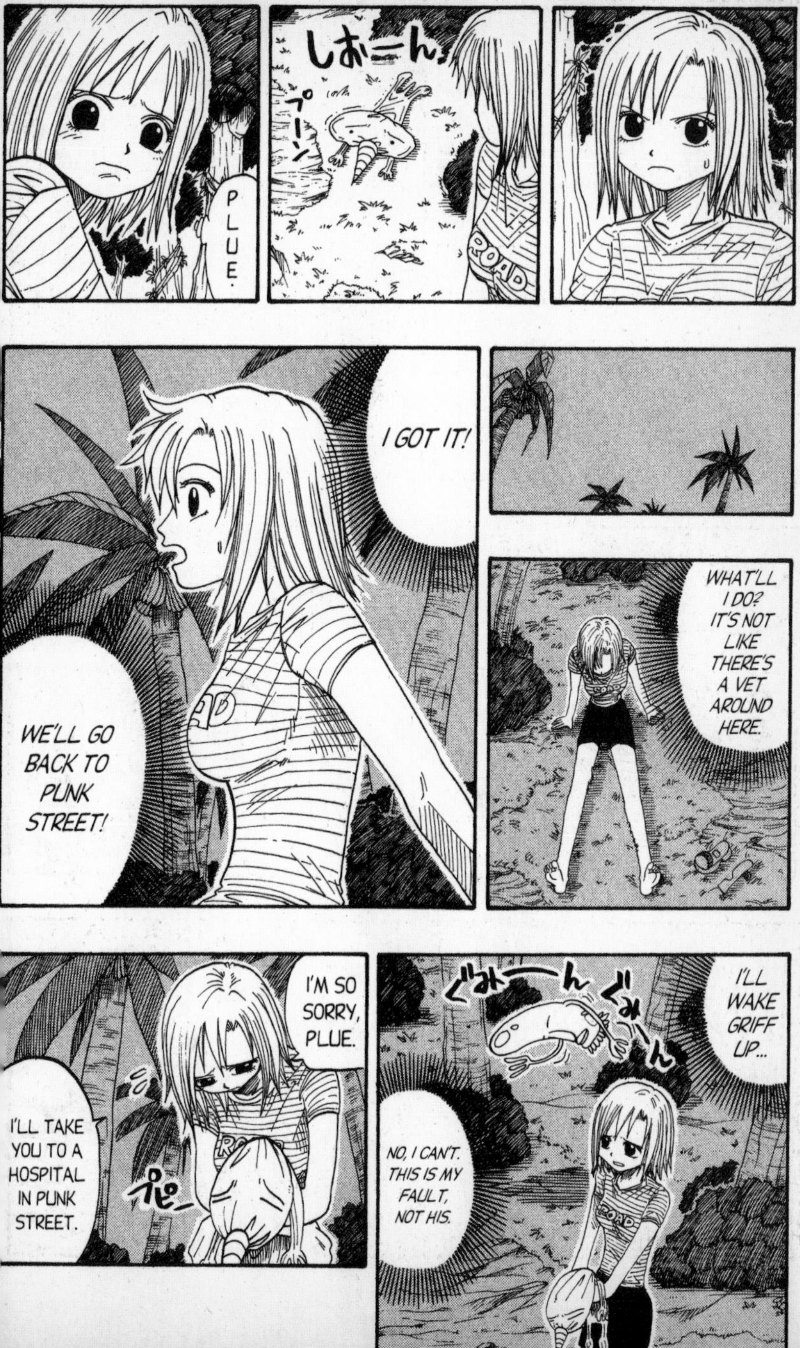

しおーん
プーン
PLUE.
WHAT'LL I DO? IT'S NOT LIKE THERE'S A VET AROUND HERE.
I GOT IT!
WE'LL GO BACK TO PUNK STREET!
ぐみーん ぐみ～ん
I'LL WAKE GRIFF UP...
NO, I CAN'T. THIS IS MY FAULT, NOT HIS.
I'M SO SORRY, PLUE.
I'LL TAKE YOU TO A HOSPITAL IN PUNK STREET.
ピー

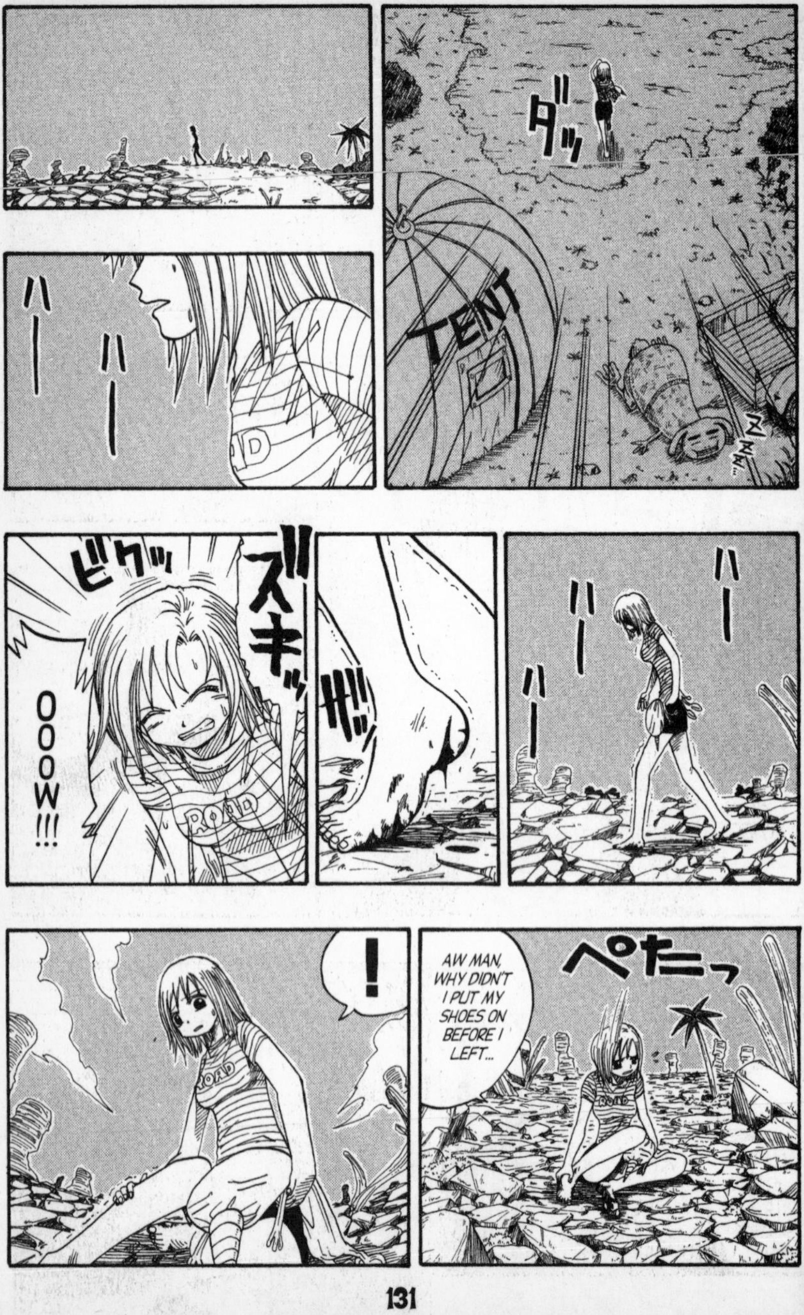

ダッ
TENT
ZZZ...
ハーハー
ハーハーハー
ズキッッ!!
ビクッ
OOOOW!!!
ぺたっ
AW MAN, WHY DIDN'T I PUT MY SHOES ON BEFORE I LEFT...
!

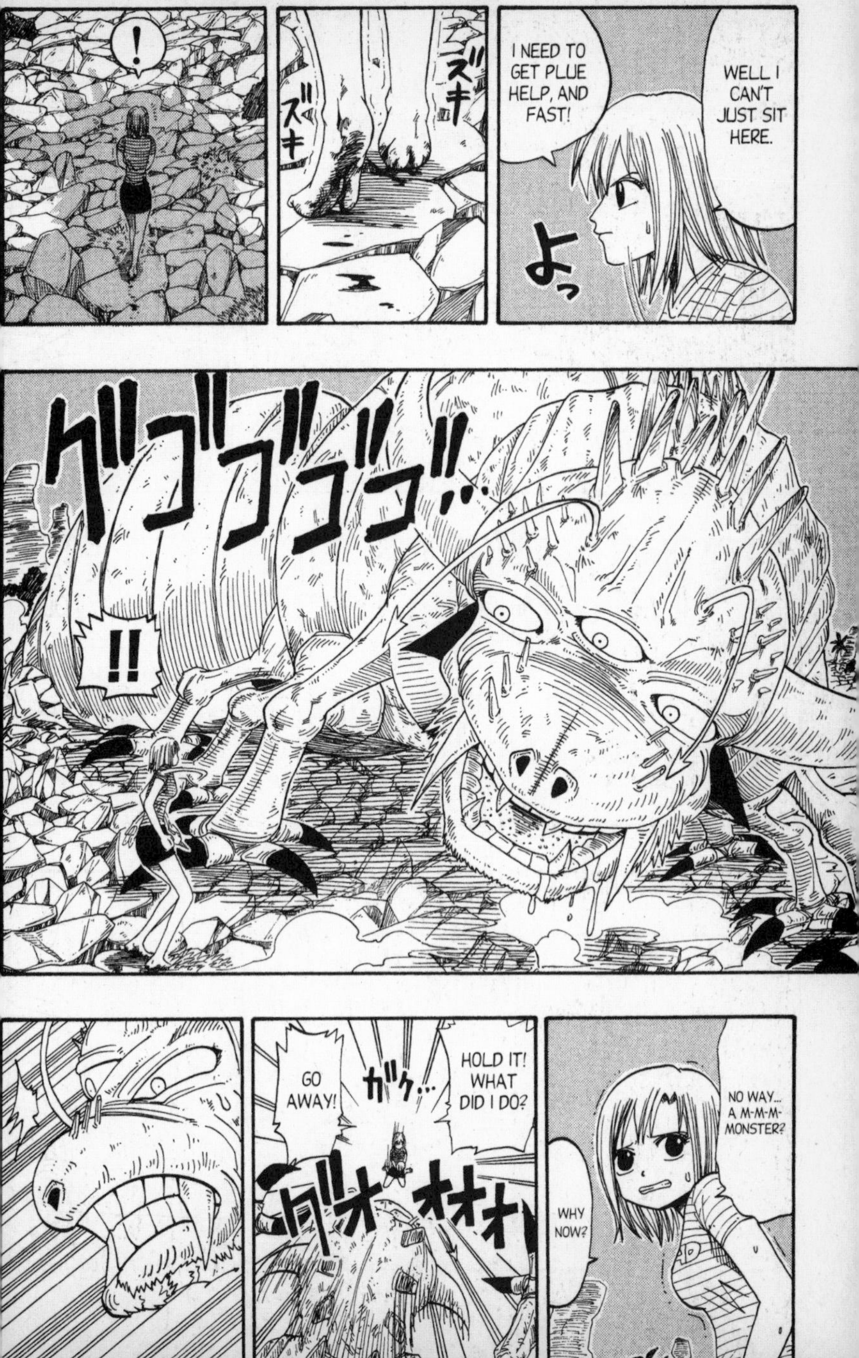
WELL I CAN'T JUST SIT HERE.
I NEED TO GET PLUE HELP, AND FAST!
よっ
ズキ
ズキ
!
グゴゴゴ!!
!!
NO WAY... A M-M-M-MONSTER?
WHY NOW?
HOLD IT! WHAT DID I DO?
ガク…
GO AWAY!
ガオオオオ

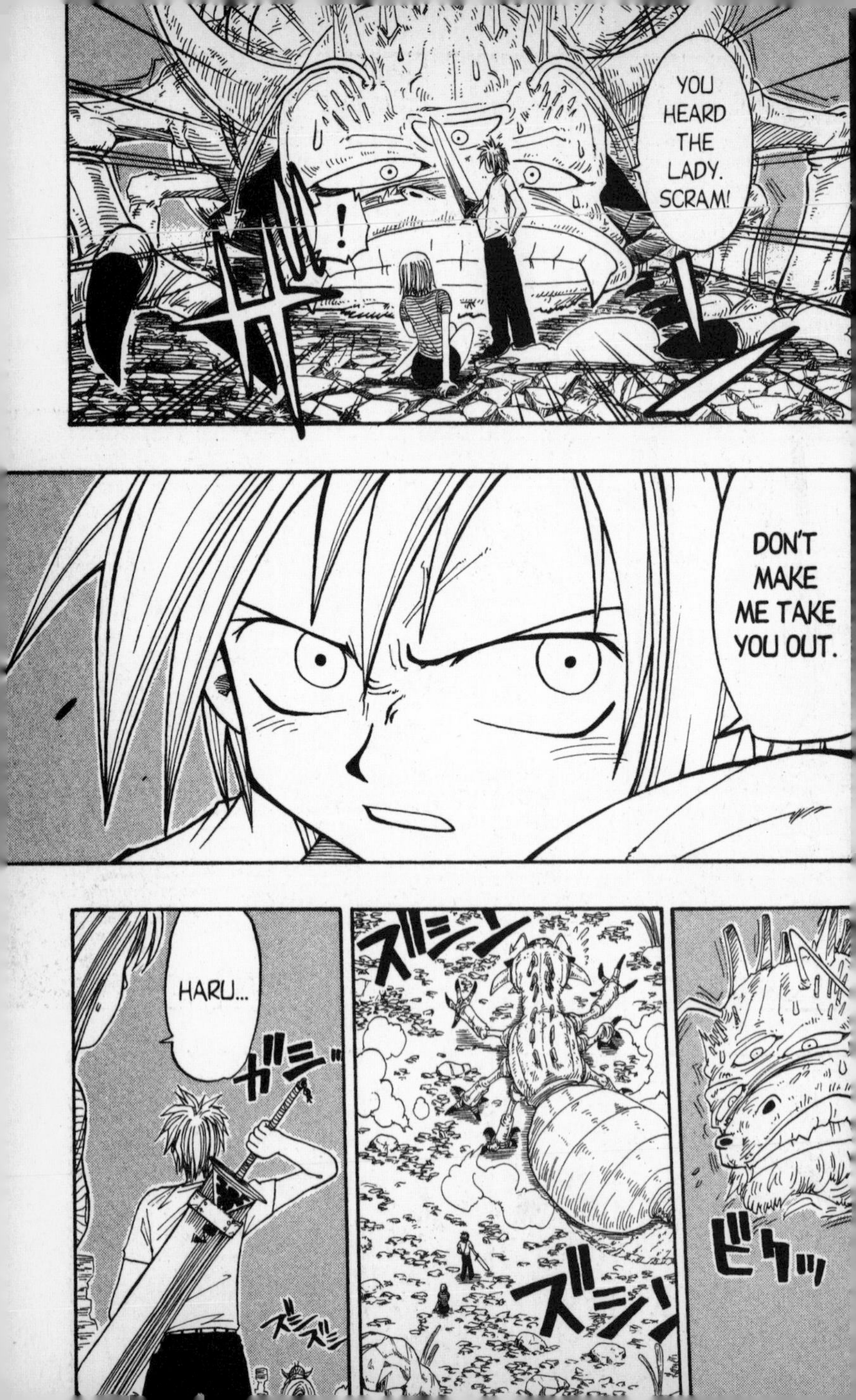
YOU HEARD THE LADY. SCRAM!
DON'T MAKE ME TAKE YOU OUT.
HARU...

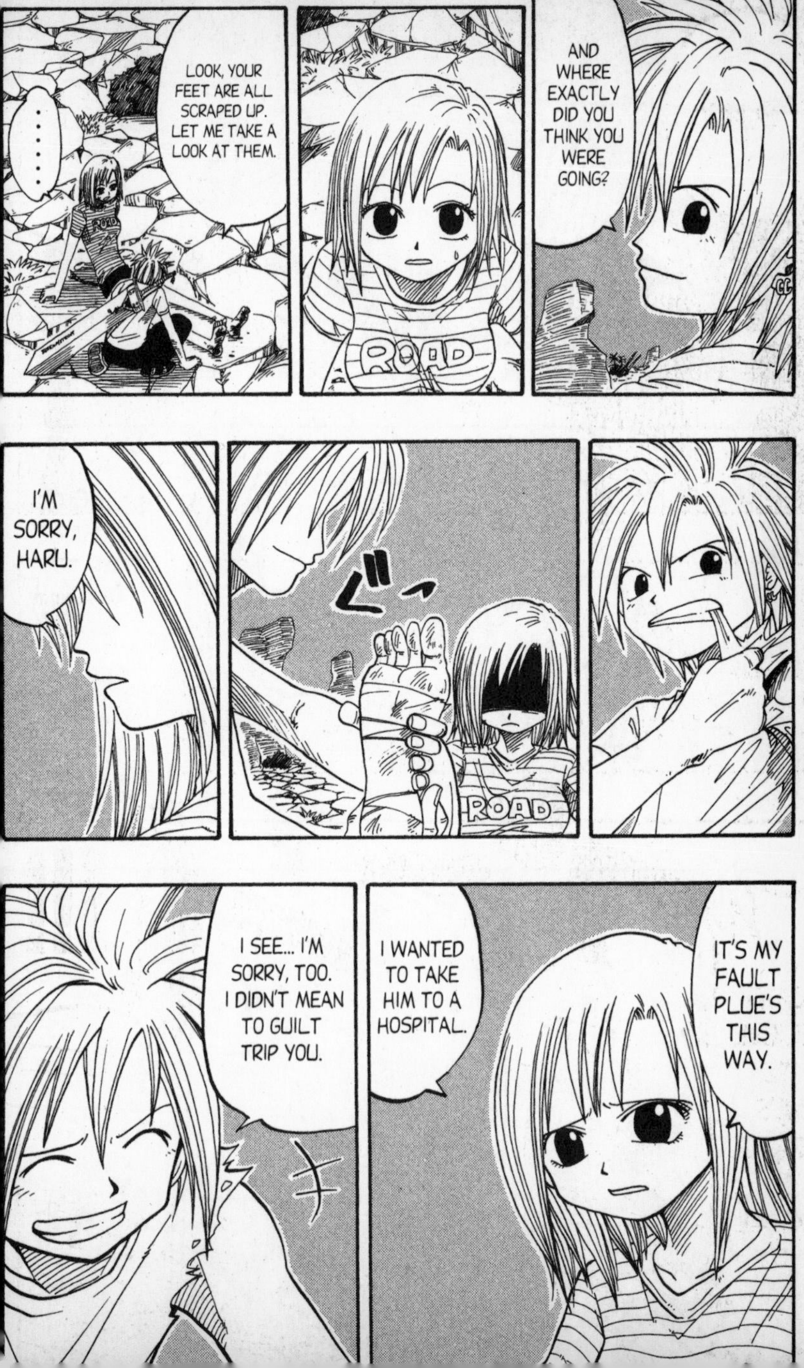
AND WHERE EXACTLY DID YOU THINK YOU WERE GOING?
LOOK, YOUR FEET ARE ALL SCRAPED UP. LET ME TAKE A LOOK AT THEM.
......
I'M SORRY, HARU.
IT'S MY FAULT PLUE'S THIS WAY.
I WANTED TO TAKE HIM TO A HOSPITAL.
I SEE... I'M SORRY, TOO. I DIDN'T MEAN TO GUILT TRIP YOU.

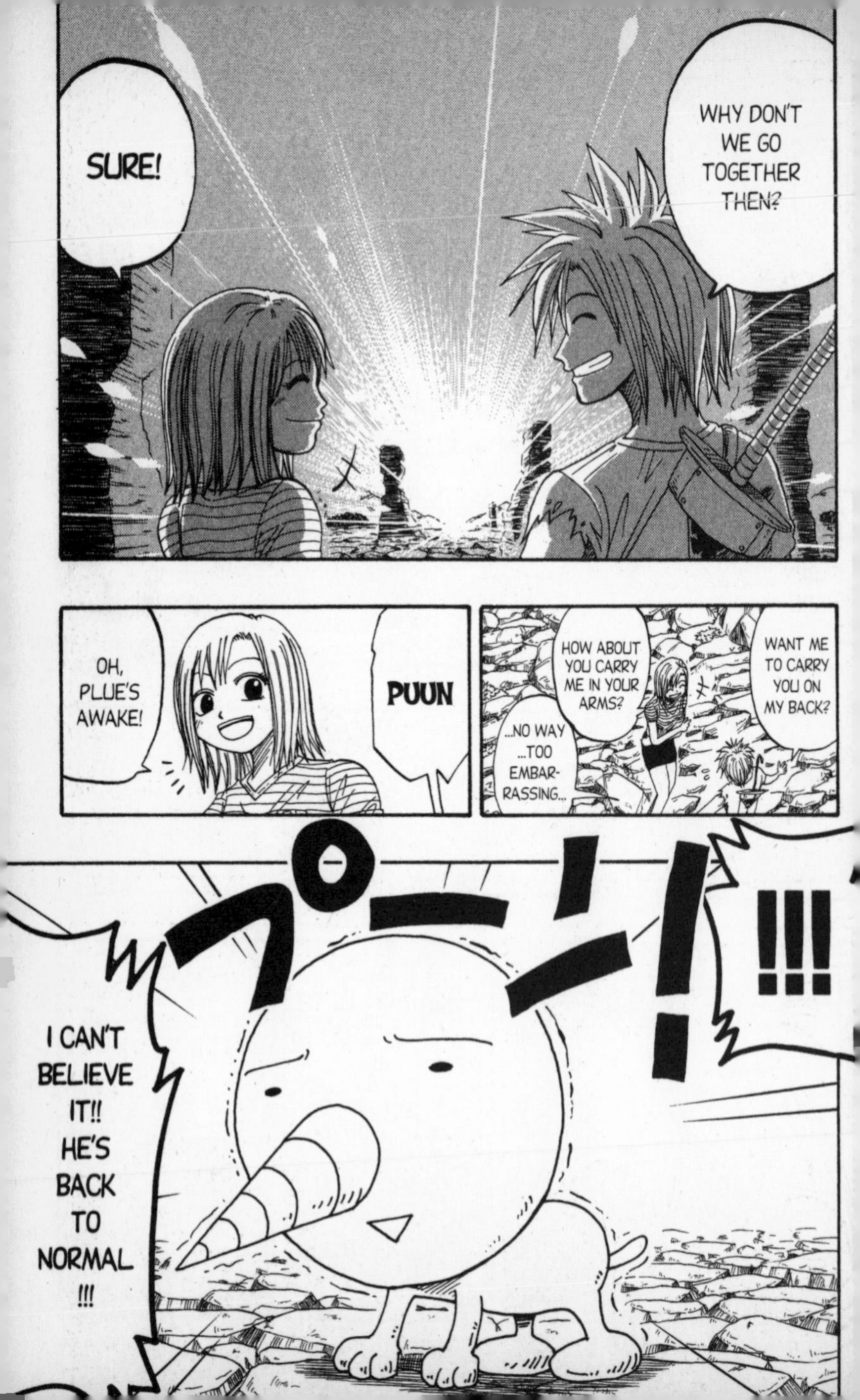
WHY DON'T WE GO TOGETHER THEN?
SURE!
WANT ME TO CARRY YOU ON MY BACK?
HOW ABOUT YOU CARRY ME IN YOUR ARMS?
...NO WAY ...TOO EMBARRASSING...
PUUN
OH, PLUE'S AWAKE!
プーン!!!
I CAN'T BELIEVE IT!! HE'S BACK TO NORMAL!!!

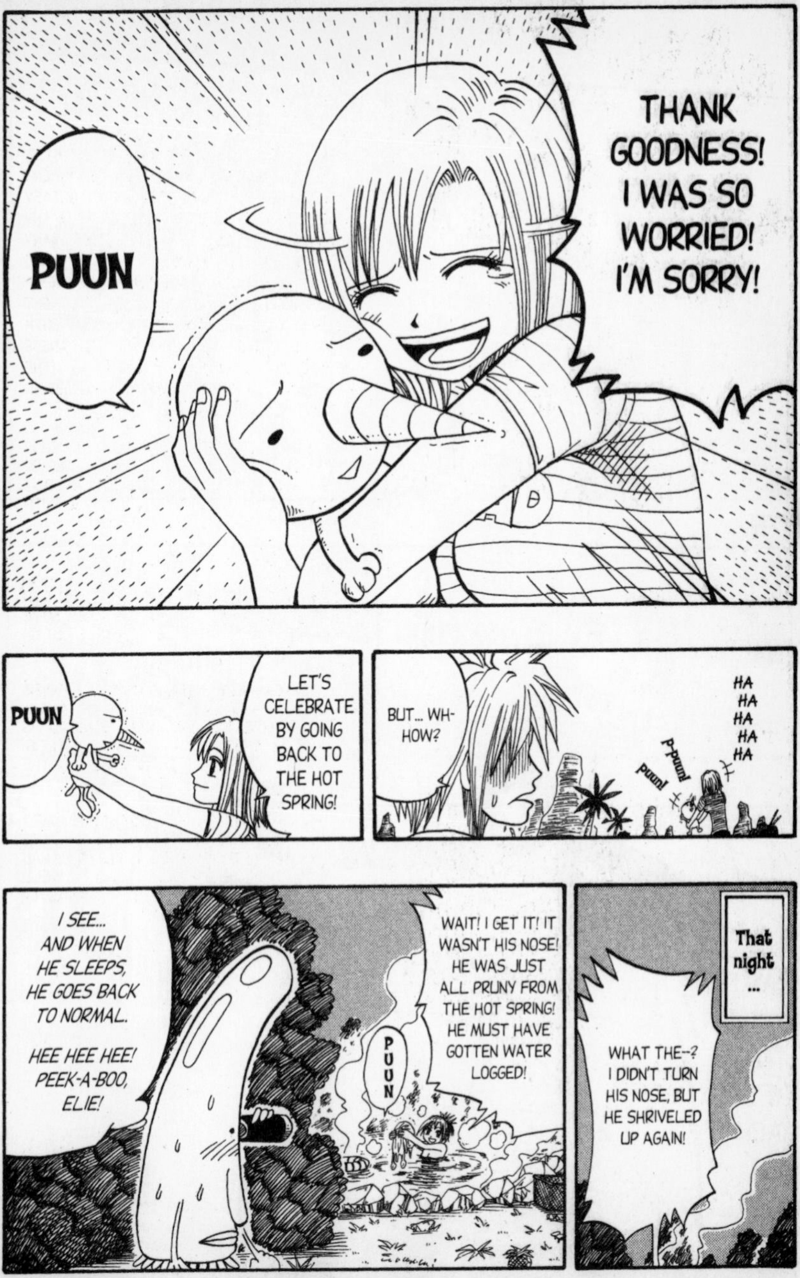
THANK GOODNESS! I WAS SO WORRIED! I'M SORRY!
PUUN
HA HA HA HA HA
P-puun!
puun!
BUT... WH- HOW?
LET'S CELEBRATE BY GOING BACK TO THE HOT SPRING!
PUUN
That night ...
WHAT THE--? I DIDN'T TURN HIS NOSE, BUT HE SHRIVELED UP AGAIN!
WAIT! I GET IT! IT WASN'T HIS NOSE! HE WAS JUST ALL PRUNY FROM THE HOT SPRING! HE MUST HAVE GOTTEN WATER LOGGED!
PUUN
I SEE... AND WHEN HE SLEEPS, HE GOES BACK TO NORMAL.
HEE HEE HEE! PEEK-A-BOO, ELIE!

ORIGINS OF THE CHARACTER NAMES

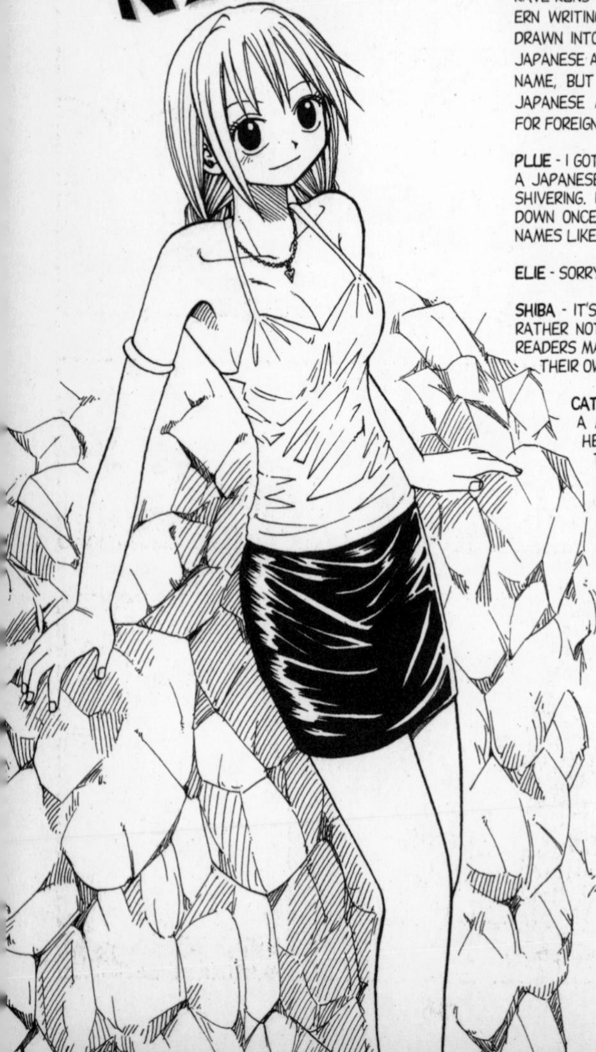

HARU - SINCE HE'S THE LEAD CHARACTER, I WORRIED ABOUT HIS NAME THE MOST. WHEN I DECIDED TO SET THE STORY IN A FANTASY WORLD, I ALSO DECIDED I WOULDN'T USE ANY JAPANESE NAMES. BUT THERE AREN'T MANY FANTASY-WORLD COMICS IN THE MAGAZINE RAVE RUNS IN, SO I WONDERED, IF I USE WESTERN WRITING, THE READERS MIGHT NOT GET DRAWN INTO THE STORY. SO I MADE IT BOTH JAPANESE AND FOREIGN BY USING A JAPANESE NAME, BUT WRITING IT IN KATAKANA (THE JAPANESE ALPHABET TYPICALLY RESERVED FOR FOREIGN WORDS).

PLUE - I GOT THIS FROM "PURUPURU," WHICH IS A JAPANESE SOUND EFFECT FOR SHAKING OR SHIVERING. I JUST WROTE, NO, SCRIBBLED IT DOWN ONCE A LONG TIME AGO... SAME WITH NAMES LIKE "SHABUTARO" AND "KONBO."

ELIE - SORRY, IT'S A SECRET.

SHIBA - IT'S NOT EXACTLY A SECRET, BUT I'D RATHER NOT GIVE IT AWAY JUST YET. SOME READERS MAY HAVE FIGURED THIS ONE OUT ON THEIR OWN.

CATTLEYA - THE NAME OF A FLOWER. A MEMBER OF THE ORCHID FAMILY. HER MOTHER'S NAME, SAKURA, IS THE NAME OF A FLOWER, SO I FIGURED I'D GIVE THE DAUGHTER THE NAME OF A FLOWER TOO.

MUSICA - AS I WROTE IN VOLUME 2, THIS MEANS "MUSIC" IN ITALIAN. I THOUGHT IT SOUNDED NICE. I HAD DECIDED HIS NAME WELL BEFORE THE CHARACTER APPEARED.

NAKAJIMA - IT JUST FIT!

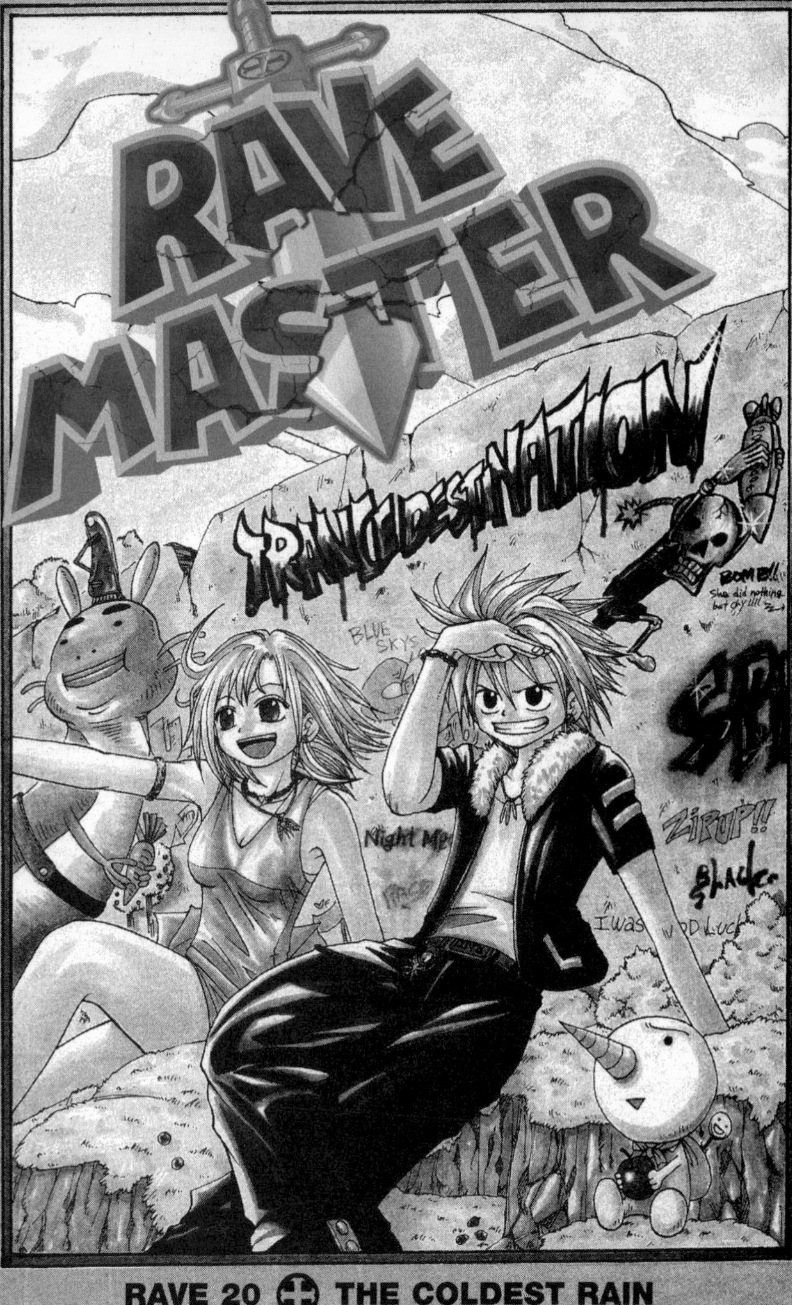
RAVE MASTER
BLUE SKYS
BOMB!!
ZIPUP!!

RAVE 20 ✠ THE COLDEST RAIN

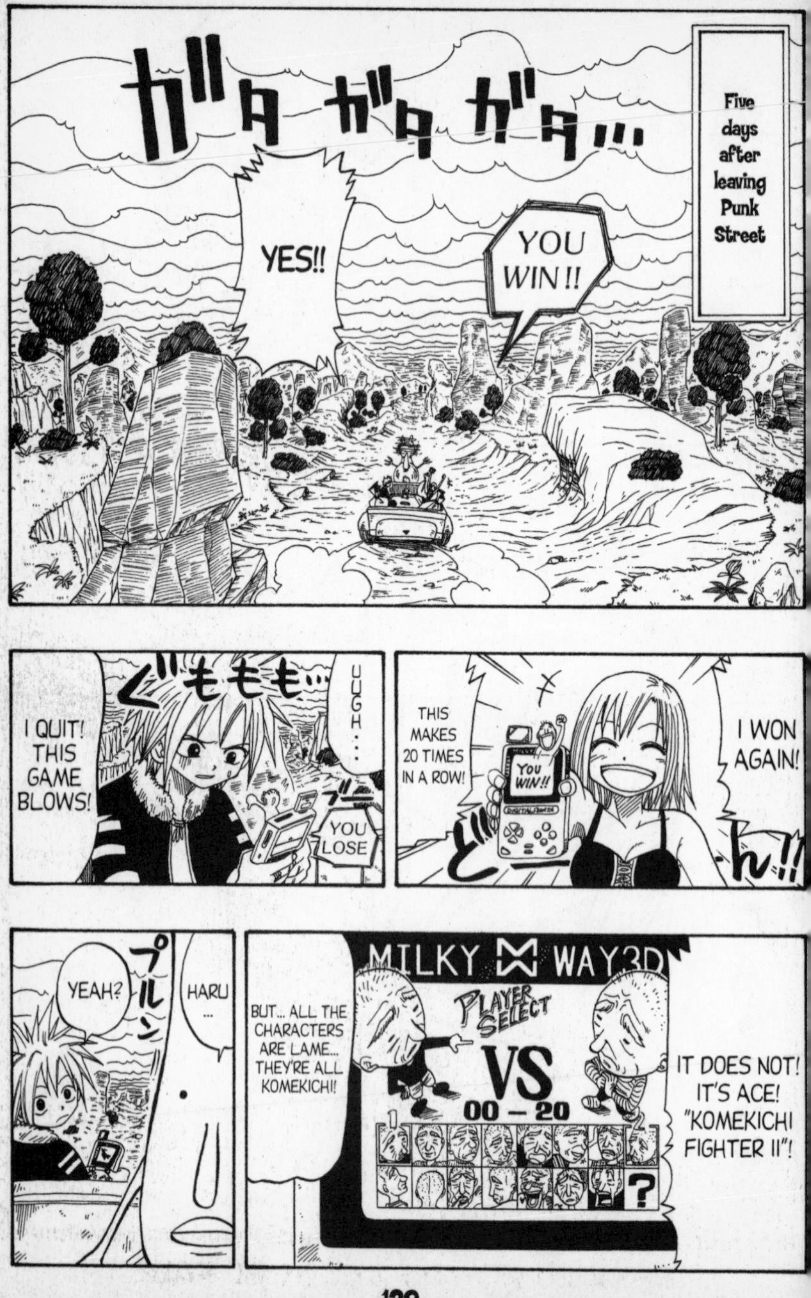

Five days after leaving Punk Street
ガタガタガタ…
YOU WIN!!
YES!!
I WON AGAIN!
THIS MAKES 20 TIMES IN A ROW!
YOU WIN!!
どーん!!
UGH…
ぐもももも…
I QUIT! THIS GAME BLOWS!
ブー
YOU LOSE
MILKY WAY3D
PLAYER SELECT
VS
00 – 20
BUT… ALL THE CHARACTERS ARE LAME… THEY'RE ALL KOMEKICHI!
IT DOES NOT! IT'S ACE! "KOMEKICHI FIGHTER II"!
HARU …
プルン
YEAH?

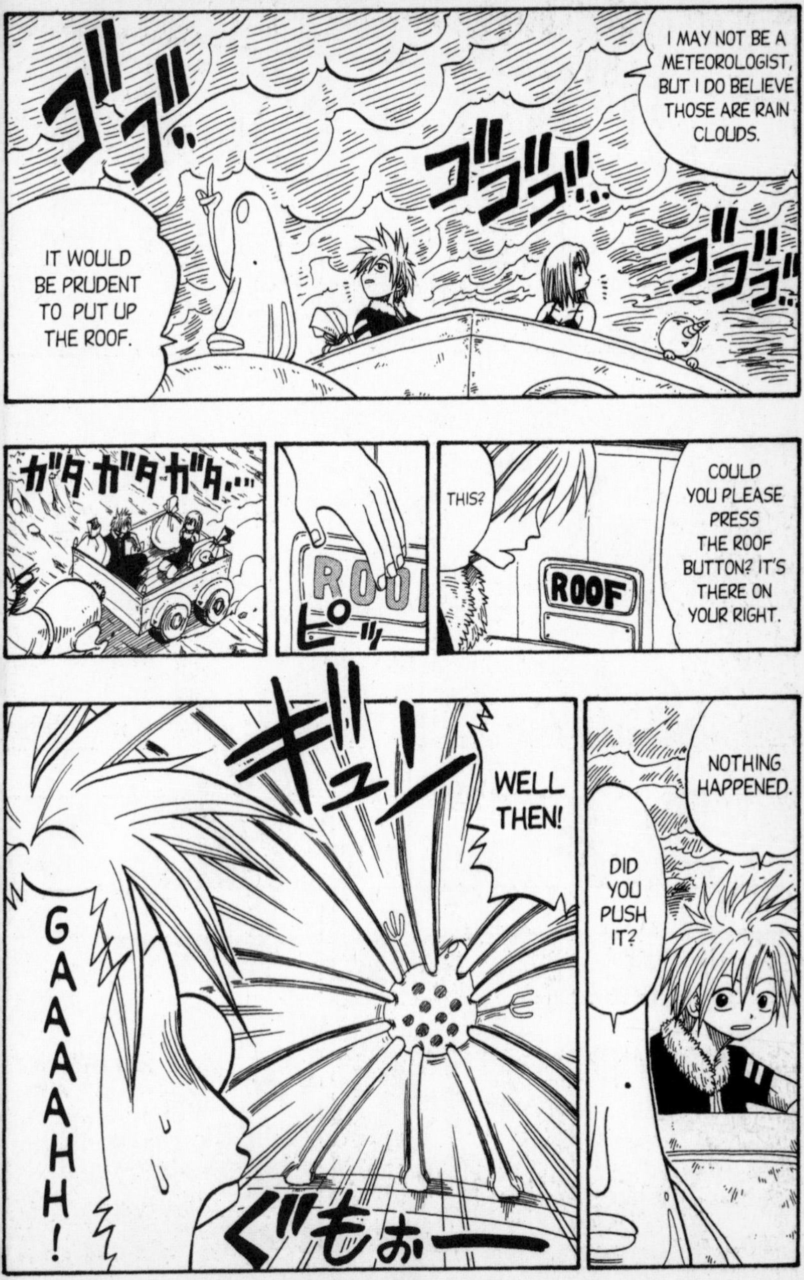
I MAY NOT BE A METEOROLOGIST, BUT I DO BELIEVE THOSE ARE RAIN CLOUDS.
ゴゴゴ…
ゴゴゴ!!…
ゴゴ…
IT WOULD BE PRUDENT TO PUT UP THE ROOF.
COULD YOU PLEASE PRESS THE ROOF BUTTON? IT'S THERE ON YOUR RIGHT.
ROOF
THIS?
ピッ
ガタガタガタ…
NOTHING HAPPENED.
DID YOU PUSH IT?
WELL THEN!
ギュ!
GAAAAAH!
ぐもぉー

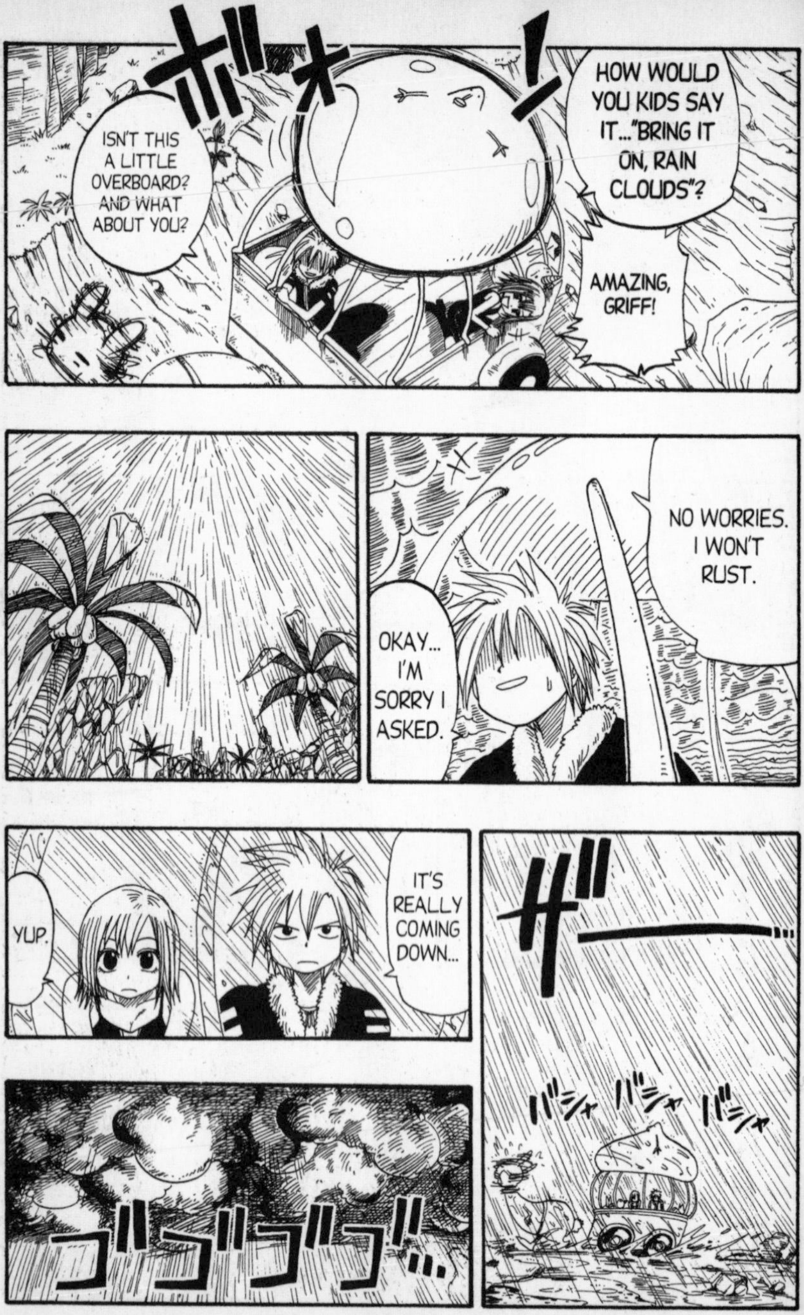
ボオー!
HOW WOULD YOU KIDS SAY IT..."BRING IT ON, RAIN CLOUDS"?
AMAZING, GRIFF!
ISN'T THIS A LITTLE OVERBOARD? AND WHAT ABOUT YOU?
NO WORRIES. I WON'T RUST.
OKAY... I'M SORRY I ASKED.
ザー...
バシャ バシャ バシャ
IT'S REALLY COMING DOWN...
YUP.
ゴゴゴゴ!...

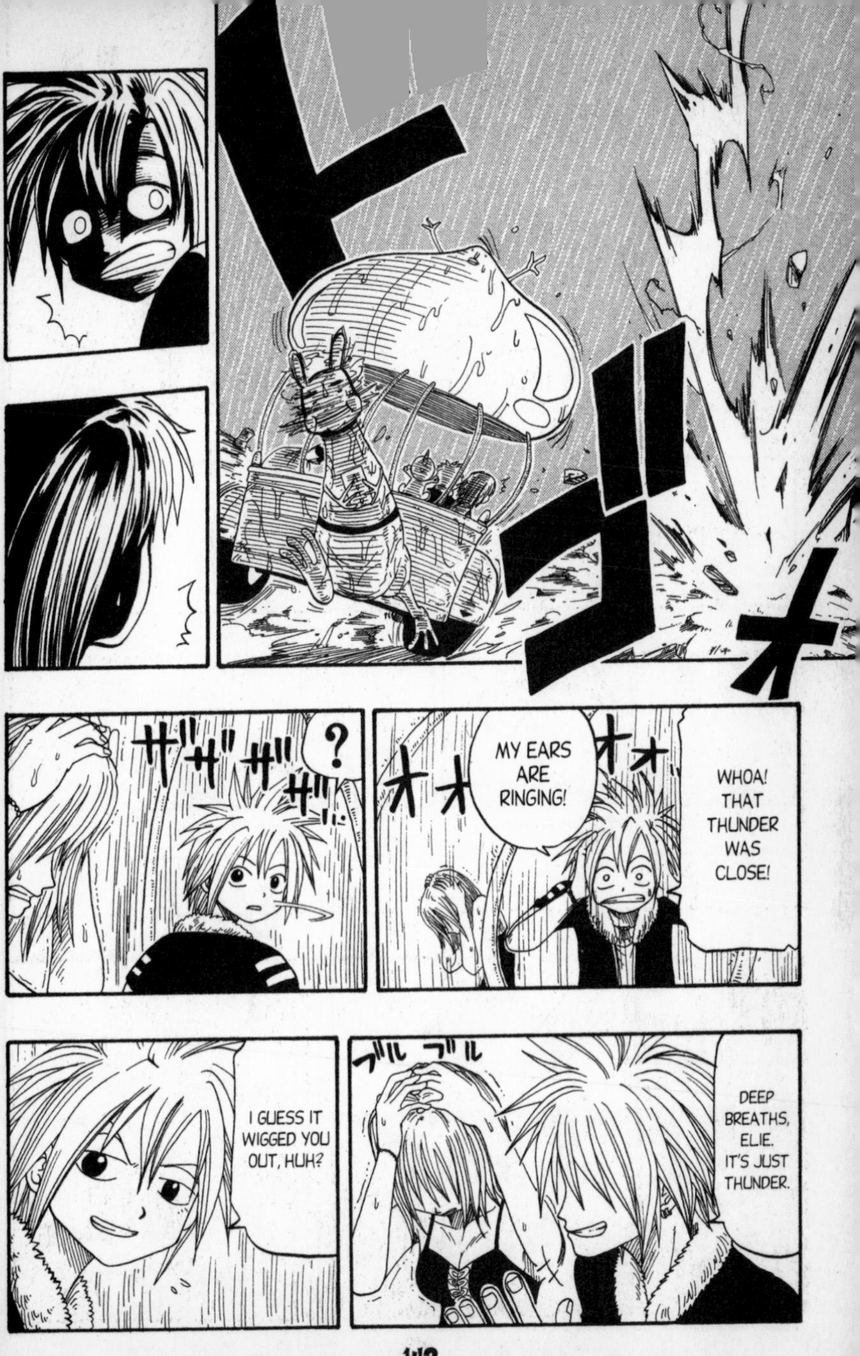
WHOA! THAT THUNDER WAS CLOSE!
MY EARS ARE RINGING!
?
I GUESS IT WIGGED YOU OUT, HUH?
DEEP BREATHS, ELIE. IT'S JUST THUNDER.

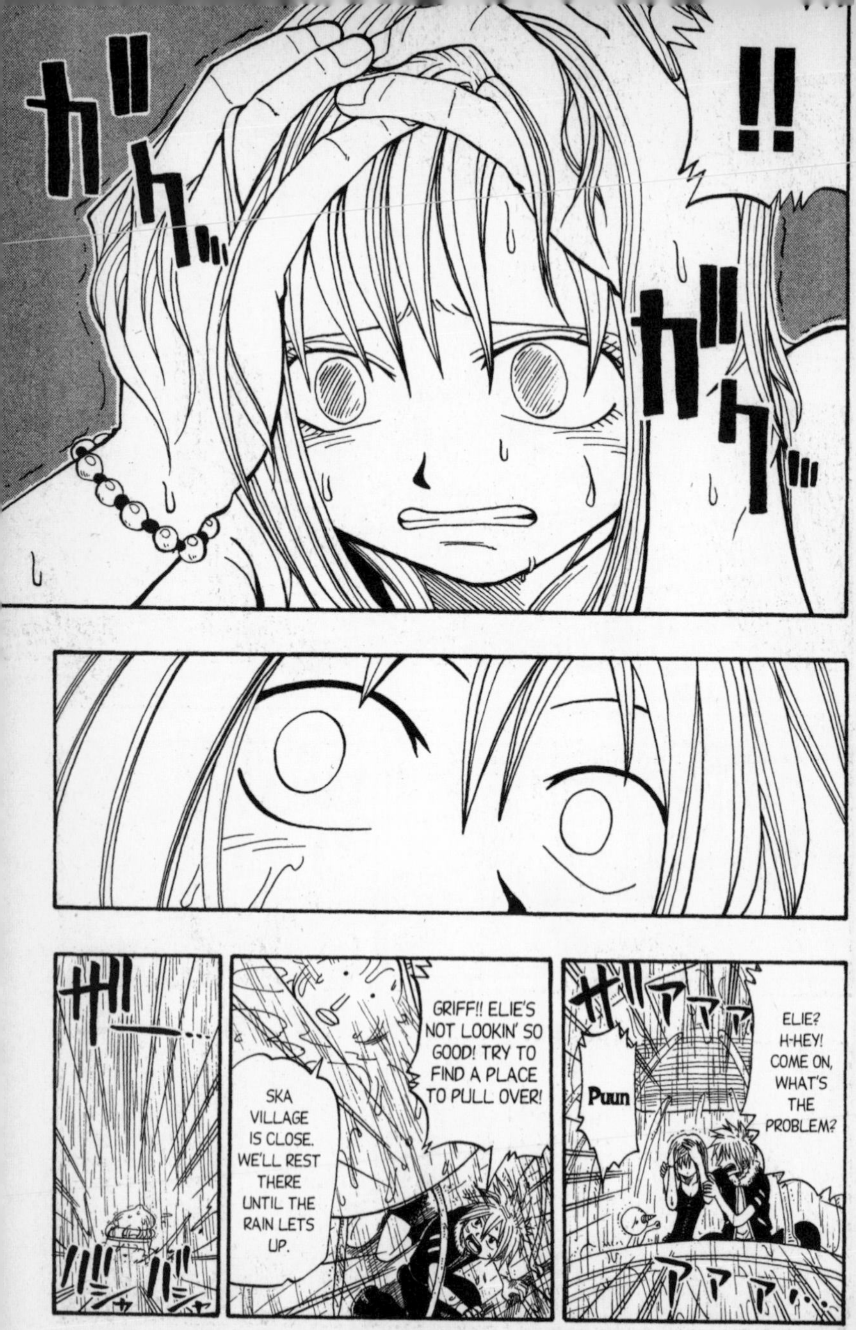
!!
ガクガク
ガクガク
ザアアア
Puun
ELIE? H-HEY! COME ON, WHAT'S THE PROBLEM?
アアア…
GRIFF!! ELIE'S NOT LOOKIN' SO GOOD! TRY TO FIND A PLACE TO PULL OVER!
SKA VILLAGE IS CLOSE. WE'LL REST THERE UNTIL THE RAIN LETS UP.
ザー…
バシャバシャ

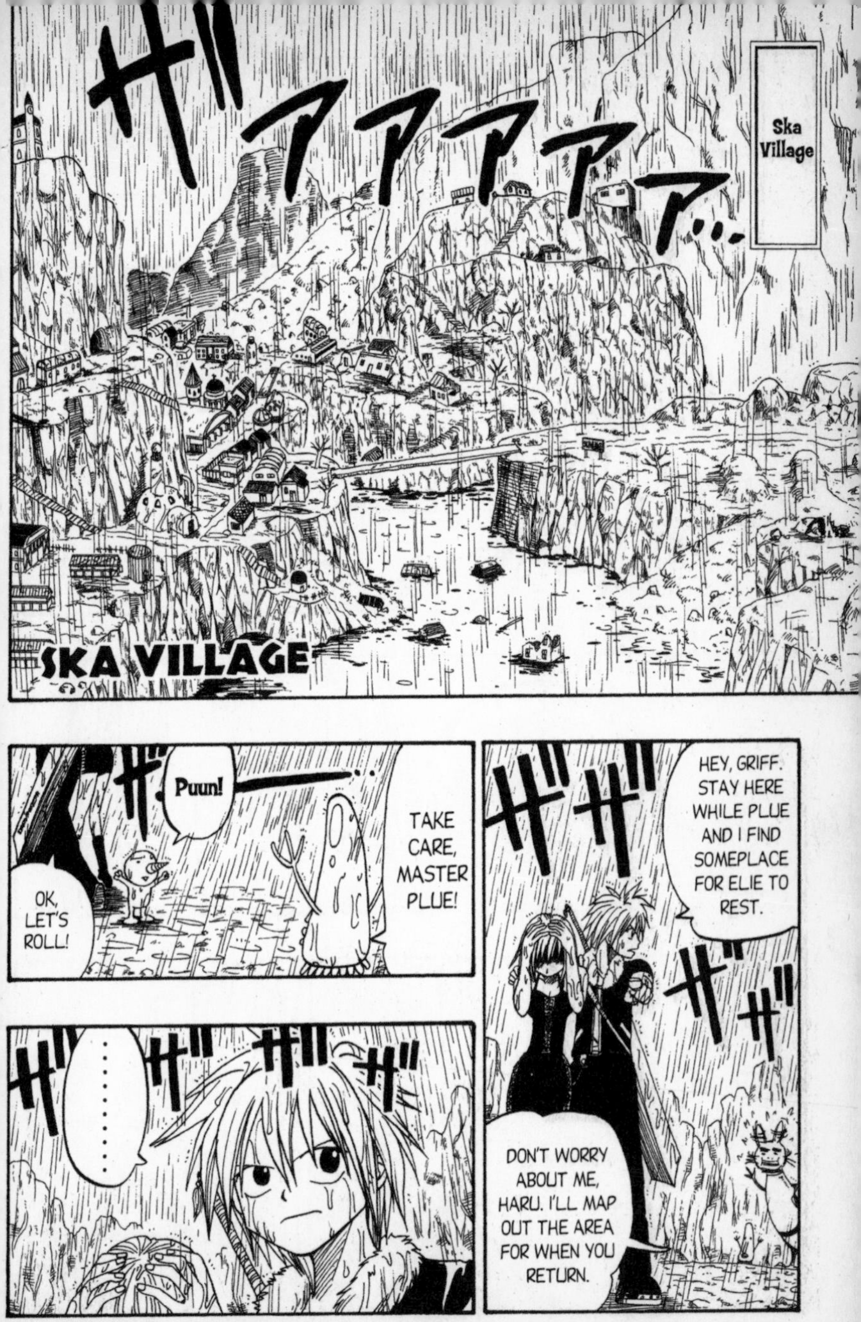

Ska Village
ザァァァァ…
SKA VILLAGE
HEY, GRIFF. STAY HERE WHILE PLUE AND I FIND SOMEPLACE FOR ELIE TO REST.
DON'T WORRY ABOUT ME, HARU. I'LL MAP OUT THE AREA FOR WHEN YOU RETURN.
TAKE CARE, MASTER PLUE!
Puun!
OK, LET'S ROLL!
……

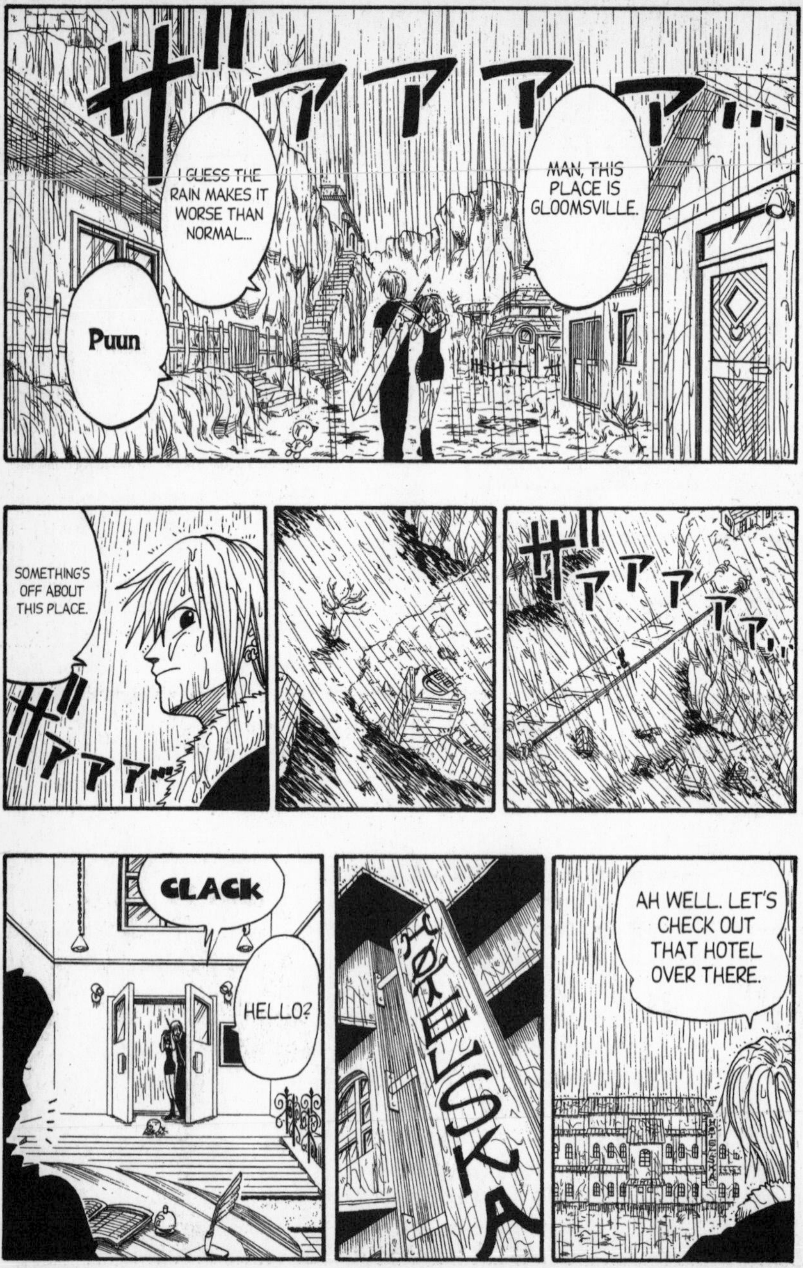
MAN, THIS PLACE IS GLOOMSVILLE.
I GUESS THE RAIN MAKES IT WORSE THAN NORMAL...
Puun
SOMETHING'S OFF ABOUT THIS PLACE.
AH WELL. LET'S CHECK OUT THAT HOTEL OVER THERE.
CLACK
HELLO?

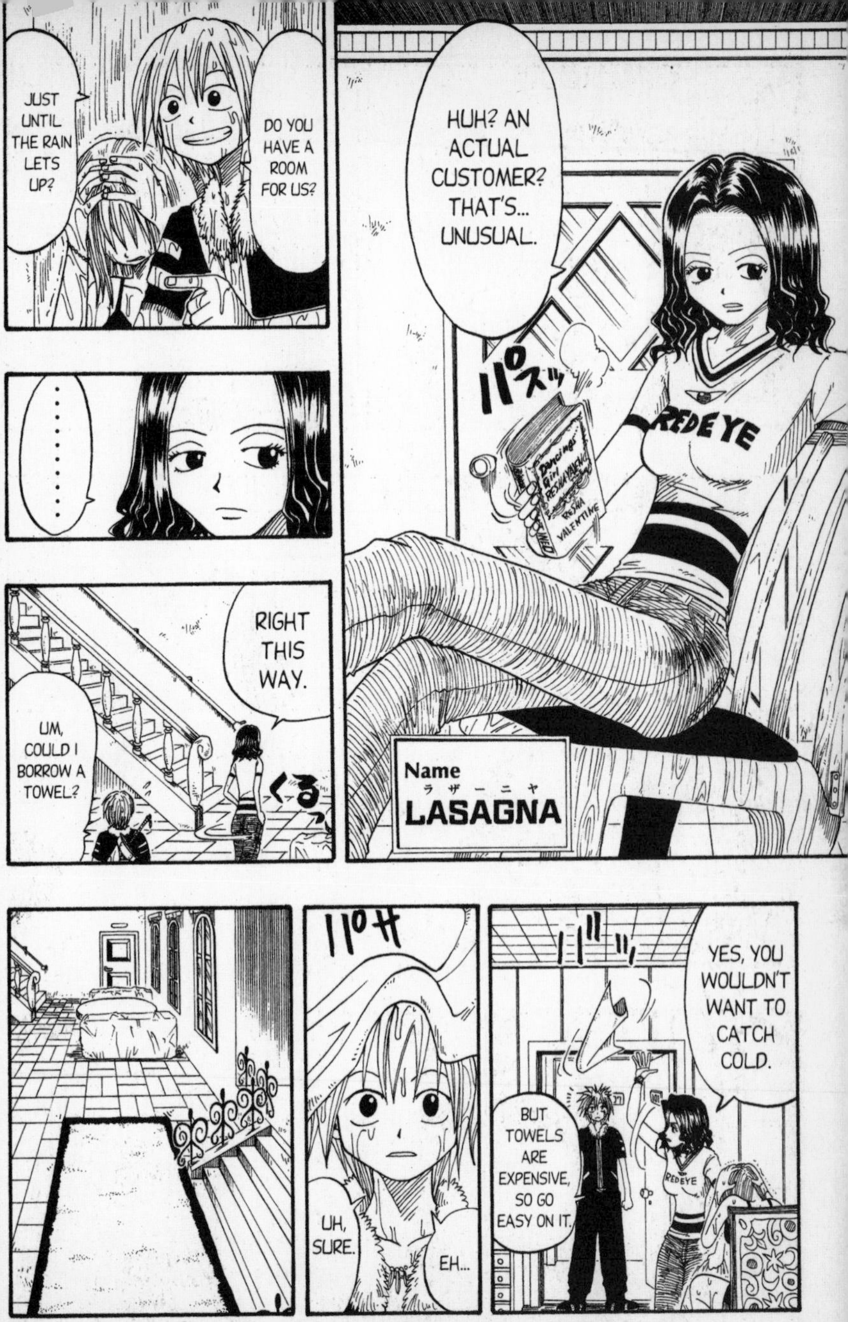
HUH? AN ACTUAL CUSTOMER? THAT'S... UNUSUAL.
パスッ
REDEYE
Name
ラザーニヤ
LASAGNA
DO YOU HAVE A ROOM FOR US?
JUST UNTIL THE RAIN LETS UP?
......
RIGHT THIS WAY.
くるっ
UM, COULD I BORROW A TOWEL?
バッ
YES, YOU WOULDN'T WANT TO CATCH COLD.
BUT TOWELS ARE EXPENSIVE, SO GO EASY ON IT.
REDEYE
パサ
EH...
UH, SURE.

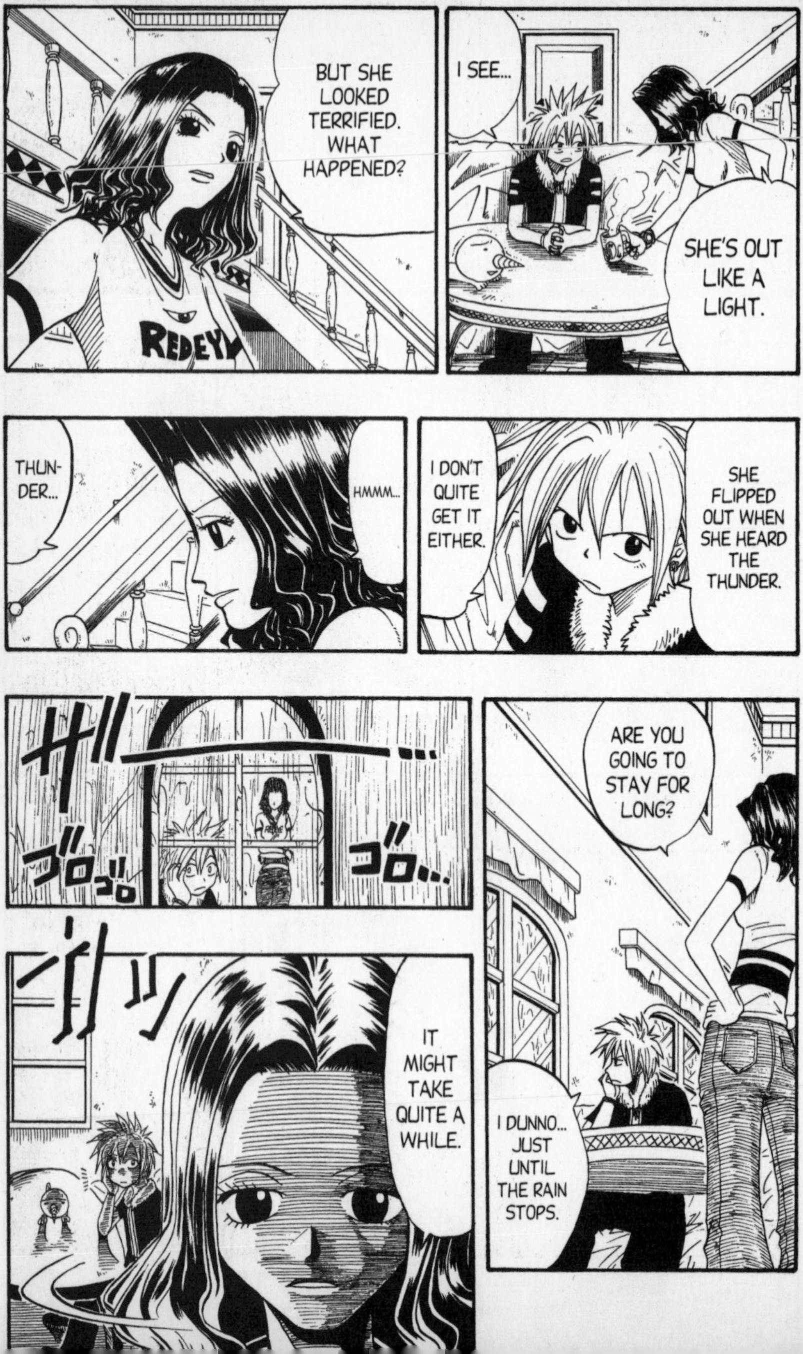
I SEE...
SHE'S OUT LIKE A LIGHT.
BUT SHE LOOKED TERRIFIED. WHAT HAPPENED?
SHE FLIPPED OUT WHEN SHE HEARD THE THUNDER.
I DON'T QUITE GET IT EITHER.
HMMM...
THUN-DER...
ARE YOU GOING TO STAY FOR LONG?
I DUNNO... JUST UNTIL THE RAIN STOPS.
ザー...
ゴロゴロ
ゴロ...
IT MIGHT TAKE QUITE A WHILE.

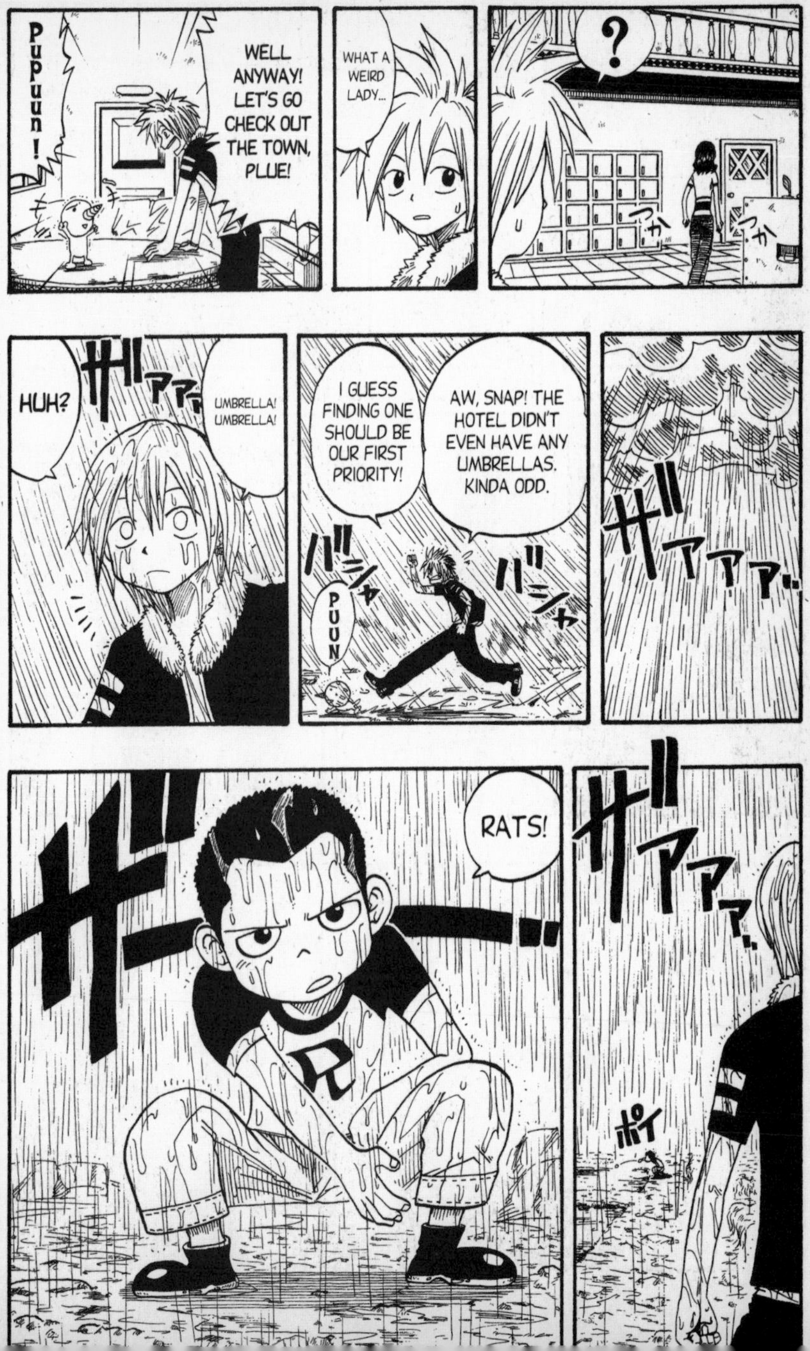
?
つか
つか
WHAT A WEIRD LADY...
WELL ANYWAY! LET'S GO CHECK OUT THE TOWN, PLUE!
Pupuun!
ザァアアア
AW, SNAP! THE HOTEL DIDN'T EVEN HAVE ANY UMBRELLAS. KINDA ODD.
I GUESS FINDING ONE SHOULD BE OUR FIRST PRIORITY!
バシャ
バシャ
PUUN
UMBRELLA! UMBRELLA!
ザァアァ
HUH?
ザァアア
ポイ
RATS!
ザー

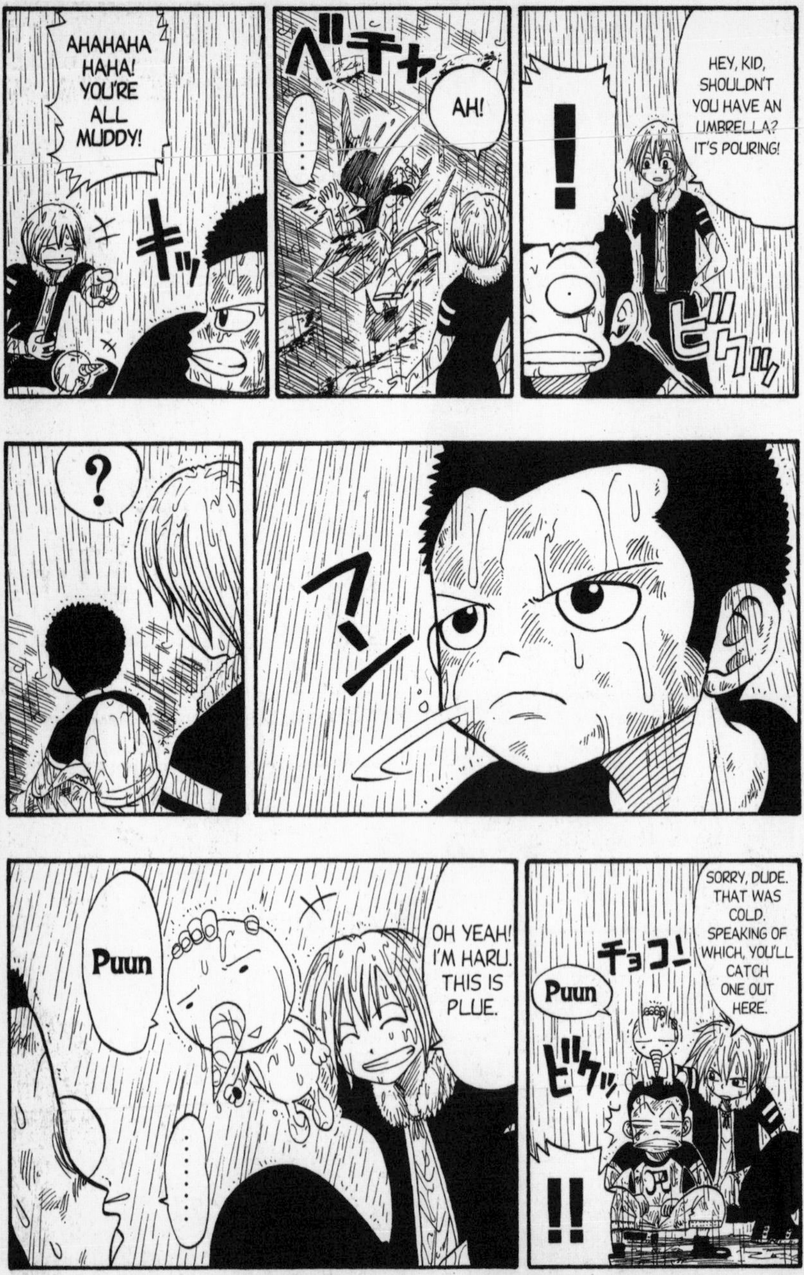
HEY, KID, SHOULDN'T YOU HAVE AN UMBRELLA? IT'S POURING!
!
ビクッ
ベチャ
AH!
......
AHAHAHA HAHA! YOU'RE ALL MUDDY!
キッ
?
SORRY, DUDE. THAT WAS COLD. SPEAKING OF WHICH, YOU'LL CATCH ONE OUT HERE.
チョコン
Puun
ビクッ
!!
OH YEAH! I'M HARU. THIS IS PLUE.
Puun
......

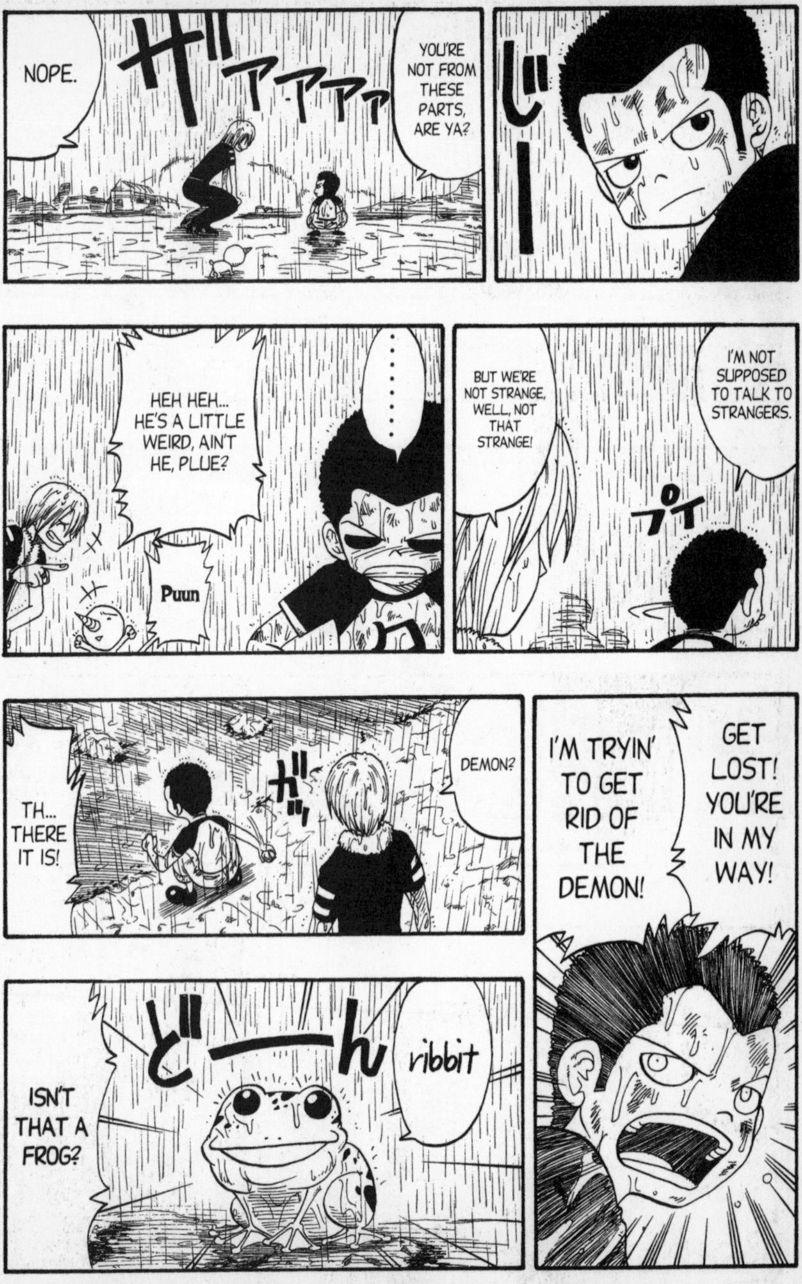
じー
YOU'RE NOT FROM THESE PARTS, ARE YA?
ザアアアア
NOPE.
I'M NOT SUPPOSED TO TALK TO STRANGERS.
プイ
BUT WE'RE NOT STRANGE, WELL, NOT THAT STRANGE!
......
HEH HEH... HE'S A LITTLE WEIRD, AIN'T HE, PLUE?
Puun
GET LOST! YOU'RE IN MY WAY!
I'M TRYIN' TO GET RID OF THE DEMON!
DEMON?
ガッ
TH... THERE IT IS!
ribbit
どーーん
ISN'T THAT A FROG?

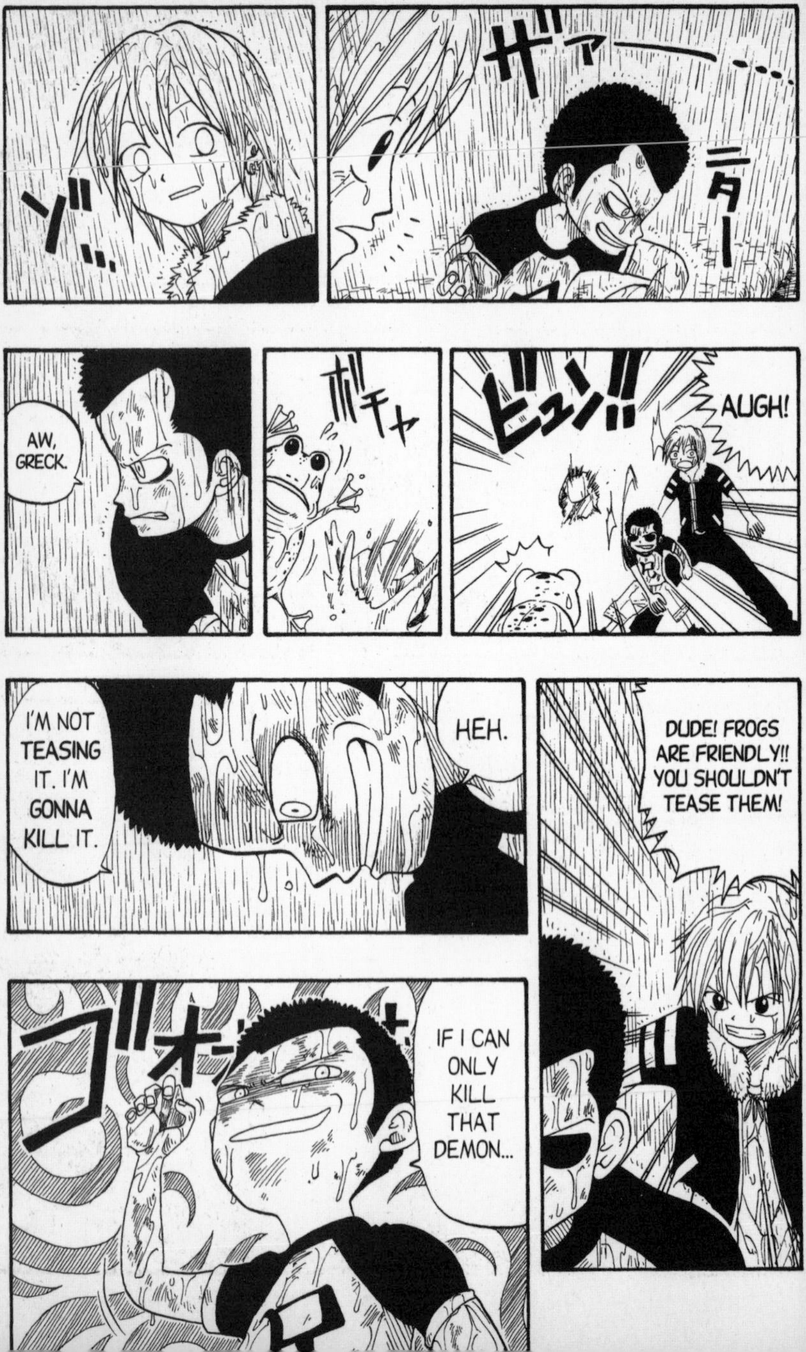
ザァーー…
ニター
ゾ…
ビュン!!
AUGH!
ボチャ
AW, GRECK.
DUDE! FROGS ARE FRIENDLY!! YOU SHOULDN'T TEASE THEM!
HEH.
I'M NOT TEASING IT. I'M GONNA KILL IT.
ゴオー
IF I CAN ONLY KILL THAT DEMON...

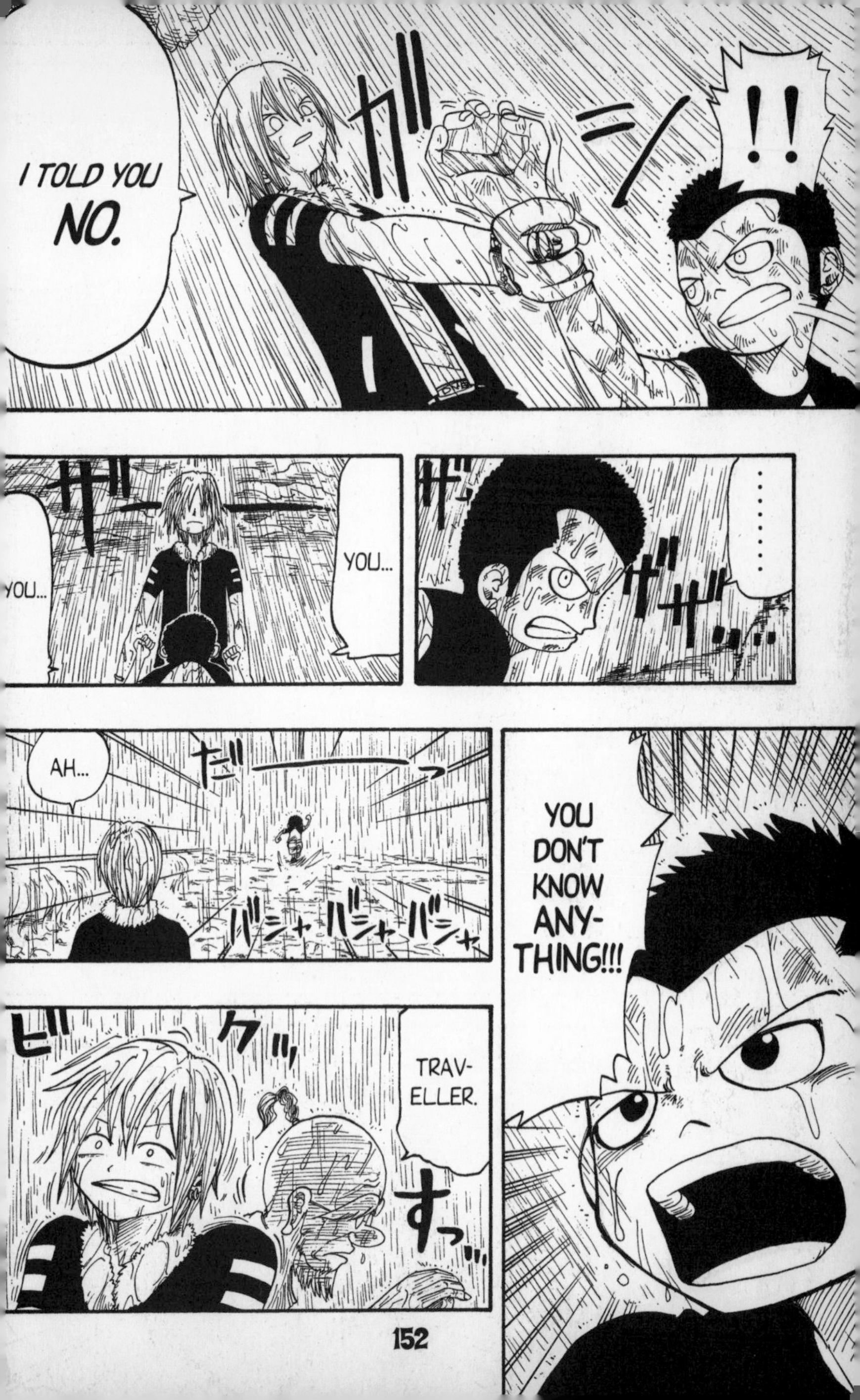

I TOLD YOU NO.
!!
......
YOU...
YOU...
YOU DON'T KNOW ANYTHING!!!
AH...
TRAV-ELLER.

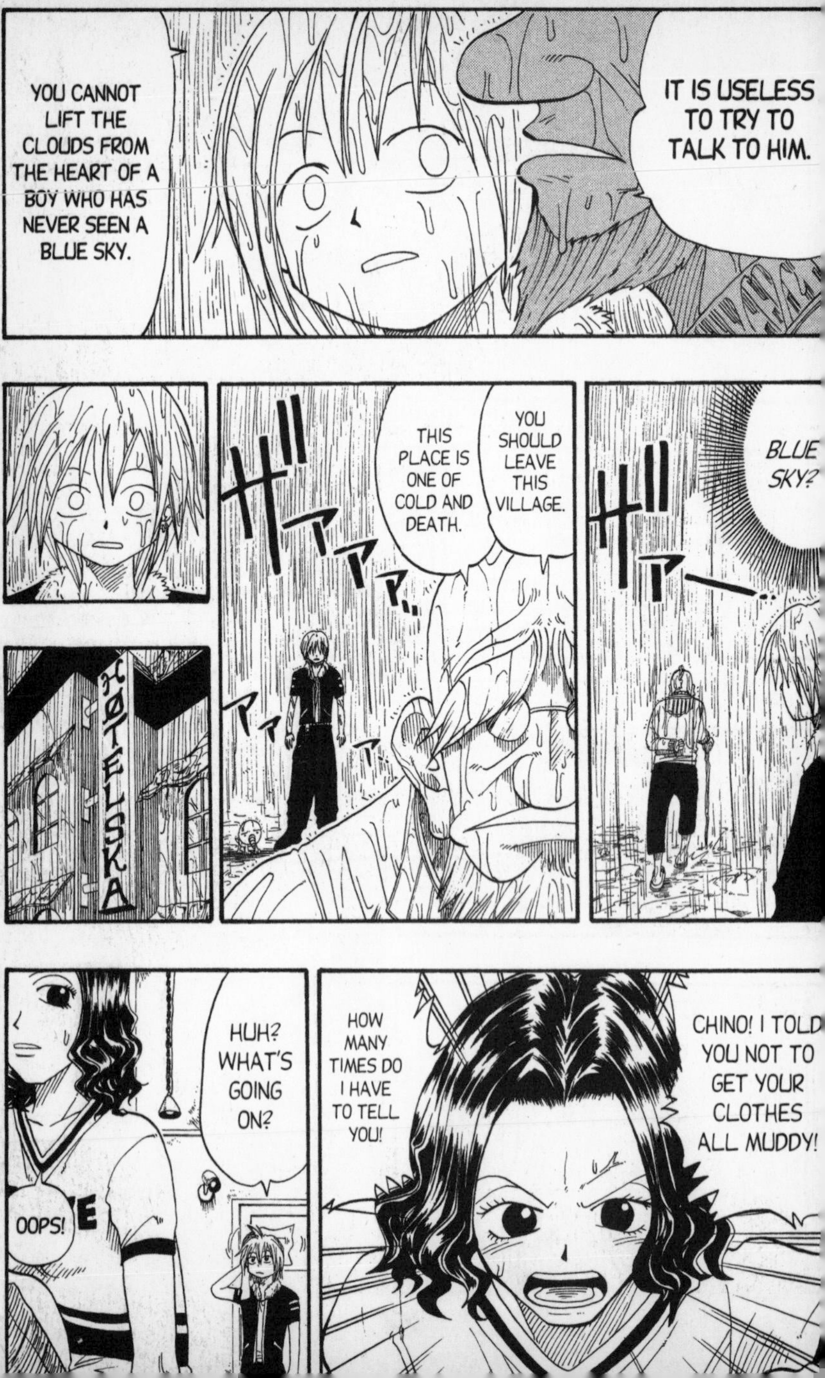

IT IS USELESS TO TRY TO TALK TO HIM.
YOU CANNOT LIFT THE CLOUDS FROM THE HEART OF A BOY WHO HAS NEVER SEEN A BLUE SKY.
BLUE SKY?
YOU SHOULD LEAVE THIS VILLAGE.
THIS PLACE IS ONE OF COLD AND DEATH.
HØTELSKA
CHINO! I TOLD YOU NOT TO GET YOUR CLOTHES ALL MUDDY!
HOW MANY TIMES DO I HAVE TO TELL YOU!
HUH? WHAT'S GOING ON?
OOPS!

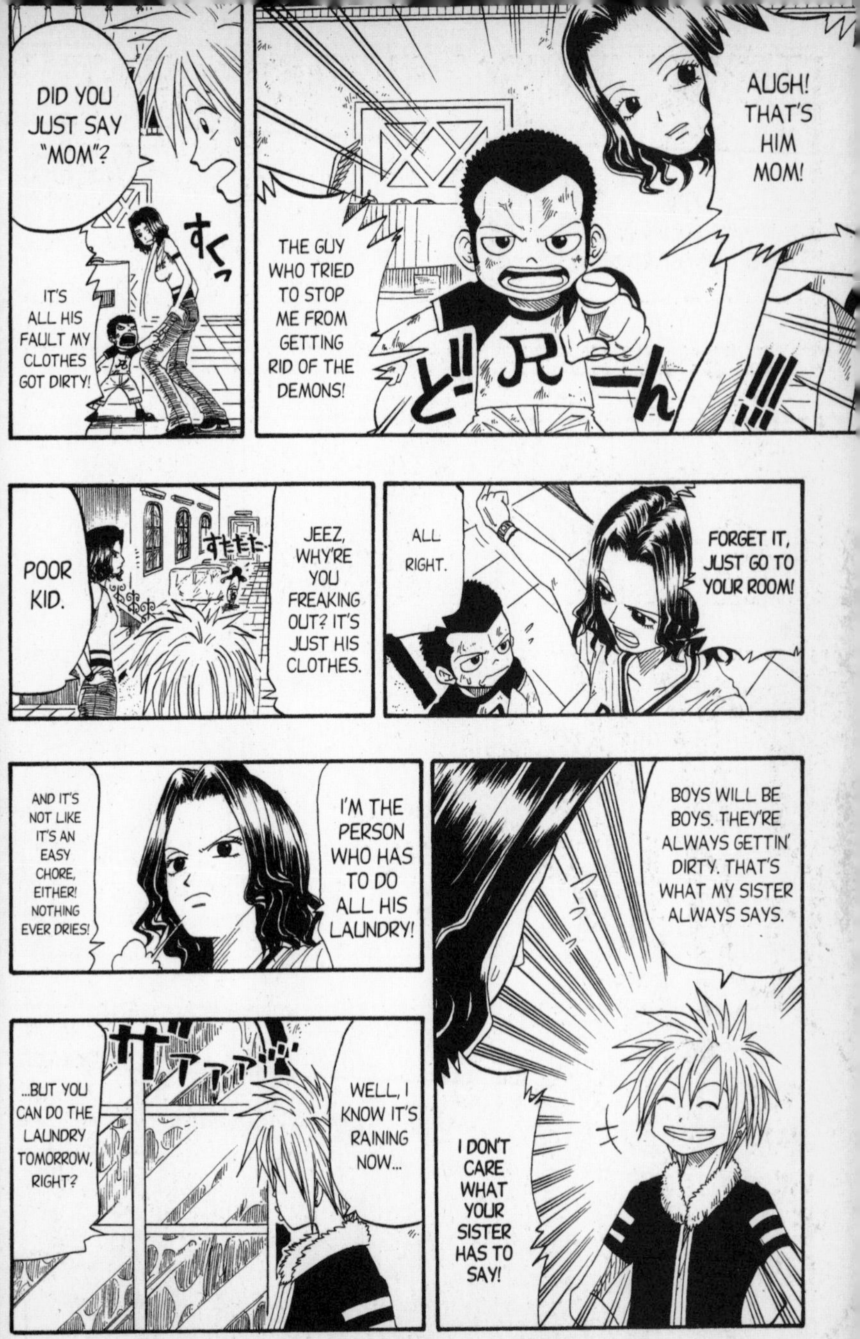
AUGH! THAT'S HIM MOM!
THE GUY WHO TRIED TO STOP ME FROM GETTING RID OF THE DEMONS!
どーん!!!
DID YOU JUST SAY "MOM"?
すくっ
IT'S ALL HIS FAULT MY CLOTHES GOT DIRTY!
FORGET IT, JUST GO TO YOUR ROOM!
ALL RIGHT.
JEEZ, WHY'RE YOU FREAKING OUT? IT'S JUST HIS CLOTHES.
すたたた
POOR KID.
BOYS WILL BE BOYS. THEY'RE ALWAYS GETTIN' DIRTY. THAT'S WHAT MY SISTER ALWAYS SAYS.
I DON'T CARE WHAT YOUR SISTER HAS TO SAY!
I'M THE PERSON WHO HAS TO DO ALL HIS LAUNDRY!
AND IT'S NOT LIKE IT'S AN EASY CHORE, EITHER! NOTHING EVER DRIES!
ザアアア
WELL, I KNOW IT'S RAINING NOW...
...BUT YOU CAN DO THE LAUNDRY TOMORROW, RIGHT?

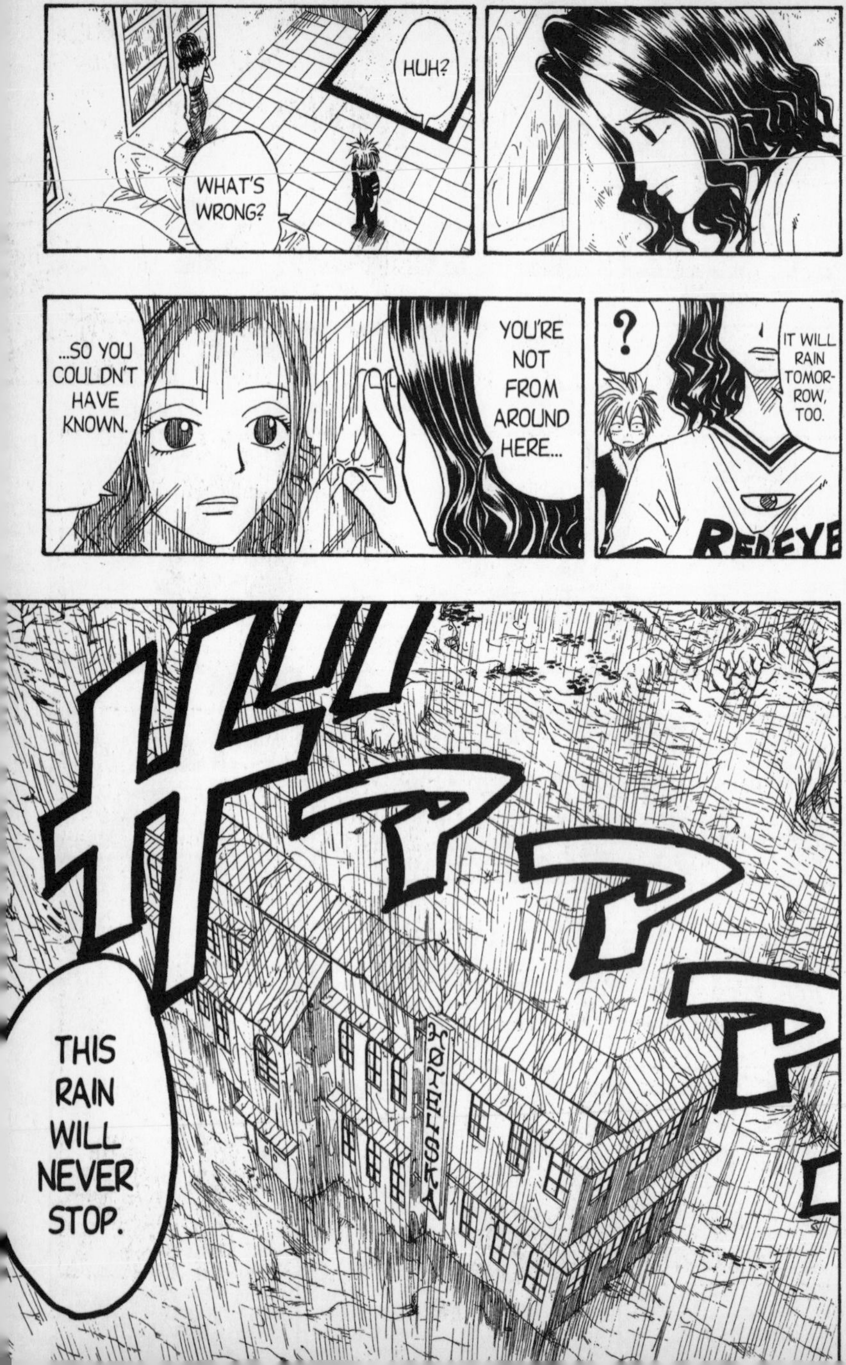
HUH?
WHAT'S WRONG?
IT WILL RAIN TOMORROW, TOO.
?
YOU'RE NOT FROM AROUND HERE...
...SO YOU COULDN'T HAVE KNOWN.
ザアアア
THIS RAIN WILL NEVER STOP.

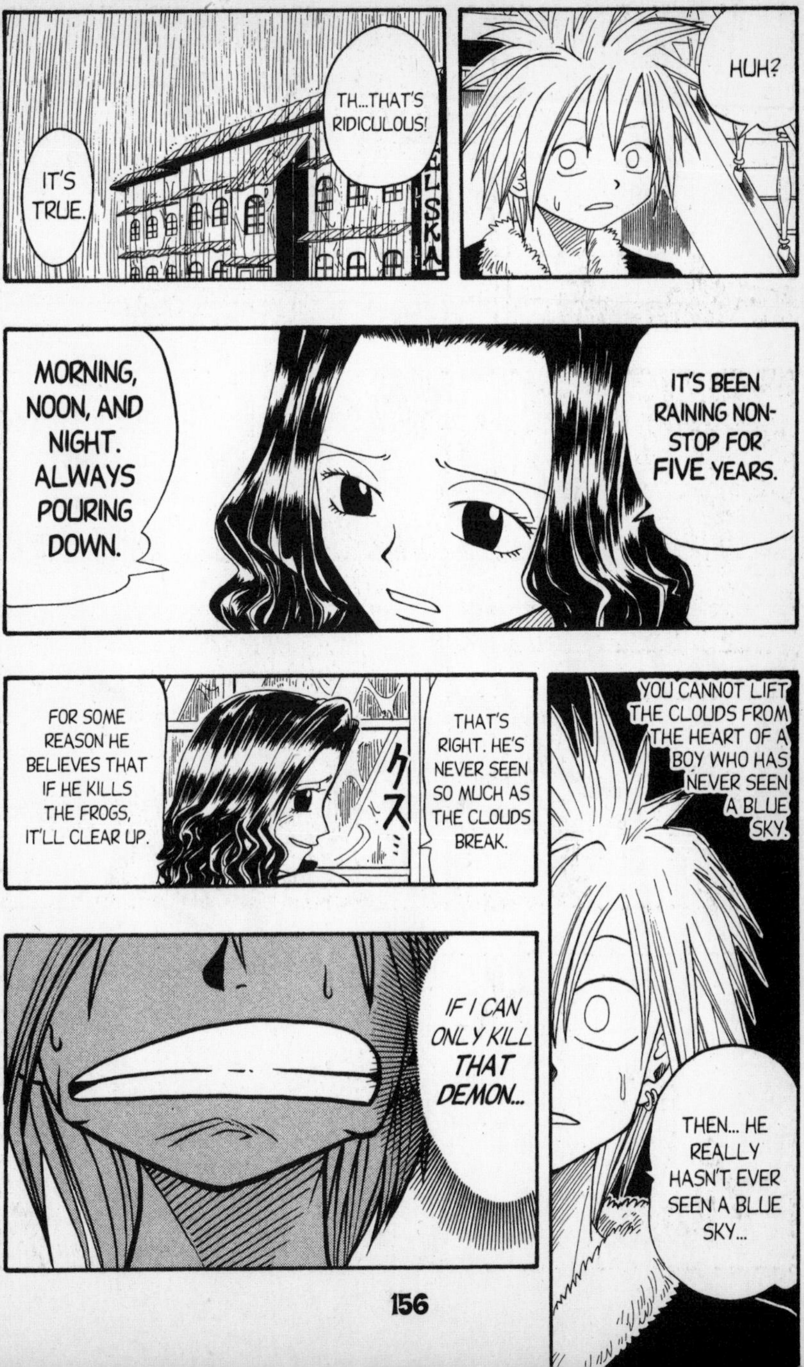
HUH?
TH...THAT'S RIDICULOUS!
IT'S TRUE.
IT'S BEEN RAINING NON-STOP FOR FIVE YEARS.
MORNING, NOON, AND NIGHT. ALWAYS POURING DOWN.
YOU CANNOT LIFT THE CLOUDS FROM THE HEART OF A BOY WHO HAS NEVER SEEN A BLUE SKY.
THEN... HE REALLY HASN'T EVER SEEN A BLUE SKY...
THAT'S RIGHT. HE'S NEVER SEEN SO MUCH AS THE CLOUDS BREAK.
クス
FOR SOME REASON HE BELIEVES THAT IF HE KILLS THE FROGS, IT'LL CLEAR UP.
IF I CAN ONLY KILL THAT DEMON...

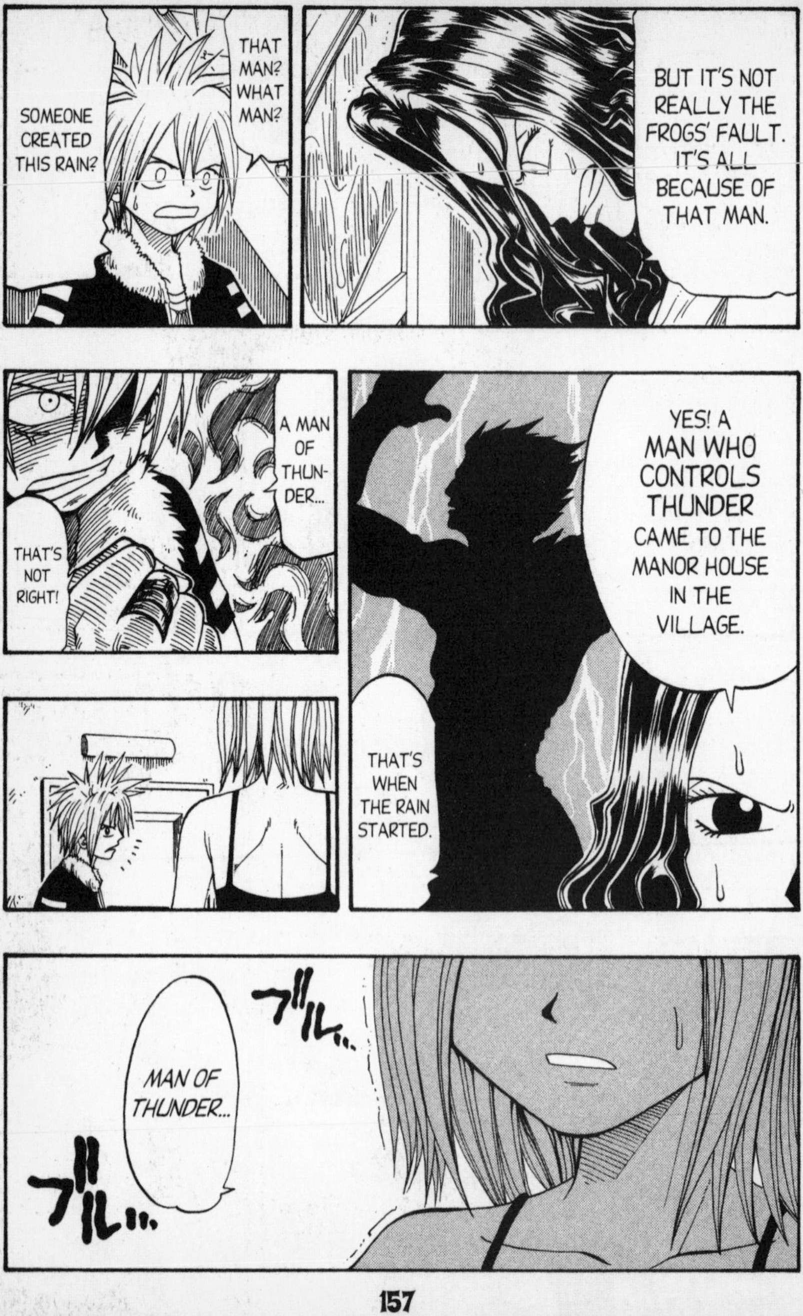
BUT IT'S NOT REALLY THE FROGS' FAULT. IT'S ALL BECAUSE OF THAT MAN.
THAT MAN? WHAT MAN?
SOMEONE CREATED THIS RAIN?
YES! A MAN WHO CONTROLS THUNDER CAME TO THE MANOR HOUSE IN THE VILLAGE.
THAT'S WHEN THE RAIN STARTED.
A MAN OF THUN-DER...
THAT'S NOT RIGHT!
ブル..
MAN OF THUNDER...
ブル..

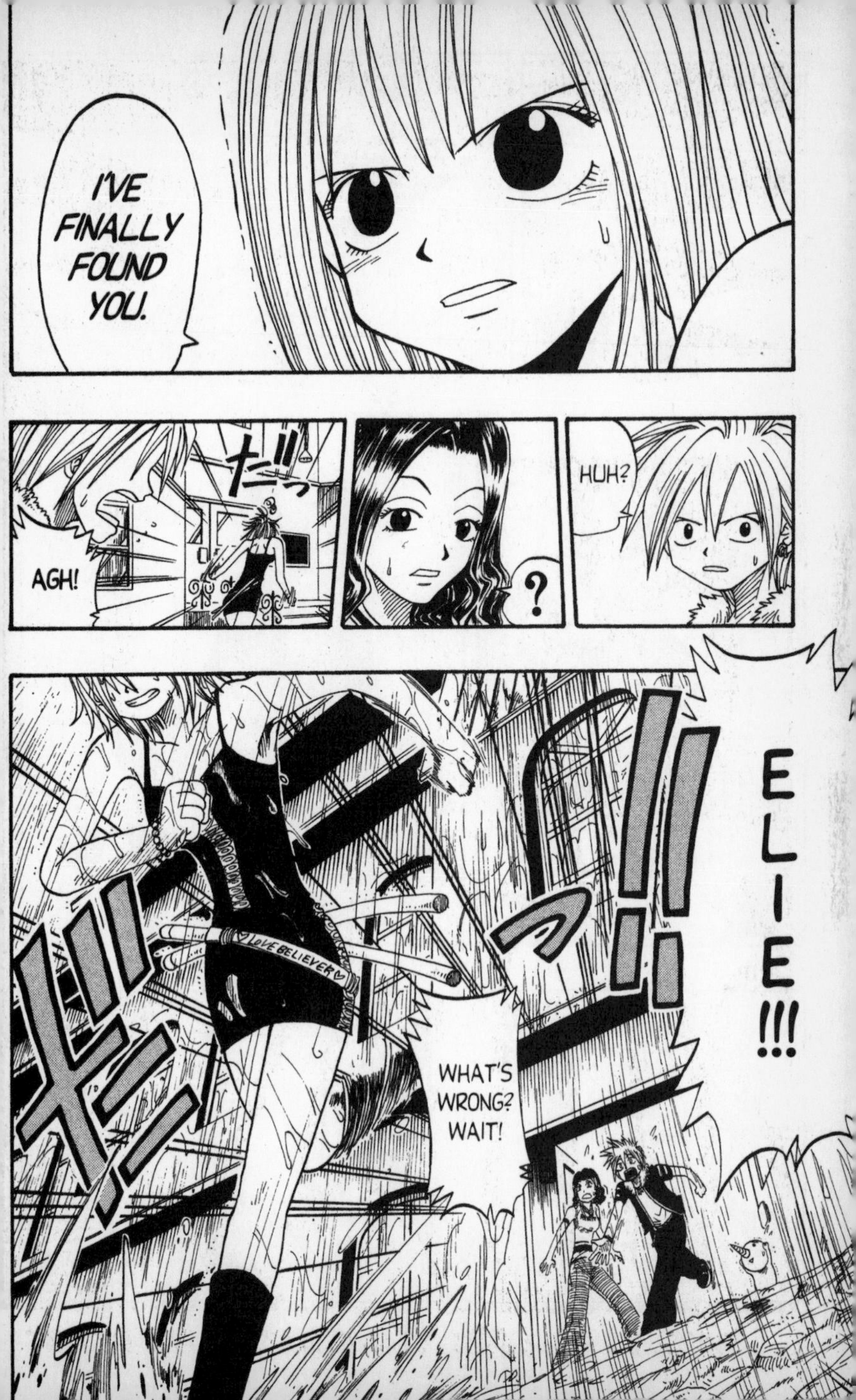
I'VE FINALLY FOUND YOU.
HUH?
?
AGH!
ELIE!!!
WHAT'S WRONG? WAIT!

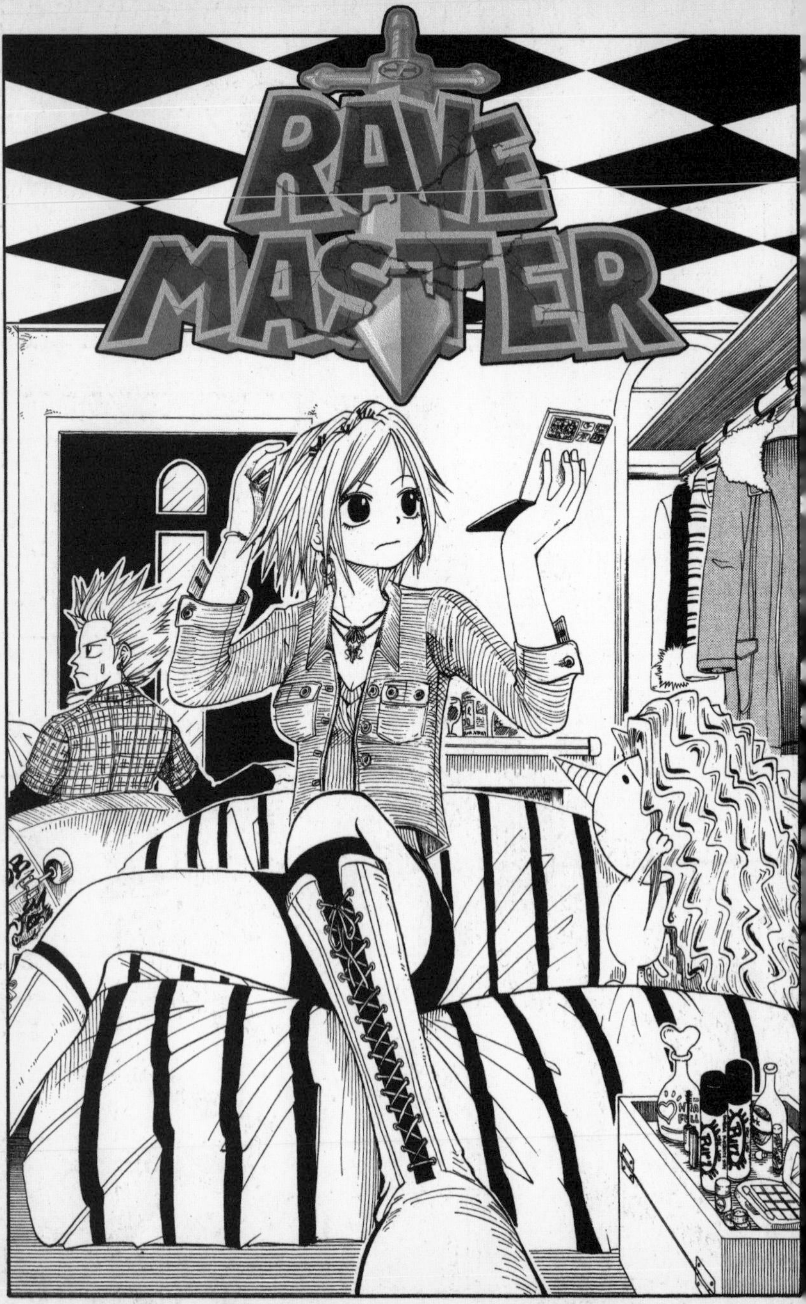
RAVE MASTER

RAVE 21 ✠ GRAY CLOUDS OVER MY HEART

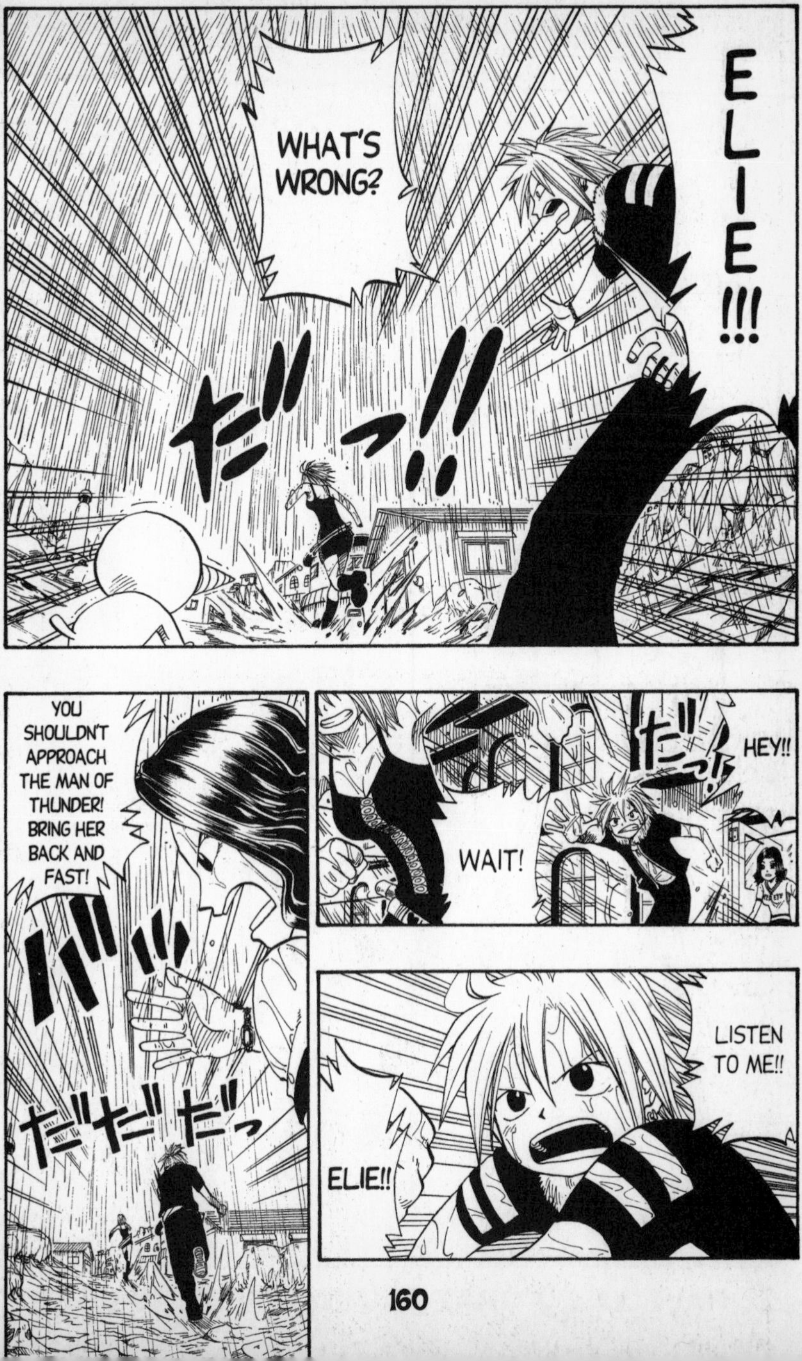
ELIE!!!
WHAT'S WRONG?
だっ!!
HEY!!
だっ!
WAIT!
LISTEN TO ME!!
ELIE!!
YOU SHOULDN'T APPROACH THE MAN OF THUNDER! BRING HER BACK AND FAST!
バッ
だだだっ

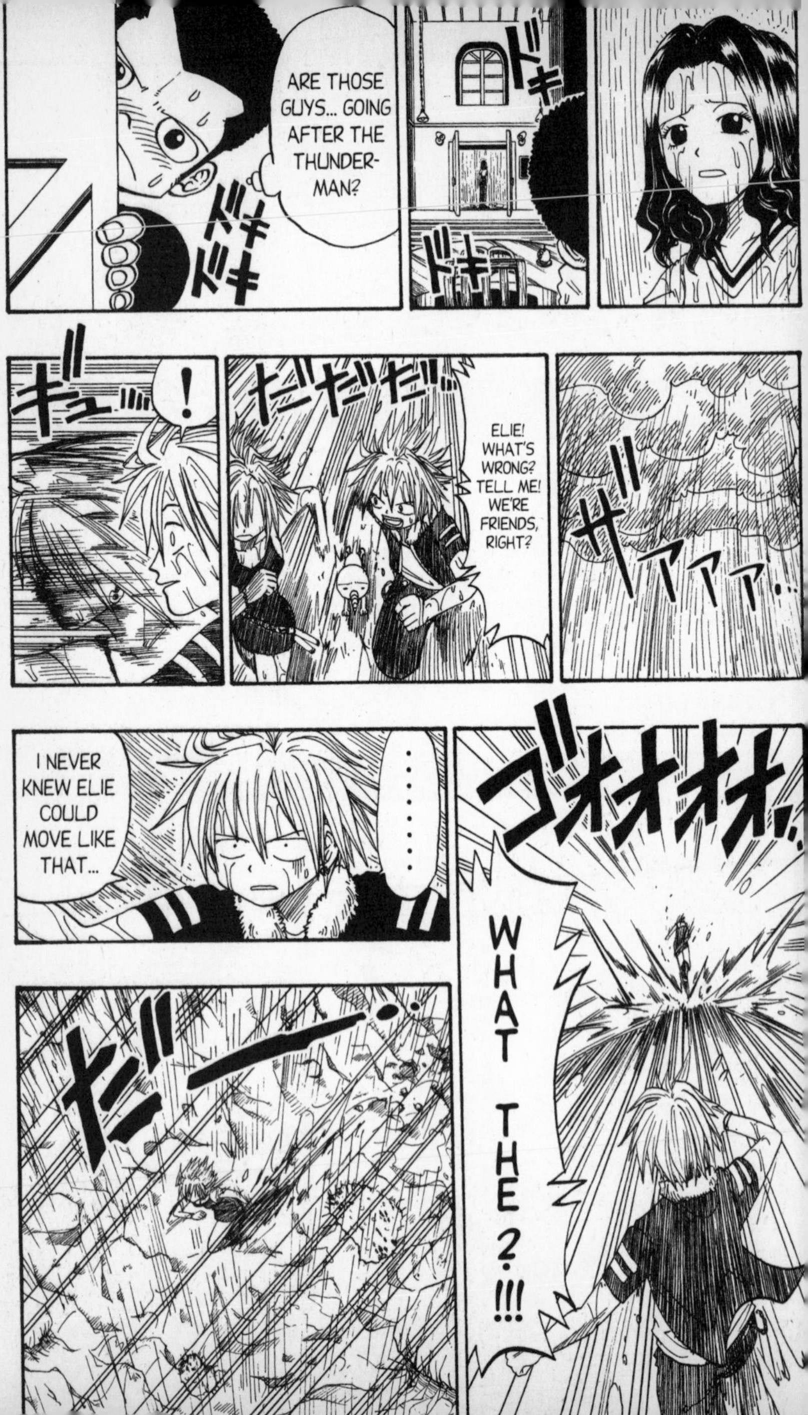
ドキ
ドキ
ARE THOSE GUYS... GOING AFTER THE THUNDER-MAN?
ドキドキ
ザァァァ…
だだだ
ELIE! WHAT'S WRONG? TELL ME! WE'RE FRIENDS, RIGHT?
ギュ
!
ゴオオオオ
WHAT THE ?!!!
......
I NEVER KNEW ELIE COULD MOVE LIKE THAT...
だーっ

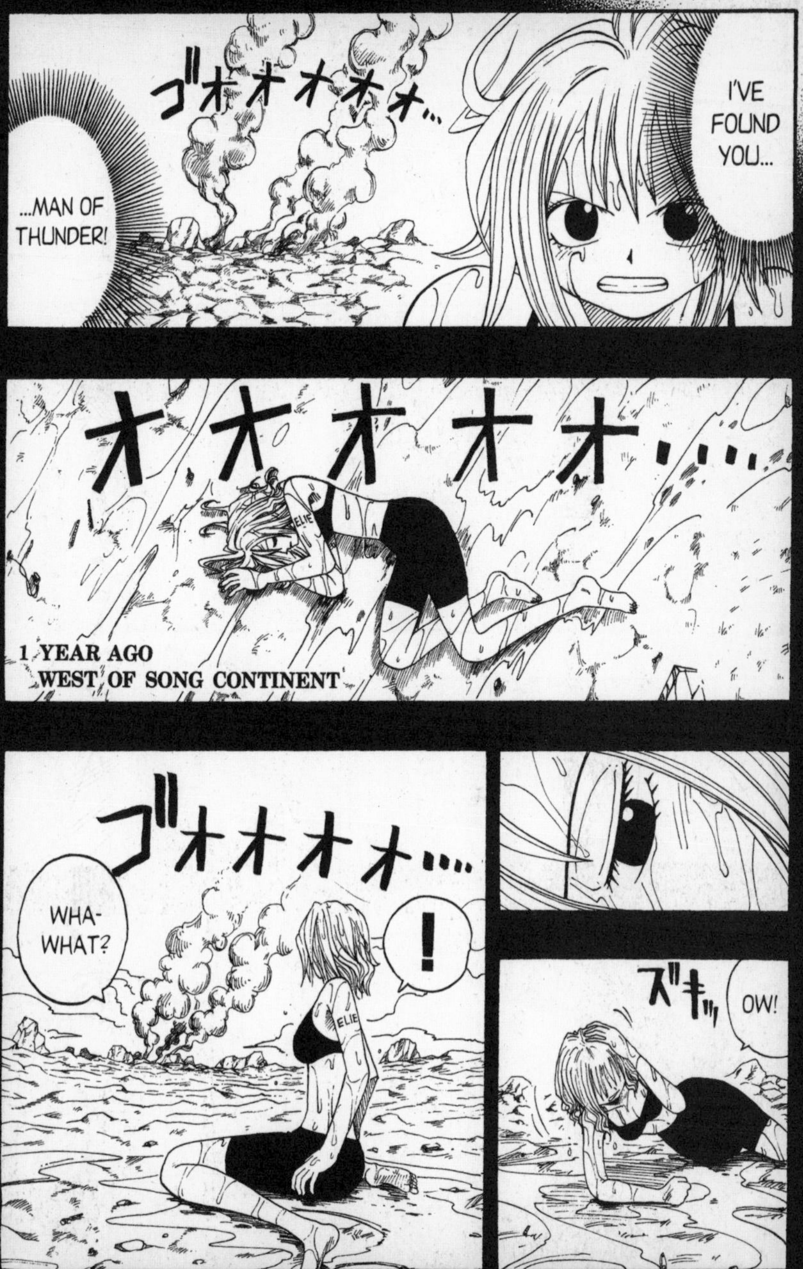
I'VE FOUND YOU...
ゴオオオオオ…
...MAN OF THUNDER!
オオオオオ…
1 YEAR AGO
WEST OF SONG CONTINENT
ズキッ
OW!
ゴオオオオ…
!
WHA-WHAT?

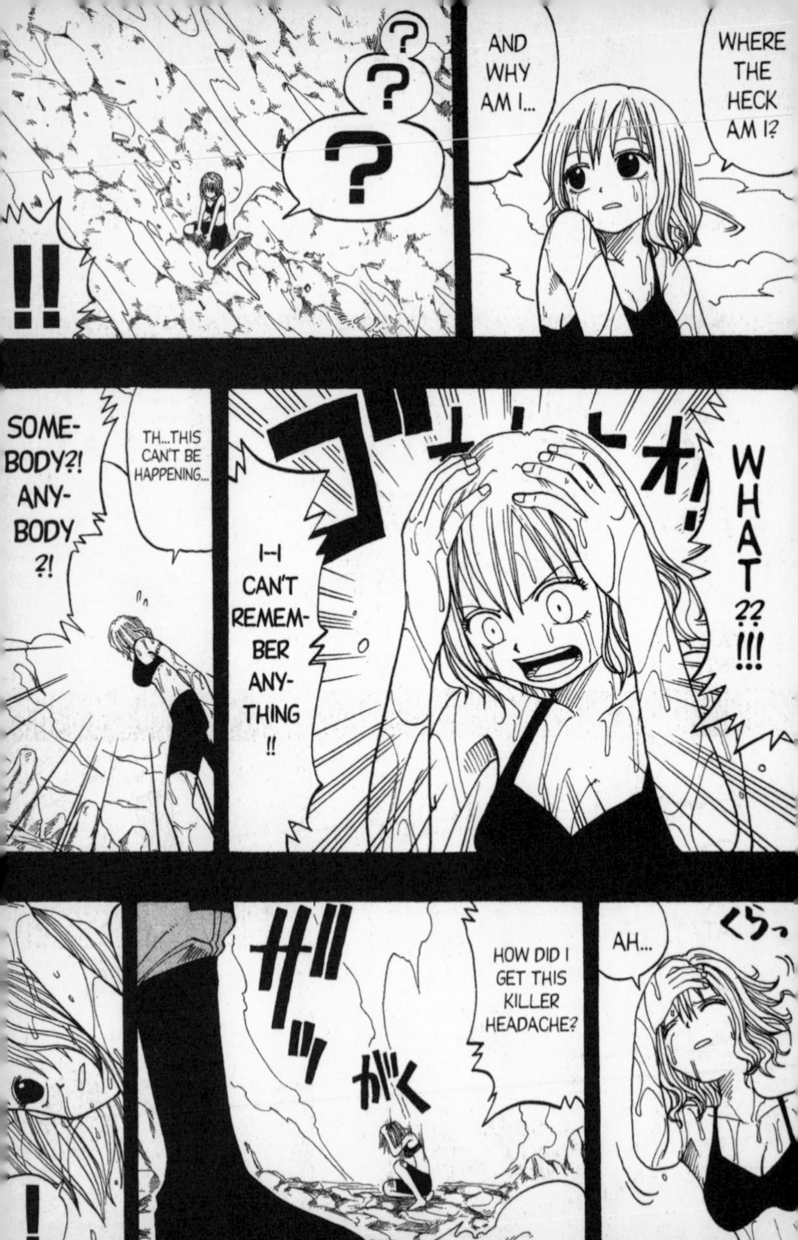
WHERE THE HECK AM I?
AND WHY AM I...
?
?
?
!!
WHAT ?? !!!
I-I CAN'T REMEMBER ANYTHING !!
TH...THIS CAN'T BE HAPPENING...
SOME-BODY?! ANY-BODY ?!
くらっ
AH...
HOW DID I GET THIS KILLER HEADACHE?
ザッ
がく
!

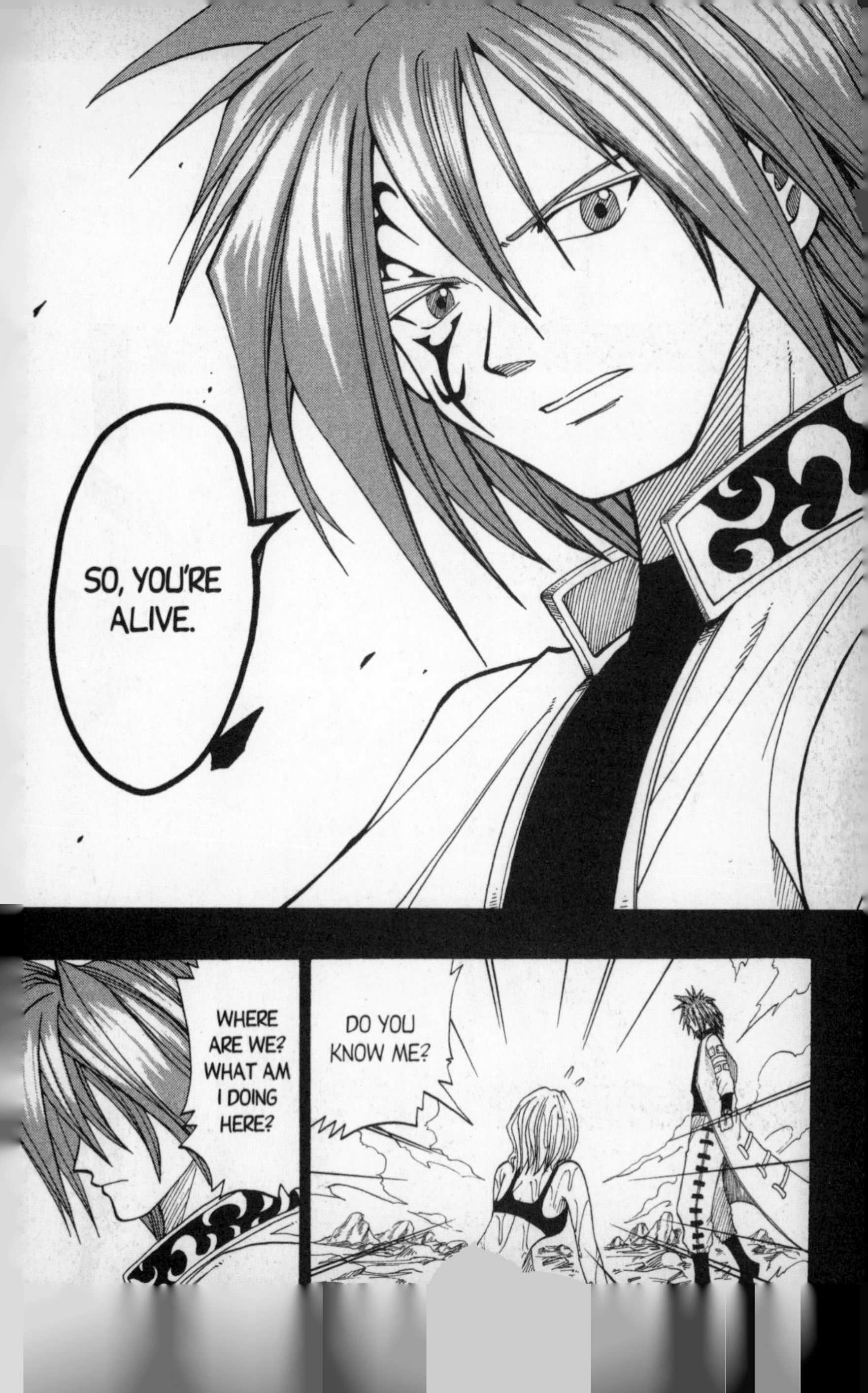
SO, YOU'RE ALIVE.
DO YOU KNOW ME?
WHERE ARE WE? WHAT AM I DOING HERE?

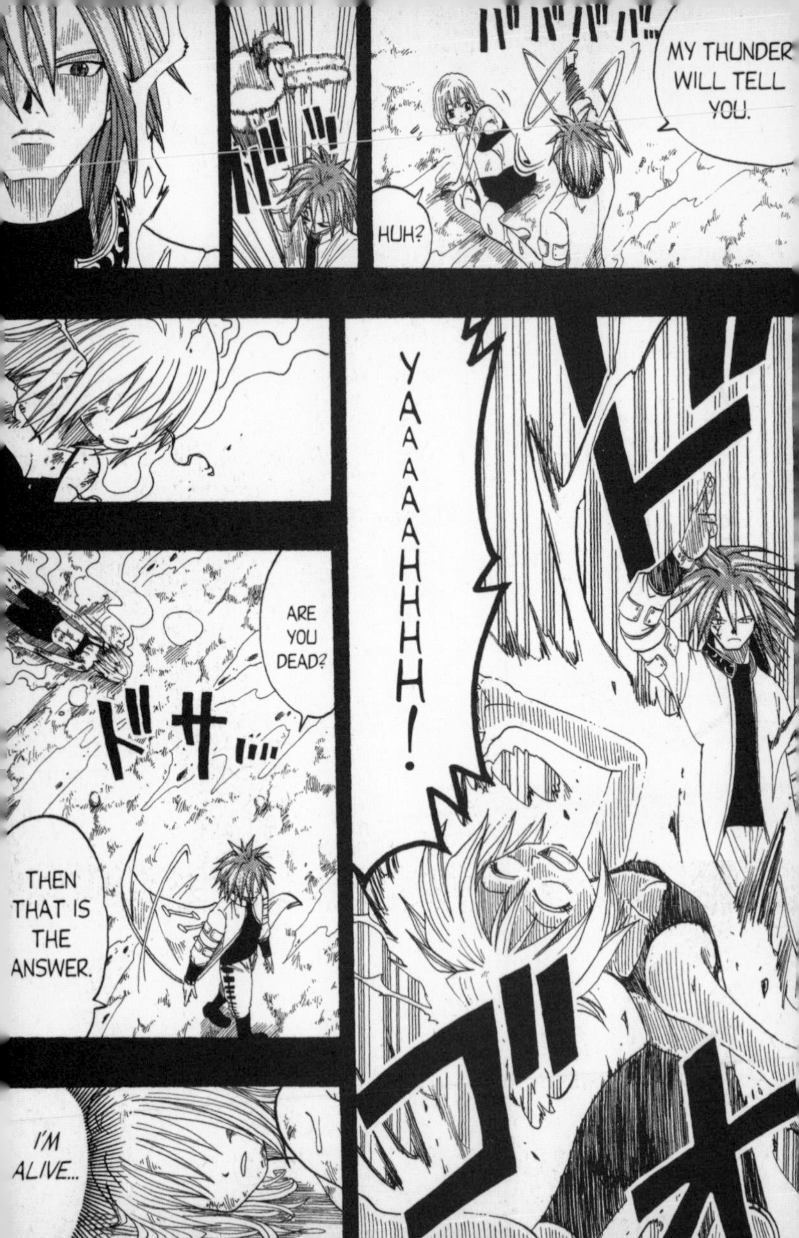
MY THUNDER WILL TELL YOU.
HUH?
YAAAAAAHHHHH!
ARE YOU DEAD?
THEN THAT IS THE ANSWER.
I'M ALIVE...

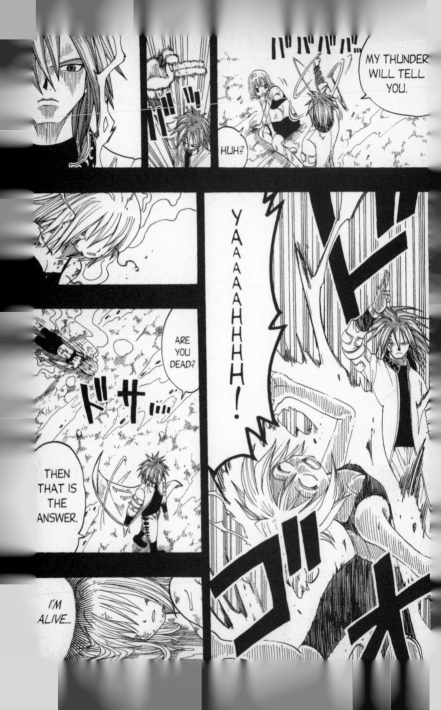

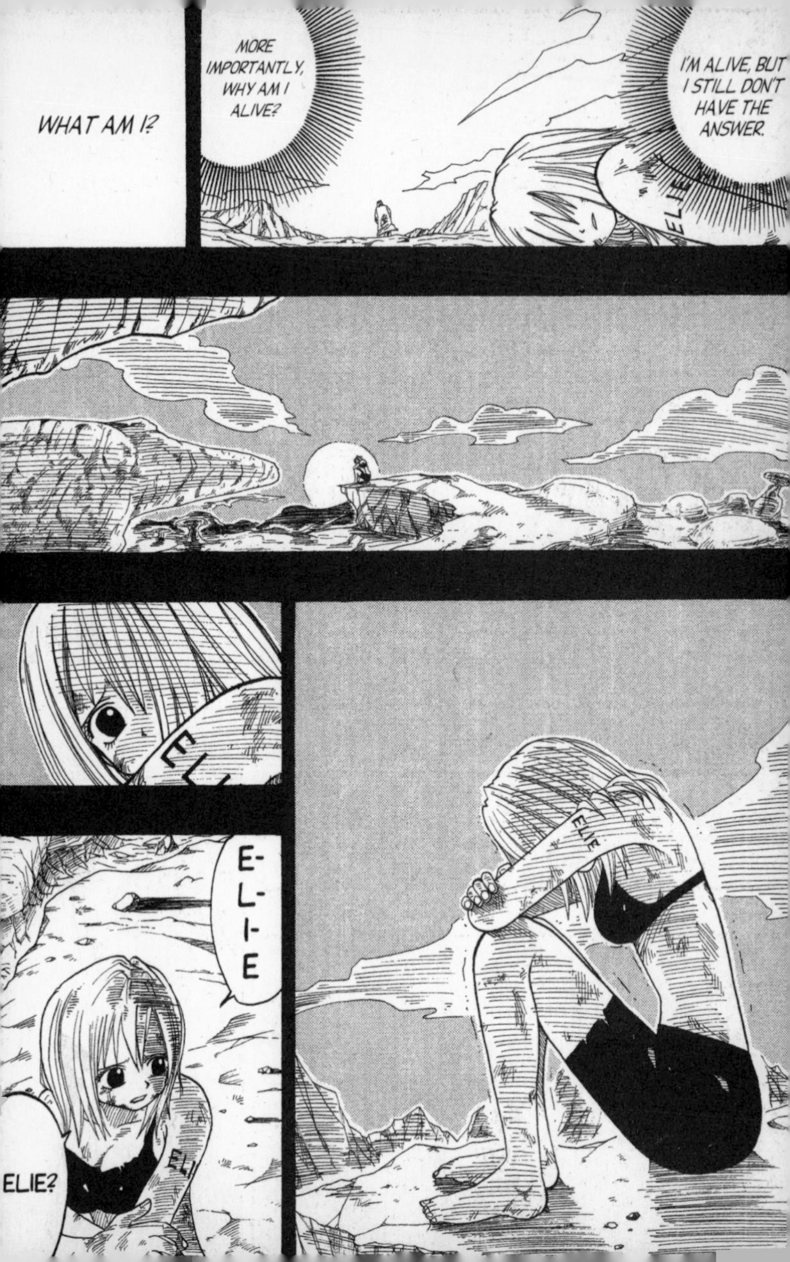
I'M ALIVE, BUT I STILL DON'T HAVE THE ANSWER.
MORE IMPORTANTLY, WHY AM I ALIVE?
WHAT AM I?
E-L-I-E
ELIE?

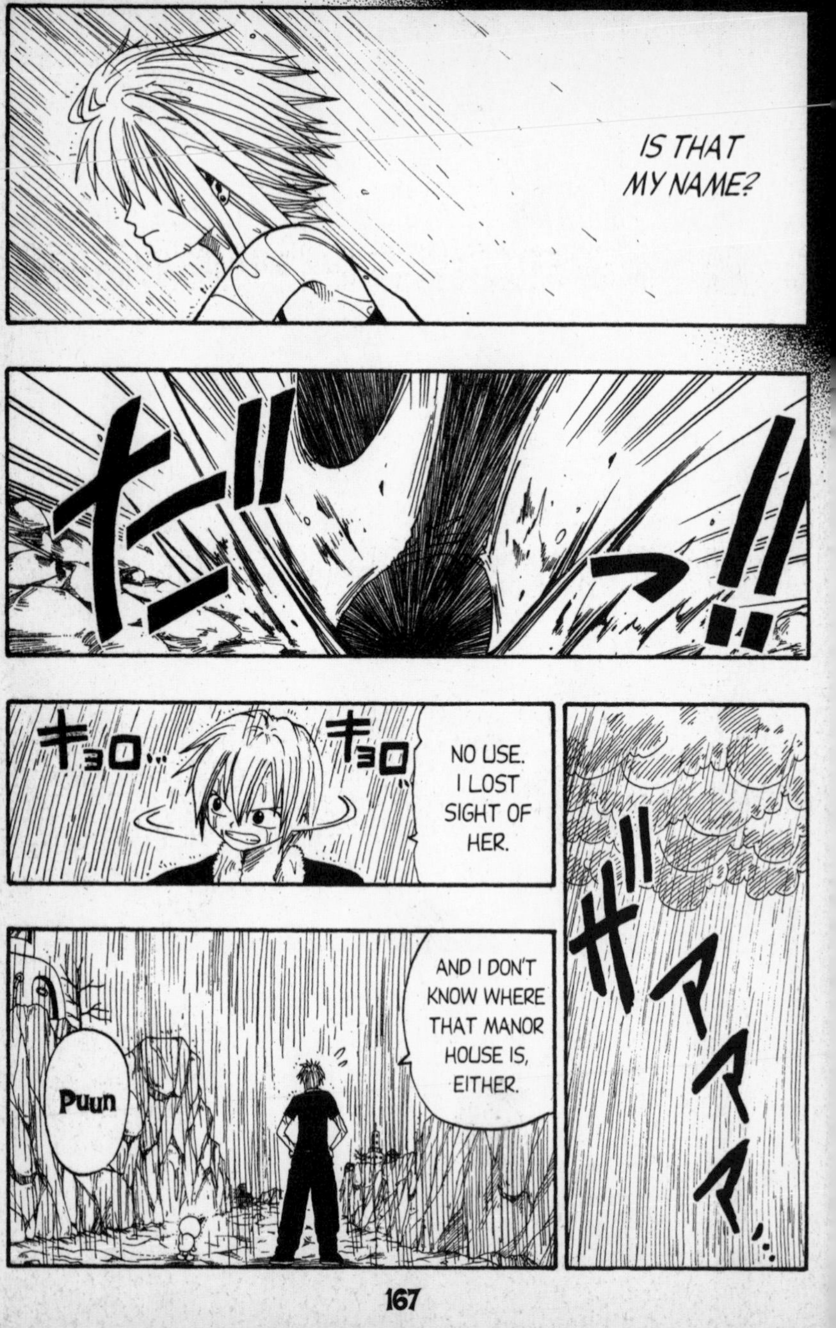
IS THAT MY NAME?
ザァァァ
NO USE. I LOST SIGHT OF HER.
キョロ
キョロ…
AND I DON'T KNOW WHERE THAT MANOR HOUSE IS, EITHER.
Puun

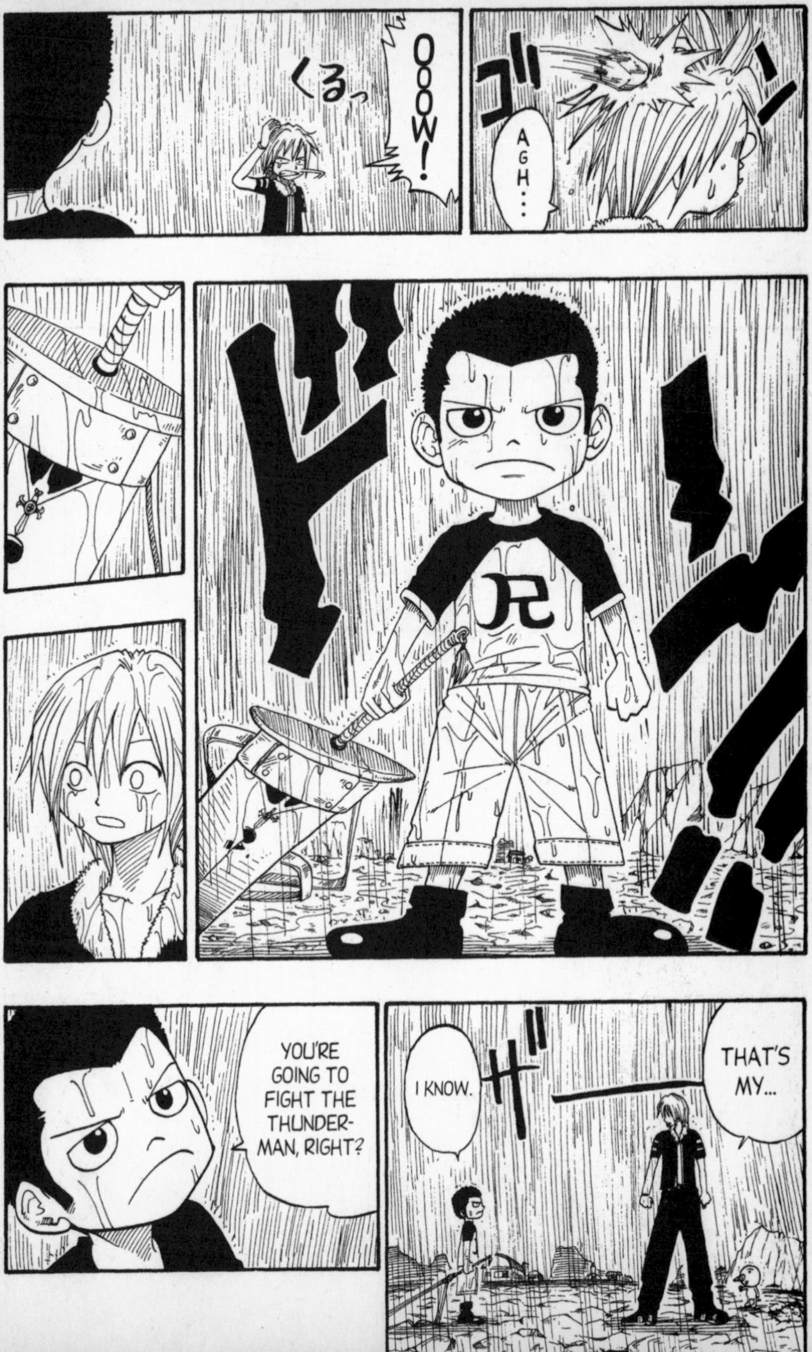
ゴ
AGH...
OOOW!
くるっ
THAT'S MY...
ザ
I KNOW.
YOU'RE GOING TO FIGHT THE THUNDER-MAN, RIGHT?

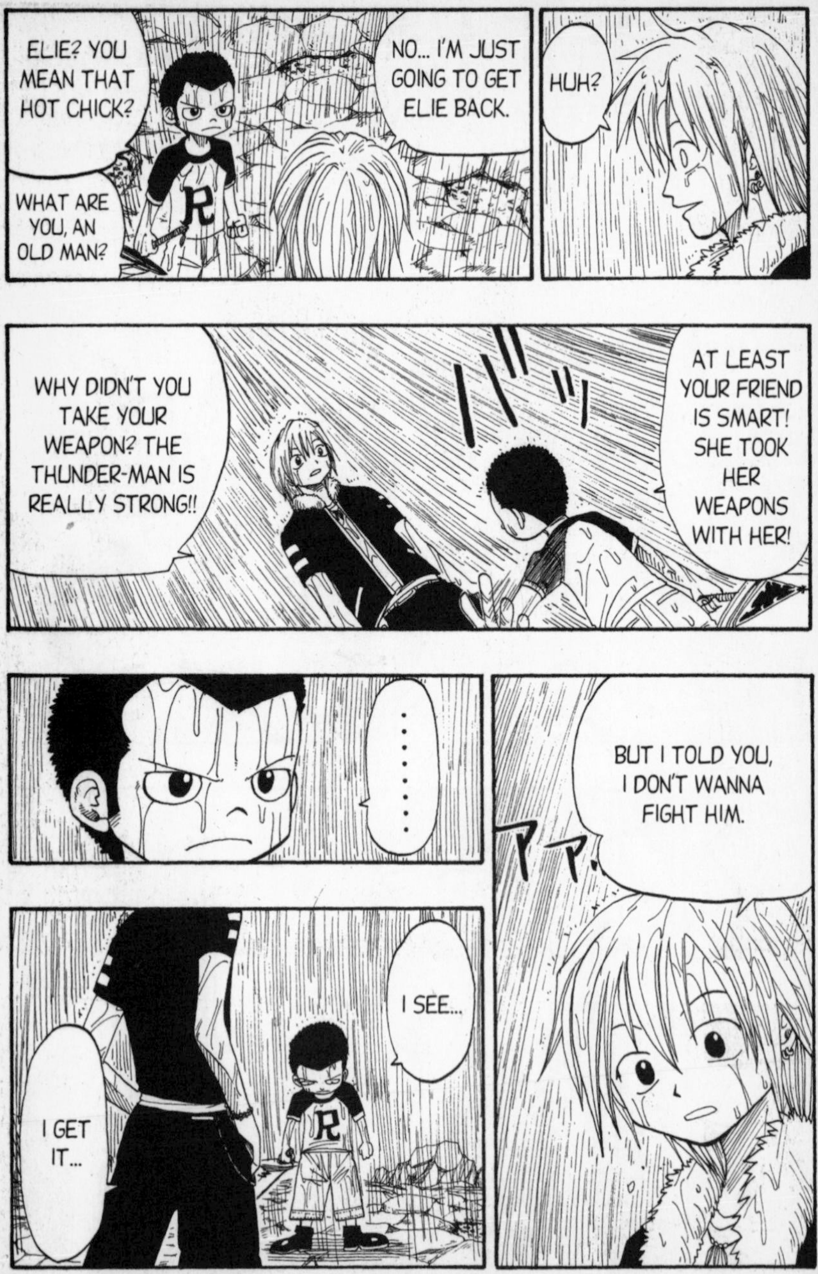
HUH?
NO... I'M JUST GOING TO GET ELIE BACK.
ELIE? YOU MEAN THAT HOT CHICK?
WHAT ARE YOU, AN OLD MAN?
AT LEAST YOUR FRIEND IS SMART! SHE TOOK HER WEAPONS WITH HER!
WHY DIDN'T YOU TAKE YOUR WEAPON? THE THUNDER-MAN IS REALLY STRONG!!
BUT I TOLD YOU, I DON'T WANNA FIGHT HIM.
....
I SEE...
I GET IT...

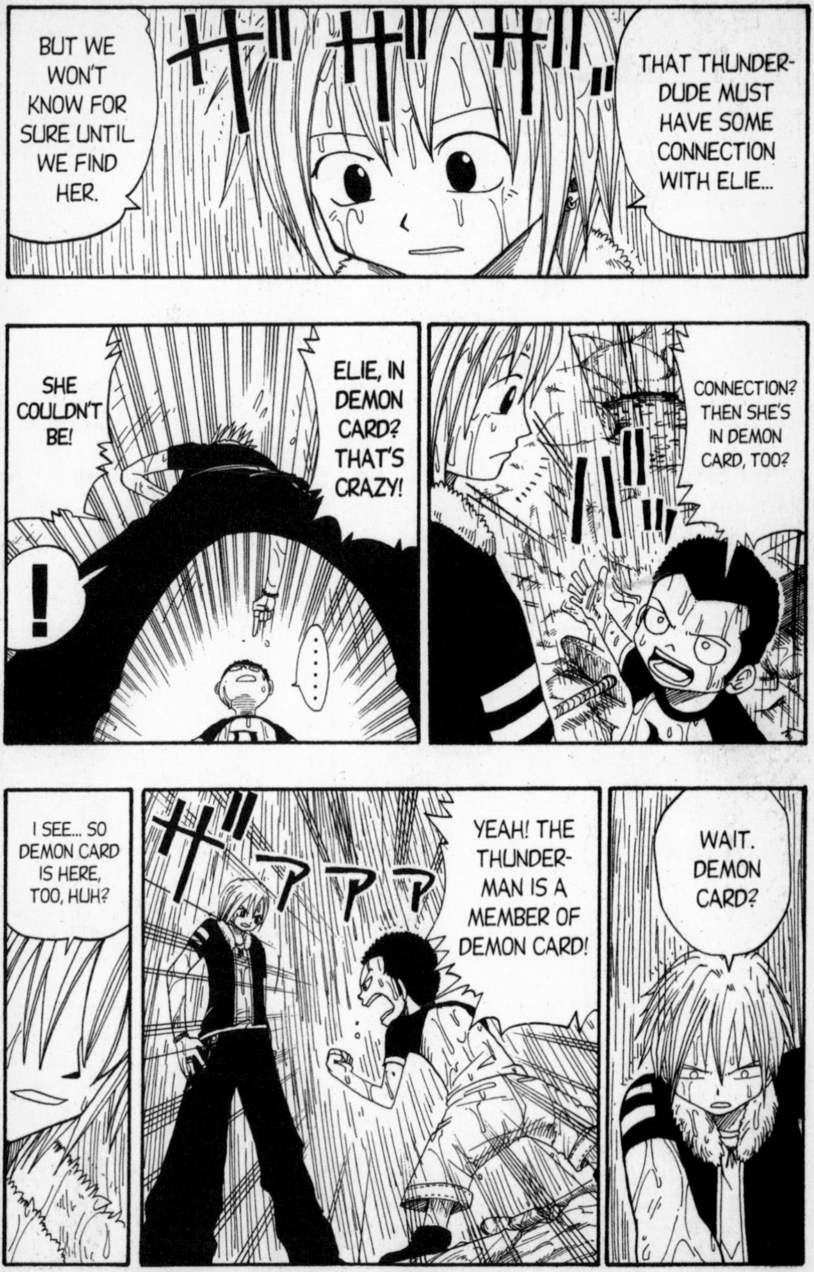
THAT THUNDER-DUDE MUST HAVE SOME CONNECTION WITH ELIE...
BUT WE WON'T KNOW FOR SURE UNTIL WE FIND HER.
CONNECTION? THEN SHE'S IN DEMON CARD, TOO?
ELIE, IN DEMON CARD? THAT'S CRAZY!
SHE COULDN'T BE!
!
.....
WAIT. DEMON CARD?
YEAH! THE THUNDER-MAN IS A MEMBER OF DEMON CARD!
I SEE... SO DEMON CARD IS HERE, TOO, HUH?

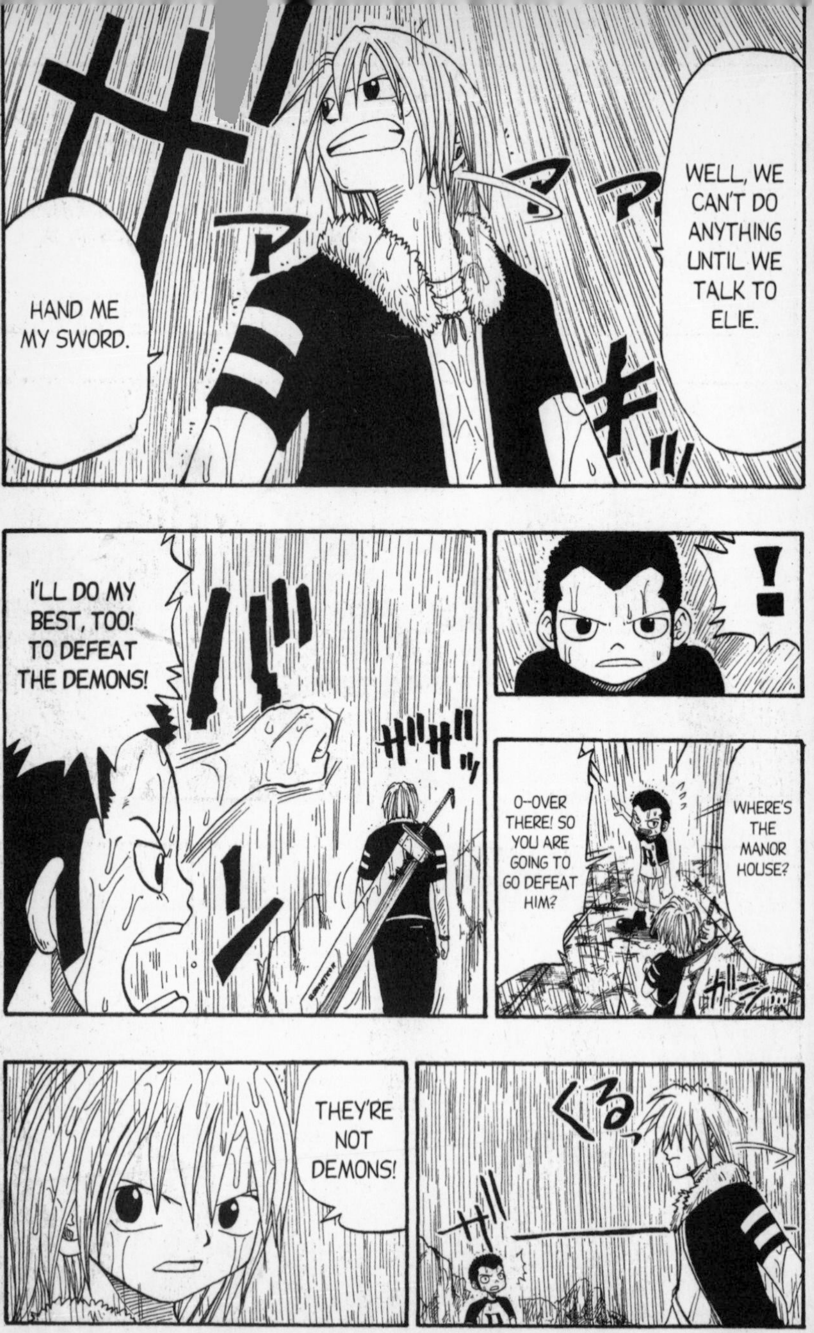
WELL, WE CAN'T DO ANYTHING UNTIL WE TALK TO ELIE.
HAND ME MY SWORD.
!
WHERE'S THE MANOR HOUSE?
O--OVER THERE! SO YOU ARE GOING TO GO DEFEAT HIM?
I'LL DO MY BEST, TOO! TO DEFEAT THE DEMONS!
くる
THEY'RE NOT DEMONS!

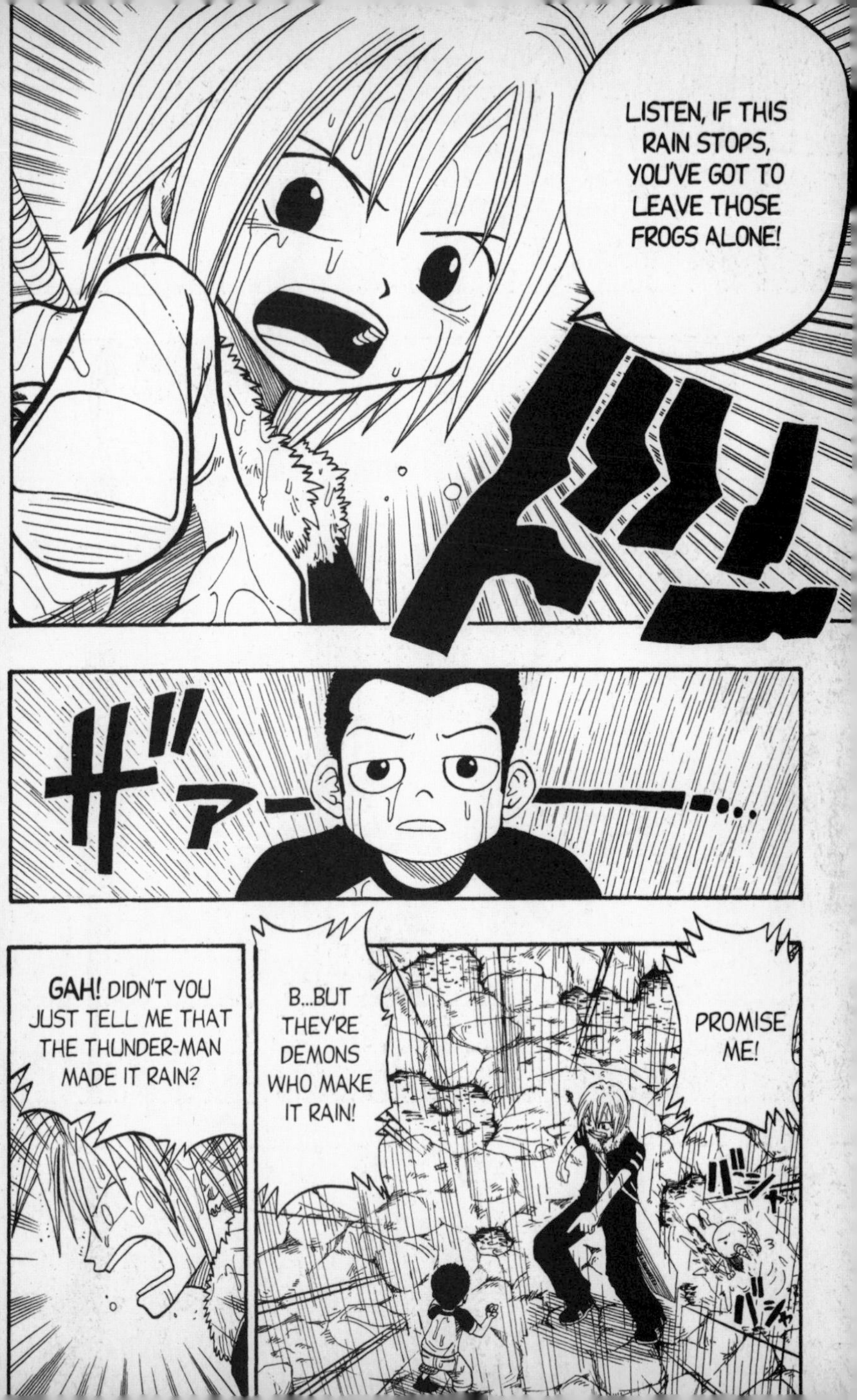
LISTEN, IF THIS RAIN STOPS, YOU'VE GOT TO LEAVE THOSE FROGS ALONE!
ザァーーー…
PROMISE ME!
B...BUT THEY'RE DEMONS WHO MAKE IT RAIN!
GAH! DIDN'T YOU JUST TELL ME THAT THE THUNDER-MAN MADE IT RAIN?

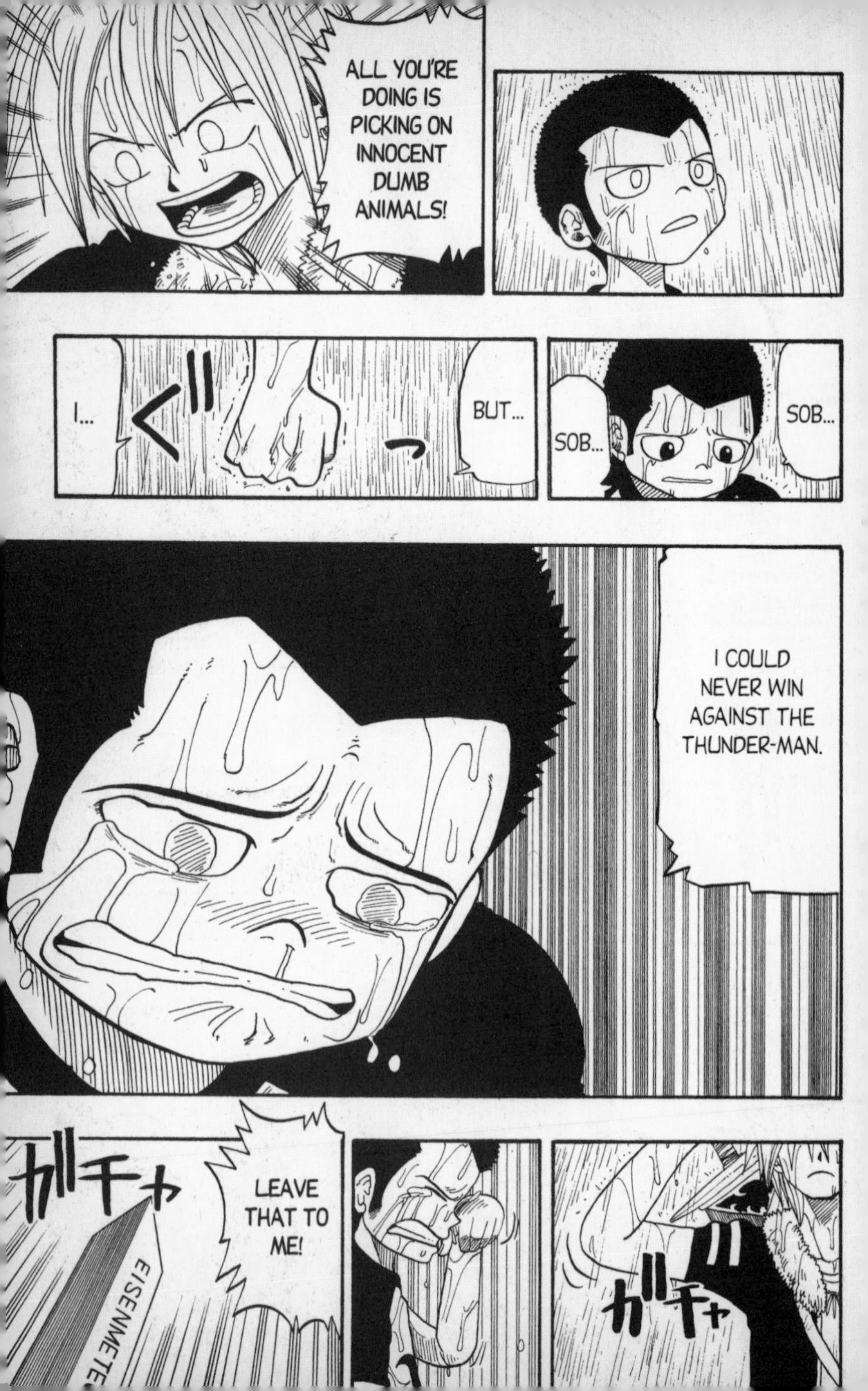
ALL YOU'RE DOING IS PICKING ON INNOCENT DUMB ANIMALS!
SOB...
SOB...
BUT...
ぐっ
I...
I COULD NEVER WIN AGAINST THE THUNDER-MAN.
ガチャ
LEAVE THAT TO ME!
ガチャ
EISENMETE

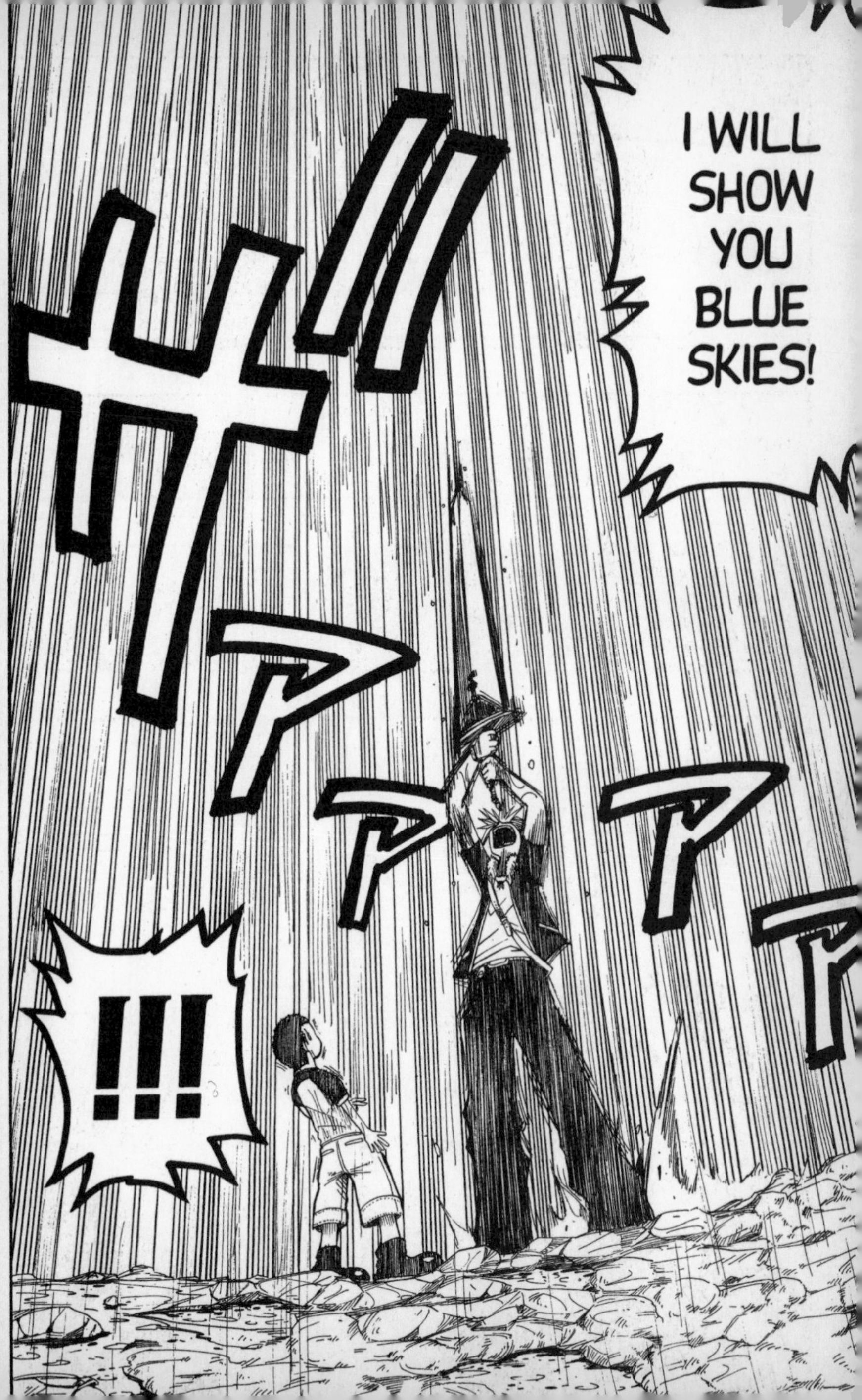
I WILL SHOW YOU BLUE SKIES!
!!!

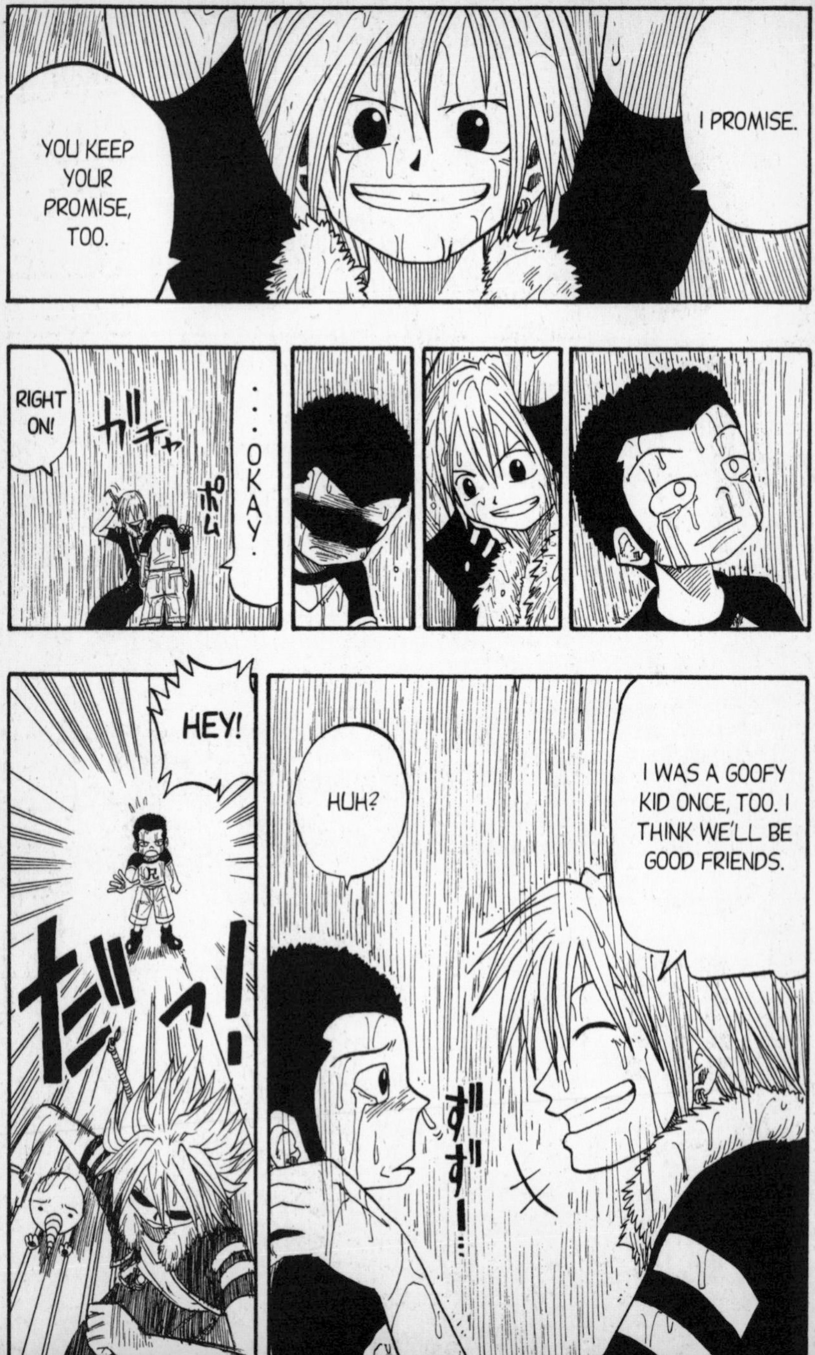
I PROMISE.
YOU KEEP YOUR PROMISE, TOO.
...OKAY.
RIGHT ON!
ガチャ
ポム
I WAS A GOOFY KID ONCE, TOO. I THINK WE'LL BE GOOD FRIENDS.
HUH?
ずずー
HEY!
だっ!

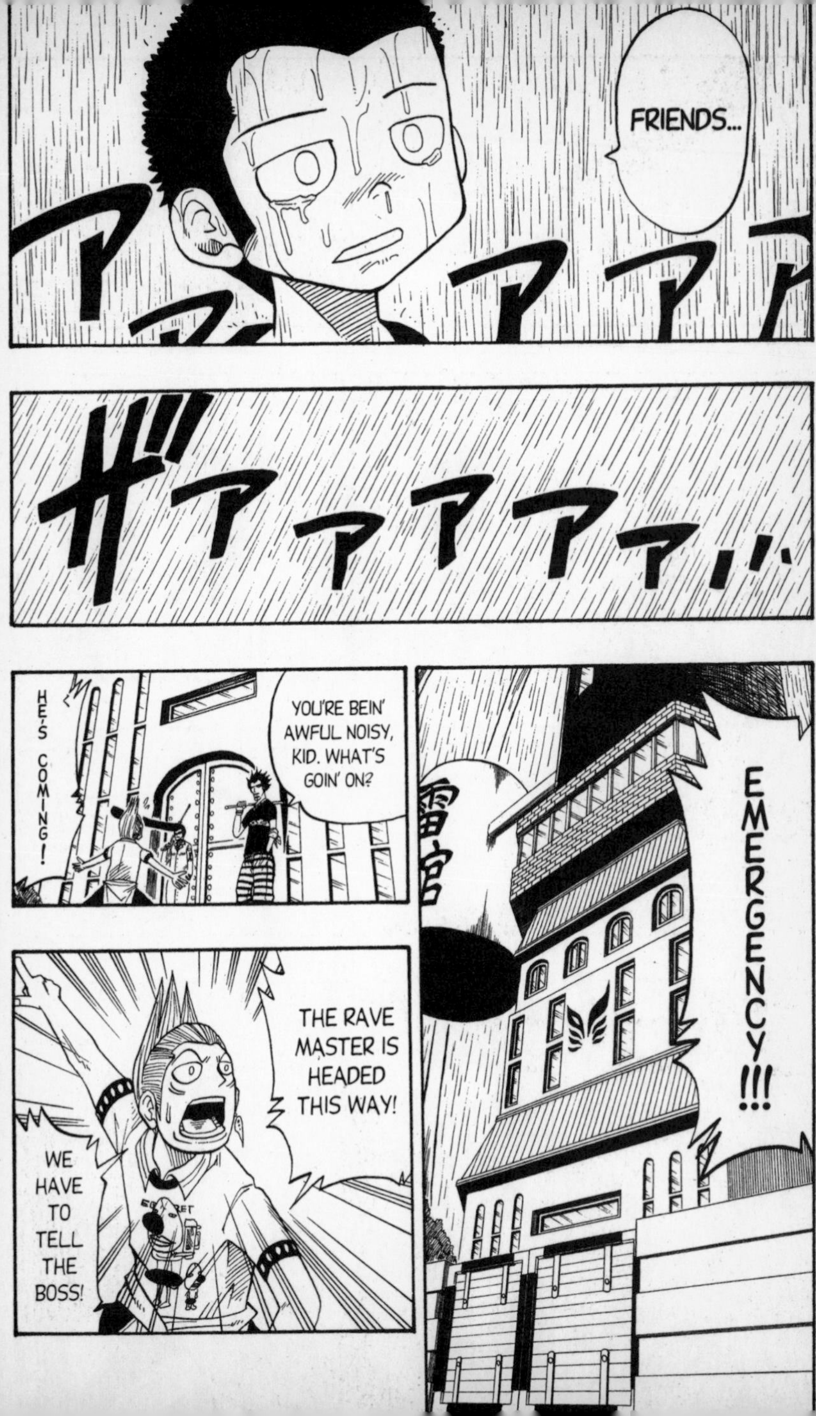
FRIENDS...
ザアアアアァ
EMERGENCY!!!
YOU'RE BEIN' AWFUL NOISY, KID. WHAT'S GOIN' ON?
HE'S COMING!
THE RAVE MASTER IS HEADED THIS WAY!
WE HAVE TO TELL THE BOSS!

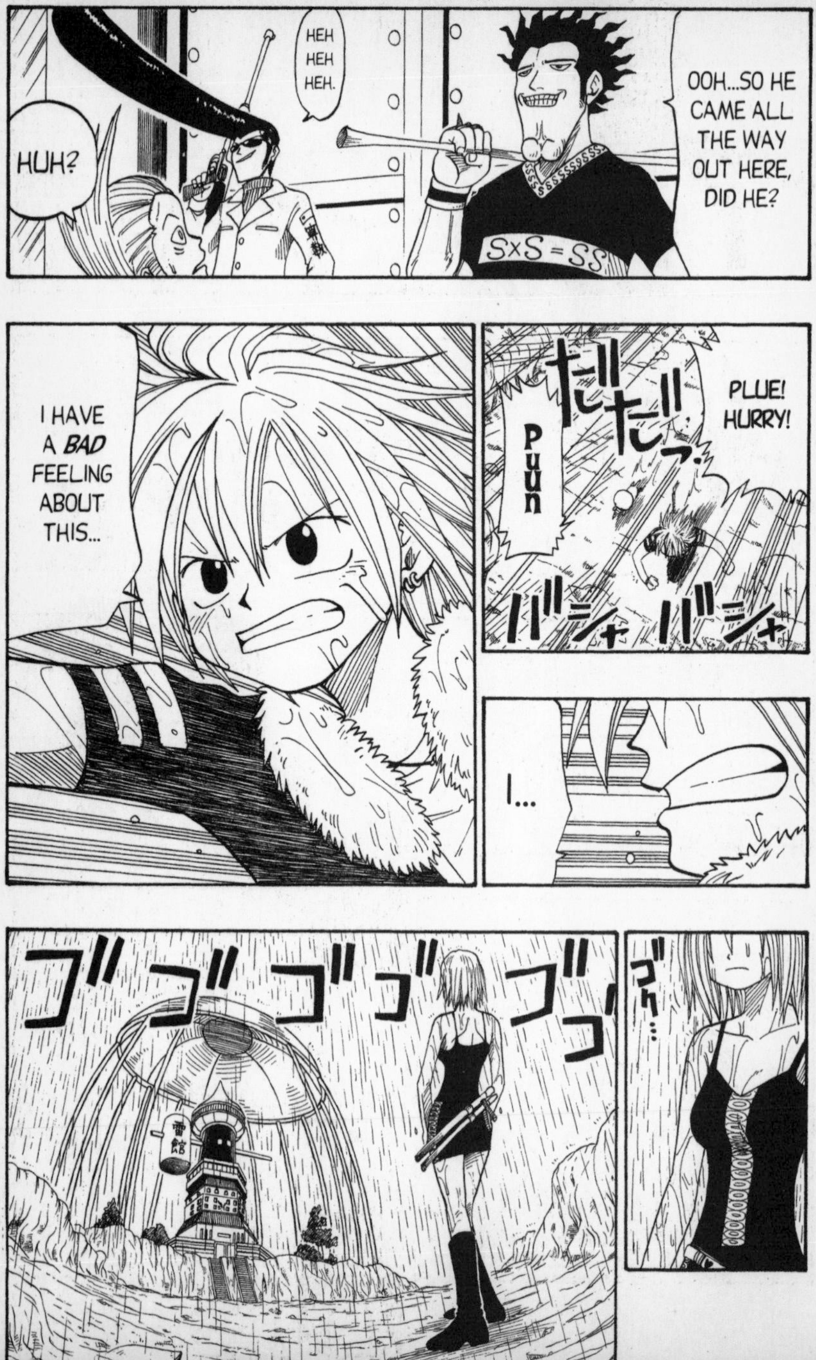
OOH...SO HE CAME ALL THE WAY OUT HERE, DID HE?
HEH HEH HEH.
HUH?
PLUE! HURRY!
だだっ
Puun
バシャ バシャ
I...
I HAVE A *BAD* FEELING ABOUT THIS...
ゴク…
ゴゴゴゴ

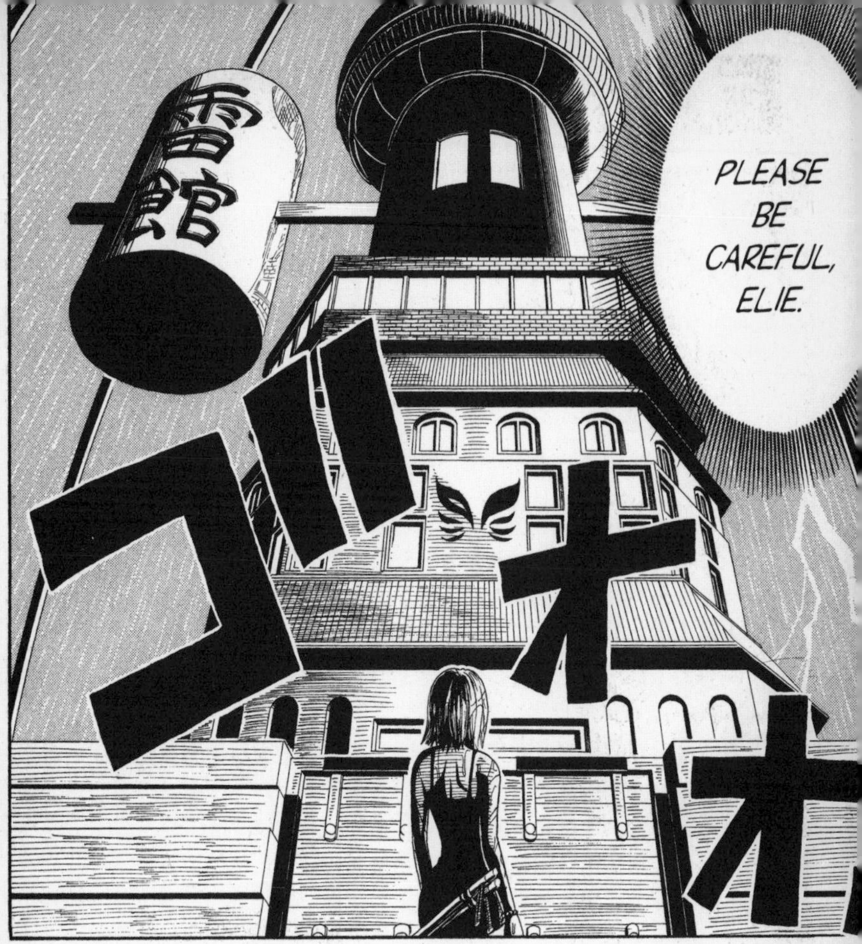
雷館
ゴオオ
PLEASE BE CAREFUL, ELIE.

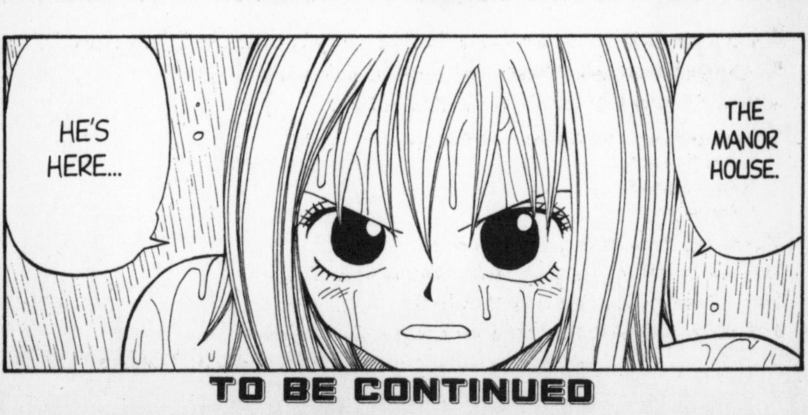
THE MANOR HOUSE.
HE'S HERE...

TO BE CONTINUED

EXTRA COMIC

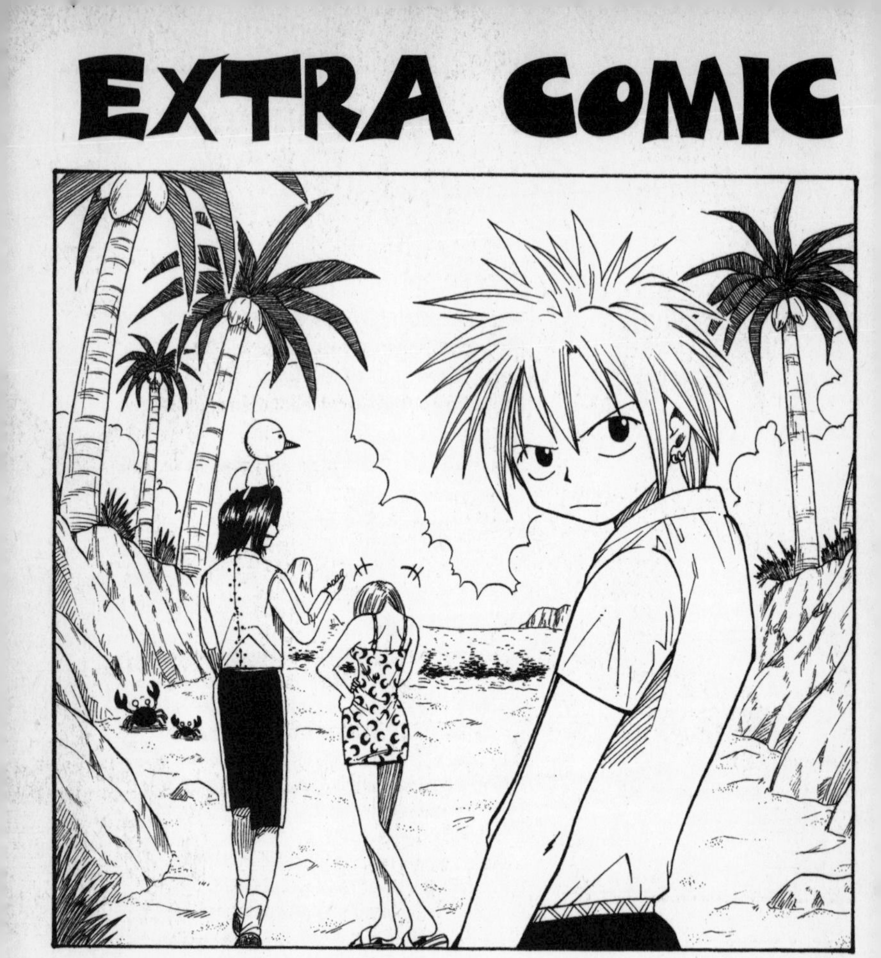

Did you know there is a hidden 4-panel story in Chapter 6 (in Volume 2)?

Some people have already noticed it and wrote to me about it, but now I'll explain it for the people who didn't notice it.

1. On page 37, panel 1. See those two guys fighting just above Elie's head?
2. Page 39, panel 2.
3. Page 40, panel 3.
4. Page 40, panel 5.

(By the way, those two guys are my bosses!)
I like putting fun little things like that in Rave once in a while.
I hope you enjoy them. I had fun putting them in.
Well, Volume 3 is almost over. Bear with me for just 8 more pages!

–Hiro Mashima

Head of Silverythm Gang: Silverclaimer Musica

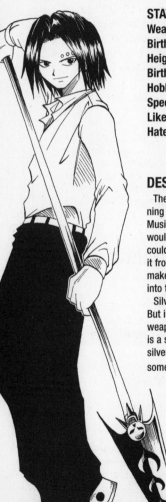

STATS

Weapon: Silver (Stronger than normal silver, though!)

Birthday / Age: July 20, 0048 / 18

Height / Weight / Blood Type: 174 cm / 61 kg / 0

Birthplace: Punk Street (but raised in Blues City)

Hobbies: Making silver accessories

Special Skills: Mackin' on the ladies, petty theft

Likes: Girls, arcades

Hates: Men who pick on girls

DESCRIPTION

There's two Musicas now! During the planning stages, I wondered, "How about making Musica a blacksmith?" But of course then he would have to be an older man. Or perhaps I could make him a female? But after looking at it from a few different angles, I just decided to make it easier on myself and put two Musicas into the story.

Silverclaimers are a step above alchemists. But in real life, silver can't be used as a weapon. So the silver that silverclaimers use is a special silver that is stronger than normal silver. So a strong silverclaimer can make some very special things out of silver.

Cart-driver: Griffon Kato (Griff)

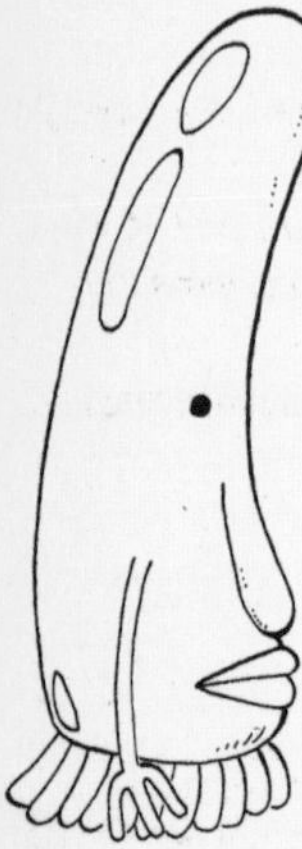

STATS
Weapon: None
Birthday / Age: September 29, 0063 / 3
Height / Weight / Blood Type: 45 cm / 2 g / none
Birthplace: It seems he won't tell…
Hobbies: Birdwatching (well, not exactly birds...)
Special Skills: Changing shape
Likes: Mayonnaise
Hates: 6:30 (for some unknown reason)

DESCRIPTION
Well, well, what the heck is this thing? [laughs] When I was drawing him, I just got more and more out of control and ended up with an outrageous character. Fans might think that he appeared on some of the chapter opening pages before he appeared in the actual story, but actually, the characters are different.

Horse: Tanchimo

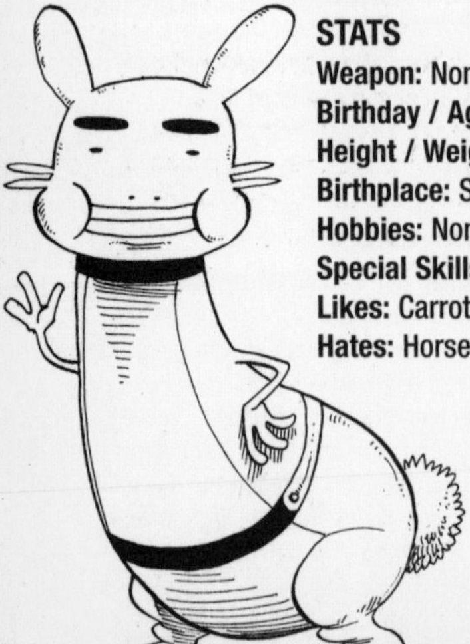

STATS
Weapon: None. But give him a break—he's a horse.
Birthday / Age: April 15, 0062 / 4
Height / Weight / Blood Type: 198 cm / 325 kg / Wireman
Birthplace: Some farm
Hobbies: None
Special Skills: Running
Likes: Carrots
Hates: Horses that are faster than him

DESCRIPTION
His name isn't mentioned in the story, but it's Tanchimo. It doesn't mean anything. And he's really a "horse." A horse with a head that moves very fast.

Mother & Son from the Hotel Ska: Lasagna and Chino

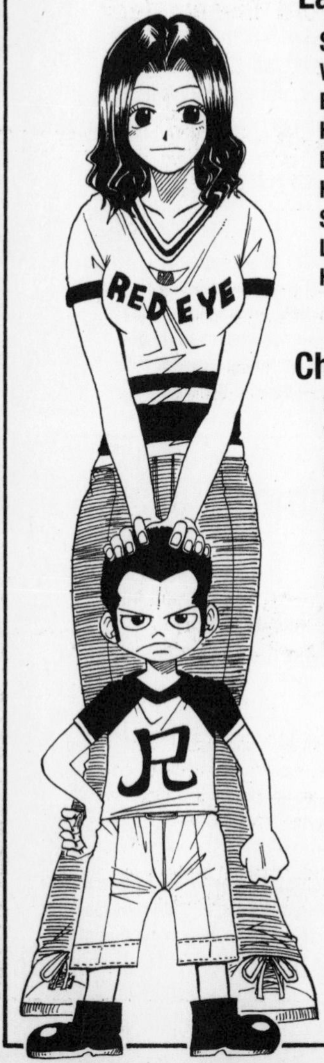
RED EYE

Lasagna

STATS

Weapon: None
Birthday / Age: December 5, 0040 / 26
Height / Weight / Blood Type: 172 cm / 50 kg / A
Birthplace: Ska Village
Hobbies: Reading (particularly historical novels)
Special Skills: Volleyball (Her mom was a pro!)
Likes: Children, customers who stay for a long time
Hates: Customers who leave the room a mess

Chino

STATS

Weapon: None
Birthday / Age: July 14, 0061 / 5
Height / Weight / Blood Type: 86 cm / 30 kg / AB
Birthplace: Ska Village
Hobbies: Watching TV
Special Skills: Running
Likes: Oolong Tea
Hates: Rain

DESCRIPTION

Their names don't come up too much in the story, but here they are.

The mother is young, isn't she [laughs]? She had her child at 21. At first I thought I would make her older, but then I decided I liked the idea of a young wife and made her young.

By the way, the father has left the house, and hasn't come back to the village in years.

Ten Form Sword: Ten Powers

1. Ordinary Form—The Metal Sword, Eisenmeteor

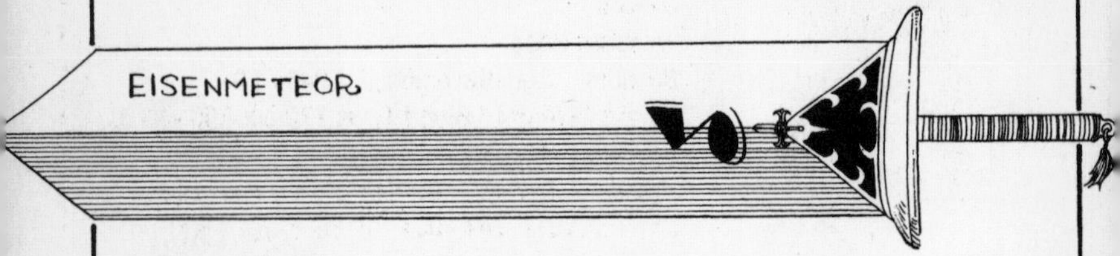
EISENMETEOR

DESCRIPTION

A regular metal sword. It's a bit big, but it's suitable for cutting through things. It's pretty heavy, so it takes some getting used to. In this normal form, this sword can be used by anyone, not just Haru.

It's really just an ordinary sword. Then why is it one of the ten forms? Well, if all of the forms were special, then even a Rave Master would get exhausted using it.

2. The Explosive Sword

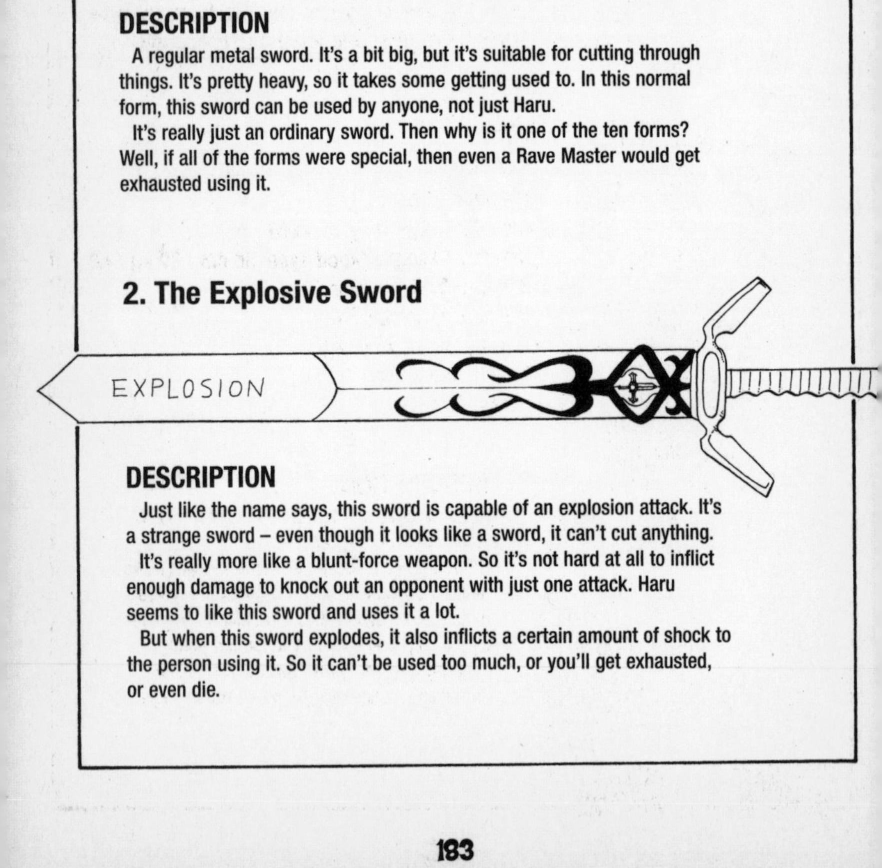
EXPLOSION

DESCRIPTION

Just like the name says, this sword is capable of an explosion attack. It's a strange sword – even though it looks like a sword, it can't cut anything.

It's really more like a blunt-force weapon. So it's not hard at all to inflict enough damage to knock out an opponent with just one attack. Haru seems to like this sword and uses it a lot.

But when this sword explodes, it also inflicts a certain amount of shock to the person using it. So it can't be used too much, or you'll get exhausted, or even die.

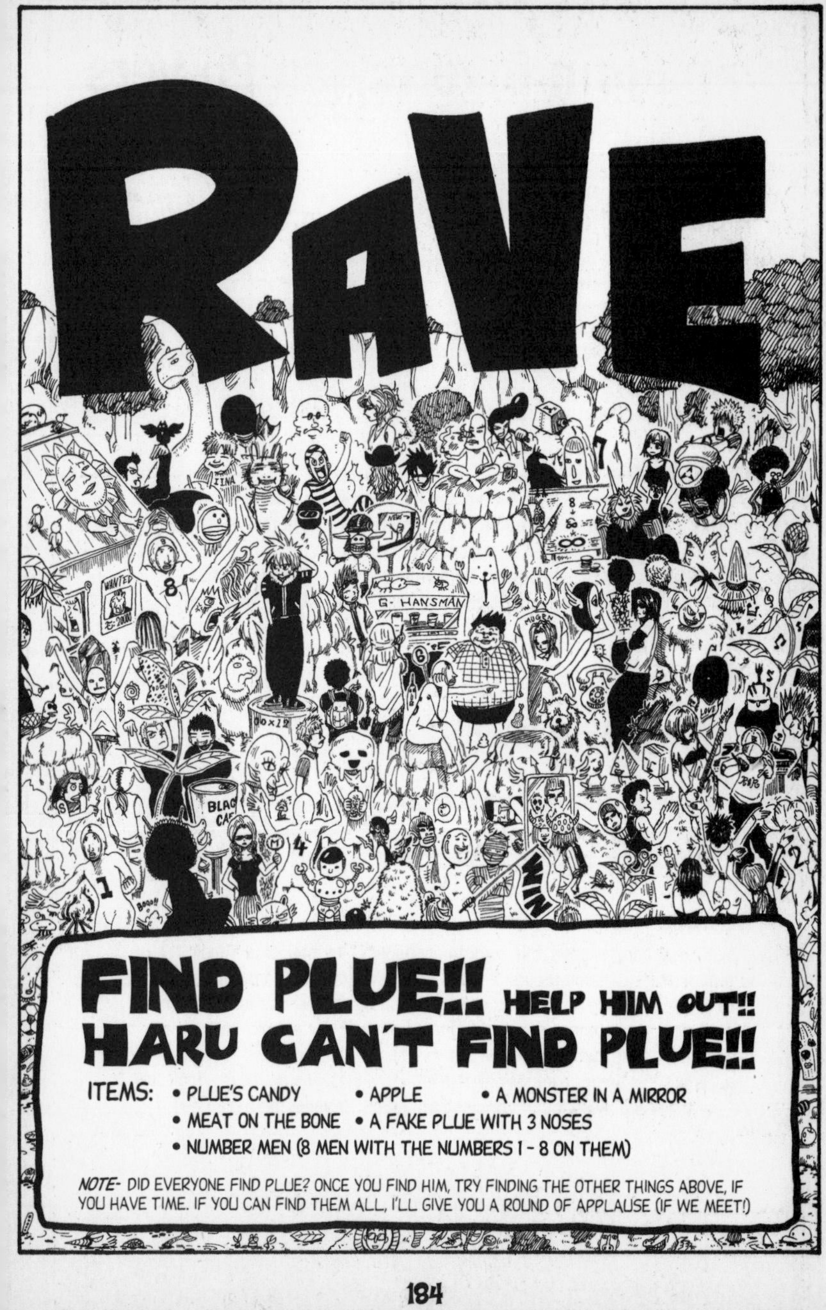
RAVE
FIND PLUE!! HELP HIM OUT!!
HARU CAN'T FIND PLUE!!
ITEMS: • PLUE'S CANDY • APPLE • A MONSTER IN A MIRROR
• MEAT ON THE BONE • A FAKE PLUE WITH 3 NOSES
• NUMBER MEN (8 MEN WITH THE NUMBERS 1 - 8 ON THEM)
NOTE- DID EVERYONE FIND PLUE? ONCE YOU FIND HIM, TRY FINDING THE OTHER THINGS ABOVE, IF YOU HAVE TIME. IF YOU CAN FIND THEM ALL, I'LL GIVE YOU A ROUND OF APPLAUSE (IF WE MEET!)

RAVE0077

LEVIN MINDS THE HOUSE

#3 The Intruder

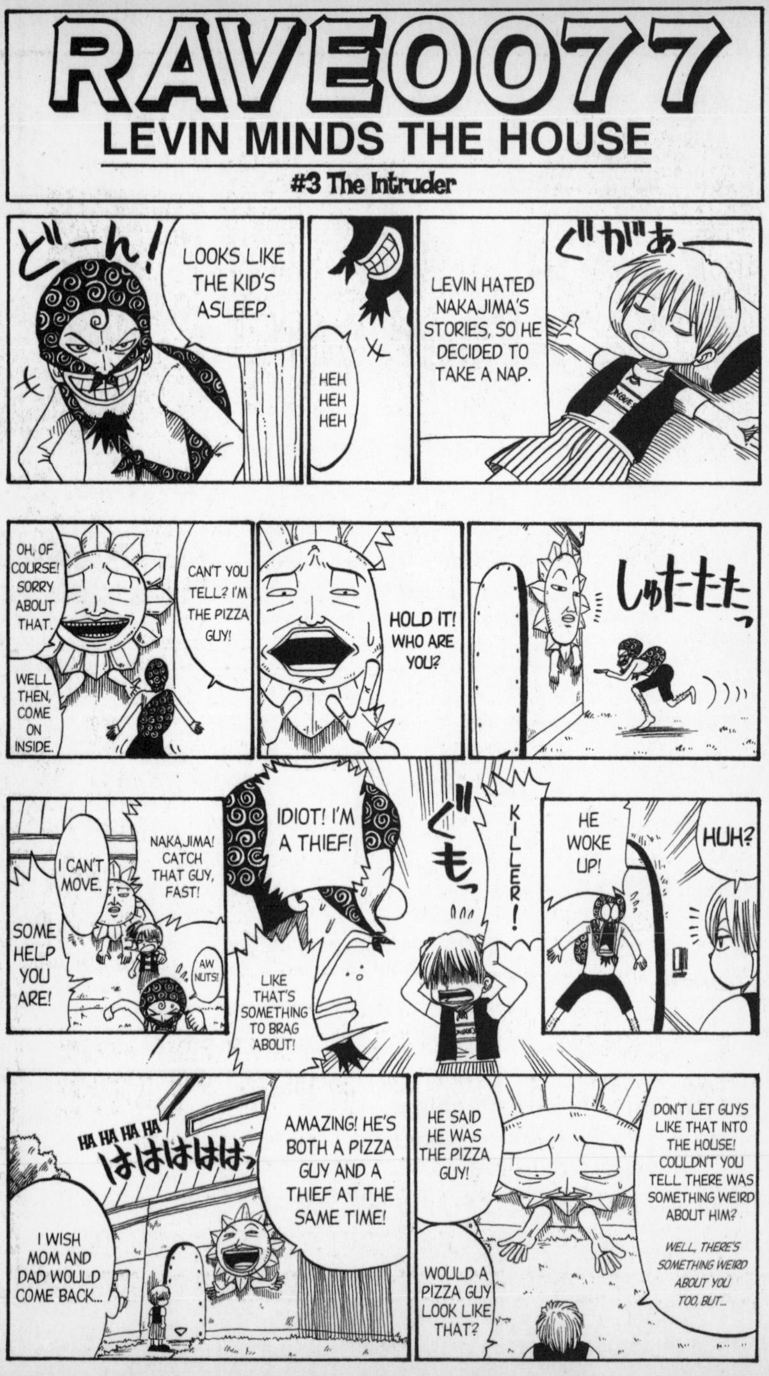

ぐがぁー
LEVIN HATED NAKAJIMA'S STORIES, SO HE DECIDED TO TAKE A NAP.
HEH HEH HEH
どーん!
LOOKS LIKE THE KID'S ASLEEP.
しゅたたたっ
HOLD IT! WHO ARE YOU?
CAN'T YOU TELL? I'M THE PIZZA GUY!
OH, OF COURSE! SORRY ABOUT THAT.
WELL THEN, COME ON INSIDE.
HUH?
HE WOKE UP!
!!
KILLER!
ぐもっ
IDIOT! I'M A THIEF!
LIKE THAT'S SOMETHING TO BRAG ABOUT!
NAKAJIMA! CATCH THAT GUY, FAST!
I CAN'T MOVE.
SOME HELP YOU ARE!
AW NUTS!
DON'T LET GUYS LIKE THAT INTO THE HOUSE! COULDN'T YOU TELL THERE WAS SOMETHING WEIRD ABOUT HIM?
HE SAID HE WAS THE PIZZA GUY!
WOULD A PIZZA GUY LOOK LIKE THAT?
WELL, THERE'S SOMETHING WEIRD ABOUT YOU TOO, BUT...
AMAZING! HE'S BOTH A PIZZA GUY AND A THIEF AT THE SAME TIME!
HA HA HA HA
ははははっ
I WISH MOM AND DAD WOULD COME BACK...

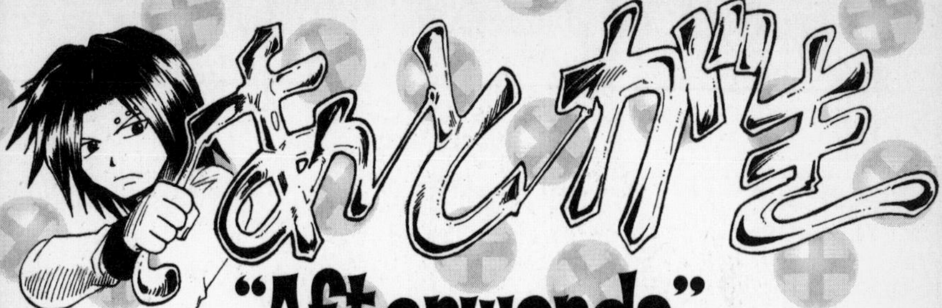
あとがき

"Afterwords"

THERE WAS A SIGNING IN SHIBUYA WHEN VOLUME 2 WENT ON SALE. THANK YOU VERY MUCH TO ALL OF THE FANS WHO CAME! WELL, IN THIS LINE OF WORK, I DON'T REALLY MAKE MANY PUBLIC APPEARANCES, SO I WAS REALLY NERVOUS. BUT ONCE IT GOT STARTED, I HAD LOTS OF FUN. I HADN'T HAD MUCH OPPORTUNITY TO MEET THE FANS IN PERSON BEFORE. I GUESS I'LL ANSWER SOME OF THE QUESTIONS THE FANS ASKED AT THE SIGNING.

Q: HOW DO YOU PRONOUNCE PLUE?
A: IT DOESN'T REALLY MATTER. BUT I PRONOUNCE IT LIKE "BLUE." IT'S A LITTLE HARD TO EXPLAIN IN WRITING [LAUGHS].

Q: IS BIS GOING TO BE IN THE STORY ANY MORE? I THINK HE'S GREAT!
A: I DON'T THINK SO.

Q: WHAT COLOR IS BIS' MOHAWK? IT'S BEEN DRIVING ME CRAZY!
A: HEY, DON'T COME BACK AGAIN!

Q: WHY IS DEMON CARD LOOKING FOR RAVE WHEN ONLY HARU CAN USE IT?
A: WELL, THAT'S BECAUSE RAVE IS [BLEEPED OUT BY THE EDITOR] AND DEMON CARD IS [BLEEPED OUT BY THE EDITOR].

ANYWAY, THE SIGNING WAS FUN! I HOPE YOU ALL COME BACK IF WE GET THE CHANCE TO DO IT AGAIN. WELL THEN, THAT'S ALL FOR NOW!

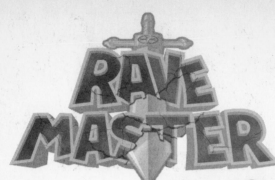

RAVE MASTER

Volume 4 Preview

4
RAVE MASTER
TOKYOPOP
Hiro Mashima

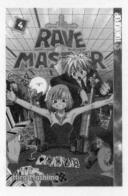

An old man once wielded Rave
But evil escaped, and the world wasn't saved
Rave came to a boy, and his name is Haru
He wields the Ten Powers sword and his guide is Plue
Isn't it exciting...don't you think?
But now there's raaaaiiin that won't go away
Chino's really sad—he's never seen a sunny day
And Elie's running to where the Thunder-Man stays
What happens next...go figure
Haru ran after Elie, fearing the worst
But he'll get to the heart of why Ska Village is cursed
He'll fight Demon Card agents named Rosa and Go
A director and actress whose films really do blow
And isn't it exciting...don't you think?
But the raaaaiiin will soon go away
'Cuz Haru's here and he will save the day
And he'll keep searching 'til he finds another Rave
What happens next...go figure
Demon Card has a way of sneaking up on him
He and his friends get to Rave Point
and everything's going right
Demon Card got there first and they're digging a mine
Haru goes undercover and blows everything up
With his Explosion Rave
Dr. Shnieder attacks them when they're in a cave
Things aren't looking good—Haru needs to be saved
And isn't it exciting...don't you think?
A little too exciting...well, you'll have to find out

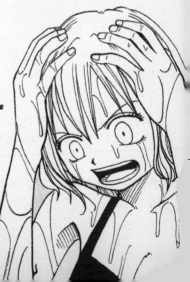

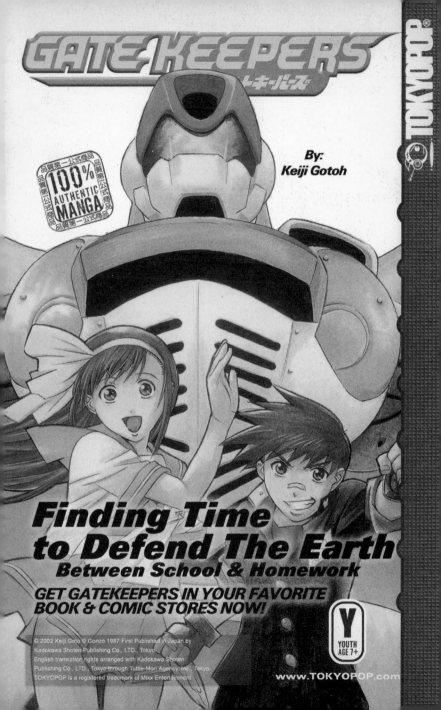

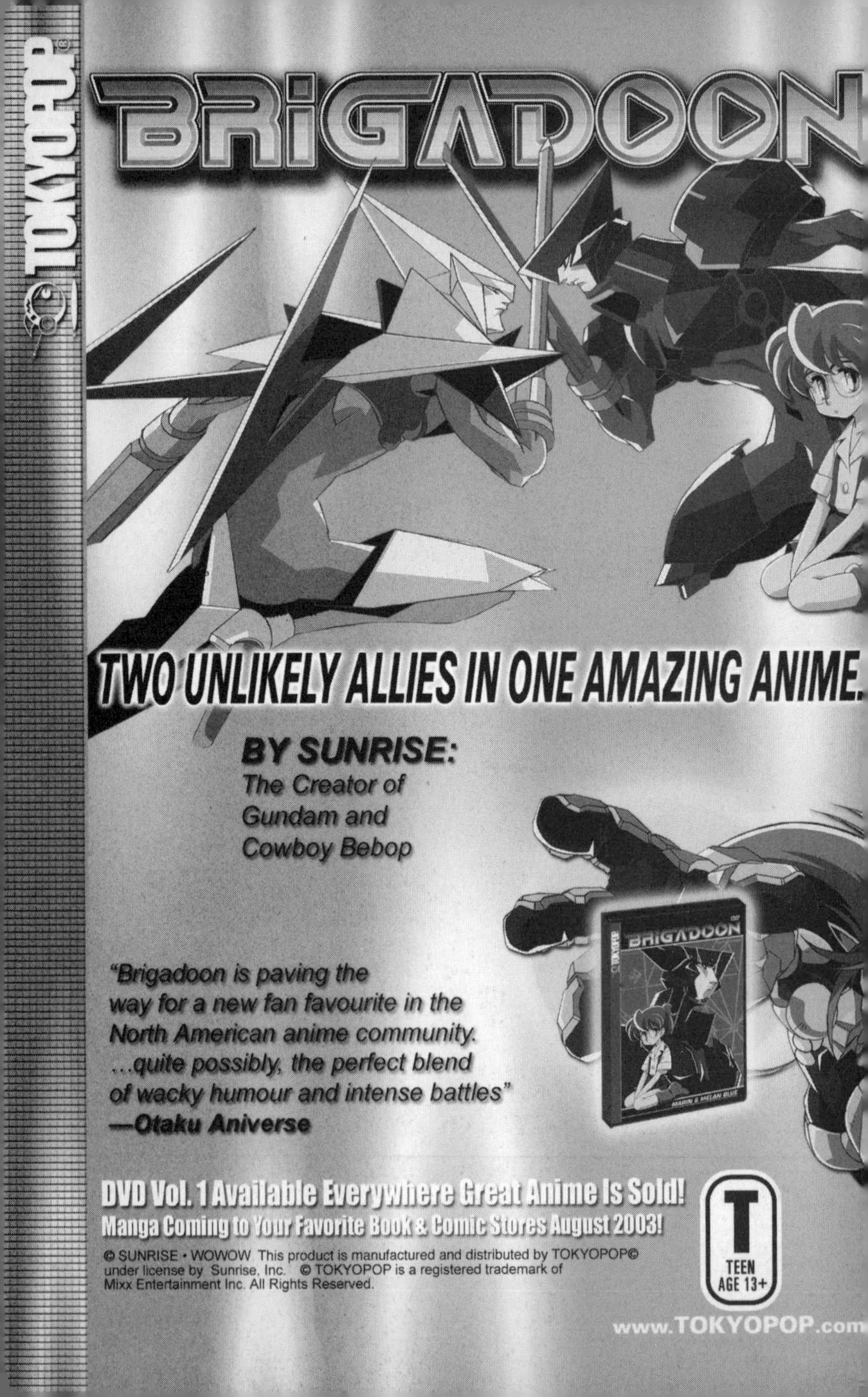

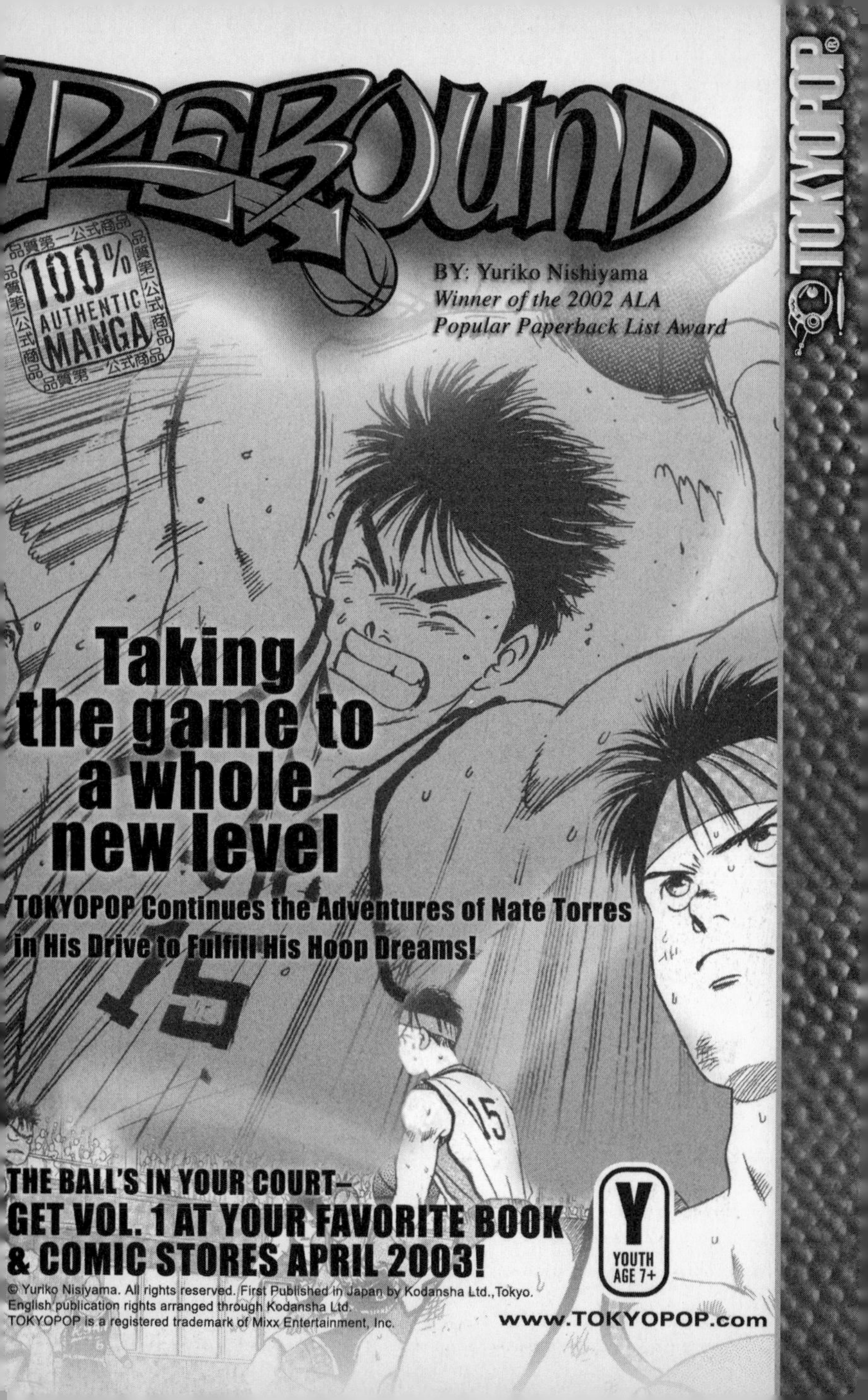
REBOUND
100% AUTHENTIC MANGA
BY: Yuriko Nishiyama
Winner of the 2002 ALA
Popular Paperback List Award
Taking the game to a whole new level
TOKYOPOP Continues the Adventures of Nate Torres in His Drive to Fulfill His Hoop Dreams!
THE BALL'S IN YOUR COURT–
GET VOL. 1 AT YOUR FAVORITE BOOK & COMIC STORES APRIL 2003!
Y
YOUTH
AGE 7+
© Yuriko Nisiyama. All rights reserved. First Published in Japan by Kodansha Ltd.,Tokyo.
English publication rights arranged through Kodansha Ltd.
TOKYOPOP is a registered trademark of Mixx Entertainment, Inc.
www.TOKYOPOP.com
TOKYOPOP

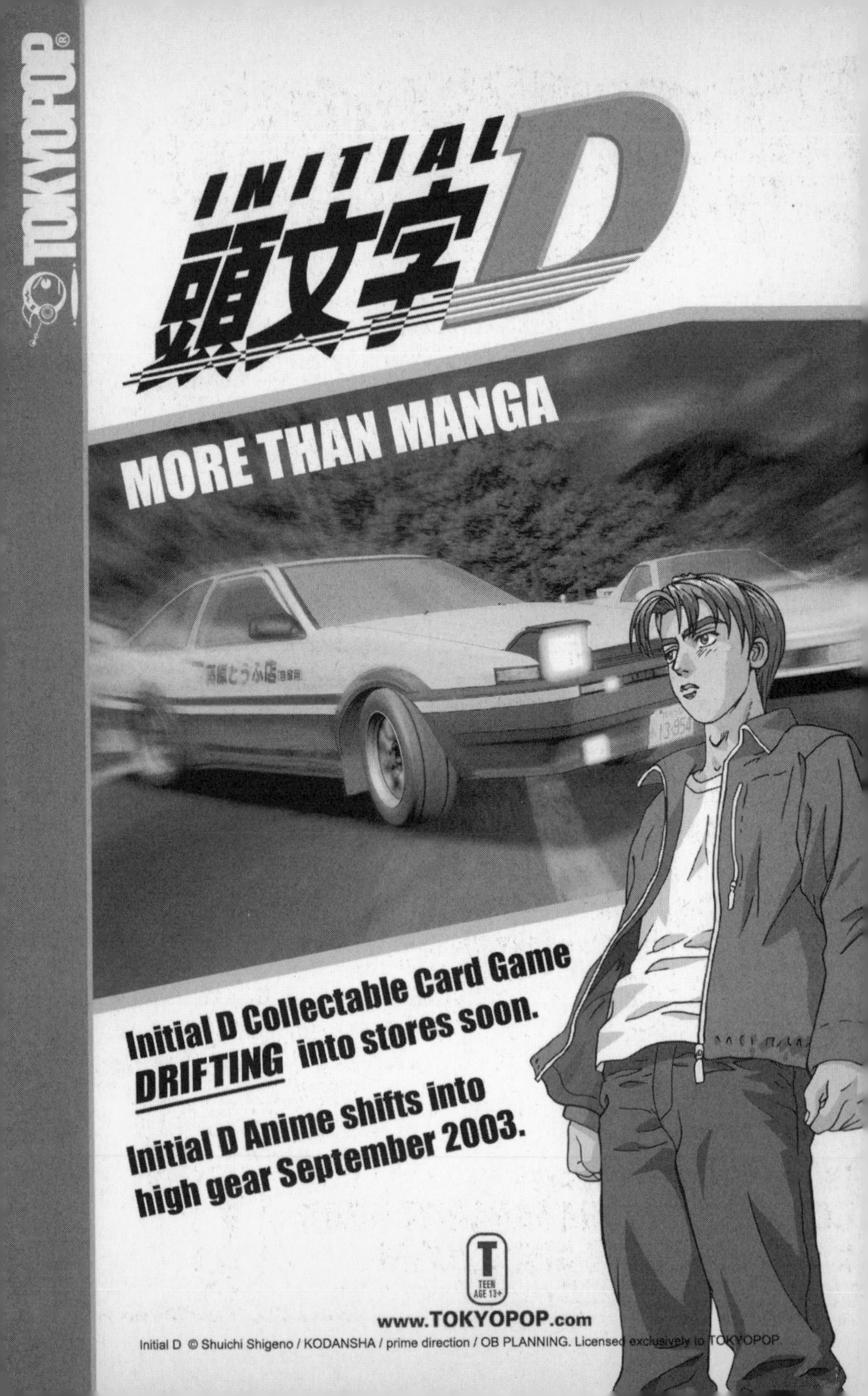
TOKYOPOP
INITIAL
頭文字D
MORE THAN MANGA
Initial D Collectable Card Game
DRIFTING into stores soon.
Initial D Anime shifts into
high gear September 2003.
T
TEEN
AGE 13+
www.TOKYOPOP.com
Initial D © Shuichi Shigeno / KODANSHA / prime direction / OB PLANNING. Licensed exclusively to TOKYOPOP.

STOP!

This is the back of the book.
You wouldn't want to spoil a great ending!

This book is printed "manga-style," in the authentic Japanese right-to-left format. Since none of the artwork has been flipped or altered, readers get to experience the story just as the creator intended. You've been asking for it, so TOKYOPOP® delivered: authentic, hot-off-the-press, and far more fun!

P9-BZP-308

DIRECTIONS

If this is your first time reading manga-style, here's a quick guide to help you understand how it works.

It's easy... just start in the top right panel and follow the numbers. Have fun, and look for more 100% authentic manga from TOKYOPOP®!

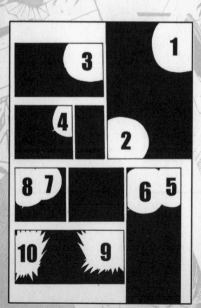

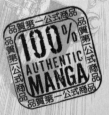